ARTISTIC ART HISTORIES IN SOUTHEAST ASIA

ARTISTIC ART HISTORIES IN SOUTHEAST ASIA

Modernisms in Contemporary Practices

Roger Nelson

SOUTHEAST ASIA PROGRAM PUBLICATIONS
AN IMPRINT OF CORNELL UNIVERSITY PRESS   ITHACA AND LONDON

First published 2026 by Cornell University Press

Librarians: A CIP catalog record for this book is available from the Library of Congress.

ISBN 9781501788833 (hardcover)
ISBN 9781501788840 (paperback)
ISBN 9781501788857 (pdf)
ISBN 9781501788864 (epub)

GPSR EU contact: Sam Thornton, Mare Nostrum Group B.V., Doelen 72, 4831 GR Breda, NL, gpsr@mare-nostrum.co.uk.

Contents

List of Figures

INTRODUCTION

Toward Alterity

A woman presents a joss stick as an offering to a stone sculpture that, sited outdoors, is encircled by verdant vegetation. The woman, filmed in 2023, is the internationally celebrated contemporary artist Thao Nguyen Phan (1987—), while the sculpture was made decades prior by the modernist artist Diem Phung Thi (1920–2002), who is now little-known outside specialist circles in Vietnam. This scene appears in a three-channel video artwork by Phan, that has been exhibited across Asia and Europe (fig. I.1).[1] As I watch this tender moment in the video, a man speaking in a voiceover says that "through Ho Chi Minh's connection, Diem Phung Thi was sent to France" following the death of her first husband "on the battlefield" in the First Indochina War. Later, while more joss sticks burn, Phan's hands caress the surfaces of Diem's reniform and rounded sculptures, some monumental in scale and some small enough to disappear into the soft flesh of a ripe papaya (fig. I.2). These dreamlike images are interspersed with Phan's delicate watercolor paintings depicting Diem's artworks, as well as archival footage of the late sculptor speaking about her life and work. The man from the voiceover reappears later in an interview with Phan.[2] While he speaks, she browses the archives that he cares for. The man describes Diem's invaluable but invisible behind-the-scenes work for the Paris Peace Accords in 1973, revealing that her life was entangled with Vietnam's long struggle for political decolonization. In another voiceover, a woman's voice poetically recounts the (perhaps imagined) words of Diem Phung Thi herself: "Everything I touch is as solid as a rock while fugitive as a bubble."

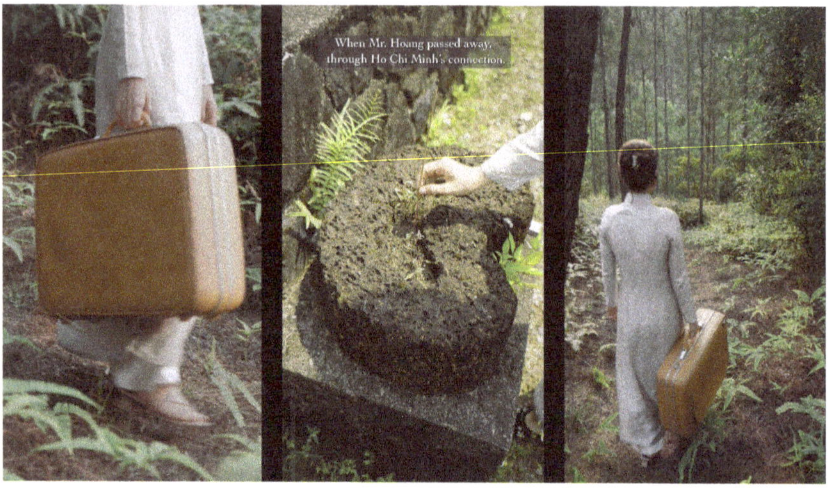

FIGURE. I.1. Thao Nguyen Phan, *Reincarnations of Shadows*, 2023–ongoing. Three-channel video with sound, 16 mins, 50 seconds. Digital still. © Thao Nguyen Phan, courtesy of the artist.

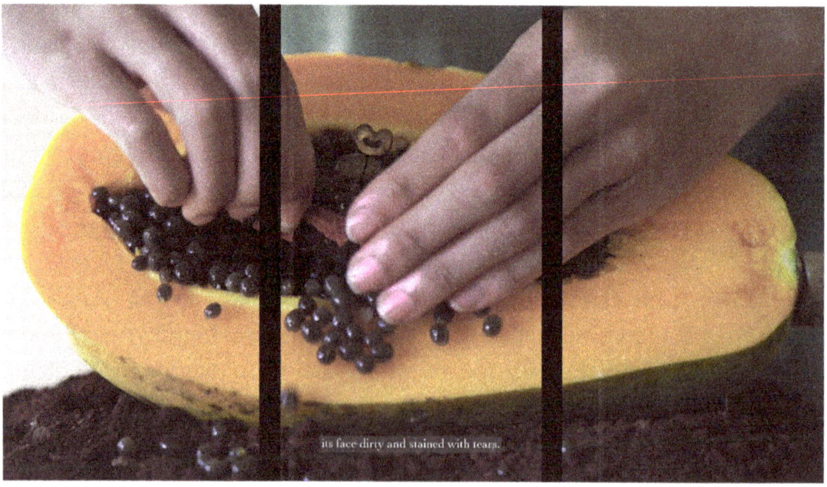

FIGURE I.2. Thao Nguyen Phan, *Reincarnations of Shadows*, 2023–ongoing. Three-channel video with sound, 16 mins, 50 seconds. Digital still. © Thao Nguyen Phan, courtesy of the artist.

Artistic art histories is the name I give to contemporary artworks like this, that are deeply engaged with under-studied modernisms. These contemporary practices are driven by research and also by thinking and theorizing. Artists today not only study their modernist forebears, they also bring the art of the past back to life by revealing its renewed relevance to the concerns of the present. These concerns are subjective as well as collective, personal as well as shared, poetic as well as political. Artistic art histories appear across the planet we share, but in Southeast Asia they are signally shaped by the idiosyncrasies of the region's distinctive discourses on modern art, as they have emerged since the 1960s. Artistic art histories in Southeast Asia emerge from this discursive alterity while also sustaining it. In this book, while focusing on artistic art histories in this region, I aim to deprovincialize the knowledges and practices emerging from Southeast Asia and suggest ways in which they may have a larger relevance, including for global art histories. I argue that the contributions artists (in Southeast Asia) make to art-historical knowledge—within their practices—also contribute to the ongoing decolonizing of the discipline of Art History.

In *Reincarnations of Shadows* (the work described previously), Thao Nguyen Phan undertakes several different kinds of artistic and art-historical research on Diem Phung Thi. As with many artistic art histories, this research is necessary because, despite Diem's historical significance, she has hardly been studied by scholars. As Phan writes, "the art history course I took in college did not mention her."[3] Phan's research encompasses many methods, at once conventional and unexpected, rigorous and speculative. In her refreshing and idiosyncratic approach, she epitomizes what art historian and curator Patrick D. Flores calls "an art-historical alterity" that reimagines art history's "norm and its fiction, its écriture."[4] For instance, Phan consults archives in both personal and institutional collections. Moreover, with her camera, she carefully examines artworks with the slow and sustained gaze of a close reading attuned to form. She conducts interviews and visits various locations that were significant to the late artist. She discusses the political and historical contexts in which Diem lived and worked, both in Vietnam and in France, linking the artist's practice to larger struggles to politically decolonize. Phan shares private, intimate details from Diem's life, as well as connecting these microhistories to major, public events of world-historical importance. She makes drawings and paintings depicting Diem's sculptures. She carefully touches their surfaces repeatedly and reverentially but also playfully and with a spirit of experimentation and exploration. Phan even dresses in a period costume to resemble and imaginatively embody Diem; and in this role, the contemporary artist almost literally follows in the footsteps of her modernist forebear, traversing various sites in central

Vietnam that were important in the late artist's life. "I feel like we're interested in the same things," Phan says of what she calls her "obsession" with Diem.[5] The two artists even share the same birthday—albeit almost seven decades apart—which is a coincidence that nurtures in Phan a sense that her connection to Diem runs deep and transcends rational understanding.[6]

The artistic art histories I discuss in this book—in which contemporary artists do art-historical work and engage with art-historical ideas and information—often involve extensive research of various kinds. As in the example of Thao Nguyen Phan's work on Diem Phung Thi, artists may undertake many research activities that are like those usually done by academic art historians working in universities or museums. But artists are also able to embark on other more experimental and speculative kinds of study that scholars may not feel ready to attempt. For instance, embodied research—such as Phan's touching of Diem's sculptures and her play-acting the role of the late artist—typically comes more easily for artists, whereas many scholars may feel reticent to fully embrace this approach. Moreover, artists seem to be more ready to draw on personal connections—even familial relationships, as is the case for several of the artists I discuss in this book—which enable special access to artworks, archives, interviews, and sites. These personal and kinship ties may also facilitate other kinds of subjective and autotheoretical research and engender related insights that are enlivened by the creative license artists enjoy.

As well as conducting research, artists making artistic art histories are also thinking and theorizing in and with their works. More than simply presenting raw data (as may be the case in some other forms of "research-based art"), they craft narratives that critically intervene in art-historical discourse to make statements about the art of the past and about its continuing relevance for the present.[7] Artistic art histories are a form of what the art historian and curator T. K. Sabapathy calls "critical activity" about art, which, he says, "need not necessarily be defined in terms of, or limited to, literary forms."[8] That is, as well as being artworks themselves, artistic art histories also offer fresh, active, and critical insights into other artworks. They complicate and deepen existing understandings of the art of the past. When encountering artistic art histories, it is palpable that, as the scholar, artist, and curator Mieke Bal proposes, "art thinks." This mode of practice compels us to, in Bal's words, take "contemporary art seriously, as art, and as a form of art history and cultural philosophy, as studies in ways of looking that go beyond the theory/practice opposition."[9] This is foundational to my approach in this book; artistic art histories reward careful study not only for their artistic merits but also for their historiographical and theoretical contributions. These artworks are also art histories. Although artistic approaches to art-historical work do not replace scholarly methods, these practices do augment, complicate, and inventively enlarge academic norms for studying the art of the past.

To think of artworks as artistic art histories opens productive possibilities for reimagining the relationship between practice and research as part of an ongoing process of decolonizing knowledge. Resisting the binary that separates (artistic) practice from (art-historical) research may contribute to recasting artists and other practitioners as not merely objects to study, but instead as agentive subjects who generate theoretical and methodological insights and innovations. In this book, I show that that artistic art histories set in motion a poetics of inclusion that redresses epistemic injustices, a concept I elaborate in the epilogue. The book focuses specifically on ways of knowing the art of the past in Southeast Asia, and it intervenes most substantially in the discipline of Art History (as well as related fields like curatorial studies). Yet at stake in my claims about the knowledge that artists enable and enact are the much larger and interdisciplinary domains of practice-based research and research-led practice, which this book seeks to take seriously and examine sensitively.

Southeast Asia is a particularly fertile site for studying the phenomenon of artistic art histories, even though this mode of practice also proliferates globally, because of the region's diversity, avowed peripherality, and dispersal. Regarding Southeast Asia's diversity, historians observe a "glorious multiplicity" expressed in geography, languages, religions, and political systems.[10] Of the region's peripherality, Flores lyrically suggests that "the coordinate of the southeast [is] possibly a double negation: not north, not west" and thus also "a productive locus: that which is not the centre, twice."[11] Southeast Asia is usually understood as a geographic zone. Today, it typically comprises the member-states of ASEAN—the Association of Southeast Asian Nations—although in the past, its borders were less clearly defined and extended into what is now usually considered East Asia and South Asia. The region has also been reconsidered, however, as a "geopoetic" constellation of imagination and affiliation.[12] Flores argues that Southeast Asia is not a stable place or even idea, but rather is always contingent and "in the process of constant forming."[13] Scholars have noted "the impossibility of fixing the region's boundaries and coordinates and the impracticality of totalizing perspectives."[14] In these understandings, Southeast Asia is unmoored from a fixed geography and instead conceived, at least in part, as a sensibility that may be dispersed through various overlapping places and populations, including among the many diasporas associated with the region.

Artistic art histories are also particularly resonant and significant in Southeast Asia because they draw on and contribute to the region's unique tradition of scholarship on modern art. The first books to discuss modern art in the region, appearing in the 1960s in Chinese and English, were both written by artists—Marco Hsü (1908–1993) and Claire Holt (1901–1970)—who exhibited alongside some of the figures they wrote about.[15] In the decades since, many of the most important and impactful texts on the region's modern art have been written by artists and (more recently) by curators. In Southeast Asia, the making and exhibiting of art and the writing of art histories are not just proximate activities; they are practices and passions that overlap, entwine, and sustain each other. This book is not chiefly concerned with texts written *about* art by artists but instead about art-historical work done *within* artworks. Yet these practices—artistic art histories—emerge from and contribute to the distinctive nature of art-historical scholarship within Southeast Asia as it has developed over more than half a century.

The contemporary art of Southeast Asia may appear frequently in biennales and other large-scale exhibitions globally, including in the North and the West, but neither the contemporary nor the modern art of the region has found much purchase within Western art histories, possibly because of the slipperiness and dispersal of the region itself. Without this burden of inclusion within most canonical Western art-historical narratives, artistic art histories in Southeast Asia are free not only to tell their own stories but also to play a substantial role in shaping the wider art-historical discourse in the region.

The artists I discuss in this book adopt a panoply of methods for approaching art-historical work and draw on quite varied forms of research. They have all been exhibited and celebrated on prominent local and international platforms, such as biennales, both within Southeast Asia and beyond, yet all of them have been relatively under-studied by scholars.[16] I have chosen to focus on these artists—and on close readings of a smaller number of specific works, rather than a broader and more general survey—because of the ways in which their rich, complex, and intelligent practices reveal and enable a consideration of the diverse forms and research methods that artistic art histories have adopted across Southeast Asia, and in its diasporas, over the course of almost a century. Their approaches encompass respectfully honoring their forebears, citing their peers and predecessors through intermedial visual quotations, staging speculative and heterochronic encounters with the art of the past, autotheorizing from their own lived experiences, and teaching art histories in a context where they are rarely included in university curricula. I will discuss each of these approaches taken within artistic art histories in more detail later on when I outline the structure of the book.

As well as adopting a range of different approaches to research, the artists in this book also work across several different media. The manifold forms that their artworks take has been another consideration guiding my choice of these artists. Some, like Thao Nguyen Phan in her work on Diem Phung Thi, combine multiple modes of research—encompassing archives, interviews, site visits, and speculative reenactments—and produce works in a range of media, including videos, paintings, and installations. Others, like Sriwhana Spong (1979–) and filmmaker Davy Chou (1983–), draw on all these various methods while foregrounding their own personal and familial relationships to the artists they study. Working chiefly in film, Spong and Chou also explore digital research methods and foreground their own diasporic experiences. Some artists, like Emiria Sunassa (1894–1964) and Hilmi Johandi (1987–), mostly limit their research to studies of images and work chiefly as painters. By contrast, Fyerool Darma (1987–) imaginatively calls on other senses beyond the visual. Meanwhile, Ho Tzu Nyen (1976–) works with archives and images and uses the reach of mass-broadcast television as a medium to question the reach of art and art-historical narratives within a Southeast Asian context. Some artists, including Araya Rasdjarmrearnsook (1957–) and Svay Ken (1933–2008), draw extensively on their own lived experiences. Svay Ken's paintings and Araya's works in an array of media insist on the importance of first-person testimonies while challenging the stability of an artistic subjectivity and suggesting the interdependence of any creative practice.

The artists I discuss in this book live and work in several different periods and places and adopt a wide range of forms and techniques. My approach is both transnational and transhistorical. Being based in or making art in various places across Southeast Asia (including in Ho Chi Minh City, Hue, Sanur, Phnom Penh, Jakarta, Singapore, and Chiang Mai) and in diasporas beyond and practicing between the 1940s and the 2020s, many of the artists I discuss in this book do not know each other personally or even through each other's works. I focus on them in order to foreground their singular, idiosyncratic practices that link older, nationally defined modernisms with newer, more globally oriented expressions of contemporaneity. These artists do not typify the region's cultures or represent a canon, and I am not proposing that they constitute a movement or a style. They hail from places both within and beyond the region: this is my contribution to undoing the binary separating local from diasporic artists. Moreover, they are affiliated with both maritime and mainland parts of Southeast Asia: this is my attempt to counter the conventional scholarly distinction between these geographic zones, which imagines them to be disconnected when in fact they are porous and intrinsically interconnected.[17] Despite their temporal and geographic spread, they do not form a historically or regionally representative or cohesive group. While they often "represent" Southeast Asia at prominent international biennales and other exhibitions, they are not a comprehensive representation of the heterogeneity of artistic practices in the region.

Some of these artists are unambiguously contemporary, while others might be more comfortably considered modernist. By discussing modern and contemporary art together, this book insists that they are not fixed and distinct periods but instead are correlated, even coextensive, and mutually illuminating. Scholars studying Southeast Asia have pointed to the increasingly permeable interrelationship between modern and contemporary art. Shifting between the modern and contemporary can be "refreshingly open-ended" and create "an active space between the two," as art historian Kevin Chua proposes, enabling the possibility of "moving back and forth between past and present."[18] As another scholar writes regarding the art-historical context of Thailand, there are no "'clean breaks' separating the *national modern* from a *global contemporary*."[19] Sabapathy also notes the "historically inflected intersections" between the modern and the contemporary; he says that they "are intriguing even as they may be jangling."[20] The sonic image of jangling invokes a polyphony that may be musical, or dissonant, or both. In this book, I consider the jangling between the modern and the contemporary as it resounds in artistic art histories to be a synergy, which is often harmonious in tone.

Artistic Art Histories and Artistic Research in Southeast Asia

Artistic art histories may overlap with yet remain distinct from other modes of practice known as *artistic research*, more specifically from the frequent engagement with other kinds of history within contemporary art of Southeast Asia. Noting this tendency, curator June Yap proposes that many artworks have what she calls "the historiographical feature, where the aesthetic expression may be conjectured as examining the nature and production of history."[21] That is, Yap argues that contemporary art in Southeast Asia is not just concerned with the events of the past but rather with the framing of these events in historical narratives. This insight, which is inherently political, has enabled my work here. So too has the art historian Eva Kernbauer's coining of the term *artistic historiography*, that she "situates within the context of engagements with history more generally," noting both that history is "a politically controversial and heterogeneous field" and that "artistic explorations of history have played an increasingly important role over time."[22] While Kernbauer does not address the art of Southeast Asia directly, her thinking aligns with Yap's and with art historians, such as Michelle Antoinette, who notes that "artists often test the limits of established histories."[23] While Antoinette mostly discusses works engaged with social and political events, she also notes that "contemporary Southeast Asian artists have looked to the local histories of modern art before them."[24] Her focus is on what she calls "the conscious search by artists for clues to the constitution of 'the contemporary' in Southeast Asia."[25] This creates a space for me in this book to instead emphasize the way artists engage with "the modern" in this region, often by revitalizing and reanimating lesser-known modernist artists, bringing their practices and histories back to life.

Artistic research is abundant in Southeast Asia and in the region's diasporas, as in many other contemporary art worlds globally, yet the phenomenon has been less extensively studied and theorized. One scholar specializing in this concept, Danny Butt, advocates for the potential of artistic research to "provide a space that can welcome indigenous knowledges which can provide flexible models of space and time," drawing on research across the Asia Pacific including in Indonesia.[26] He recognizes that "the recent history of artistic research in the Anglo-Saxon world has largely been a quest for acceptance into a science-dominated paradigm of university knowledge," yet in my view more work needs to be done on how understandings and valorizations of artistic research in regions like Southeast Asia may differ from the North and West.[27]

I propose the concept of artistic art histories as a companion to the more widespread notion of artistic research because it emphasizes the historiographical as well as theoretical contributions that artists make, alongside their research. Finding and sharing information is just one part of the larger significance of these practices. For example, Thao Nguyen Phan's work on Diem Phung Thi seeks (to paraphrase one scholar of artistic research) "to make knowledge its subject" and "*to act epistemically*" in a way that is related to "decolonial epistemologies."[28] I take this to mean that the artist is interested in contemplating ways of knowing about the art of the past and in ways of delinking our knowledge from methods and assumptions that originate in coloniality. In this way, artistic art histories like Phan's may be quite different in their origins, motivations, and attitudes than some articulations of artistic research, which the scholar and artist Kamini Vellodi contends first emerged due to bureaucratic decisions at institutions in the North and West.[29] In the past two or three decades, the concept of artistic research has proliferated; it has often been observed that "regular visitors of contemporary art biennials, modern and contemporary art museums" and similar sites will easily recognize "that contemporary art is a mode of knowledge production."[30] In this book, I show that the knowledge that contemporary art enables and enacts includes art-historical ideas and information, and that contemporary art is often a mode of art-historical thinking and theorization, and a contribution to the ongoing decolonizing of art histories.

The mode of practice I call *artistic art histories* is found globally but takes on special significance in Southeast Asia because it emerges from and contributes to a distinctly Southeast Asian version of art history, as I mentioned previously. There are several reasons for this. First, as a scholarly discipline, art history is relatively incipient and malleable in Southeast Asia, especially when concerned with modern and contemporary art. Many colonial scholars working in the region were chiefly concerned with premodern art and artefacts, and the practice of studying the history of more recent and living art and artists in the region has emerged relatively recently. Although the first books to discuss modern art in a Southeast Asian nation appeared in the 1960s, comparable art-historical accounts of most other nations in the region, including those written by Southeast Asian scholars, emerged only in the 1990s and 2000s.[31] This is also when the first transnationally comparative, regionalist accounts of Southeast Asia's art first appeared.[32] Moreover, art history often remains centered outside of universities in the region, for example, in archives initiated by independent collectives of artists and researchers or else in museums.[33] Because of its relative recentness and autonomy, art history maintains a flexibility of forms in Southeast Asia. The discipline has not ossified into the "remarkably uniform" manner that art historian James Elkins laments in much "North Atlantic" art-historical writing.[34] Instead, it often remains strikingly eccentric. Art history, as it is practiced in Southeast Asia, is quite simply not the same as art history as it is practiced in the North and the West. This creates an opportunity for artists to make significant contributions to the way art histories are studied and told through their practices.

A second reason for the special importance of artistic art histories in Southeast Asia is that scholars in the region have long contended that art-historical narratives are enmeshed within larger social, political, cultural, and other historical contexts of the region and therefore with decolonization. For example, Flores writes of his aim "to situate art in the premises of history" and "to locate history in art" and evocatively suggests that the "movement" of art through time and history "always takes the rhythm of a grinding against the forces of society."[35] The art historian Simon Soon similarly writes of "historical contingencies" as well as "art resulting from a common historical experience" and "historical affinities" shared in many countries across the region.[36] Sabapathy is more specific in his linking of art histories to political histories, pointing to the relationship between modern art and processes of political, epistemic, and cultural decolonization. Writing in 1982 at a conference organized by ASEAN, he affirmed that the "development of modern art in Southeast Asia" is related to larger (post)colonial histories, such as the following:

> self-determination in structuring new states, securing a semblance of harmony between the old and the new, and safeguarding of cultural identity. These processes exert enormous pressures, explicitly and implicitly, on the purpose and meaning of modern art activity.[37]

It is clear that the art-historical and the historical are enmeshed and entwined, in many scholarly accounts of modern art in Southeast Asia, particularly in relation to coloniality. This is also the case in many artistic art histories, as I will show in this book. For example, when Thao Nguyen Phan's video highlights how Diem Phung Thi was affected by both the First Indochina War and the Vietnam War (also known as the American War), she is continuing this entangling of modern art and modern political history. Moreover, when running her fingers along the surfaces of Diem's works, Phan is also reaching for a way to decolonize her practice of artistic art histories. "When I discover artists who are not in art history textbooks, it's very exciting for me, because it shows another one of the many ways to look and learn about art and history," Phan says. "And it's not just in a western-oriented way."[38]

A mutually reinforcing relationship between artistic and curatorial practice and scholarship is a third reason why Southeast Asia is a particularly rich site for studying artistic art histories. Sabapathy has noted that "exhibitions are dominant sites for the production of discourse on contemporary art in Southeast Asia."[39] Thus, catalogues and other kinds of curatorial texts are often important sources of art-historical thinking, contributing to the eccentricity and multiplicity of forms that art histories take in the region. Although more research is needed on the histories and tendencies of curatorial practice in Southeast Asia, some important foundational work has been done.[40] Flores has noted the particular prominence of artist-curators during and after the 1970s.[41] More recently, scholar-curators (like Flores himself) have become more prominent.[42] These figures build on foundations laid by earlier generations, writers of art-historical works who also practiced as artists.[43] Many of the key figures working as critics and teaching art history in the region, particularly in the late twentieth century, were also artists. While widely known, this phenomenon has been under-examined in scholarship. Flores has suggested that "it is . . . the art historian and the curator who have been responsible in sketching out the forms of knowing the region in a terrain of a postcolonial art history in crisis."[44] While astute, this stops short of recognizing the role played by artists.

The presence of artists among the ranks of art historians is certainly not new nor unique to Southeast Asia. Practice and discourse have always relied on each other since the early stirrings of what would later become the discipline of art history with the artist-scholars Zhang Yanyuan (815–877), Giorgio Vasari (1511–1574), and others. In his study of the history of the discipline (chiefly in the West), art historian Christopher S. Wood notes that Zhang's approach "legitimates art as a kind of knowledge" while Vasari "set up a feedback loop between writing and art-making."[45] Today, artistic art histories proliferate globally, including in the North and the West. For example, the American artist

Isaac Julien's five-channel video installation, *Once Again . . . (Statues Never Die)* (2022) speculatively reexamines the relationship between Black philosopher Alain Locke and white American art collector Albert Barnes. Commissioned by the Barnes Foundation, where it premiered in 2022, this artwork was a highlight at the Sharjah Biennial in 2023 and the Whitney Biennial in 2024, indicating the prominence of this mode of practice at major exhibitions globally.

Yet artistic art histories seem to be particularly prominent, and especially significant, in the decolonizing world or Global South, where, as in Southeast Asia, the production of art-historical knowledge is intimately related to the ongoing processes of epistemic decolonizing. My thinking about artistic art histories is indebted to the scholarship on and practices of artists from elsewhere in Asia and beyond. The art historian Saloni Mathur's discussions of the Mumbai-based artist Vivan Sundaram's practice have been particularly inspiring, as have the works of New Delhi-based artist Pablo Bartholomew done in dialogue with his father, the critic Richard Bartholomew.[46] Mathur has adapted a critical vocabulary from Sundaram's work and made it her own while both Sundaram and Bartholomew have made palpable the emotional and ineffable entanglement of research and affect when an artist engages with the art histories of another artist to whom they have a personal, familial relationship. Some other examples of artists making artistic art histories globally are Yuki Kihara (working in Sāmoa and Aotearoa New Zealand), Ala Younis (working in Kuwait, the UAE, and Germany), Mario García Torres (working in Mexico), The Otolith Group (working in the UK and India), Gala Porras-Kim (working in the UK and US), Richard Bell (working in Australia), and many others too numerous to name here. The field is ripe for further study, and I hope that this book's discussion of artists in and related to Southeast Asia may also contribute to thinking about these and other artists practicing in other regions globally. I take courage from the daring of Yuki Kihara's claim that her artworks are "*improving* on Gauguin," that she "engage[s] with art history as a sculptural material," and that she knows things that art historians do not.[47]

Deprovincializing and Decolonizing

Artistic art histories are particularly prevalent and significant in Southeast Asia, but they are not unique to this region. Moreover, the artists I discuss in this book are just some of the many proponents of this mode of practice. My choice of artists is necessarily subjective and partial, even while it also attends to the jangling of modernisms as they appear within contemporary practice.

By choosing to study a varied group of artists who are not linked by a shared culture but instead exemplify the rich diversity of contemporary artistic practices in Southeast Asia and its diasporas, I aim to deprovincialize the region's art histories. I do this by showing their interconnectedness with each other and with ideas and practices that extend across the planet, coming together with particular potency in the decolonizing world. The concept of *deprovincializing* is inspired by scholars including Achille Mbembe, who calls for African thinking and experience to be deprovincialized, that is, to be recognized as source of theoretical insight that can be useful far beyond the African continent.[48] I propose deprovincializing Southeast Asia (and other regions across the Global South) as a possible next step after the irreversible (if incomplete) task of "provincializing Europe" and the West.[49] Art-historical research and practice—which is closely linked to processes of epistemic decolonizing, as I will argue throughout this book—has a significant role to play in this deprovincializing option.[50] Artworks from Southeast Asia and the ideas they engender can illuminate and enter into dialogues with artworks and ideas in other parts of the world too.

Deprovincializing ideas and practices from Southeast Asia is one tenet within the more colossal project of decolonizing ways of thinking, studying, and knowing. Much like political and other forms of decolonization, epistemic decolonizing is usually understood as an always ongoing process.[51] The process is complicated in Southeast Asia by the multiple and often overlapping colonial regimes that have dominated different parts of the region for centuries. Unthinking empires in Southeast Asia often involves celebrating the many miraculous forms of knowledge that have been violently denigrated under colonial epistemologies. "The legends of my ancestors were being put to shame," says the protagonist of Pramoedya Ananda Toer's novel (written in Indonesian while the author was a political prisoner), because "science was giving birth to more and more miracles."[52] Decolonizing knowledge is a continuous endeavor toward valuing a richer array of epistemic miracles and ways of knowing, beyond what is typically considered "science," including the legends of ancestors. Epistemic decolonizing, according to many Indigenous scholars, may involve working to decenter colonial ways of knowing while also recognizing that coloniality has sought to define and control knowledge.[53]

It is by grappling with this dual challenge that decolonizing ways of knowing may become also a process of deprovincializing sources of knowledge. In this book, I position contemporary artistic practices as miraculous in their ability to enable insights into under-studied modernisms in Southeast Asia. I understand these artistic art histories as contributing to processes of deprovincializing and also decolonizing knowledge in, from, and for this region.

Doing and Making, and Bringing Art Histories Back to Life

Artists' engagements with art-historical narratives are provisional and continuous. They refuse colonial epistemologies that claim comprehensive certainty and finality. Instead they foreground micro-histories, tentative speculations, and the strategic entwining of personal and shared historical narratives. Among the manifold approaches that artistic art histories may take, several recurring tendencies stand out, and these constitute the structuring concepts of this book. When artists engage in art-historical work, they reveal the art of the past to be lively, even alive; they foreground the many human and nonhuman lives and life-forces that create and animate artworks and also art histories. Artists (in Southeast Asia, as elsewhere) often share the view, articulated by a group of painters in Baghdad in 1969, that "the past is not a dead object that we study; rather it is a stance that goes *beyond time*."[54]

I understand artistic art histories as provisional and continuous—beyond time—and this is reflected in my use of the present participle to describe the epistemological and heuristic strategies taken by artists; in their works, they are *honoring*, *citing*, *staging*, *autotheorizing*, and *teaching*. Through these and other means (and this list is also, of course, provisional and incomplete), artists are *doing* and *making* the practice of art history. This is particularly possible in Southeast Asia because of the relative recentness and malleability of the discipline in this region, as mentioned previously. By simultaneously doing and making, artists in, from, and otherwise affiliated with Southeast Asia are imagining and reimagining the possibilities and parameters of an art history of and for this region, which is related to and yet also distinct from the kinds of art histories that are done and made elsewhere, including in the former colonial centers of the North and the West. In many languages, including many of Southeast Asia's vernaculars, a single word is used for both doing and making. Some examples include the words *làm* in Vietnamese, *tham* in Thai, *buat* in Malay, *thveu* in Khmer, and *faire* in French; all these verbs can mean to do and to make. This simple linguistic alignment facilitates a sense that through their practice of doing art history, artists in Southeast Asia are also actively participating in making the discipline for the region. This doing and making is also a process of undoing and unmaking colonial ways of knowing and thereby contributes to the ongoing process of decolonizing art-historical practice.

Artists doing and making art histories are entwining the aesthetic with the epistemic, which is often reflected in an intermediality of forms and a multisensory and embodied approach to knowing. The artists I discuss in this book seem to share the art historian Cara L. Lewis's commitment to approaching aesthetic form as "a verb as well as a noun" and thereby enabling "a vision of form not only as a state of *being* but also as a kind of *doing*."[55] That is, for the makers of artistic art histories, the aesthetic form of an artwork actively participates in how it enables and enacts meaning, including thinking and theorizing about the art of the past. Discussing writing (rather than art), Black feminist scholar Jennifer C. Nash has proposed that "beautiful writing" reflects a commitment that is at once "aesthetic, ethical, and political," suggesting that form can shape meaning in ways that are at once affective and ideological.[56] Mieke Bal has written extensively on "the integration of philosophy (thinking) and (close) analysis (doing)" and celebrates the value of ambiguity as "crucial to meaning-making."[57] She insists that "theory, and more broadly, thinking [are] a crucial part of intermediality" and sees this theory and thinking as happening on the part of artists as well as their audiences, emerging from "the dynamic between the works as objects, their perceivers, and the time in which these come together" and also "accompanied by the social buzz that surround both."[58] That this thinking and theorizing are multisensory and embodied—that is, they are a kind of knowing that happens in the fingertips and bellies of artists and their audiences as well in their ears and eyes—is underscored by the repeated emphasis on tactile encounters in many of the artworks discussed in this book, as in the example of Thao Nguyen Phan's hands gently caressing Diem Phung Thi's sculptures, discussed previously.

Artists in Southeast Asia are not alone in conceiving and creating regional art histories. Their work is sometimes produced in dialogue with scholars and independent researchers, as well as curators. Research-intensive curatorial projects at independent spaces have been particularly significant in expanding the parameters of what art histories are and can be in the region.[59] While in the past decade or so there has been a striking surge of interest in art-historical research in Southeast Asia, this is largely centered outside of traditional Western-style academies, in both small-scale organizations and large, state-funded museums such as the National Gallery Singapore. Southeast Asia's art histories belong not only—not even primarily—to academics employed by universities but also and equally to artists; the contours and textures of the discipline are continually imagined in contemporary artists' studies and accounts of often overlooked modernist art histories and in their works that engage with obscure but inspiring art-historical precedents.

When artists engage with art-historical information and ideas in their works—when they make artistic art histories—they bring the region's modern art back to life. The artists that this book discusses choose to focus on Southeast Asia's lesser-known modernist artists and artworks in their practices.

Images, objects, concepts, and stories that had been languishing in obscurity—often inaccessible to or overlooked by scholars, students, and publics—are revitalized and illuminated anew through their reappearance in contemporary artworks. Within artistic art histories, the region's modernist artists are invested with a new relevance to the present and to the personal and subjective experience of contemporary artists and their publics today.

My use of the phrase "back to life" to describe these twinned processes of reanimation of historical thinking and subjectivization of theoretical thinking draws on two other uses of the phrase: one is from Vann Molyvann and the other is from Sara Ahmed. Writing in very different contexts, the two figures are brought into proximity due to my own personal and research interests in modernist architecture in twentieth-century Cambodia and feminist theory in the twenty-first-century anglosphere, reflecting my own insider-outsider status as a long-term resident in Southeast Asia who is not Southeast Asian by birth. Put another way, in using "back to life" to try to think through and articulate the kinds of art-historical and theoretical doing and making that artistic art histories enable, I am also participating in these processes of reanimation and subjectivization.

The acclaimed architect and cultural official Vann Molyvann (1926–2017) described his vision for a decolonized modernity distinct to Cambodia in its first years after independence from almost a century of colonial rule. He affirmed the following:

> Modernity should not be inspired superficially by Western ideas that destroy all traces of the past. New building should bring tradition and heritage *back to life*.[60]

With this statement (as with much of his practice), Molyvann is rejecting the kind of modernism (in architecture as well as art and other fields) that he had encountered in Paris, where he studied during the late 1940s and early 1950s, during the final days of colonial rule.[61] The scholar Marshall Berman, in his discussion of chiefly Western modernities and modernisms, describes an "impersonal drive that seems to be endemic to modernization" that he characterizes as "the drive to create a homogenous environment, a totally modernized space, in which the look and feel of the old world have disappeared without a trace."[62] Instead of this destructive form of modernization, Molyvann is decolonizing the modern by proposing a locally inflected modernity in which "tradition and heritage" (Berman calls this "the look and feel of the old world") is treasured and utilized—brought "back to life"—in the development of new, modern forms.

Molyvann's instinct was shared by many of his peers in Southeast Asia, including modern artists in the region. The art historian and critic Alice

Guillermo writes (describing the Philippine context) that "to become meaningful modernism must necessarily draw on impulses from the matrix of the native culture."[63] Similar ideas of multiple and discrepant modernities and modernisms have also been discussed by art historians in other Asias, as well as in other regions across the decolonizing world or Global South, and in the North and the West.[64] When contemporary artists engage with Southeast Asian modernisms in their practice, they revisit and revitalize the possibility for modernisms, in Guillermo's terms, "to become meaningful." Through their focus on overlooked artists and other figures, artists reanimate the region's modernisms, bringing them back to life.

Artistic art histories also bring obscure modernist artists and artworks from the past into proximity with the lived experience of contemporary artists today; they are personal and (sometimes implicitly, sometimes avowedly) autotheoretical. In this sense, they follow the scholar Sara Ahmed's (1969–) affirmation:

> The personal is theoretical. Theory itself is often assumed to be abstract: something is more theoretical the more abstract it is, the more it is abstracted from everyday life. To abstract is to drag away, detach, pull away, or divert. We might then have to drag theory back, to bring theory *back to life*.[65]

Ahmed calls for scholars as well as feminists in other fields to feel empowered to draw on their own subjective senses of the world as a resource for their theoretical thinking. As well as reanimating Southeast Asian modernisms, artistic art histories also follow Ahmed's call, bringing the art of the past into intimate proximity with the lived, often personal and even messy present-day experiences of contemporary artists and their publics.

To return to the example of Thao Nguyen Phan's engagement with the modernist artist Diem Phung Thi, Phan brings Diem back to life, both in the sense of reanimation as propounded by Molyvann and of subjectivization as articulated by Ahmed. Since her death in 2002, Diem's practice had been largely unknown outside of small, specialist circles before Phan began researching her. As a result of the contemporary artist's work, however, several collectors and institutions in Vietnam have acquired Diem's work.[66] Phan has single-handedly reactivated interest in her formerly forgotten forebear, bringing Diem's practice back to life through her art-historical research and artworks. Moreover, Phan's approach also foregrounds the liveliness of Diem's artworks themselves. In the scene in the video that I described previously, Phan makes an offering of incense to a stone sculpture, suggesting that although inert, Diem's work is also invested with a spiritual life. Moreover, her footage highlights the plants abundantly growing in and around Diem's outdoor sculpture, which are also simple signs of liveliness. Phan also brings Diem back to life by highlighting the late artist's relevance to Diem's own practice and experience. When Phan dresses and performs as Diem, by acting the role of the late artist, she suggests the strongly felt affinities she perceives between their lives and practices.

The Politics and Poetics of Inclusion

Thao Nguyen Phan's avowed obsession with Diem Phung Thi is deeply personal—as reflected in her revelation that the artists share the same birthday—and also driven chiefly by an aesthetic affinity that is irresistible, intuitive, and exceeds rational systems of knowledge. Art historian Catherine Grant describes such artistic and art-historical (as well as ideological and other) attachments in terms of fandom, noting that "to be a fan of something often indicates an over-attachment, an excessive engagement that goes beyond the intellectual."[67] This is typical of artistic art histories, in which lines of inquiry are pursued because of deeply-felt fascination and instinct as much as or more than any other factor. After all, artists are always making choices in their work, and these choices can rarely be explained in purely logical or objective terms but also demand to be reckoned with on aesthetic and affective terms. Thus, artists' engagements with art histories may reveal some possibilities for scholarly art historians who are increasingly grappling with questions of what artists and narratives to pay attention to and at what cost. The call for art histories to be more inclusive is as challenging as it is pervasive.

Phan's interest in Diem does not appear to be motivated by a desire to be inclusive. While Phan may champion efforts for Diem's work to be included in more museum collections, this is motivated by her appreciation for Diem's art rather than an interest in her identity. This sets an artist like Phan's approach apart from the politics of inclusion as it is often practiced by art historians and institutions.

Affirmations of inclusion in scholarly art histories can often elide the many exclusions that must also be made in any account of art, especially art beyond the relatively narrow echelons of the so-called Western canon. Of course, no book or exhibition, not even the broadest survey, could ever hope to include every artist, but having recognized this basic fact, we may also notice some patterns and preferences that mean that some individuals and types of practice are more likely to feature in putatively global art histories while others are not. Despite the repeated insistence on the need to be inclusive, the criteria for what to include (and, by unavoidable necessity, what to exclude) are rarely discussed.

Calls for inclusion are generally well-intentioned but nevertheless often descend to what Araya Rasdjarmrearnsook describes as a kind of superficial "yelling," in which scholars "accidentally adopt politicians' traits."[68]

How should art historians decide which artists to pay attention to, and how should they explain or even justify these decisions? By practicing a poetics (alongside or even instead of a politics) of inclusion, artists reveal some possibilities for reframing questions such as these.[69] Because artistic art histories are accounts of the art of the past made by artists rather than scholars, it is to be expected that their decisions about what to study are often guided by aesthetics and impulse rather than or as well as other considerations. Capturing the affective drives governing such work, Grant suggests that some "artists work as fan scholars."[70] Yet because artists also critically engage with the histories of the art they study, they also reveal the intertwining of the aesthetic, the historical, and the political.

Artists may feel more free than scholars when making their choices about what to include and what to exclude. For artists to choose what to focus on in their artworks is clearly a question of choice and creative license (akin to what Grant calls the "creative, productive space of engagement" of fandom).[71] By contrast, for scholars to decide how to be inclusive in their studies may often feel more like a matter of authority or political sensitivity. The intuitive, personal, and poetic sensibility that artists adopt may not always be available to scholars, but it nevertheless reveals a possibility, perhaps even a prospect to which we may aspire. I hope to follow the lead of such artists and use my writing to contribute toward a collective effort to bring art histories back to life, both in the sense of reanimating and subjectivizing the stories of the art of the past. In this book, I seek to amplify the contributions made by the artists I have chosen for detailed discussion.

The question of an inclusive art history is complicated in Southeast Asia by the nascent nature of the discipline. Many modernist artists in this region (like Diem Phung Thi) remain barely known outside of small, specialist circles. Whereas scholars working in and on the so-called Western canon may seek out artists to study primarily because they have been marginalized in most art-historical accounts, for artists and scholars working in and on Southeast Asia, the relative obscurity of an artist may not be a deciding factor at all. Yet while art histories are relatively incipient here, the situation is changing rapidly. For this reason, it is more important than ever to consider how to contribute to the ongoing decolonizing of the ways of knowing that underpin art histories in this region: to devise and deploy epistemologies that do not rely on, perpetuate, or serve coloniality.

Art Histories in the Twenty-first Century in Southeast Asia

Now is the time to rethink what kinds of theoretical and research approaches are most meaningful for art histories in this region because art-historical inquiry is burgeoning in Southeast Asia in the twenty-first century, and its energetic growth is decolonizing in its impulses and intentions. Individuals, collectives, institutions and governments in varying ways all demonstrate a clear, if uneven, awareness of the importance and philosophical value in studying art histories. Others are recognizing the commercial value of the region's art histories too. In 2022, the first Southeast Asian-owned gallery opened in New York's Chelsea district, on the same street as established blue-chip American-owned galleries, and within the last few years, record prices have been set at auction for several modernist artists in the region, including women such as Georgette Chen (1906–1993) and Anita Magsaysay-Ho (1914–2012). Relative to other parts of the world in which art histories have had a longer history, these intellectual and financial commitments and investments may seem paltry and belated. But relative to the region's own history—there was scant scholarship, education, or commerce in art histories just a few decades prior—the sudden surge of interest is unmistakable. There may not yet be a real change in museum collections or scholarship in the North and the West, yet within Southeast Asia, there is a substantial, qualitative shift and embrace of art histories.

The motivations behind the art-historical efflorescence of the twenty-first century range widely, from state-sponsored nation-building and the attraction of tourists to critical and even oppositional recoveries of politically suppressed narratives. Moreover, their methods encompass a broad spectrum of approaches, including the building of collections, the digitization of archives, exhibition-making, publications, formal studies, and many other informal endeavors as well. Yet despite their often divergent ideological agendas and their vastly different scales in both human and financial terms, as well as their varying emphases on different artistic media or geographies or time periods, these manifold moves to do art-historical work in Southeast Asia all contribute to a groundswell of often impassioned interest in the region's art histories. It is in this context that artistic art histories have flourished in this region.

Southeast Asia is famously characterized by its diversity, yet across a spectrum of vastly different populations and disparate material resources, many of the region's national governments are investing in art-historical projects of various kinds. In many cases, governments may be chiefly interested in art that they believe reflects a nationalist agenda, but the effects of their investments may often exceed these narrow motivations. In Singapore, which is the wealthiest country in the region (in terms of GDP per capita) yet with 5 million residents has the second-smallest population, the government invested half a billion dollars in the establishment of the National Gallery Singapore (NGS), which opened in 2015.[72] NGS boasts the world's largest public collection of modern and contemporary art from Southeast Asia, and this collection has been continuing to grow rapidly in the years since the museum opened, as a result of a generous ongoing budget for acquisitions.[73] In Cambodia, which is the second-poorest country in the region (in terms of GDP per capita) and home to 17 million people, the government has energetically pursued the restitution of looted artworks and artefacts, successfully negotiating for the return of large, impressive, and highly valuable premodern and precolonial statues from private collections and prestigious museums in the West.[74] In Malaysia, which is the third-richest country in the region and home to 33 million people, the government-funded Islamic Arts Museum paid a record-breaking price in 2019 for an 1880 artwork by the Turkish artist Osman Hamdi Bey (1842–1910). Titled *Young Woman Reading* or *Girl Reciting the Quran*, the oil on canvas painting was bought for USD 7.4 million and soon after being purchased was loaned to the British Museum for an exhibition.[75] In Thailand, the region's fourth-richest country with a population of some 72 million people, the government offers fully-funded scholarships for Thai students to study postgraduate art history at expensive universities in the US, UK, and elsewhere. Upon completion of their doctoral degrees, these students are guaranteed prestigious (if relatively low-paid) tenure-track positions at the country's top universities, where they are required to work for an agreed minimum period in order to repay the government's investment in their education. At least one university in Singapore offers a similar scheme.[76]

Universities and educational institutions across the region have also demonstrated a commitment to art histories. Sometimes, this has also involved investment. In Singapore, for example, there has been steady growth in both undergraduate and postgraduate art history teaching over the past decade and a half. In 2010, T. K. Sabapathy lamented that the only art-historical courses at universities in Singapore were "boutique offerings" and that the "story of the practice of history of art as a disciplinary field in Singapore is frozen."[77] A decade later, however, the situation was substantially different. One of the country's largest art schools, the Lasalle College of the Arts, began offering a master's degree in Asian art histories in 2010 and a bachelor's degree in art histories and curatorial practices since 2024. One of the two main public universities, Nanyang Technological University, boasts a small art history department with both undergraduate and graduate programs in art history. The other main public university, the National University of Singapore, has offered a minor in art history since 2017, with most of the teaching for the first few years done by curators employed at the NGS and Singapore Art Museum. In 2023, a new University of the Arts Singapore was inaugurated, established on a model similar to the University of the Arts London. In Malaysia, the top university has not invested heavily in art history, but nevertheless, the discipline is growing steadily as it has been recognized as an income stream for the institution. The University of Malaya in Kuala Lumpur receives dozens of applications from international students—most from East Asia—wanting to study art history at a postgraduate level. In Thailand in 2022, the top art school, Silpakorn University, completed an extensive renovation of its historical buildings located next to Bangkok's Grand Palace.

Despite these and many other instances of government and university commitments to art histories, many artists and researchers in Southeast Asia remain dissatisfied with official institutions and have formed independent organizations dedicated to art-historical work. For example, in Kuala Lumpur, the Malaysia Design Archive was established in 2008 "to trace and document Malaysian 'endangered' design legacy, to preserve our historical past, as well as to create a resource of Malaysian art and design work."[78] In Phnom Penh, the Bophana Audiovisual Resource Center was established in 2006 to collect and offer free public access to "film, television, photography and sound archives on Cambodia."[79] In Yogyakarta, the Indonesian Visual Art Archive was founded in 2007, with a collection that "consists of photographs, audiovisual recordings and printed documents that record the various art practices from pre-independence till today."[80] In Yangon, the Save Myanmar Film organization was established in 2017.[81]

Other researchers and practitioners have chosen to establish collectives, rather than organizations, dedicated to art-historical studies in a further demonstration of the breadth of enthusiasm for art histories across a wide range of scales. For example, the Hyphen – collective was established in 2011 "as a sustainable conversational space regarding aesthetic practices" with three (and later five) members based in various cities across Indonesia. They have since engaged in national and international "exhibition-making, various forms of publishing, archiving, research, open-ended conversations, karaoke, barbecue nights, feasts, etcetera."[82] Their most prominent international showing was at the 58th Carnegie International curated by Sohrab Mohebbi in Pittsburgh in 2022, where they were awarded one of two juried prizes for their capsule exhibition within the exhibition.[83] The collective's research centers on various artists, collectives, and exhibitions dating between the 1950s and the 2010s, with a focus on the late twentieth century. In Phnom Penh, the Roung Kon Project was established in 2016 "by a group of architects and architecture students" to study, document, and collect archival materials related to 1960s cinema buildings in Cambodia.[84] In Ho Chi Minh City, a collective of three curators, together with artists and collaborators in 2017 presented an exhibition, essay, and website for "documenting the role and contribution of artist friendships in furthering the development of experimental languages in Vietnam."[85]

In addition to all these collectives, independent organizations, institutions, and governments, the number of individuals with a passionate interest in art history has also been growing during the twenty-first century across Southeast Asia. This claim is impossible to substantiate with data, but it is felt by many organizers of talks and lectures and other art-historical events that draw crowds far exceeding expectations, and it facilitates questions and discussions that are deep and impassioned. This is a logical effect and corollary of the various forms of infrastructural investment mentioned previously. Despite the lingering pessimism of some art historians and others in the region—especially those able to compare the state of art histories here with other parts of the world, particularly in the West where many go for studies—it is clear that art histories are flourishing in Southeast Asia.

But why this surge of interest in diverse forms of alternative art-historical work, and what does this have to do with decolonization? I have already argued that, for many scholars, the history of modern art in Southeast Asia is "is linked with processes related to the attainment of political independence [and] self-determination."[86] In this statement from 1982, Sabapathy is speaking chiefly of artists working in the twentieth century. Might it be that the development of art histories in Southeast Asia in the late twentieth century and especially in the twenty-first century is also linked to these "processes" of striving for independence and autonomy, in short, decolonization? Might the sprouting and blooming of art-historical research, sometimes led by state institutions but very often driven by individuals, especially artists and curators and collectives, be a manifestation of the continuing and incomplete task of epistemically unthinking empire and imaginatively decolonizing Southeast Asia? In this book, these questions hover in the background of my close study of specific artworks.

Like a number of other participants in Southeast Asia's art-historical discourses, I am not Southeast Asian by birth, and I write this book cognizant of my own positionality and experiences, and I am aware that I am both limited and enriched by these.[87] I draw inspiration from the recent methodological turn to "the personal-theoretical, incidental, gut-centered nature of autotheoretical research," and also from the older Indigenous-led affirmation that the activity called "research" is also "a significant site of struggle between the interests and ways of knowing of the West and the interests and ways of resisting of the Other."[88] Specifically, I write as a migrant living and working in this region (for over fifteen years, first in Cambodia and since 2017 in Singapore) and as a lifelong student of Southeast Asia's art without a familial or cultural connection to this part of the world.[89] I recognize that my lived experiences shape my understandings; these include aspects of my identity as they intersect with various forms of privilege, including being white and middle class, as well as my professional trajectory that has involved repeated shifts and overlaps between curatorial and scholarly work, including employment at a state-funded museum and a state-funded university, as well as freelance curatorial work across the region and beyond.[90] I write as both an insider and as an outsider, often negotiating both roles simultaneously. These positions sometimes function to exclude me from some kinds of experience and knowledge and sometimes to enable access and insight. Recognizing these limits and possibilities, in this book, I aim to highlight and elevate the ideas and voices of artists (as well as scholars, curators, and others) in, from, and affiliated with Southeast Asia.

Parenthesized Yet Centered (in Southeast Asia)

In diversely varied ways, the artists discussed in this book may be considered Southeast Asian, although some (especially those raised or based outside the region) may not primarily describe themselves in this way. For some artists, this condition of being from or working in or being otherwise affiliated with the region is central to their sense of self and their way of articulating their practice and to the way their practice is usually described by curators, critics, journalists, and scholars.[91] For other artists, especially those participating in the circuits of discourse and display called the "global contemporary," Southeast Asia may be more peripheral or secondary to the understanding of their practice.

In his ongoing, multiplatform project titled *The Critical Dictionary of Southeast Asia* (2017–ongoing), the artist Ho Tzu Nyen asks, "What constitutes the unity of Southeast Asia—a region never unified by language, religion or political power?"[92] This book will not attempt to answer this largely rhetorical question. Instead, like many others working in and on the region and its art, I regard Southeast Asia as a "geocultural problematic,"[93] an unfolding concept and imaginary, rather than a fixed location, and one largely constituted by its diversity. Yet I share with other scholars of Southeast Asia a belief that "a regional perspective is useful because it provides a vantage that is neither so tightly focused on one locale that it ends up insisting on that place's uniqueness, nor is it so beholden to generalising impulses that it fails to ring true with on-the-ground observations."[94] Thinking at a regional scale lends itself well to theorizing from the particular. Moreover, regional approaches to thinking about art are often linked to efforts at epistemic decolonization.[95]

The artworks I discuss in this book are not positioned as case studies, which is a term that implies that they may represent or typify larger civilizational trends or cultural formations. They instead have been chosen for their ability to generate and enrich a sense of what artistic art histories are and what kinds of knowledge and understanding they can enable. As part of my effort to avoid burdening the artists I discuss here with the responsibility of representing the region, I approach artworks as "theoretical objects," to use a term developed by Hubert Damisch, Mieke Bal, and others, by which I mean that artworks are things to think about theoretically as well as being sources of theoretical insight themselves.[96] Another, perhaps more elegant way of saying this (and recognizing the active subjectivity of artists) is that I approach art itself as being a form of critical activity, recalling the words of Sabapathy, who proposes that "critical activity need not necessarily be defined in terms of, or limited to, literary forms."[97] Yap puts it pithily, describing historiographically-engaged practices as being "art as *method*."[98] My approach, like the approach taken by Bal, Yap, and others, is to think with rather than only about art.

I have chosen to include the geographical and conceptual category—Southeast Asia—in the title of this book for several reasons, even though I make no claim to comprehensive or representative coverage of the entire region. The first and simplest reason is to specify the book's area of specialization and focus. Even with the rise of global art histories and calls to decolonize the discipline, many art-historical (and other) books announce their conceptual focus without any mention of their geographic focus. This may risk perpetuating colonial notions of Western universality. As Kuan-Hsing Chen has famously declared, many canonical Western scholars were "actually doing European studies" since "European experiences were their system of reference." Chen urges scholars to "recognize how extremely limited the current conditions of knowledge are" and thereby to learn "to be humble about our knowledge claims."[99] I announce the purview of this book as being "in Southeast Asia" (a region that is as imaginary, dispersed, and "geocultural" as it is geographical) in an effort to be specific and humble about its knowledge claims.

Yet I also invite readers to imagine that specification as parenthesized, that is, to temper or decenter it. While I do not wish to perpetuate what Chen calls the "universalist assertions of theory," I also do not wish to contribute to the ghettoization of studies of Southeast Asia's art histories.[100] Instead, as I've mentioned, I aim to contribute to the ongoing deprovincializing of the region and its art. By suggesting that we imagine the region as parenthesized, I make a winking gesture toward "bracketing" in phenomenological philosophy, which in essence calls for a suspension of judgment. I recognize that being Southeast Asian remains in many settings "a limit to, rather than a guarantee of, suitability" for study by art historians without an existing specialization in this region, to borrow a phrase from another book in which (real, not imagined) titular parentheses play a striking rhetorical role.[101]

While art-historical studies languish in many parts of the world, in Southeast Asia, the discipline is flourishing with an energy and expansiveness that is unprecedented in the region. It is for this reason that the practice of artistic art histories matters a great deal in Southeast Asian contexts. Here, the discipline is making itself and being made, and artistic practice is participating significantly in that provisional and continuous process of decolonizing and imaginative creation.

Back to Life: The Structure of the Book

In this book, I emulate the way that contemporary artists bring their modernist forebears back to life by structuring the chapters around some of the various provisional and continuous actions that are performed through artists' strategies of doing and making artistic art histories. This is reflected in my use of present participle verbs, which suggest a state of being active, incomplete, and ongoing: honoring, citing, staging, autotheorizing, and teaching. Each chapter concentrates on close and careful studies of a small number of artists and artworks. Yet in each chapter, I also offer a brief discussion of some other practices that elaborate a context for these more focused analyses. Throughout, knowing is multisensory and embodied. As the scholar Chairat Polmuk has argued, embodiment may be theorized multiply, with reference not only to anglophone affect studies but also Buddhist thought.[102] My thinking alongside and with artists and their practices is an instance of what scholars have termed "theorizing together," in which theorizing is at once practical (like riding a bike), explicit, reflexive, and often collaborative.[103]

The book's narrative begins with individual histories, then expands to consider broader historical narratives before simultaneously returning to the personal and turning to the theoretical. In this way, the structure of the book reflects a commitment—which I share with the artists who I discuss—to theorizing outwards from the subjective and particular. The art historian Ashley Thompson playfully and provocatively writes of "a small that is large," and although for her this is chiefly "a deconstructive complication of the very notion of scale," I also understand Thompson's attention to "small and large at once" to be a way to attend both to "irreducibly singular" qualities in works of art and also their greater, theorizable implications.[104] Close readings propel my claims. I begin, in chapter 1, with a discussion of two artists whose approach to artistic art histories is highly personal; they study their own grandfathers. I then move from the personal to the inter-personal, with chapter 2's focus on direct artistic citations of other artists' works. In chapter 3, I expand to consider artists' relationships to broader narratives of modern art in Southeast Asia. This enlarging continues in chapter 4, which examines artists' engagements with wider theoretical concerns, yet this also marks a return to the emphatically personal approach of the artists discussed at the beginning of the book.

In chapter 1, I examine the ways in which contemporary artists engage with the art histories of Southeast Asian modernisms as a means of *honoring* the contributions of their forebears. Practices of honoring are concerned with offering respect while still retaining the possibility of coded critique. This process of honoring is often deeply personal, even while it also intersects with larger shared histories, and it is rooted in Southeast Asian cultural norms that also underpin the other approaches to artistic art histories as described in the chapters that follow. I propose the *sampeah kru*—a dance-ritual performed in Cambodia, which may be literally translated as a greeting to teachers both living and dead, human and spirit—as a queer theoretical model for understanding practices of honoring.

This chapter centers on a 2019 video artwork by Sriwhana Spong (1979–) and a 2011 feature-length film by Davy Chou (1983–), both of which honor the work of their grandfathers, whom they never met, yet whose work resonates with and in some ways enables their own contemporary practices. Both Chou and Spong use digital research methods and draw on their diasporic upbringings and sensibilities. Both Spong and Chou's works navigate experiences of living in diaspora while also illuminating histories that have been largely overlooked by scholars. For these artists and others who adopt a practice of honoring, artistic art histories really matter; the stakes are high, including for reasons that are deeply personal for the artists as well as reasons that are tied to shared historical violence related to colonialism. This is why I approach honoring in the first chapter as a precursor to those that follow.

Coded and covert strategies of criticality are also articulated through the practice of *citing*, which is the subject of chapter 2, thereby expanding the book's focus from the personal to the interpersonal. My concept of citing (as distinct from received, Western ideas like appropriation) is elaborated with reference to paintings made by the pioneering modernist painter Emiria Sunassa (1894–1964). In Indonesia in the 1940s, she made several paintings based on published photographs by the canonical European artist Walter Spies (1895–1942), who had lived and worked in Bali since the 1920s. As well as being one of very few women to professionally exhibit in the period—in Indonesia or anywhere in Southeast Asia—Emiria was also a prominent anticolonial activist. Her practice of citing Spies encompasses both a display of mastery, calling forth her artistic sources, and also an act of daring, taking from them without acknowledgement. Drawing in part on Southeast Asian vernacular terms, I offer a theory of citing that emphasizes the decolonizing implications of Emiria's reliance on Spies' compositions and her defiance of his (white, masculine, artistic, and anthropological) authority.

Chapter 3 is concerned with *staging*, a speculative and creative contemporary strategy for recovering and resurfacing art histories that may otherwise have been lost due to limitations in archival or other sources. Thus, the chapter expands the book's focus from interpersonal approaches to artists engaged with broader historical narratives. By staging encounters between history and fiction, the archival and the imagined, artists can critically speculate about the legacies of under-studied modernisms within present-day art and culture and imaginatively embroider gaps in the art-historical record, which often result from colonial and other forms of historical violence. I propose that staging is dramatic (staged like a play or a movie), heterochronic (encompassing several stages in history), experimental (staged like an experiment or essayistic attempt), and contingent (resembling temporary staging or scaffolding). This chapter centers on a close reading of another project by Thao Nguyen Phan—first exhibited in a 2022 solo show at Tate St Ives and in the 2022 Venice Biennale—in which she turns her attention away from the modernist sculptor Diem Phung Thi, to instead focus on little-known modernist architects whose buildings are emblematic of postcolonial nation-building in Vietnam and Cambodia. Phan's staging sees her inventing a laborer who worked on some of these structures. Her work is discussed in dialogue with Hilmi Johandi's (1987–) use of colonial-era posters in a public installation and Fyerool Darma's (1987–) engagement with archival sound recordings held in colonial archives in Berlin.

The dual status of art-historical narratives and sources as both personal and shared recurs throughout the book. This reflects the affective qualities and high stakes of artistic art histories in Southeast Asia. In chapter 4, I discuss the practices of several artists as instances of *autotheorizing*; thus, the book's focus expands from the historical to turn to the theoretical while also returning to personal stories, which is the focus of chapter 1. In chapter 4, I explicate the concept of autotheorizing by integrating recent discussions of autotheory in the anglophone academy (by scholars such as Lauren Fournier) with enactments of the practice in Southeast Asia, including in the region's vernacular languages. Araya Rasdjarmrearnsook's (1957–) uncategorizable writing is a key theoretical source guiding my understanding of her installation and moving image artworks, as well as paintings by the self-taught hotel worker-turned-painter Svay Ken (1933–2008) in Phnom Penh. These artistic art histories suggest that autotheorizing is a key strategy that underpins many of the provisional and continuous methods elaborated in previous chapters. This autotheorizing takes various forms; some (like Araya's) are more outward looking and engaged with the work of peers and predecessors, while others (like Svay Ken's) are more autobiographical in approach.

The various approaches to artistic art histories discussed in this book offer conceptual and theoretical tools for understanding the enduring significance of the art of the past and its appearance in the narratives of today. All the artists in the book conduct research, but this is not their main contribution. Rather, their practices offer new ways of thinking about art histories (in Southeast Asia). In doing this, these artistic art histories are not only researching, thinking, and theorizing, but also teaching. This takes on particular importance given the relative scarcity of art-historical education within universities in the region.

In a short epilogue, I consider the relationships between the practice and pedagogy of art histories. A four-part television program about art-historical figures made by Ho Tzu Nyen (1976—) and broadcast nationally in Singapore in 2005 guides my thinking about the provisional and continuous practice of *teaching*. Ho's approach resonates with but also complicates Araya's polemical suggestion that "the only place left to talk about art is in the art class."[105] By focusing on teaching in the epilogue, I also ask what kinds of *knowing* are enacted in artistic art histories in the context of the unending work of decolonizing, epistemic and otherwise. I borrow the concept of epistemic injustice from philosophy to suggest that artistic art histories may help enlarge spaces for thinking and theorizing within art and for its histories.

1

HONORING

Will I smell it first or will I hear it first? This is what I remember wondering as I found the right doorway and began to climb the steep stairs to my friend's apartment in Phnom Penh.[1] I was on my way to a *sampeah kru*, and I knew from past experiences that these are sensorially rich events: fragrant and sonic spectacles of performance, devotion, and honoring. Part dance and part ritual, a *sampeah kru* is done every Thursday morning by performing artists in Cambodia and the diasporas to honor and offer respect to their *kru*—teachers and other artistic forebears, including humans, spirits, and deities. Similar practices are known throughout much of the region; for example, in Laos and Thailand, a *wai khru* is also sometimes performed by healers, boxers, students, and other practitioners.

As I climbed the stairs, I was suddenly and simultaneously hit by the viscous odor of incense and fresh jasmine and the abundant and polyphonous sound of the Khmer *pinpeat* orchestra; more than visual or cerebral, this was an embodied encounter. An elegantly jostling crowd of dancers, musicians, artists, and friends was gathered in the upstairs apartment that served as a rehearsal and performance space for the choreographer Prumsodun Ok (1987–) and his dance company, which was called Natyarasa (2015–2023). Describing themselves as "Cambodia's first gay dance company," Natyarasa characterized their work as an attempt to "re-stage Khmer classical dances with a vital freshness" and "infuse our tradition with a contemporary spirit."[2] They danced to bring this ancient artform back to life, and queerness was central to the liveliness of their practice of reanimation and subjectivization. The dancers all identified as queer, and in their work they demonstrated both respect for the conventions of their artform and a readiness to alter and even subvert those same conventions. For the *sampeah kru* on that December morning, they had invited a group of musicians and choreographers from Japan to begin collaboratively exploring the little-known history of a centuries-old exchange between the performing arts cultures of the two countries, a process of inter-Asia research that may lead to a new performance that may be another instance of artistic art histories.[3]

This chapter is about *honoring* as a strategy, which recurs in many artistic art histories in Southeast Asia. Many contemporary artists choose to study and celebrate modernist forebears who have been overlooked in most conventional, academic art-historical accounts. For various reasons—sometimes personal, sometimes spiritual, and often decolonial and political—artists choose to devote their artworks to a provisional and continuous process of honoring. This honoring is a strategy and attitude adopted instead of or as well as art-historical methods that might be more familiar or expected in most Western or scholarly approaches (ranging from social art history to anthropology to formalist art criticism), such as explicit critique. For cultural and political reasons, open criticism of artistic predecessors is not always possible or preferable in Southeast Asia as elsewhere in the Global South or decolonizing world. Instead of seeing this as a circumstance of lack or shortcoming, I argue that the concept of honoring enables an implicitly critical kind of nostalgia, which is often a means of healing after (personal or collective) historical violence. Honoring, like other approaches taken in artistic art histories, brings the art of the past back to life, reanimating it and foregrounding its subjective significance in the present day.

My interest in honoring as an attitude, an aesthetic gesture, and an epistemic and political attitude—chiefly inspired by the *sampeah kru* dance-ritual—is also nourished by intersectional resonances I perceive in Black feminist discourse on honoring in literary and theoretical practices. Jennifer C. Nash, in her study of what she calls "beautiful writing" done by Black feminist scholars, positions that "unprecedented commitment to poetic language as crucial to honoring Black women's freedom dreams and practices of living."[4] I am drawn to Nash's articulation of honoring as it offers a generative language for making sense of the artistic practices I see proliferating in Southeast Asia. These artists are—perhaps in a way that is similar to, even while also certainly distinct from, Black feminist theorists—"honoring . . . sacred creative and intellectual work" done by their forebears.[5] They are also "honoring dream, memory and its imperfection, fantasy, and the idea of fate."[6]

In this chapter, I first discuss the *sampeah kru* ceremony as one possible model for thinking about artistic practices of honoring. I then discuss two films in detail, one by the artist Sriwhana Spong and one by the filmmaker Davy Chou. Both Spong and Chou have made significant works centered on their grandfathers, who they never met yet whose artistic and cinematic practices relate to and in some ways even enable their own. By honoring their grandfathers, Spong and Chou reveal the enmeshing of personal and larger shared histories, both within Southeast Asia and across its diasporas (where both Chou and Spong grew up). In their works, they draw on family members as informants while also making use of various digital methods for research; both oral histories and digital databases are important sources for conventional art histories, too, and Chou and Spong offer inspiring examples of how to interweave these two very different approaches. Like the *sampeah kru* at Prumsodun's apartment, which I could not see or think about without first being enveloped in its smells and sounds, the honoring that is done by Spong and Chou is embodied and contemporary while also being innovative and subtly critical.

Sampeah Kru as Theoretical Model

Writing in what he claims is the first history of Khmer dance to be written by a practitioner, Prumsodun Ok proudly affirms the following:

> I belong to a lineage of artists more than 1,000 years old. I practice an art form developed as a prayer in movement for rain and fertility, one that symbolizes the highest in Khmer notions of beauty and identity.[7]

The importance of lineage is reflected in the *sampeah kru*, which Prumsodun explains "*honors* pedagogical relationships at its core."[8] In this conception of ancestry and inheritance, some among each passing generation of students will become teachers, renewing the cycle of artistic and spiritual practice (fig. 1.1). The *sampeah kru* "is a moment in which love, history, hope, and knowledge are passed on from teacher to student, teacher to student. It is a moment of gratitude and of reflection; it is a moment of celebration and *honoring*."[9] This ceremonial dance, Prumsodun insists, "is a significant moment of intergenerational connection, a time and space in which dancers both young and old connect to our ancient lineage and its legacy."[10] The dance scholar Toni Shapiro-Phim concurs, describing the *sampeah kru* dance ritual as "a salutation (*sampeah*) to the spirits and teachers (*kru*), both living and deceased," that reflects "the power and significance of the teacher-student bond in the handing down of accumulated wisdom."[11]

The ancient and continuing practice of honoring teachers and other *kru* offers one possible theoretical model for examining contemporary practices of

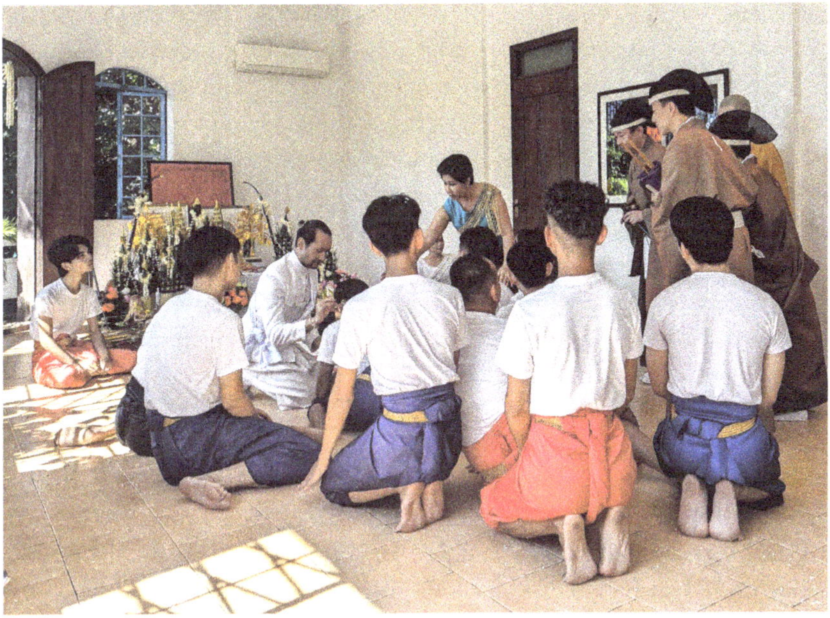

FIGURE 1.1. Prumsodun Ok and his teacher Sophiline Cheam Shapiro with dancers and musicians at a *sampeah kru* at Prumsodun's apartment, Phnom Penh, December 2022. Photograph by the author.

honoring within artistic art histories. Elaborating on the kind of exchange embedded within the practice of *sampeah kru*, Shapiro-Phim says,

> In return for the gratitude and respect they show through weekly offerings of incense and elaborate pre-performance and annual ceremonies, and for the acknowledgement of their proper place in the artistic and spiritual hierarchies, dancers receive blessings for continued growth and protection from their teachers and, it is hoped, from the spirits of the dance.[12]

In this understanding and within this belief system, the aestheticized and ritualized form of honoring teachers and spirits ensures many forms of continuity: for a dancer's practice, the development and growth of that practice, and the health of the community at large. In Thailand, versions of the *wai khru* ceremony are also practiced at hospitals to help guide and strengthen healers in their treatment of the unwell.[13]

During times of violence and upheaval, practices of honoring such as *sampeah kru* have been essential to the mental and spiritual health of dancers. In Cambodia during the Khmer Rouge genocide of the late 1970s, dancers performed *sampeah kru* as one of the only means at their disposal to resist the policies of the regime—which forbade prerevolutionary artforms such as Khmer dance—and also to survive the threat of illness and starvation. Recalling that period, one dancer said that she "felt that if she could perform a *sampeah kru* she might survive" and so she secretly completed the ritual, after which, "slowly, she recovered."[14] In this account, the practice of honoring is essential to an individual's life and survival in a very literal sense; the dance-ritual may be felt to actually bring an artist back to life.

The *sampeah kru* has also been crucial for collective cultural survival. Shapiro notes that the ceremony is "about gratitude, acknowledgement and remembering" and explains that "'remembering' takes on added meaning in the context of the losses suffered by the Khmer," and that, in the two decades after the 1975 to 1979 genocide, the *sampeah kru* "is about 'putting back together' before being able to move forward."[15] Although the scale of Cambodia's suffering during the genocide is unique, many other parts of Southeast Asia have also endured historical violence, including during colonialism and decolonization. Therefore, while Cambodia's need for "putting back together" is singular, a similar urge for collective, cultural repair is also felt elsewhere in the region and among its diasporas. The scholar Andreas Huyssen recognizes that "in many cases, the violence is still much closer to home in the Global South today than it has ever been for most post-war European or North American citizens," and he characterizes the artistic response to and attempt to heal from this violence as "memory art."[16] The practice of the *sampeah kru* during and after the genocide in Cambodia suggests that customary artistic forms may offer precedents and sources for Southeast Asian manifestations of this "memory art." Shapiro also proposes that "communication with the *kru* and participation in dance performances may also have provided models for ritualized resistance at the level of everyday practice under various political regimes."[17] In this sense, Prumsodun and his Natyarasa dance company may have been drawing sustenance from honoring their teachers and forebears to help them withstand the challenges of practicing as an openly queer ensemble. Shapiro studied dance communities in Phnom Penh during the late 1980s and early 1990s, and her detailed account of a *sampeah kru* performed in 1990 shares many similarities with my own experiences of the dance ritual during the late 2000s, 2010s, and early 2020s.[18]

At Prumsodun's apartment in December 2022, I encountered a similar atmosphere of reverence and celebration and similar ceremonial acts and symbolic offerings yet also some important differences. For one, the dancers in the Natyarasa company all identify as queer, most as gay men. By contrast, the dancers Shapiro observed in 1990 all identified as women, as has been the norm in

Khmer dance for centuries. Prumsodun's introduction of male-identified dancers has been controversial within the Cambodian community.[19] As well as the gender of the dancers, the musical component of the *sampeah kru* I joined in December 2022 also differed from the norm when the visiting Japanese musicians joined in the performance. As their wind and percussive instruments swung in and out of harmony with the Khmer instruments in the *pinpeat* orchestra, Prumsodun read a text he had written specially for the occasion, which combined customary Khmer and Pali prayers with new incantations of his own devising. As he frequently does in his writings, interviews, conversations, and teachings, Prumsodun gave particular prominence to his teacher, the choreographer Sophiline Cheam-Shapiro, as well as Sophiline's teachers, Chea Samy and Chheng Phon. He did not name any of the senior dancers currently involved with the Royal Ballet company, implicitly marking his independent and partly diasporic lineage as one distinct from the official, palace-sponsored mainstream.

This highlights the possibility for coded criticality alongside and within the practice of honoring that is central to the *sampeah kru*. While *kru* can comprise living and deceased teachers as well as spirits and deities, it is up to the practitioners performing the dance ceremony to decide which *kru* to name and include in offerings of respect and gratitude. Writing of *wai khru* as they are performed by healers at hospitals in northern Thailand, one scholar notes that "the principal purpose of the *wai khru* . . . is not to honor the Buddha, but rather the lineage of divine and human teachers that have more directly contributed to one's healing practice."[20] Identifying who that lineage comprises (and by implication, who is *not* considered part of one's lineage) is a subtly critical act.

This is a poetics of inclusion (and exclusion) which is political, too. To exclude a key figure may be considered to be disrespectful, or perhaps even to be dishonoring, but it may also be excused as a necessary and normal effect of an artistic decision that is chiefly aesthetic in nature. Exclusion as a form of critique is acceptable because it is encoded in an artistic gesture. By contrast, open denigration of other dancers or artists, especially of more senior practitioners, is generally considered culturally inappropriate in Cambodia, Thailand, and many other Southeast Asian contexts, so quieter and more implicit forms of critique such as this are important in ways that may not always be easily legible to some outsiders.

Just as the dance ritual enables the possibility of implicit and coded critique alongside honoring and within processes of remembering, it is also open to the possibility of innovating customary forms, combining the traditional with the experimental and contemporary and bringing these back to life through a process of creative and sometimes queer reanimation. Prumsodun's integration of the visiting Japanese musicians with a conventional Khmer *pinpeat* orchestra is an example of this. So too is his respectful acknowledgement of several contemporary visual artists and foreign scholars who were attending that December morning in the same ritualized chanting within which his dance teachers and other more expected *kru* figures were also named. These innovations in the form of the *sampeah kru* reflect Prumsodun's own intermedial practice, which comprises not only classical and contemporary dance and choreography, but also filmmaking, writing, and other forms of artistic endeavor.

By reminding his students in the Natyarasa company of the names and significance of his teachers, his teachers' teachers, and the spirits and deities who guide them all, perhaps Prumsodun was also performing artistic art histories in his *sampeah kru* that morning. Because the students, as well as other attendees like myself, were asked to actively participate in certain moments of the ritual, such as the passing of symbolic objects like the *babil* (or *popil*) candle holder around the room, we were encouraged not only to memorize names but also to physically embody the lessons of these teachers who we were collectively and collaboratively honoring.[21] Indeed, Prumsodun's teacher Sophiline, who was also present at the ceremony, used it as an opportunity to correct and improve the posture and choreography of other dancers over the course of the event. Together on that December morning, we inhaled the lineage like the incense that hung heavy in the air; it animated our bodies like the music that reverberated through the walls.

In these ways, the honoring that is practiced in the *sampeah kru* is affective and embodied as well as implicitly critical, innovative, and contemporary. Therefore, it offers one possible theoretical model for thinking about similar strategies at work in other kinds of honoring within the forms of contemporary practice I call artistic art histories. This chapter examines some examples of these; a related attitude recurs in artworks discussed in later chapters, particularly in Svay Ken's work, which is examined in chapter 4. As will become clear, when artists do art-historical research, thinking, and theorizing in their works, they are able to adopt many methods that may be alternative to, or even exceed, those typically taken up by scholarly art historians.

First, though, I need to consider my own place in this account. I have already suggested that an encounter with a *sampeah kru* is so sensorial as to be difficult to describe without reference to first-person subjective experience. But what is my personal relationship with Spong's video and Chou's film, both of which center on their grandfathers who they never met? Both works entangle personal and shared histories, but the similarities between them are coincidental. Spong and Chou did not know each other (or each other's work) when they produced the films I discuss. Over a prolonged period of thinking alongside these works, I have slowly come to realize that my understanding of them is colored by another coincidence: the fact that I, too, never met my grandfather, and that the trajectory of his life was also shaped by his individual circumstances and by larger historical forces of violent displacement. My grandfather was born in Germany in 1900 in a Jewish family. He fled the country soon after Hitler came to power in 1933, moving first to the United Kingdom and then, when war began to seem inevitable, to Aotearoa New Zealand, a place that he apparently chose because of its remoteness from Europe. His family members fled to other far-flung places more commonly associated with the Jewish diaspora at that time, including New York and Shanghai. Although my grandfather's medical practice flourished in Auckland, his status as a refugee and as a (former) citizen of an enemy nation was hard to shake. For example, due to absurdly ignorant and racist laws, he was prohibited from using radio equipment during the wartime years, and until his death, he carried cash in large quantities "just in case" of some (always unspecified) peril. My grandfather died a few years before I was born, but I often wonder whether growing up with stories about his life contributed to my interest in and care for refugee experiences and stories of displacement and my sense that the personal and the historical are always intertwined. History, too, is lived and felt; this also includes art histories, including those done and made by artists.

"The Poem is a Temple": Sriwhana Spong's *The painter-tailor*

In 2019, the artist Sriwhana Spong (1979–) made a single-channel video titled *The painter-tailor*, which is a fertile example of honoring within the practice of artistic art histories.[22] Over thirty-two minutes, the work pays tribute to the story of Spong's late grandfather, an artist named I Gusti Made Rundu (1918–1993, hereafter referred to as Gusti Rundu), and specifically his last painting, which is also his only work to remain in the collection of the artist's family. Spong's work shares new art-historical information and ideas about Gusti Rundu's practice while also emphasizing his emotional and personal importance to Spong and her extended family in Bali.

Spong has made several other works that may be considered artistic art histories, although without Southeast Asian references. One example is *Costume for a Mourner* (2010), a digital video, which "reimagines a scene from Sergei Diaghilev's 1925 Ballets Russes production of *Le chant du rossignol (The song of the nightingale)*," a ballet that is "based on Hans Christian Andersen's 1844 tale of a mechanical songbird given to the emperor of China by the emperor of Japan," and that, in its 1925 production, "featured an orchestral score by Igor

Stravinsky, choreography by Léonide Massine and later George Balanchine, and an orientalist set and costumes designed by Henri Matisse."[23] More recently, a trio of moving image works Spong made during her doctoral studies all enact a kind of dialogue with texts that were written by historical figures who the artist describes as "mystic women," calling their publications "translations of their authors' direct encounter with the divine."[24] It is notable that Spong repeatedly takes up the artistic practice (including choreography and writings) of her predecessors as the subject matter of her works—that is, she makes artistic art histories—and also that collaboration is a recurring concern both at the level of narrative and methodology in these works. We return to the matter of collaboration after considering other aspects of *The painter-tailor.*

Chou shares with Spong a desire to make films on a diverse range of subjects, not all of which have any direct relation to Southeast Asia. His 2022 feature film, *Return to Seoul*, centers on a woman who was born in Korea but raised by adoptive parents in France. By contrast, Chou was raised by his Cambodian-born parents in France, where he was born. Both Spong and Chou have no personal or familial ties to many of the stories that they engage with in their work, and their films about their grandfathers occupy a singular position within their oeuvres. For both artists, growing up in the diasporas seems to have enabled a flexible and fluctuating sense of cultural affiliation and a cosmopolitan subjectivity.

It is important to recognize from the outset that Spong is not a "Southeast Asian artist" in any straightforward sense. Both her complexly diasporic positionality (raised in Aotearoa New Zealand with Balinese and other heritages and now living in London) and her strategically intermittent engagement with her cultural background within her artworks serve to highlight the instability of the category of "Southeast Asian art" and its unviable simplicity within the context of contemporary transnational subjectivities and practices. While *The painter-tailor* is the first video Spong filmed in Bali, she made several other works that refer to Balinese culture and her familial ties to the island, including *Muttnik* (2005), a video depicting flowers and fruits arranged like Balinese spirit offerings, and *Instruments A–J* (2015/16–ongoing), which the artist describes as being "inspired by the percussive instruments of Balinese Gamelan."[25] It may be tempting to see these works and *The painter-tailor* as an attempt to solve what Spong describes as "a double riddle: What is the measure of the distance that makes me inauthentically Indonesian, the measure of the distance that makes me authentically Indonesian?"[26] But the artist's practice is of course more than this; it is personal but also art-historical, and many other things besides. And anyway, as Spong continues, these are "futile questions."[27]

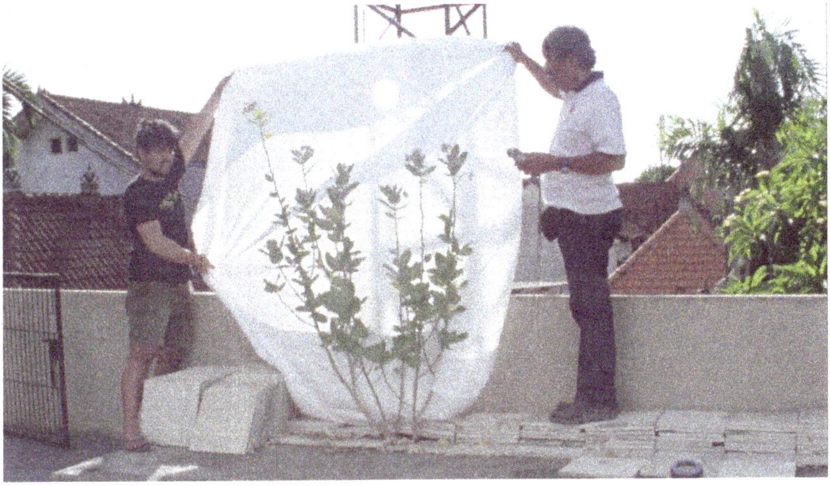

FIGURE 1.2. Sriwhana Spong, *The painter-tailor*, 2019. Single-channel video with sound, 32 mins 10 secs. Digital still. © Sriwhana Spong, courtesy of the artist.

As suggested by its title, *The painter-tailor* reveals that as well as being an artist, Gusti Rundu also worked as a tailor: with these two vocations, he was able to support his family through tumultuous decades of historical violence and economic difficulty (fig. 1.2). Spong's work may be considered a kind of worker's history, a history from below.[28] The painter-tailor's son—who is also Spong's father, and who narrates much of the film—explains that while Gusti Rundu had already been a painter before the Second World War, "during the [time when] the Japanese conquer[ed] the island, he was making shirt[s] for the soldier[s]." He later alternated between painting and making clothing to sell to tourists. This work was "very hard," the son-and-father explains in his laconic voiceover, but he did it "so he can keep the family." Like much of the narration, this is said with a tone of palpable gratitude and affection. In part, *The painter-tailor* appears to be honoring this material contribution made by Gusti Rundu in supporting his (and by extension, Spong's) family.

As is the case with most artistic art histories (in Southeast Asia), the subject of Spong's film is relatively under-studied. He is mentioned only in passing in the scholar Adrian Vickers's widely cited monograph on Balinese art as being one of "the main artists of the Sanur school, which numbered around sixty painters."[29] Sanur is the village in eastern Bali where Gusti Rundu lived and where what Spong calls her "ancestral family home" remains today; many villages in Bali have developed their own distinctive style or "school" of painting.[30] Although he appears within the archives of the pioneering art historian of Indonesia, Claire Holt, Gusti Rundu is not mentioned in her canonical 1967 book on Indonesian art.[31] The photographs from Holt's archive, which appear in Spong's video, place Gusti Rundu in close contact with key figures of modern art in Bali, including his celebrated contemporary, the Dutch-Indonesian painter Arie Smit (1916–2016). Yet whereas there are several books on Smit (in English and Indonesian), scant traces of Gusti Rundu appear in print.[32] By focusing on her grandfather's final painting, Spong is honoring not only his contributions to her family but also his proficiency as an artist, which has rarely been studied by scholars.

Gusti Rundu is certainly nowhere near as well-known as Spong herself, reflecting the relatively poor visibility of Southeast Asia's modernist art histories in contrast to the notably greater diversity of some circuits of contemporary art.[33] Spong's professional achievements embody the transnational trajectory of a "global contemporary artist," including significant exhibitions and experiences in Aotearoa New Zealand and internationally.[34] Educated in Auckland and Rotterdam, Spong has shown her work at the Busan Biennale (2024), Istanbul Biennial (2022), the Auckland Art Gallery Toi o Tāmaki (2020), the Jewish Museum in New York City (2015), the Art Gallery of New South Wales in Sydney (2013), and the Biennale of Sydney (2012), among others. She has held solo exhibitions in Aotearoa New Zealand, the United Kingdom (where she lives and works), and Germany. Spong describes her relationship to her Balinese heritage (and perhaps, by extension, to Southeast Asia) as complex and changing. "[P]rior to embarking on this project," she writes in her 2021 doctoral thesis, "I used to think I had to patch the leaks, to close the distances created by being raised . . . estranged from my Balinese heritage."[35] This is reflected in her practice.

Spong seems to recognize and prize the ability of words and voices to capture shifts and slippages, and the limits of verbal communication, especially in transcultural contexts. These include her own work in Bali, recalling that *The painter-tailor* was the first video she had ever filmed on the island. In one of the few scholarly essays on Spong's practice, the curator and critic Wong Binghao stresses that "the generative tension of vague (in)decipherability is key to Spong's artistic stratagem."[36] When we hear Spong's voice in *The painter-tailor*, it is almost out of range of the microphone, yet is unmistakably accented with the distinctively flattened vowels of Aotearoa New Zealand English, which contrasts sharply with the sonorous Indonesian English spoken by her father. Speaking to her just a few years later, or hearing her voice recorded in other video works, I notice that Spong's accent continues to shift (as does my own). She is diasporic, twice over, first by being raised in Aotearoa rather than Bali, and now by living in London rather than in Auckland. These positionalities are not fixed but remain mutable and mobile.

This reflects the complexity of contemporary cosmopolitan experiences. The scholar and writer Alice Te Punga Somerville uses poetry to convey something of feeling "too this for that, too that for this."[37] The poet Sawako Nakayasu registers the beautiful possibilities of incomplete communication in a chapbook titled *Say Translation is Art*, writing, "Say who, you. Say who, I."[38] There are limits to language (in Nakayasu's terms: "Say 'bad' translation. Say 'F' translation. Say ephemeral translation"), and these limits can be valuable and instructive.[39] The generative "failures" of words can also prompt us to look to artworks in all their ineffability.[40] In a discussion of terms invented by artists in various parts of Southeast Asia during the late twentieth century to describe their approach to the modern and the contemporary, Flores writes of "the strain that the language absorbs" and suggests that some turns of phrase may "[convene] in an intractable way what appears and what cannot be seen."[41]

In *The painter-tailor*, Spong delights in showing us Gusti Rundu's final painting in a gorgeous profusion of shots, in shifting settings, and from varying angles and distances, revealing different aspects of its composition and also emphasizing its dual importance as an artwork and an heirloom. Before we see the painting, we are given glimpses of the home in which it lives: an elegant and sprawling compound, with a Balinese house built around a lush central courtyard. In conversation, Spong describes this as her family's ancestral home in Sanur. The long shots of the house and garden linger lovingly; this too is a kind of honoring, with the artist's gratitude mixed with curiosity. Spong offers several views of the courtyard before gradually giving us our first sighting of Gusti Rundu's painting, which is shown hanging above a bed, dappled in soft sunlight (fig. 1.3). The square-shaped painting is large, wider than the double bed, and although it hangs high on the wall, the lower edge of the picture is obscured behind the wooden bedhead. This indicates the artwork's emplacement within the intimate, domestic setting of the family home, which is further underscored when we notice an air-conditioning controller mounted on the same wall just a few inches to the left of the painting, and a large, framed photograph hanging opposite it on the adjacent wall that depicts a child and a dog.

This tableau suggests that the painting is effectively part of the family. It lives alongside the bed on which Spong's human and non-human relatives sleep and dream, and Gusti Rundu's artwork is perhaps woven into those dreams, just as in Spong's artwork, the art-historical is folded into the familial and the personal. The painting is honored and treasured by adults and children, including the two men who we later see carefully carrying the work outside so that it can be viewed more clearly in the courtyard. The narrating son-and-father

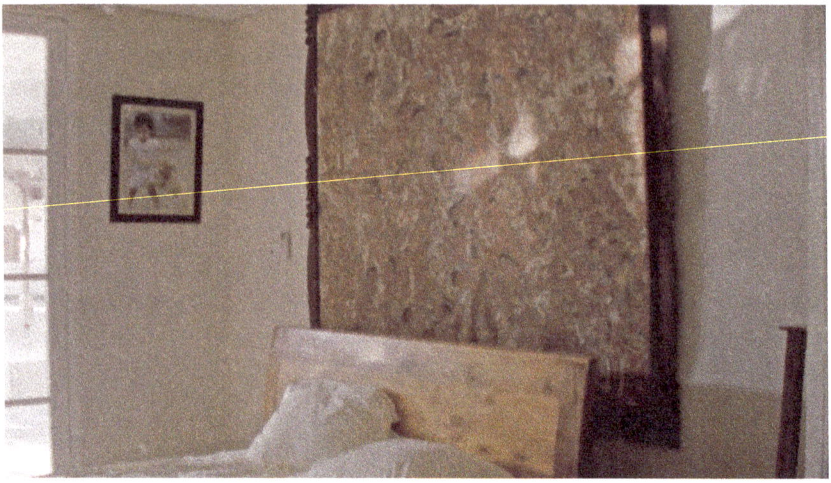

FIGURE 1.3. Sriwhana Spong, *The painter-tailor*, 2019. Single-channel video with sound, 32 mins 10 secs. Digital still. © Sriwhana Spong, courtesy of the artist.

explains, "to keep a painting is quite difficult. You have to have a place for it . . . Good air circulation, and good things." Kinship, especially queer kinships that extend beyond human relatives to encompass animals and artworks, require care and ecological sensitivity.

Even the three family dogs seem to be fondly honoring and respecting the painting; they give us a surprising "dog's-eye-view" of it when we see the work filmed from cameras that Spong has attached to their collars (fig. 1.4). The footage from these cameras is hilarious and unexpected. Shots with jaunty angles are framed by canine whiskers and a dripping pink tongue. The dogs run up to lick some of the human occupants of the courtyard. This recalls the narrator's confession in *This Creature* (2016), a video work Spong shot in London just three years prior (which also mentions Bali), that she has "recently developed a desire to lick things." Spong's interest in multisensory, embodied knowledge is longstanding and visceral. Yet the dogs somehow know not to get too close to the painting, suggesting an (innate or trained) understanding of the need to respect its preciousness.

As well as honoring the treasured place of the painting within the family's life, there is an implicit critique in Spong's use of the dog's-eye-view cameras. While Gusti Rundu's paintings often simply depict animals, Spong is interested in going further and imaginatively occupying a nonhuman perspective. Instead of merely depicting creaturely companions, she tries to find strategies to give animals agency in shaping some of her artworks. Of course, the dogs did not

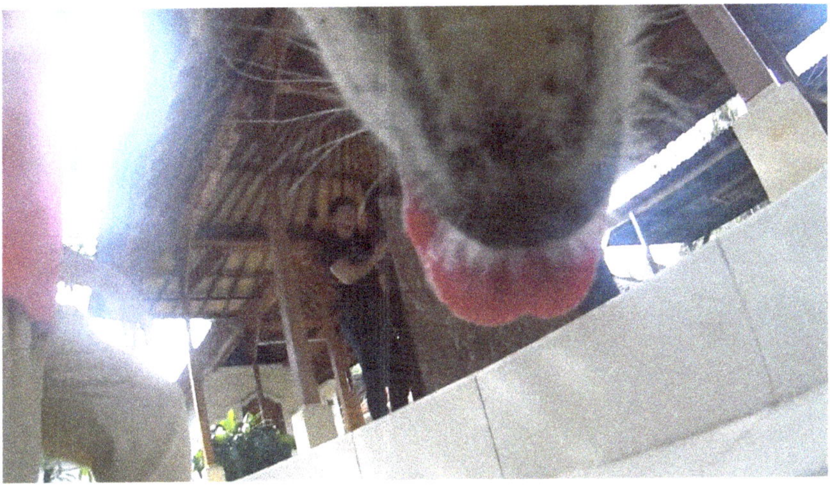

FIGURE 1.4. Sriwhana Spong, *The painter-tailor*, 2019. Single-channel video with sound, 32 mins 10 secs. Digital still. © Sriwhana Spong, courtesy of the artist.

choose to wear the cameras, and the footage shot on the cameras attached to their collars may not really allow us to see as dogs do.[42] But as well as suggesting this impression, the quirky and comically jarring angles of this footage and the routes taken by the animals cannot be completely planned or mastered by the artist. Instead, these are left to chance and controlled more by the canine rather than human contributions. At one point in her recorded conversation with her father, Spong comments that he has three dogs, just as his father Gusti Rundu had before him. There is a palpable reverence and care here, a respectful sense of quiet wonder at the inter-generational affinities in her family. But even in this process of honoring, there is still room for critical perspectives that are enabled by Spong's different life and educational and professional experiences as a contemporary artist engaged with recent scholarly and curatorial discourses around nonhuman agencies and perspectives.[43] Despite working in very different ways, both artists have a lifelong affinity for incorporating animals into their works. Gusti Rundu is known for having "pioneered the style of depicting multiple animals," while Spong is described as being "so attracted to animals, so interested in excavating her own encounters with them . . . [she] seems always to approach animals not as something to be controlled but as somebody to be encountered."[44] By incorporating animals into the making of *The painter-tailor*, Spong is at once honoring her grandfather's work, bringing it back to life by signaling its proximity to her own practice, while also implicitly critiquing the limits of his approach.

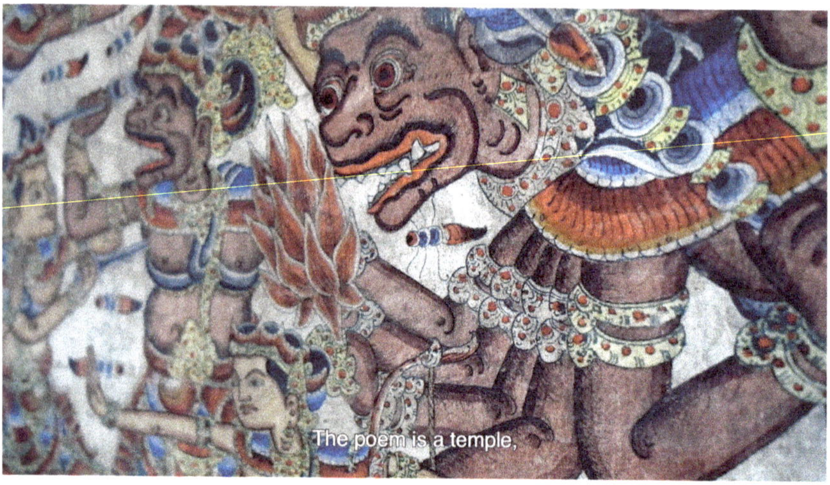

FIGURE 1.5. Sriwhana Spong, *The painter-tailor*, 2019. Single-channel video with sound, 32 mins 10 secs. Digital still. © Sriwhana Spong, courtesy of the artist.

The sentimental value for Spong's family and art-historical significance of Gusti Rundu's painting is reiterated when we later learn that it is Gusti Rundu's final work. The narrating son-and-father explains in his voiceover that the painting had been a "struggle to finish" because the artist had made it "when he was quite sick." Despite these circumstances, the work is a highly accomplished composition, which Spong is careful to emphasize in her camerawork. In addition to the medium shot of the work hanging in the bedroom and several wider-angle views of it being held up by two men in the courtyard, we see various details of the painting in no fewer than ten different close-up shots (fig. 1.5). In some of these scenes, Spong films the surface of the painting gently rippling in a breeze.

The fluttering of the painting is not solely an aesthetic or artistic flourish but also contributes to an art-historical understanding in a way that honors the artist and his work. First, its rhythmic, liquid-like motion is a reminder of the distinctive materials and techniques used in Balinese paintings, which are typically painted on fine cloth rather than canvas, and stretched loosely. Second, the rippling effect also underscores the dynamism of Gusti Rundu's characteristically dramatic composition. By capturing the wind, which can be felt on the skin as well as causing the fluttering of the painting that can be seen with the eyes, Spong engenders a multisensory appreciation for the work. In this way, her film works like a *sampeah kru*, honoring a lineage in an embodied and not purely visual way.

Text surtitles superimposed over this succession of close-up shots, written by Spong, inform us about the painting's subject matter while highlighting the intermedial connections the artist perceives between the visual, the literary, and other arts. The text begins:

> I Gusti Rundu's last painting depicts the death of Bhoma from the 12th Century epic tale the *Bhomāntaka*.

In the absence of written sources on the artist or the work, Spong learned this by directly contacting Vickers, the previously mentioned scholar who specializes in Balinese painting. Deftly shifting from art-historical information to artistic imagination inspired by a creative reading of the *Bhomāntaka*, Spong's text continues with the following:

> In the poem's first stanza, the unnamed poet utters a wish: 'Let this temple now be made of poetic language, a worthy place for Kāma (the God of Love) to be given visible form.' The poem is a temple, an architecture into which Kāma descends and takes up residence in the material world. The text is a temple. The body of the speaker is a temple's holy ground, which makes the body of the listener holy ground also. Perhaps? But if so, where are the edges of this holy ground? And could a painting be a temple also? Or a film?

With this text, Spong seems to be speculating about how customary Balinese understandings of spirituality and honoring as articulated in classical literary form may be theoretically reanimated within contemporary artistic practice, including in her own film.[45] She positions herself ambiguously, neither specifying nor disavowing her status as Balinese. By implication, she also opens the possibility for Balinese cultural artefacts, such as the *Bhomāntaka*, to have a profound and even magical and spiritual effect on what she calls (in the text quoted above) "the body of the listener" regardless of the identity of that person.

The implicit connection between Gusti Rundu's practice as a painter and his granddaughter Spong's practice as an artist who makes films is further elaborated later in the work. The narrating son-and-father, who had previously been a source of art-historically valuable information about Gusti Rundu, now offers an insightful and admiring analysis of the artist's work.

> You see his painting [is] so big. How can he cope with all the figure[s], you know? It's incredible. I can't do it, you know? Maybe do half of it, even [then I] won't finish. How can he do a figure there, and joined to there, and come out there? [laughter] I hope you can do that? In the future? [unintelligible question from Spong, not included in subtitles] Yeah maybe, maybe not exactly that, but something as good as that? Maybe in a different way? [Spong: Mum's always asking me to paint. Both: laughter]

Here, the narrator emphasizes the dense and vital composition of Gusti Rundu's work, in which numerous figures—humans, animals, and spirits—jostle together. He also demonstrates a subtle and sophisticated sensitivity to Spong's difference. The narrating son-and-father seems to recognize that Spong is a different kind of artist than Gusti Rundu (distinguished perhaps by her generation, her practice, her positionality, or perhaps all these factors). She is not a painter, and therefore she might not aspire to emulate her grandfather by doing "exactly that," but instead by working "in a different way."

A similar sense of carrying on but also departing from an artistic lineage is seen in Chou's film. Like Spong, he suggests that his own practice is made possible by the work of his forebears, including his own grandfather. But also like Spong, Chou nevertheless stylistically signals his own difference from the work of his predecessors—a difference that, for both artists, is not only aesthetic but also generational and diasporic, too. I will return to these points later in the chapter when I shift focus to Chou's film.

In addition to Gusti Rundu's painting itself and the oral testimony of the late artist's son, Spong draws on two other art-historical sources for *The painter-tailor.* One is an unnamed local museum in which Spong films visitors viewing two smaller works by Gusti Rundu, both of which feature his characteristically crowded compositions of animals. The architecture of the museum and the way people move through its somewhat stiff, furniture-less rooms mark it as a public space, clearly distinct from the comfortable private and domestic environment of the family home (fig. 1.6). Similarly public is a digitized album of photographs (with captions) assembled by the pioneering art historian of Indonesia, Claire Holt, that is publicly available on the website of the New York Public Library.[46] Using screen-recording software, Spong films the impersonal, disembodied process of browsing this album, which comprises images taken by Holt as well as by the Russian-born German artist Walter Spies (who we will meet again in the next chapter), mostly between the 1930s and 1950s.

Like the physical space of the museum, this virtual space of the digitized album is clearly legible as public, a distinction that may be a source of pride for Spong, or discomfort, or both. Images of Spong's grandfather are accompanied by carefully written captions, indicating that the album was intended not as a private memento but as a record for posterity (fig. 1.7). Unlike the family home and even the museum, which is located nearby on the island of Bali, the digitized album was produced by a white Russian-American and is housed far away in an American institution. Whereas Spong has uniquely privileged access to the oral account given by her father because of their familial relationship, by contrast, any member of the public could potentially see the artist's works in the museum or view the photographs in the archive. This may be a reason to be

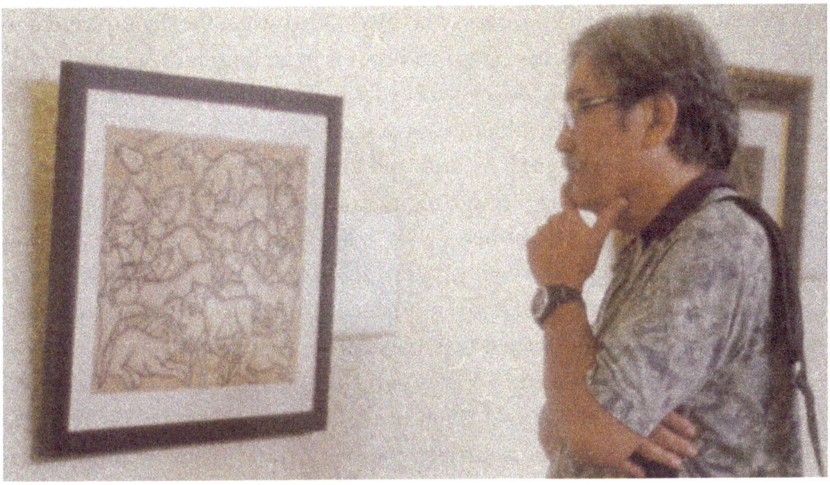

FIGURE 1.6. Sriwhana Spong, *The painter-tailor*, 2019. Single-channel video with sound, 32 mins 10 secs. Digital still. © Sriwhana Spong, courtesy of the artist. The scene shows another artwork by Gusti Rundu on display at Museum Puri Lukisan in Ubud, Bali.

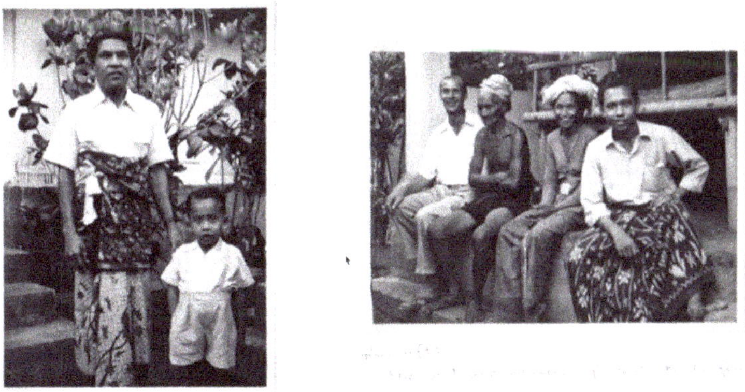

FIGURE 1.7. Sriwhana Spong, *The painter-tailor*, 2019. Single-channel video with sound, 32 mins 10 secs. Digital still. © Sriwhana Spong, courtesy of the artist.

proud of Gusti Rundu's place in "official" history and his international profile. Yet there is a sense of awkwardness and discomfort when the digital hand and cursor browsing Holt's archive stops and zooms in on images of Spong's grandfather and family. How did these traces of people's private lives end up in the public realm? Was their permission ever sought?

Chou also draws on digital research and foregrounds the embodied process of zooming in and scrolling through digital sources within his film. Despite the widespread availability of Southeast Asia–related materials in online archives both within the region and in the West, the use of digital methods in art-historical research remains relatively unusual in Southeast Asia. An online repository of images and related text, called The Virtual Museum of Balinese Painting, which was initiated by Vickers and his colleagues, is one notable and rare example.[47] Both Spong and Chou not only show the potentials of digital tools but also eloquently demonstrate the possibilities for entwining digital with other methods, including a reliance on oral testimonies and even personal, familial relationships.

Spong's decision to draw on diverse art-historical sources—detailed examination of the artwork itself as well as oral testimony, a visit to a small local museum, and an online visit to a large foreign institutional archive—typifies the kind of multimodal approach taken by many scholars of Southeast Asia's modern art histories. With collections of artworks and archives often incomplete, art historians working in and on Southeast Asia's art tend to piece together a narrative from components that are manifestly disparate in nature and dispersed geographically. Interviews and observations (including, sometimes, participant observations) are often used to supplement textual and visual sources. In a widely cited scholarly account of modern artists in Hanoi, the art historian Nora A. Taylor even suggests that, in Vietnam, "art history records are rare, thus it is much easier to interview living artists than to consult written documents."[48] We see interviews used throughout many artistic art histories, including in the work of filmmaker Davy Chou later in this chapter and in the practices of other artists and collectives in the chapters that follow.

In the context of this widespread art-historical reliance on interviews, Spong's handling of her father's oral testimony in *The painter-tailor* offers a potentially significant methodological model. Through her interweaving of her recorded conversation with her father with her close and careful study of her grandfather's last painting, Spong reminds us gently but insistently that the subjective claims of interviewees can always be tested against the interpretive possibilities offered by sustained attention to artworks themselves. She simultaneously champions and honors her father's account while also allowing us to see its blind spots and limitations. Faced with a scarcity of sources on Gusti Rundu, Spong does not rely on her father alone but instead turns to a creative reading of the literary classic, the *Bhomāntaka*.[49] Upon finding photographs in the archives of a scholar held at an American institution, Spong neither ignores nor overemphasizes this discovery but instead situates it within a range of other public as well as private sources, effectively provincializing the Russian-American scholar and American institution while celebrating and honoring the personal and familial as valid and important sites of art-historical insight alongside the study of artworks.

The methodological interweaving of disparate art-historical sources in *The painter-tailor* is aesthetically underpinned and harmonized by Spong's use of multiple types of film footage within the work. Sections shot with a 16mm analog camera have warm tones, slightly desaturated colors, soft and almost grainy edges, and occasional flares or other chromatic glitches (fig. 1.8). Sections shot with a digital camera are crisp and clear. Sections shot using a digital GoPro camera attached to the collar of a dog have an extended depth of field and occasional momentary glitches in brightness balance. These different types of footage convey shifting moods and several ways of looking. Although the diverse technologies have all been transferred to HD digital video, their varying textures, hues, and speeds remain tangibly apparent.

Although as a single-channel video, *The painter-tailor* is experienced visually, aurally, and temporally, and its enmeshing of diverse formats of footage invokes a more layered and embodied appreciation of the imagery, sound, and time.

FIGURE 1.8. Sriwhana Spong, *The painter-tailor*, 2019. Single-channel video with sound, 32 mins 10 secs. Digital still. © Sriwhana Spong, courtesy of the artist.

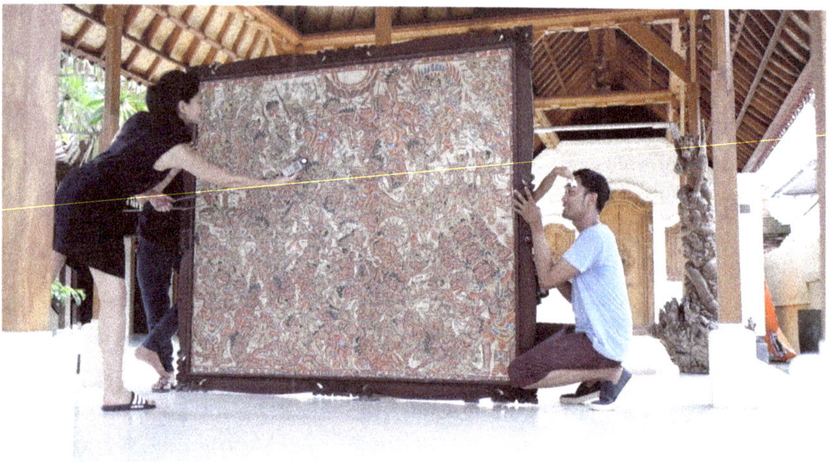

FIGURE 1.9. Sriwhana Spong, *The painter-tailor*, 2019. Single-channel video with sound, 32 mins 10 secs. Digital still. © Sriwhana Spong, courtesy of the artist.

For example, hearing the panting of a dog as we see its dangling, dripping tongue and past that its view of Gusti Rundu's painting, I imagine that I can smell the creature, feel its soft fur and warmth. Seeing plants bend and the painting flutter in a gentle breeze and observing someone's hand gently mop the warm brow of one of Spong's cousins, who is holding the painting (fig. 1.9), I imagine that I can feel the movement of the seaside Sanur air cooling the perspiration on my skin. Watching the video on a loop, cycling through analog and digital and back again, I gradually gain a sense of the many and varied embodied ways of looking at and thinking about Gusti Rundu's painting and his life and honoring its importance to his family, to Spong, and to the histories of modern art in Southeast Asia.

These many and varied ways of honoring Gusti Rundu add a richness to Spong's work but also lend to it a kind of generatively queer instability. The artist's expansion of the notion of kinship—to encompass her father, various relatives and collaborators, the family dogs, and the painting itself—may be considered a kind of kincoherence or kin-aesthetics. These terms, proposed by scholars Teagan Bradway and Elizabeth Freeman, serve to complicate and update "kinship theory," which they note was foundational to (mostly anglophone, mostly Western) queer studies in texts published between the 1970s and the early 2000s.[50] They suggest *kincoherence* as a concept that "fuses the mutually constituting and complicating forces, desires, practices, relations, institutions, and forms that render kinship a horizon of violence and possibility," implying that the familiar and recognizable nature of the neologism may help to flesh out the "fraught and overdetermined nature" of kinship.[51] They similarly propose *kin-aesthetics* as a concept to name "activities [that] make and unmake the social field," elaborating the term as "containing not only *kin* but also *kinetics* and *aesthetics*" and referring to "processes of *figuration*, whether they take place as social practice or in imaginative texts."[52]

In *The painter-tailor*, Spong honors Gusti Rundu by situating him in relation to her in terms of kinship. Yet she also recognizes in this relationship a kind of kincoherence; she writes that she never met her grandfather, and we may imagine that this separation could be experienced as or related to a kind of historical violence, possibly including economic disparity (as despite its enduring popularity for tourism, Bali remains fiscally under-developed when compared with the Indonesian national GDP or the GDP of a "developed" nation like Aotearoa New Zealand).[53] Spong also approaches Gusti Rundu's practice with kin-aesthetics; she emphasizes the physical facticity and compositional qualities of her grandfather's final painting and even uses it as a social device to gather her family in their ancestral home. Spong pays tribute to her grandfather, but her honoring is not without implicit criticality. This position of respectful critique is engendered in part from her own doubly distanced diasporic positionality and by her technical evocation of multisensory embodiment. Like a *sampeah kru* dance ceremony, Spong's work operates at several levels and engages several senses.

Spong's strategy of splicing together footage generated using different technologies recurs in several of her other films, including in two of the three works made during her doctoral studies, concurrently with *The painter-tailor*. These two works are titled *a hook but no fish* (2018) and *Interior Castle (a blueprint)* (2019); both feature a mixture of 16mm analog film and digital video transferred to HD video. The third work in the trilogy, titled *This Creature* (2016), differs in that it is filmed only using HD digital technology, but it shares something else in common with *The painter-tailor*. Whereas the latter work is filmed predominantly within Spong's ancestral family home in Sanur, the former work is shot almost entirely within Hyde Park in London. In both cases, the artist uses carefully cropped camera angles to direct our gaze to particular and sometimes peculiar details and corners, and in both cases, the sites are significant in framing the narrative and affective aspects of the works, too.

All these works, like most films and most of Spong's projects, are also collaborative in nature. In the credits at the end of *The painter-tailor*, the artist names not only the sound composer but also five camera operators, leaving it ambiguous which of these are human and which are canine. This recognizes the contributions made by Spong's human and nonhuman family while also suggesting that this provisional and continuous process of honoring is enriched by varied forms of intelligence working together in tandem: human and non-human, affective and intellectual, scholarly and literary, archival and oral, historical and artistic. In part, this collaboration is necessary to produce the film. In part, it is necessary to conduct the art-historical research for the film. In part, it is inspired by the collaborative nature of Balinese culture. Spong describes her project titled *Instruments A–J* (2015/16–ongoing), as "inspired by the percussive instruments of Balinese Gamelan," in which the instruments are "records of the places I make work in and the people I collaborate with."[54] Just as the *sampeah kru* ceremony is participatory, embodied, critical, and contemporary, a similar tenor governs Spong's respectful approach to honoring in *The painter-tailor.*

"A mysterious world": Davy Chou's *Golden Slumbers*

In 2011, the filmmaker Davy Chou (1983–) released his first feature film, a documentary titled *Golden Slumbers* (or *Le sommeil d'or*). It addresses the histories of Cambodian cinema from the decades before the genocide perpetrated by Pol Pot and the Khmer Rouge regime between 1975 and 1979 when many filmmakers were killed, all cinemas were closed, and most films were lost. With characteristic, careful hesitancy—reflecting the still-nascent state of studies on this topic and the still-scarce nature of sources—the film informs us that "the first Cambodian feature film was *likely* made in 1960" and that "*about* four hundred movies were made in Cambodia between 1960 and 1975. Phnom Penh alone had over thirty movie theaters."[55] Drawing chiefly on interviews with three surviving filmmakers, an actor, and two cinéphiles, *Golden Slumbers* builds on these shaky foundations of historical knowledge, tentatively navigating a path into Cambodian cinema histories, which are, as Chou says, "a secret world."[56]

Golden Slumbers is a lyrical example of honoring within the practice of artistic art histories in an expanded sense, and like Spong, Chou has a personal, familial connection to this tale. He too was raised in a diaspora, being born and raised in France before relocating to Cambodia in 2009. His grandfather, Van Chann, was a film producer during the 1960s, and Chann's daughter (Chou's aunt), Sohong Stehlin, is one of the first people interviewed within *Golden Slumbers* (fig. 1.10). Her position as a familial relation of both the subject of the film and its maker is analogous to the position of Spong's father in *The painter-tailor.* This is the lineage, as is honored in a *sampeah kru.* "I felt like I had just discovered a mysterious world," Chou says, "not understanding how it could

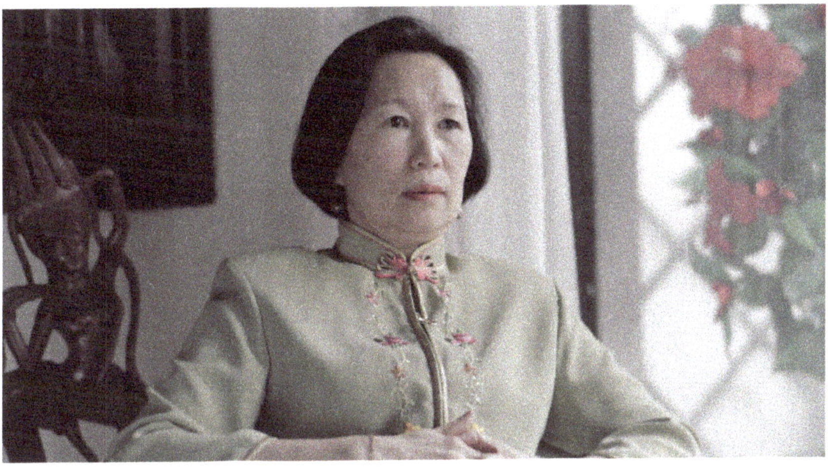

FIGURE 1.10. Davy Chou (director), *Golden Slumbers*, 2011. Documentary film, 96 min. Digital still. © Vycky Films.

have been hidden from me for such a long time." It was not until he began to make movies himself that the extent of his grandfather's legacy as producer of some 40 films was shared with him by his family.[57] Like Spong, Chou never met his grandfather.[58] Also like Spong, and in keeping with the theoretical model of honoring that is suggested by the *sampeah kru* dance-ritual, Chou's approach to the little-known movies from the 1960s and early 1970s is at once respectful, embodied, critical, and contemporary.

Significantly, just as Spong's work examines how Gusti Rundu's final painting relates to her own artistic practice, Chou's film makes clear that his engagement in cinema histories is also energized by his avid interest in fostering the present and future of filmmaking in Cambodia. This includes Chou's role as founder of Kon Khmer Koun Khmer (colloquially known as 4K, which they translate as "Cambodian Films, Cambodian Generations"), a loose group first gathered in 2009 who describe themselves as "a self-sustained team of young students and artists with [a] main focus on film production and arts management."[59] We see the 4K group several times during *Golden Slumbers*, their easy and youthful countenances contrasting acutely with the older interviewees, who recount and relive often difficult memories. Significantly, the film closes with a climatic sequence in which the 4K group watch clips from some of the few surviving films from pre-1975 Cambodia (fig. 1.11). This is the first time Chou has shown any footage from the movies that are the subject of *Golden Slumbers*, and this withholding of this imagery until the end of the film, and

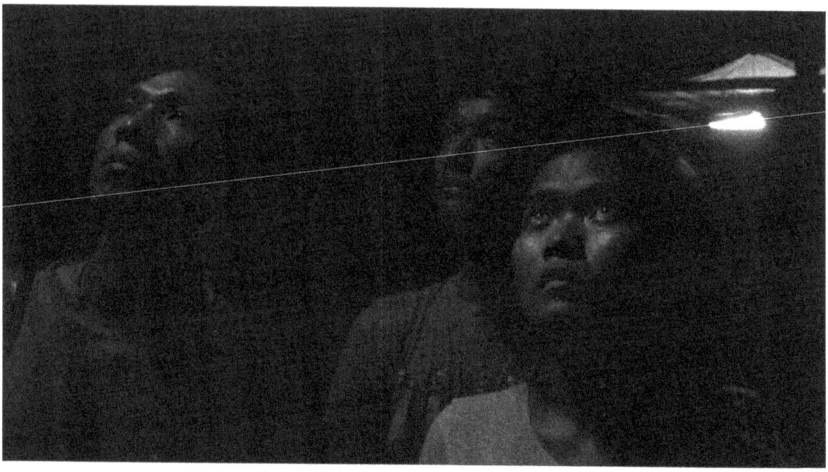

FIGURE 1.11. Davy Chou (director), *Golden Slumbers*, 2011. Documentary film, 96 min. Digital still. © Vycky Films.

the decision to finally allow us to watch it only as though we are seeing these films through the eyes of the 4K group, strongly suggests that the real value of this cinema heritage, for Chou, is to inspire new, younger generations of filmmakers in Cambodia. The plan is working; one of the 4K group featured in the film, Kavich Neang, has gone on to release several films, one of which, *White Building* (2021), was the first-ever Cambodian production to premiere in the official selection at the Venice Film Festival, and it won an award there.[60] *White Building* is a story centered on an architecturally significant modernist apartment building that was inhabited by artists and thus may also be considered an example of artistic art histories. The film's focus on the social aspects of art's histories aligns it with canonical Western social art historians, such as Arnold Hauser and Thomas E. Crow. *White Building*'s success affirms Chou's vision for honoring Cambodia's cinema. In a funding application written during the production of *Golden Slumbers*, Chou writes that "[making] this story known on an international level would be the best tribute to pay to this sacrificed generation of filmmakers and actors."[61]

I remember seeing *Golden Slumbers* several times during its early screenings in Phnom Penh and discussing it with artist friends over grilled snacks late into the evening. We were used to seeing short documentaries addressing topics like poverty and trauma, that had been prescribed by the foreign-run NGOs who funded these small productions; this was what much of Cambodian cinema had been like in the 2000s and early 2010s. The impact of Chou's film felt so forceful as to be almost physical. For some of us, it brought tears, and for others, only distracted and quietly intense stares into the expanses of memory and sorrow. As much as the film is a joyful celebration of a generation of filmmakers in Cambodia, it is also a tragic lamentation of the loss of those films and those people.

The film's quiet insistence on the importance and value of art and culture, and of honoring and continuing these traditions, recalls scholar Toni Shapiro's account of Cambodian survivors of the genocide who she met in the early 1980s. Describing her experience of working in a small refugee camp in Indonesia in 1982 amidst conditions of physical depravation and scarcity, sometimes even lacking drinking water, Shapiro writes of being "struck by the fact that among such a small population (about 300 Khmer), and under such conditions, there was a drive to dance, to perform . . . the same phenomenon was occurring in camps [elsewhere]."[62] She records refugees in the late 1980s describing dance as "the soul (*proleung*) of the Khmer people" that must be taught to the "children born and raised in the camps" so that they "know what it means to be Khmer."[63] Even after a genocide in which an estimated 80 to 90 percent of dancers (and artists of all kinds) had been killed, the practice and history of dance and its lineage could be taught, and its *kru* could be remembered and honored with the *sampeah kru* and other forms of teaching. But how could this be done with film? Around 40 of the 400 films made in Cambodia before 1975 have survived. How could this singular disaster, and the unspeakable human devastation that accompanied it, now be inspiring such beautiful and sophisticated new artists, new filmmakers, and new ways of honoring the art and cinema of the past?

Often, the histories of art and cinema are studied and written about separately by scholars with different training and in different departments, but this siloing of cultural forms often does not make sense in many Southeast Asian settings, including Cambodia, for two key reasons. The first reason is that there was an abundant cross-fertilization between modernist visual art and cinema and other modes of practice during the heady decades leading up to and following independence from colonial rule. For example, Cambodia's best-known visual artist before 1975, Nhek Dim (1934–1978), collaborated with the country's most popular singers, Sinn Sisamouth (1932–1976) and Pen Ran (c. 1944–c. 1979) whose songs animate the soundtracks of films from the period and appear in the soundtrack of *Golden Slumbers*. Moreover, Nhek Dim's paintings appear as part of the mise-en-scène in films directed by Norodom Sihanouk (1922–2012), who, as well as being prince and head of state, was an active filmmaker.[64] Elsewhere in the region, Myanmar's most celebrated modern artist, Bagyi Aung Soe (1924–1990) also starred in over

40 films.[65] Similarly, Vietnam's Tran Trung Tin (1933–2008) is celebrated outside the country for his paintings and drawings but is best-known within Vietnam as a film actor.[66] The second reason for the inseparability of art histories and cinema histories in much of Southeast Asia is that there are rarely separate university departments for the study of these fields. In many parts of the region, including in Cambodia, neither are officially studied within state universities, and the amateur or independent researchers who specialize in histories of either art or film tend to also maintain an active interest and involvement in the other practice, too. In these and other ways, the fertile intermediality of the early years of decolonization continues today.

Davy Chou reflects these rich exchanges within and between different contemporary media. We have already seen that the 4K group he founded comprises artists as well as other students and fans of film. In *Golden Slumbers* and several of his other productions, he has collaborated with the celebrated visual artist Kanitha Tith (1987–) as his art director. She also appears in a nonspeaking role in the film as part of the 4K group. The two have also collaborated on several art projects initiated by Kanitha. For example, Chou was responsible for the camera and sound documentation of Kanitha's performance *How Heavy is Time?* (2020) at the Rijksakademie in Amsterdam.[67] When in Phnom Penh, Chou and other members of the Anti-Archive film production company that he cofounded in 2014 regularly attend exhibitions, open studios, and other contemporary art events.[68] Similarly, contemporary artists and curators are regularly among audiences at film screenings. In short, there is a close relationship between the contemporary art and cinema communities in Cambodia, as elsewhere in Southeast Asia, that echoes and continues the intermedial intersections that characterized the development of modernist practices in the twentieth century despite the violent historical ruptures of the intervening decades.

The opening sequence of *Golden Slumbers* encapsulates the film's personal and semi-autobiographical qualities and its embodied approach to honoring little-known cinema histories. Shot from a moving vehicle on a dark country road, with the footage shuddering arrhythmically as the camera is jolted over the uneven surface of the unpaved road, the extended take is hypnotic and seductive yet also eerie and disorienting (fig. 1.12). The road travels through an indistinct Cambodian landscape, but it also offers a symbolic journey into the world of the film. For Chou—who first visited Cambodia in 2008, the same year he made his first short film—as perhaps for many viewers among the Cambodian diasporas, this is also a voyage into a land at once familiar from stories told by parents and relatives, yet also foreign and unknown.[69] At some point, we realize that the footage of the road is being played in reverse. Instead of watching scenes of the road disappearing from view behind the moving vehicle, we are in

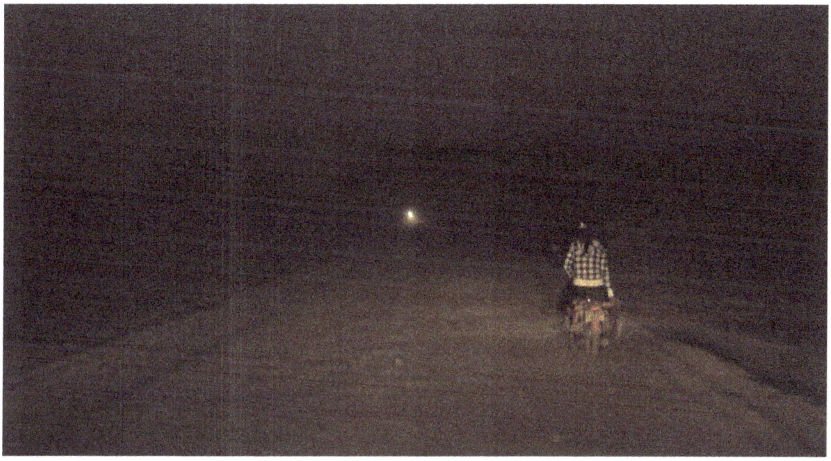

FIGURE 1.12. Davy Chou (director), *Golden Slumbers*, 2011. Documentary film, 96 min. Digital still. © Vycky Films.

fact seeing the opposite view, filmed from a camera facing frontwards. In her evocative discussion of this scene, the scholar Leslie Barnes observes that "what is filing past is the road not yet travelled" and that "the distinctions between the road ahead and the road behind—understood temporally and spatially—give way" as "we experience both the future as the immediate past and the past as present before us."[70] This sense of spatiotemporal disorientation is heightened by the aforementioned shakes and wobbles in the footage; we experience this bodily, as if feeling the jolts and jerks of the camera in our abdomens.

The opening sequence serves as Chou's tribute to the beauty and mystery of the Cambodian countryside—and by extension the "mysterious world" of cinema histories—and as his registration of the uneasy nature of his (physical, emotional, and historiographical) relationship to and journey into this world. In honoring these complex attitudes that are held simultaneously, the opening sequence invites a multisensory, embodied understanding with the visual and textual information supplemented at a deeper, affective level, much like in a *sampeah kru*.

The use of deliberately unstable cameras to produce jerky, jaunty footage is a strategy for invoking an embodied response, which is shared by Chou and Spong. Whereas Spong attaches cameras to the collars of her family dogs, Chou fixes his cameras to the back of a moving vehicle traveling along a rough-surfaced road. The effects differ, but both prize the kind of unexpected angles that make us experience the film not only with our eyes but in our bodies, too.

Chou's opening sequence also reflects his film's affinities with contemporary visual art. While *Golden Slumbers* has been sensitively studied by film scholars, it has yet to be examined within the larger context of contemporary art and culture in post-war, post-genocide Cambodia.[71] The disorientation that Chou invokes is not exclusive to diasporic Cambodians or returnees. Many people raised within the country also often experience a sense of bewilderment at its rapid transformations, and this is often reflected in artistic practice using motifs that are strikingly similar to those seen in *Golden Slumbers*. For example, just as the opening sequence of the film derives much of its visual and psychological drama from the chiaroscuro effect of motorcycle headlights shot against the inky darkness of the surrounding night, this device has also been used in contemporary art. The photographer Philong Sovan's (1986–) series titled *In the City by Night* (2010–ongoing), begun while Chou was filming *Golden Slumbers*, depicts scenes from around various Cambodian cities, which are illuminated using only the headlight from the artist's motorcycle (fig. 1.13). This results in a warm and familiar glow while also implicitly marking at once the Philong's closeness to his subjects—close enough to shine his headlight onto them—as well as his distance and his status as a passerby rather than a participant.

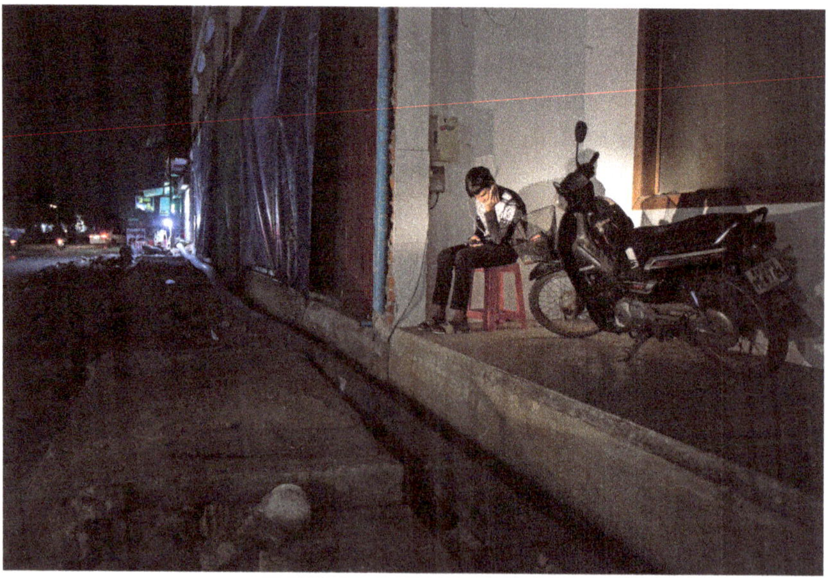

FIGURE 1.13. Philong Sovan, *The black moto_Siem Reap*, 2020, from the series *In the City By Night*, 2010–2020. Digital C print. Collection of the artist. © Philong Sovan.

Whereas Spong draws on various sources of art-historical information and ideas, supplementing her interview with her father with extensive footage of Gusti Rundu's painting as well as scenes of a local museum and a foreign archive, Chou necessarily relies almost solely on oral testimonies, yet these are also multisensory encounters. The film is anchored by extensive interviews with three former filmmakers—Ly Bun Yim (1942–), Yvon Hem (1937–2012), and Ly You Sreang (active 1960s)—as well as one star actor, Dy Saveth (1944–). Chou elicits moving performances from all of them, amplifying the affective impact of their spoken accounts through judiciously chosen locations, several of them dilapidated or semiderelict sites that were formerly cinemas. These diverse spaces are lovingly captured in a series of long takes that intersperse close-up shots of details in each of the settings with medium-shot footage of each person speaking. The theatrical venue for Ly Bun Yim's interview matches perfectly with his showy manner, dressed in a flashy suit and recounting the plots of his movies with heightened dramatic effect. Similarly, the walls of Dy Saveth's home and dance instruction studio are plastered with photographs, which underscore the perpetual presence of memories of the past in her life. By contrast, the intimate interiority of scenes with Yvon Hem speaking while seated on his bed, surrounded by his wife and children, intensify the sense of loss as he describes the death of his family in the genocide. These settings—as well as other more historically significant sites, such as a former film studio and even the place where a key scene in a lost 1960s movie was shot—together constitute a kind of affective and embodied archive, one that extends beyond text and images to encompass spaces and emotions in flux.[72] Learning about and honoring cinema histories involves not only words but more multisensory experiences.

The stark contrast between these sites, amplified by Chou's divergent stylistic approaches to each of them, highlights the differences between the various filmmakers. In honoring their work, Chou maintains the possibility for a kind of respectful critique that privileges differentiation over denigration. For example, Ly Bun Yim's emphasis on special effects in his oral account of his films is matched by Chou's use of digital editing techniques to make four images of him appear within a single shot (fig. 1.14). The comic and technologically quaint effect of this marks a strong contrast with Yvon Hem's more emotionally charged testimony, filmed mostly in his sparsely decorated bedroom, with the footage alternating between close-up shots of his face and hands and the faces of his children who look on and listen silently. Because so few filmmakers active before 1975 survived, it would not be culturally appropriate or narratively viable for Chou to choose to interview only those whose films he is able to access or considers to be of high aesthetic quality. That kind of critique is not

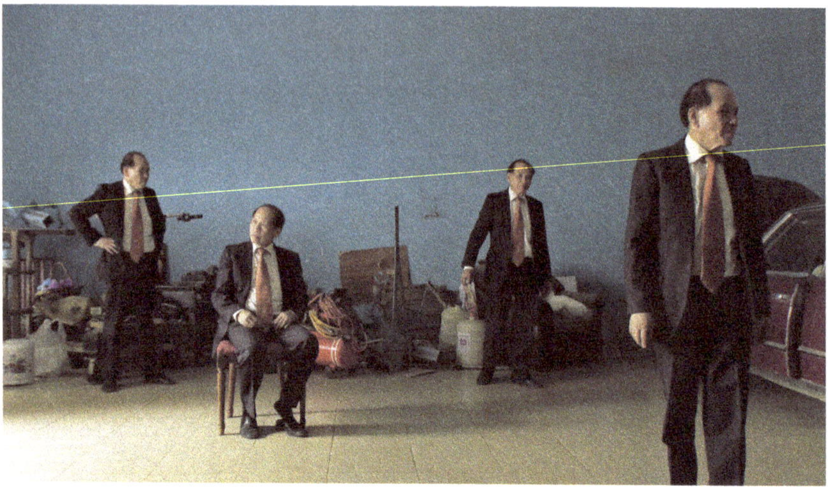

FIGURE 1.14 Davy Chou (director), *Golden Slumbers*, 2011. Documentary film, 96 min. Digital still. © Vycky Films.

possible in this context and nor is open criticism; this would be dishonoring, which would feel not only culturally insensitive but also blind to the effects of the genocide. Instead, while honoring his subjects, Chou uses location and editing to highlight the differences in their approaches to filmmaking, ensuring that his work is able to be analytical rather than solely descriptive while still maintaining a respectful tone.

Another kind of coded critique implicit in Chou's film is its omission of the cinematic oeuvre of Norodom Sihanouk, a kind of poetics of exclusion. The king (1922–2012) who abdicated the throne to rule Cambodia as a prince and head of state during the 1960s, overseeing the country during the tumultuous period of war in neighboring Vietnam, was also an avid filmmaker. He directed some 50 films during his lifetime, including several during the heyday era of the 1960s, the period that is the focus of *Golden Slumbers*.[73] Although open critical discussion of his cinematic work was politically impossible within Cambodia during his lifetime and remains fraught today, anglophone historians have left accounts of the allegedly poor quality of the films, their elitist subject matter, and the coercion he used to ensure he had a (sometimes literally) captive audience for screenings during the 1960s.[74] Chou's decision not to feature Sihanouk's films—not to openly denigrate them but also not to celebrate or dwell on them at all—is a critical omission of the kind that honoring enables. It reflects a nuanced poetics and, perhaps, politics of inclusion typical of artistic art histories.

Several of the sites Chou features in his film also appear in contemporaneous artistic and related projects, indicating the importance of modernist architectural sites as loci for diverse practices of honoring in the context of post-war healing in Cambodia. For example, several former cinemas have been studied by a collective of architects and researchers called the Roung Kon Project.[75] The Roung Kon Project also used a private apartment located within one former cinema as the venue for an exhibition they collectively curated. I have argued elsewhere that by bringing visitors into close proximity with its interior spaces while educating them about its history and (then) continuing use for the screening of films, Roung Kon Project was raising awareness about the cinema's importance at both intellectual and affective levels.[76] The scholar Margaret Jack describes this work as "infrastructural restitution" in the aftermath of the historical violence in Cambodia, which she characterizes as "a form of social and political action."[77] This too is honoring. In Jack's terms, the Roung Kon Project "praised and mourned the flourishing arts and space of the cinema from before the crisis of the Khmer Rouge in order to encourage public support for the arts and sustainable urban development in contemporary Phnom Penh."[78] The concentration of creative interest around former cinemas suggests the power of these sites to elicit memories that enable processes of honoring that are also healing. As the Roung Kon Project matter-of-factly note, after Pol Pot's troops took power in 1975, "all the cinemas were closed until the fall of [the] Khmer Rouge."[79] While many never reopened and have since been destroyed, recovering their stories is a way of confronting the legacies of that historical violence.[80] Conservation of the buildings is not possible for political and economic reasons, but other kinds of honoring help ease the pains of loss.

It is significant that in addition to interviewing filmmakers and an actor, Chou also relies extensively on oral testimony from two "cinéphiles." They provide valuable information as well as analytical insights, revealing the importance of unconventional sources when researching art and cultural histories in Southeast Asia. Whereas the filmmakers and actor speak of their experience in producing movies, the two cinéphiles, named Ouk Silayouth and Lim Vong Thavy, necessarily focus on the reception of these cinematic works. Their accounts are unambiguously personal and subjective—they frequently need each other's help to recollect films they saw over forty years prior—and in these ways they foreground the inescapable but sometimes more invisible role that memory plays in filtering the oral testimonies of the filmmakers and actor as well.

The cinéphiles are central to the narrative development and emotional impact of *Golden Slumbers*. The first words we hear spoken in the film—accompanying the eerie, bumpy footage of the road—are from one of their conversations, highlighting their significance from the outset. These words, "I have been a fan of movies since I was four or five," also stress the first-person texture of cinematic histories and the importance of reception in the sharing of these histories. In one of the most powerful scenes in *Golden Slumbers*, in which the tragedy of the genocide and the deeply felt importance of honoring are both cast in stark relief, Ouk and Lim admit to each other that their memories of the cinema are stronger than their memories of their family members who died in the genocide. "I've forgotten the faces of my family members, but I remember the actors," one man says. Faced with such profound loss and enduring pain, the cinéphiles draw comfort and strength from the honoring they perform through their memories. As Barnes has eloquently suggested, "their conversations are the refuge the cinema once was."[81] Chou is honoring the cinéphiles and, by extension, the memories of all survivors of the genocide, just as he is honoring the filmmakers, many of whom perished.

The only archival source featured in *Golden Slumbers* is an unofficial, semi-anonymous and evolving online website. Its appearance in the film highlights the frequent need to rely on unconventional materials when researching Southeast Asia's art and cultural histories and the possibilities of digital methods for research. Appearing early in the film, a YouTube page called "Khmer Oldies" features hundreds of rock and pop songs from pregenocide Cambodia that have been made freely available. It appears onscreen after black-and-white family photographs shared by Chou's aunt, Sohong Stehlin, suggesting that the public space of the YouTube page and the private space of the family album each have a role to play in piecing together the fragments of the pregenocide past in Cambodia. While watching a digital hand and cursor scroll through the YouTube page, we hear Stehlin's testimony as well as a hauntingly melancholic song that surtitles inform us is "from the film *The Father's Dagger* [directed by] So Man Chiv [produced by Chou's uncle's company] Van Chann Films [in] 1967." The implication is that no single source can contain all this historical information.

Honoring the past, which requires piecing together fragmentary remnants and traces, requires a patchwork of oral testimonies, digital archives, text, images, and sounds all filtered through loss and memory and respect for the importance of lineage, or *kru*.[82] Describing his process of research, Chou says, "My first real discovery was a blog, written by Vathana Huy, a Cambodian living in France and a real film buff. Having fled Cambodia in 1979, he set about reconstructing the filmography of Cambodian filmmakers of this golden age, and his only source was his memory."[83] Chou respects and honors the necessity of this memory.

By championing digital research tools for art-historical inquiry, Chou and Spong are pioneers. Scholars have only recently begun to consider the theoretical and historiographical implications of the rise of blogs, social media, and other digital archives for scholarship on art histories in Southeast Asia. Chou's filmic integration of an interview, a family snapshot, and a YouTube page in his creative practice of honoring predates these scholarly investigations by several years. The scholars Alexander Supartono and Alexandra Moschovi have discussed "the 'social life' of colonial photographs kept in Dutch museums and archives and the ways such imagery has been recently reconfigured, manipulated and repurposed by contemporary Southeast Asian artists" through chiefly digital tools.[84] In scholar Clare Veal's discussion of Facebook groups dealing with historical images from Thailand, she examines "the relationship between the apparently contradictory forces of contemporaneity and historicity in the archival functions of . . . Facebook groups and pages." She is chiefly engaged not with artistic practice but rather with the rise of social media platforms in which "members of these groups participate by sharing posts, generally consisting of historical photographs and videos with a brief commentary."[85] Veal's conclusion (also published in 2020) is that "understanding the circulation of historical photographs on Facebook allows us to move beyond a chronological, linear conception of history towards a consideration of the ways in which the past is continuously reconstituted through the contemporary."[86] These are important insights that I believe will become more significant as more scholars of Southeast Asia's art histories engage with digital tools and online sources. Yet Chou seems to have reached this realization before any of these scholars.

Veal's sense of the (images, and we might add, sounds of) "the past" being "reconstituted through the contemporary" echoes Mieke Bal's argument that contemporary art's engagement with the art of the past is always "an *active reworking*," and "creates new versions of old images."[87] This happens in *Golden Slumbers*; the appearance of the "Khmer oldies" YouTube page shows how songs from pregenocide Cambodia continue to be reimagined and remembered, made useful and brought back to life, not only by Chou but also by diverse publics in Cambodia, in the diasporas, and in online settings. Chou, like Spong, is creatively nourished by the artistic art histories he honors in his film. Studying the art and cinema of the past enables continuing practices in the present and for the future.

Lineage, Kin, and *Kru*

The *kru*—the teachers and spirits, living and deceased—who are honored in a *sampeah kru* dance ceremony comprise a performer's lineage, and this lineage may shift with time and circumstance. But who are the *kru* of Sriwhana Spong and Davy Chou? Their lineage and kin comprises many teachers and inspirations, and these figures are cosmopolitan and dispersed. As diasporic subjects, Chou and Spong may be expected to be in some ways distant from the Southeast Asian artistic communities they study in their works. Yet both are also bold innovators—among the very first to research and honor the historically important contributions made by their predecessors. The forebears to whom they are perhaps most closely related by familial ties as well as through their creative practice are little-known and rarely studied. Through the provisional and continuous process of honoring their grandfathers (and, in Chou's case, his grandfather's peers), both Spong and Chou are making artistic art histories that are embodied and affective, critical yet respectful, encompassing multiple modes of research including interviews and digital methods, and at once informed by the past and contemporary.

2

CITING

One of the most common strategies for contemporary artists to engage with modernist art histories is through direct visual references to the work of their predecessors. I have already mentioned several instances of this, including the appearance of I Gusti Made Rundu's paintings in Sriwhana Spong's film (discussed in the previous chapter) and the depictions of Diem Phung Thi's sculptures in Thao Nguyen Phan's video (discussed in the introduction). I call this *citing*, and this chapter discusses that phenomenon. What happens when artists reuse images, ideas, and aesthetics from other artworks? What are the "epistemic politics" of this reuse, and how does it relate to power structures of patriarchal colonialism and decolonization in Southeast Asia?[1] How can thinking of this reuse as citing ground this artistic art-historical practice in local and regional discourses that may be related to yet also remain distinct from received Western concepts such as appropriation and borrowing?

In this chapter, I first briefly introduce some examples that highlight the breadth and diversity of citations within artistic practice across the past century, and then outline my theorization of citing, which I understand as a provisional and continuous process of both calling forth and taking from artistic forebears. I then discuss in detail two paintings made by Emiria Sunassa in Indonesia in the 1940s that are both based closely on photographs by Walter Spies that were published in the 1930s. In my analysis of Emiria's citing of Spies, I emphasize the decolonizing implications of her reliance on his compositions and her defiance of his (white, masculine, artistic, and anthropological) authority. I have chosen to focus on this historic and modernist case of citing, from almost a century ago, in order to indicate the prehistories of more recent contemporary practices and to suggest the porosity between the modern and the contemporary in Southeast Asia.

Instances of contemporary artists citing works by their lesser-known modernist forebears abound in Southeast Asia and its diasporas, and this citing is often ideologically charged, imbuing many artistic art histories with a political sensibility. For example, from around 2012 to 2018, the Singapore-based artist Hilmi Johandi (1987–) repeatedly made paintings that reuse imagery from Malay films of the Merdeka era, which is the Malay language name for the years leading up to and following Malaysia and Singapore's independence from British colonial rule. This is Hilmi's way of interrogating what he calls "a culture that has interacted and changed over time, especially at a time of great political, social and cultural change throughout Singapore" and offering "nostalgic interpretations by focusing on the conflict between modernity and tradition."[2] This unapologetic nostalgia has an edge to it in the context of contemporary Singapore, where many feel that minority groups, including Malay-speaking artistic communities, are marginalized within present-day nationalist discourses.[3] Hilmi's repeated depiction of heroic cultural figures from the Merdeka era, such as musician, actor, and filmmaker P. Ramlee (1929–1973), can be understood as pointed reminders of the contributions of Malay-speaking cultures to modern Singapore. Hilmi (whose practice I will discuss in more detail in chapter 3) speaks of his aim to "instill a critical discourse that may reflect the sociopolitical nature of the spaces we inhabit," thereby emphasizing how the 1950s through 70s images cited in his paintings are intended to speak directly to the tensions and issues of the here and how.[4]

As well as contemporary artists citing their modernist forebears, there are many instances of earlier generations citing the works of their peers, thereby signaling their modernness. One example is Saya Myit (1888–1966), who is considered by scholars an early proponent of modern, Western-style oil on canvas painting in Myanmar.[5] He made several paintings during the 1920s and 1930s that I believe quote from the visual language of studio photography in the period, which was especially popular in cosmopolitan port cities like Yangon, where he lived and worked. Writing of the impact of studios on modernizing cities and cultures including Yangon, one scholar suggests that "the new medium of photography transformed social perceptions in the 1920s."[6] In some of Saya Myit's works, such as *Sitting Man with Mustache* (c. 1920s–1930s) (fig. 2.1), this intermediality involves reusing the distinctive compositional format of photo-portraiture, including shallow pictorial space and the seating of the subject next to a table dressed with objects that symbolically convey his social status. Beneath the man's feet is a colorful carpet of the kind commonly called "Irish carpets." Made in the United Kingdom for a Southeast Asian market, these woolen rugs

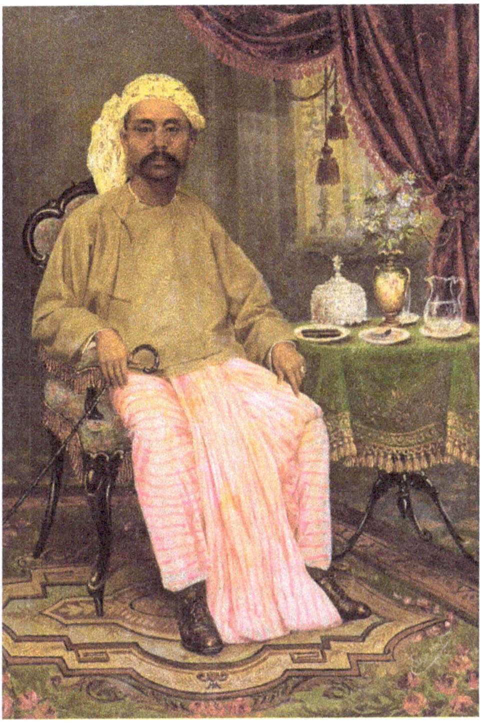

FIGURE 2.1. Saya Myit, *Sitting Man with Mustache*, c. 1920s–1930s. Oil on canvas attached to board, 73 × 51.5 cm. Collection of National Gallery Singapore. Image courtesy of National Heritage Board, Singapore.

feature ornamentation and imagery adapted from Burmese and other regional designs. Irish carpets are also omnipresent as props in photo-portraiture of the period.[7] Other works by Saya Myit, such as *Rangoon Port* (c. 1920s–1930s), also reuse props commonly found in photography studios at the time, such as a white terrier dog that, although lifelike, was probably made from ceramic.[8] The dog looks quite out of place in the busy portside scene, but through its familiarity from photography and its popularity as a middle-class pet, it functions as a symbol of modernity, much like the row of tall buildings on the Strand in downtown Yangon, seen toward the left of the picture, and the electrical streetlamp that the artist has carefully included along the right edge of the canvas.[9]

Many artists in and affiliated with Southeast Asia have also cited premodern artistic and architectural artefacts in their works. For example, the sculptor and printmaker Kim Lim (1936–1997) amassed a large photographic archive of her travels to ancient temples in Cambodia, Indonesia, and Malaysia, as well as in China, India, Japan, and beyond, from the 1960s to the 1990s. Although

Lim's artworks adopted the austere and unornamented appearance of minimalism and abstract sculpture that were popular in the UK (where she lived and worked) and elsewhere in the West during and after the 1960s, the artist herself claimed that her works were informed by her travels, that she said inspired an "'empathy' for Asian art and philosophy."[10] This affirmation of the importance of citing Asia in her work is striking since the Singapore-born Lim is known for having refused artist-curator Rasheed Araeen's invitation to join the celebrated 1989 exhibition titled *The Other Story: Afro-Asian Artists in Post-war Britain*; Lim wrote that "to participate would be to self-consciously place myself in a situation of 'otherness.'"[11]

A careful attention to Lim's photographs of ancient artefacts and her minimal sculptures made with marble, wood, and steel suggest that her visual citing worked in several ways. Not only were her sculptures inspired by her experience of spaces and shapes in premodern temples, but her composition of photographs during her travels was also a way of citing her own, earlier sculptural works, as well as her own photographs of those sculptures. For example, a photograph that Lim took of a fluted Roman column at Çavdarhisar in 1996 echoes the composition of her sculpture *Kudah*, made with marble several years earlier in 1989, which Lim also photographed.[12] The interplay of light and shadow within the parallel vertical grooves is emphasized by a raking light from one side, in both Lim's photograph of the Turkish architectural artefact and her photograph of her own artwork, which predates her trip to Çavdarhisar. This suggests that citing was a dynamic and multidirectional strategy that Lim used to covertly signal the Asian sources for her minimal sculptures, which also guided her aesthetic appreciation of other premodern architecture and cultural artefacts during her travels. Lim's highly considered approach to photographing her own sculptures, as well as these premodern artefacts, suggests that she used the citational practice of photography as a way to think through and shape her encounter with three-dimensional art.[13]

The examples of artworks by Hilmi Johandi, Saya Myit, and Kim Lim are indicative of the manifold approaches to citing taken by artists in and affiliated with Southeast Asia from the 1920s (and before) to the 2020s. With this diverse art-historical landscape in mind, I turn to outlining my understanding of citing before examining the works of Emiria Sunassa in detail.

Toward a Theory of Citing in Southeast Asia

To cite is to *call*; this is the Latin etymology of the English word. When I cite an artwork or text, either by quoting from or simply referring to it, I am calling the ideas and aesthetics of that earlier work to mind for my reader, and I am also calling those ideas and aesthetics into dialogue with my own writing. This act of citing as calling forth is also a display of mastery. When I cite other authors or artists, I am performatively demonstrating my awareness of their work, my way of understanding it, and my confidence that my own work can be read in relation to theirs. One sociologist describes citations as functioning to "support the communication of specialist knowledge."[14] This understanding presupposes an acceptance that the artwork or text in which a citation is made is a site of "specialist knowledge." We may be more likely to accept this claim when the knowledge takes recognizable forms or is produced by scholars with institutional or other validation. Therefore, the stakes of citing to call forth are substantially higher for artists than for scholars in Southeast Asia because the art-historical knowledge that artists produce is often less well-recognized, respected, and understood than that of scholars working in universities or other canonizing institutions. This is an instance of epistemic injustice, a concept I revisit in the epilogue.

Yet to cite (or to quote) is not only to call but also to *take*. This is the etymology and literal meaning of the Malay and Indonesian word for citing, *mengutip*, and also of equivalent terms in many other Southeast Asian vernacular languages; in Khmer, for example, to cite is literally to "take out" or "extract": *dak srang*.[15] When I cite (or quote) an artwork or text, I take the ideas and aesthetics from that other work, and I reuse them in my own writing. This kind of taking—perhaps we can also call it borrowing, although the word is less than ideal, as we will see later—is accepted as normal and allowable if I agree to obey the conventions of scholarly citation and formally acknowledge the source from which I am taking. If I quote or cite an artwork or text or use ideas or words or images that are not my own, generally I must provide a footnote, endnote, in-text reference, bibliography, or some other recognized mechanism for acknowledging my source. This is easy to do in scholarly writing, but it becomes more complex and challenging in other contexts, especially in artworks.[16]

If citing is understood as an act involving both calling and taking, then it is usually expected that these two facets of citation—the calling forth of another text or artwork and the taking of ideas or aesthetics from it—are to be kept in balance. In scholarly writing, an equilibrium is typically achieved through use of footnotes, or other similar recognized mechanisms, and also through adherence to the norms of scholarly writing in a particular disciplinary setting. Even within the field of art histories, these norms vary. In Southeast Asia's modern and contemporary art histories, many respected writers cite very infrequently. The art historian T. K. Sabapathy has lamented this on several occasions, noting that only "rarely" do scholars "acknowledge and build upon extant writings . . . every effort, every exegesis is, seemingly, a new beginning!"[17] By contrast, in the kind of art-historical writing that James Elkins calls "a standard North Atlantic idiom," extensive citations are expected and normalized.[18] Especially in first books by scholars published with North American university presses, it is common to find multiple citations within a single paragraph, few of them substantially engaged with in the main text. For readers trained outside of the North American system, such as myself, this proliferation of citations can feel unbalanced—too much calling forth other specialists as a kind of display of mastery and not enough taking from and deeply engaging with their ideas in any meaningful way—but I also recognize that (as Elkins affirms) there are "many small inequalities between art historical practices of writing in different places," such as "discrepancies between different authors' engagement with the literature" and so on.[19] Reinforcing this view that scholarly practices vary in different settings, a study of citation practices in the humanities notes that "references are a social and institutional phenomenon as well as an epistemological one."[20] How we cite is shaped by the contexts in which we work.

Yet while scholarly writing has developed (explicit and implicit) ways of maintaining a balance between the calling and the taking that is done with any citation, artistic practice has not. After all, artworks typically do not have footnotes or bibliographies, and nor are artworks understood or circulated within normative systems like disciplinary subfields. Some kinds of artistic practice, such as appropriation, have made this circumstance their central subject matter: appropriationist art typically takes from other artwork (or images) without being concerned about acknowledging its sources.

It is worth noting that appropriation has had relatively little impact in Southeast Asia, either as a practice or an art-historical term. It is hard to think of many artists equivalent to the American Cindy Sherman or the Japanese Yasumasa Morimura in Southeast Asia. There are some artists who have worked in a similarly ironic and parodic way—such as Semsar Siahann (1952–2005), with his reuse of the composition of Manet's *Olympia* in a 1987 painting, and Yee I-Lann (1971–), with her reuse of digitally manipulated reproductions of Kassian Cephas's nineteenth century photographs in a 2013 digital print—yet the epistemic politics of appropriation have been secondary in discussions of their work, which have instead emphasized other political issues.[21] Elsewhere in the discourses of art histories in Southeast Asia, the term appropriation is sometimes used in more generic ways, such as to refer to the integration of art-related ideas and techniques from another place (as in the art historian John Clark's suggestion that "the representation of the land, a theme beloved of conservative nationalists in many countries, was appropriated in the 1920s and 1930s by resident Dutch painters or Indonesian painters in [Indonesia]").[22] The term appropriation is also rarely used in discussions of artists in Southeast Asia using found images and objects in collage, assemblage, and other works. It is for these reasons, as well as a desire to avoid habitually adopting terminology and art-historical concepts developed in Western discourses, that I propose *citation* in place of a more familiar term like *appropriation* when discussing artists' reuse of images, ideas, and aesthetics from other artworks in Southeast Asia.[23]

My use of the term citing also invokes and honors the late art historian Ingrid Muan's influential unpublished doctoral dissertation, titled "Citing Angkor."[24] In addition to being a foundational study of twentieth-century art in Cambodia, Muan's work is also significant for its transhistorical scope, discussing art of the colonial and postcolonial eras in dialogue with each other, and thus enabling a sense of the modern and the contemporary as interrelated. In this, Muan was building on work by scholars such as Apinan Poshyananda, whose book examines art in Thailand from the mid-nineteenth century until the 1990s.[25] As suggested by its title, Muan's account centers on an understanding of how the premodern temples of Angkor are repeatedly cited and thus reexamined and (aesthetically and ideologically) repurposed within the arts of the modern era. In this transhistorical approach, Muan's work differs from Apinan's fidelity to chronology in the tradition of canonical Western art historians such as E. H. Gombrich.

While citation is not well-theorized in art-historical or other humanities discourses, the fact that artworks reuse images, ideas, and aesthetics from other artworks is well known, as is the basic observation that artworks do not have footnotes.[26] Writing in 1978 for the exhibition *Art About Art* at the Whitney Museum of American Art, the revisionist art historian Leo Steinberg notes that art's "origin in other art is not always confessable."[27] Using the example of early modern Western paintings, he continues that "there is no place in Renaissance pictures for footnotes, credit lines, or quotation marks, whether these pictures 'quote' from the moderns or from the ancients, as they habitually do," and that as a result, "the quotations, if that's what they are, go unacknowledged."[28] Expanding on his hesitation around the use of the term quotation, Steinberg affirms that "if quotation by definition requires acknowledgement, then the word had best stay out of art." He continues, "the word 'borrowing' is even less apt" since it is not possible to conceive of borrowing something "without a lender's consent, without temporarily dispossessing the owner, or promising restitution," yet all of these things can be done when an artwork reuses images or ideas or aesthetics from another artwork.[29] After all, an artist can reuse something from an artwork made long ago by an artist who is long-dead; no consent is required, nothing is physically taken from whomever owns the artwork being cited, and there is no need to return whatever it is that is being reused.

More than merely semantic, the problem with terms like quoting and borrowing is that they may limit our imaginative understanding of what is happening at a deeper, epistemic, affective (and even, as we will see later, political) level when an artist reuses something from another artwork. Steinberg asserts the following:

> our conventional jargon continues to muddle the issue by arousing our tenderest feelings about possessions. Terms such as 'borrowing' and 'stealing' empoison our judgement and they reduce the abundant spiritual intercourse between artists and art to a uniform pattern, as if an artist's recourse to precedent necessarily betrayed a deficiency; as if this aspect of creativity could be covered by a simplistic word.[30]

The suggestion that terms like borrowing and stealing fail because they are too closely associated with (Western and) capitalist concepts of property and possession is useful, because it raises the question of what connotations are attached to other possible terms, such as appropriation and quoting or citing—or, in Steinberg's terms, what tender feelings are aroused by this alternate critical vocabulary. I have already suggested that appropriation feels inapt because the term is rarely used with specificity in the discourse of Southeast Asia's modern and contemporary art histories, and because the kinds of practice usually called appropriationist in the West or in other contexts have had little impact in this region.

Why, then, have I chosen to use the term citing (which is synonymous with quoting in many Southeast Asian languages)? What are its connotations? The term is usually associated with scholarly writing, and as such, I hope that by suggesting that artistic art histories are performing a provisional and continuous act of citing, I am bringing these artworks into proximal dialogue with scholarly practices of research and writing. I wholeheartedly agree with Steinberg's affirmation that "the varieties of artistic trespass or repercussion (or whatever you call it) are inexhaustible because there is as much unpredictable originality in quoting, imitating, transposing, and echoing, as there is in inventing."[31] In my detailed discussion of Emiria Sunassa's trespass into Walter Spies's practice in the next section, I highlight this "unpredictable originality" and the ways in which it combines both taking and calling, with a distinctly decolonizing motivation and effect. Citing—as an active and intentional strategy—also gets us away from defunct notions of derivativeness and mimicry that continue to plague many accounts of modern art in Asia.[32]

Emiria Sunassa's Citational Paintings

While living in Jakarta in the 1940s, the artist Emiria Sunassa (1894–1964) repeatedly based her paintings on published photographs taken in Bali by her contemporary, the Russian-born German artist Walter Spies (1895–1942). She did this without any explicit acknowledgement of his work as a source for her own, and as a result, this recurrent habit of this significant artist has hitherto been overlooked in art-historical scholarship.[33] This act of citing was Emiria's way of inserting herself into the aesthetic discourse of the period, in which Western artists and anthropologists were beginning to engage with artistic practice in Bali to a greater extent than ever before, and to produce photographic images in Bali in ways that had never been done before. Spies was central to both artistic as well as anthropological and other scholarly engagements with Bali. By choosing to repeatedly cite his published images, Emiria was at once calling forth his influential work—thereby demonstrating her mastery, including her awareness of and critical engagement with it—as well as taking his images, thereby asserting her perceived right to these images, and her confidence to use them, presumably without seeking permission, despite her doubly subjugated status as a colonized and feminine subject. In these ways, Emiria's practice of citing Spies is not only a source of art-historical information and insight, but also a confrontation with patriarchal and colonial structures of power and knowledge. Emiria is staking out a space for her artistic subjectivity in the context of competing attempts to represent colonized subjects in Bali; alongside her reliance on Spies's photographs is a defiance of their authority. This conjoined reliance and defiance will recur throughout my discussion of her paintings.

Most studies of Emiria, grounded in feminist approaches to art histories and area studies, have focused on her biography and her gender rather than the aesthetic or epistemic qualities of her artworks. In Southeast Asia's modern art histories, Emiria holds a doubly significant place: first, for having been an active member of the pioneering modernist collective in Indonesia called Persagi, exhibiting alongside better-known male artists like S. Sudjojono (1913–1985); and second, for having been one of the only women anywhere in the region to be recognized as a professionally exhibiting artist during the 1940s.[34] She participated in prominent solo and group exhibitions, and must have been joking when she herself perversely claimed in a 1952 interview to "just paint as a hobby."[35] Claire Holt—writing in the 1967 book on "Indonesian art" that was one of the first in any language to discuss the modern art of Southeast Asia—conceded that "a few of Emiria Sunassa's works show flashes of power and originality."[36] Yet Emiria's best work, according to Holt, was shaped by the artist's biography. More specifically, it was inspired by her "personal contact" with and "impressions" of regional minority cultures, such as the Dayak peoples in Borneo, where she spent time early in her life. "As the impact of her impressions there faded," Holt asserted, Emiria's works became lacking in "strength and cohesion."[37] More recent studies have been more positive in their assessment of Emiria's oeuvre. Nevertheless, they have implicitly agreed with the view expressed by Holt (who worked for the CIA) that the artist's most significant paintings are her "indigenous portraits" of Dayak people, Papuans, and others, presumably done from memory. Feminist art historian Wulan Dirgantoro champions these as "a potential site for ruptures in nationalist and colonial discourse" in Indonesia and as having "proposed a more inclusive vision of the newly emerging nation."[38] In these readings, Emiria's works are valued for their subject matter and its relation to her biography but not for the way in which they are composed and painted.

By instead focusing on Emiria's strategy of painting in response to photographs, I seek to contribute to a reappraisal of her work, while also highlighting the possibilities for artists to participate in art-historical dialogue by citing within their artwork itself, by doing and making artistic art histories. My approach builds on and departs from the foundational scholarship of Holt and Dirgantoro, as well as Heidi Arbuckle, and others.[39] Drawing on previously overlooked archival materials relating to Emiria's paintings from the 1940s, I focus on two artworks, titled *Pucuk Layu (Wilting Stamen)*, also known as *Balinese Prince* (circa 1940s), and *Tari Kebyar (Balinese Dancer)*, also known as *Mario Penari Bali* (circa 1940–46), both of which were painted in direct response to contemporaneous photographs made by Walter Spies in Bali. The composition of Emiria's *Pucuk Layu (Wilting Stamen)* (fig. 2.2) is closely based on Spies's photograph published in 1930 (fig. 2.3); both the painting and photograph are depictions of an anonymous Balinese man. Similarly, Emiria's *Tari Kebyar (Balinese Dancer)* (fig. 2.4) is closely based on Spies's photograph published in 1938 (fig. 2.5); both the painting and the photograph depict the celebrated Balinese dancer and choreographer, Gusti Raka, performing the *kebyar* (or *kebiar*), a seated dance popularized during the 1920s by Gusti Raka's teacher, I Ketut Marya (also known as I Mario, 1897–1968), and first reported by Spies.[40]

The 1940s, when Emiria made *Pucuk Layu (Wilting Stamen)* and *Tari Kebyar (Balinese Dancer)*, marked a heated moment and critical turning point in

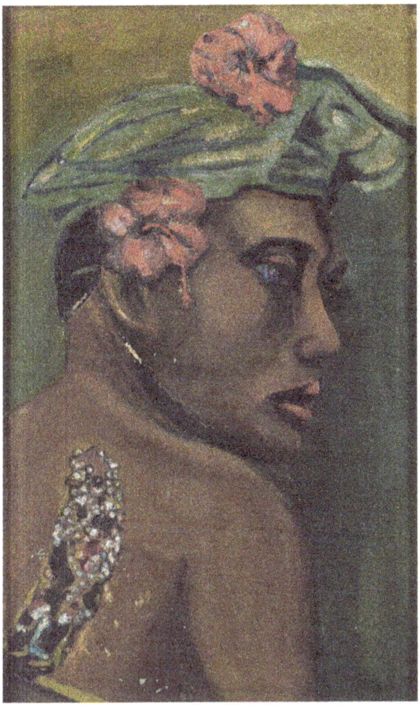

FIGURE 2.2. Emiria Sunassa, *Pucuk Layu* (*Wilting Stamen*), also known as *Balinese Prince*, c. 1940s. Oil on board, 48.3 × 29.6cm. Collection of National Gallery Singapore. Image courtesy of National Heritage Board, Singapore.

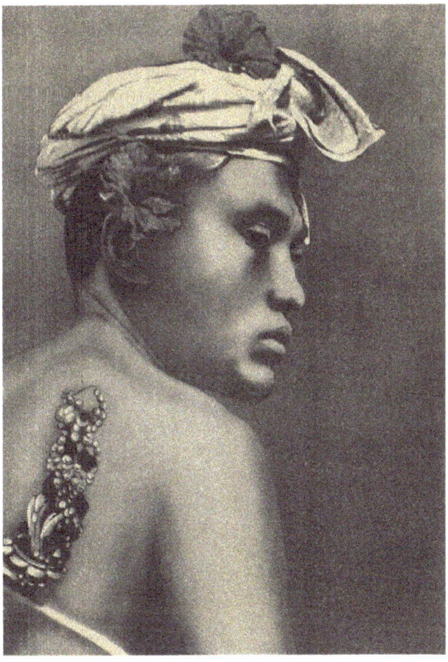

FIGURE 2.3. Walter Spies, untitled photograph published in Roelof Goris, *Bali: Godsdienst en Ceremoniën* [Bali: Religion and Ceremonies] (Batavia: Druk G. Kolff & Co., 1930).

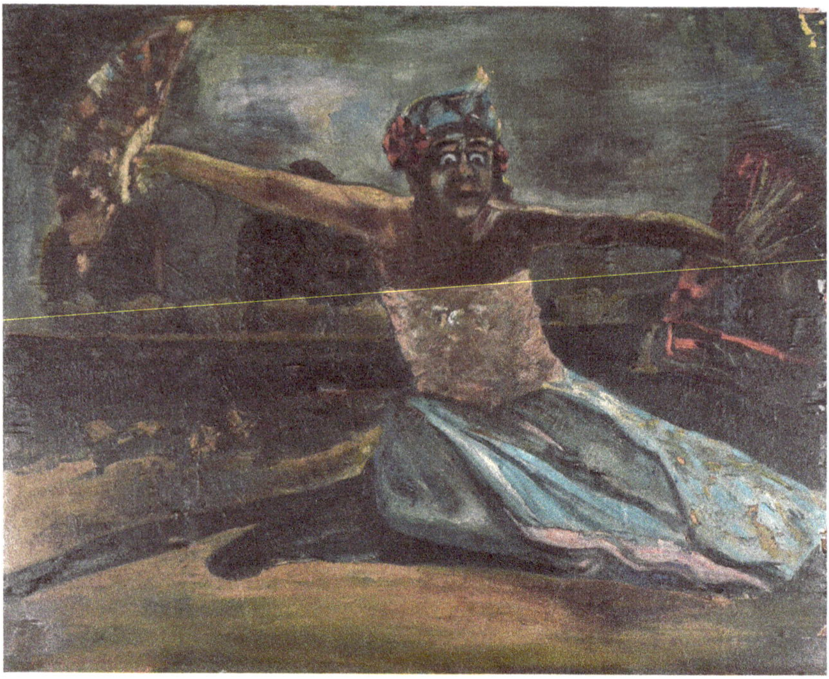

FIGURE 2.4. Emiria Sunassa, *Tari Kebyar (Balinese Dancer)*, also known as *Mario Penari Bali*, c. 1940–46. Oil on board, 59 × 75cm. Collection of National Gallery Singapore. Image courtesy of National Heritage Board, Singapore.

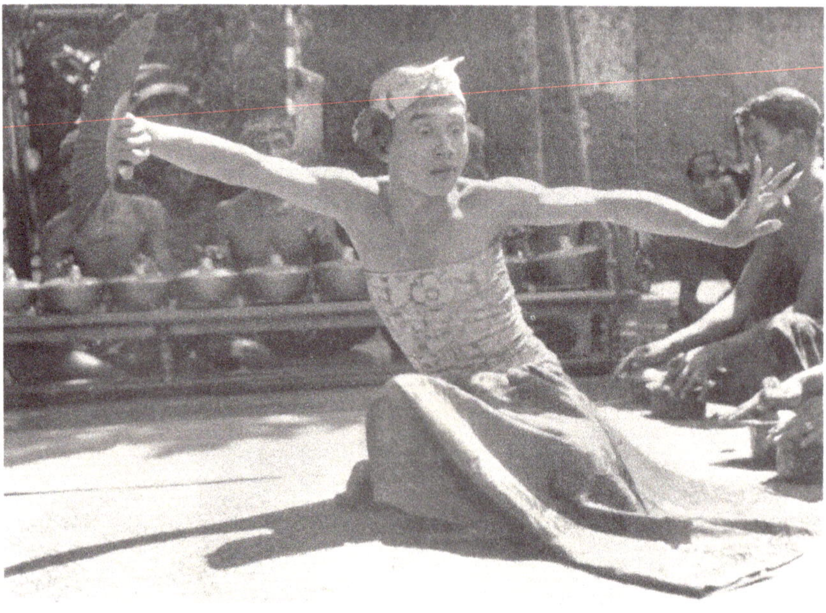

FIGURE 2.5. Walter Spies, *Goesti Raka in Kebyar*, photograph published in Beryl de Zoete and Walter Spies, *Dance and Drama in Bali* (New York: Harper and Brothers Publishers, 1938).

Balinese cultural politics, as in Southeast Asia more broadly. Since the 1920s, Bali had endured two volcanic eruptions, illnesses, and both social and economic instability.[41] Following this tumult, historian Adrian Vickers argues, debates "about the relationship between religion, art and social order . . . became increasingly violent from the 1940s onwards." Moreover many Balinese people became increasingly strategic in their adoption of "tradition" and "culture" during this period, "not slavishly following the colonial agenda by any means."[42] Concomitantly, Balinese writers, such as G.N.M. Wirjasutha, wrote radical treatises in the 1930s calling for an overthrow of the caste system and invoking the anticolonial figure of Rabindranath Tagore.[43] Emiria's paintings are implicitly aligned with and best understood in relation to this moment of sustained upheaval and anticolonial zeitgeist. In a letter written during Indonesia's struggle for independence, Emiria wrote that "things don't look too rosy in Dutch territory here, whether you look at Holland itself or its Colonies," and that the political leaders "are all standing by hopelessly, with everything turned upside down."[44]

The 1930s and 1940s was also an intense period of Western and colonial artistic and anthropological engagement with Bali, and Emiria's deliberate and repeated citations of photographs by Walter Spies—the most prominent of all foreign artists to work on the island during these decades—is a significant intervention into this art-historical context. Spies's prominence derives not only from his own painting and photographic practice but also from his role in championing Balinese artists. Soon after arriving in Bali in 1927, having lived in Java since 1923, Spies became close with painters on the island.[45] At the same time, his own paintings were shaped by the influence of Balinese pictorial conventions, including the elongation of limbs associated with *wayang* shadow puppets and dances, the densely filled narrative compositions, and the reduced palette. In 1936, Spies established an organization called Pita Maha in Ubud together with the Balinese artist and architect I Gusti Nyoman Lempad (c. 1862–1978), the aristocratic patron Tjokorda Gede Agung Sukawati (1910–1978), and the Dutch artist Rudolf Bonnet (1895–1978). Pita Maha has been described as "a meeting place and a market" for several dozen other modern Balinese painters and sculptors.[46] Although the European and Balinese artists were certainly mutually inspired by each other's work, Spies and Bonnet were the "arbiters of taste."[47]

Moreover, Spies straddled the realms of art and anthropology, which were converging in Bali during this period in an early antecedent of what would become cultural and creative anthropology. Scholars such as Margaret Mead, Gregory Bateson, Jane Belo and Colin McPhee, who were all close to Spies, were pioneering the use of photography as a tool of anthropological research.[48]

Mead and Bateson also amassed a significant collection of paintings made by "Balinese artists."[49] Spies produced photographs for publication in anthropological and tourist-oriented books. His works thus had a kind of double authority as art and as anthropological information; this double authority was redoubled by his whiteness, his role at Pita Maha, and the many other roles he played in colonial-era Bali.[50] More recently, Spies and other white residents of Bali have had an outsized visibility in historical accounts of the island's culture in the late colonial period. Heavy financial, scholarly, and cultural investment in their legacy (over and above that of the Balinese artists they worked alongside and who inspired them) in the form of "books, films, foundations and other material have ensured that the golden age of expatriate Bali lives on the world's eyes," as Vickers has argued, and this has involved considerable "smoothing over of the inconsistencies of the image."[51] Spies is certainly much more well-known than Emiria in almost every context. In this art-historical setting, Emiria's citational paintings, which freely take from and adapt Spies's published photographs, may be seen as daringly defiant.

My focus on the aesthetic and epistemic qualities of Emiria's artworks marks a shift from previous scholarship on the artist, which has instead focused on her unusual biography, including her gender, her anticolonial activism, and her contested claims to royal lineage.[52] The rich, foundational studies by feminist scholars Arbuckle and Dirgantoro are invaluable; they draw on precious oral histories and scarce archival texts to piece together Emiria's life story, including her disputed claim to rule over Papua as queen, and as princess of the nearby island of Tidore. Drawing on Arbuckle and Dirgantoro, Yvonne Low has positioned Emiria's contribution within a broader comparative feminist history of Southeast Asian art.[53] Carla Bianpoen has also championed the artist's importance as a pioneering woman in Indonesian art.[54] In their focus on the artist's gender and biography, however, all of these important scholars discuss Emiria's paintings themselves relatively briefly.[55]

Enabled by their path-clearing work, Emiria, like many other hitherto overlooked artists associated with global modernisms, is currently enjoying renewed interest among curators and museums internationally. Exhibitions that have prominently featured her work include the 2024 Venice Biennale and 2025 Singapore Biennale, as well as *Tropical: Stories from Southeast Asia and Latin America* at National Gallery Singapore in 2023, *Power & Other Things: Indonesia & Art (1835–Now)* at the Centre for Fine Arts in Brussels in 2017, *Reframing Modernism* at National Gallery Singapore in 2016, and *Familiar Others: Emiria Sunassa, Eduardo Masferré and Yeh Chi Wei, 1940s–1970s* at National Gallery Singapore in 2022.[56] Yet in these settings, too, she has been mostly prized either as a "woman artist" and/or an "Indonesian artist." Her paintings deserve to be studied more closely, including as artistic art histories.[57]

The colors in *Pucuk Layu (Wilting Stamen)* and *Tari Kebyar (Balinese Dancer)* are muted, moody, and typical of Emiria's palette in the 1940s, which demonstrates her ability to inscribe her own artistic identity over the compositions even though they are based on Spies' black-and-white photographs. *Pucuk Layu (Wilting Stamen)* comprises humid greens, soft browns, and almost-blacks, with highlights in saturated reds and lucent blues. *Tari Kebyar (Balinese Dancer)* is similar in its tonal range, with the addition of soft mint greens, dusky pinks, and flashes of white. Oil pigments in these organic shades, although applied in varying thicknesses on the cheap wooden board supports, evenly fill both pictures from edge to edge, rendering the distinction between figure and ground somewhat blurred. Dirgantoro insightfully notes that "Emiria's paintings evoked the sensual, lived experience of the local environment" and that in them "figures and the landscape reflect one another in a subtle way."[58] In some of her contemporaneous paintings, like *Bahaya Belakang Kembang Terate (Danger Lurking Behind The Lotus)* (c. 1941–6), she depicts dense and dark forests, in which human figures, like the archer who is the principal subject of that work, emerge, as if camouflaged. Contemporary Papuan artists Betty Adii and Dicky Takndare recognize the "aspiration of [Emiria's] resistance towards European colonialism" and see works such as this as "a form of solidarity that was born out of the spirit of camaraderie" even though they also "seem to only narrate Papua superficially."[59] By contrast, in both *Tari Kebyar (Balinese Dancer)* and *Pucuk Layu (Wilting Stamen)* it is difficult to discern any identifiable features of the natural environment or landscape. The background of *Pucuk Layu (Wilting Stamen)* is uninflected and blank, while in *Tari Kebyar (Balinese Dancer)* the indistinct shapes behind the dancing figure are human rather than botanical. Despite this, the subdued, vegetally-toned pigments imbue both paintings with a humid sultriness and unmistakably tropical atmosphere. The tonal range of Emiria's paintings expanded and brightened during the 1950s, but during the 1940s, including in her major solo exhibition in Jakarta in 1946, she kept largely to these sullen, muggy colors.[60]

This is just one of the many stylistic idiosyncrasies in Emiria's work (not in her biography or gender) that allow her paintings to occupy a singular position in the art histories of Southeast Asia in this period. Many of the most memorable paintings made during the 1940s by her peers in the anticolonial Persagi artists' collective rely on brighter colors and sharper tonal shifts for their impact.[61] By contrast, the murkiness of Emiria's palette means that her works demand slow, sustained scrutiny.[62] They take time to really see. Yet, once seen, they reveal themselves to be distinctively and unmistakably Emiria's. Perhaps this is why, in a 1949 text about "New Indonesian painting," the artist and filmmaker Basuki Resobowo (1916–1999) singled out Emiria, alongside Sudjojono, Affandi, and three others, as being a rare example of an artist who had achieved "freedom of the soul" through "individual freedom and the emergence of personalit[y]."[63]

In the Southeast Asian context, there is something distinctly modern about this "emergence of an individual style." Despite its independence and individuation, the pursuit of originality may also be tied to a collective, nationalist sensibility. The conjoined aesthetic and ideological obligations of an artist in this setting are evoked in a 1952 poem titled "My Duty" (*Dharmaku*) written in Indonesian by the Balinese writer Windhya Wirawan. Its final verse declares:

> If I were an artist
> I'd write history
> with dance, painting
> sculpture and song.[64]

Although Emiria's paintings refuse direct representation of political histories, they may nevertheless to be understood to "write history"—and write art history—by engaging with the modern entanglement of the individual and the collective in a "geopoetic" way.[65] They harmonize with the anticolonial zeitgeist of the 1940s, mentioned previously, especially through the complex politics inherent in their citation of contemporaneous photographs. Windhya Wirawan's poem guides us to an embodied and artistic understanding of history, while Emiria's paintings, through their use of visual citing, guide us to see their reliance on Walter Spies's photographs and their defiance of those same images.

As well as affirming Emiria's modern artistic individuality and conveying an atmosphere of tropicality, the palettes of *Pucuk Layu (Wilting Stamen)* and *Tari Kebyar (Balinese Dancer)* are significant because they make explicit Emiria's transformation of monochrome, mechanically reproduced photographic images into colored oil paintings. This has not been discussed in previous studies of the artist and her work. Although Arbuckle recounts speculation and rumors that "Emiria's paintings of Bali were 'copied' from publications or photographs about the island," she finds no evidence in the form of specific source images for any artworks.[66] Therefore, the implications of this aspect of the artist's compositional approach are elided in her account. Moreover, few scholars have addressed the intersections of photography and painting in twentieth-century Indonesia. In her 1967 book, for example, Claire Holt makes no mention of the pioneering

Javanese photographer Kassian Cephas (1845–1912), one of the earliest Asian professional photographers, nor of any other photographers. In her chapters on modern art, she almost exclusively discusses painting and, to a lesser extent, sculpture.[67] In turn, more recent studies of photography and its relationship to coloniality in Indonesia, such as the insightful work of Susie Protschky, have not focused on the intersections between the medium and painting.[68]

This bifurcation of scholarship on photography and painting is not unique to Indonesia's art histories; rather, it typifies much research on modern Southeast Asia more broadly. Many of the foundational scholarly art-historical accounts of different nations in the region focus exclusively on painting and, to a lesser extent, sculpture. Similarly, much of the more recent scholarship on early photography in the region is done by social historians, anthropologists, and others, rather than art historians, and considers the medium in relative isolation. This is despite the longstanding use of photographs as source images for paintings in Southeast Asia as elsewhere (and perhaps especially in colonized regions). As Protschky observes, for example, many of the painted portraits of the Dutch queen Wilhelmina (r. 1890–1948) made in the former Dutch East Indies were painted after photographs of paintings, while "even in the Netherlands" many paintings of the queen were done after photographs.[69] Key figures of Southeast Asia's modern art in the period, such as Mas Pirngadie (1875–1936) in Indonesia and Yong Mun Sen (1896–1962) in Malaysia, worked both as painters and photographers. With this context in mind, it is clear that when Emiria made paintings in response to and citing photographs, she was adopting a well-established and distinctly modern way of working, yet one that has not been substantially studied within Southeast Asia's scholarly art histories.[70] One contribution of artistic art histories like Emiria's work is to bring different media, like photography and painting, back into lively dialogue with each other.

The composition of *Pucuk Layu (Wilting Stamen)* is based very closely on a photograph by Walter Spies, published in 1930 in Roelof Goris's book *Bali: Godsdienst en Ceremoniën* (Bali: Religion and Ceremonies).[71] Described as a "guide book" and published in Jakarta, Goris's book would have been easily accessible to Emiria, whose first exhibition was held in a bookstore in the capital.[72] Spies's photograph, which depicts an unnamed figure, appears as a full-page reproduction; it is almost half the size of Emiria's painting, which would have made for easy reference when she composed the image. While far from photorealistic, *Pucuk Layu (Wilting Stamen)* is one of the most naturalistic of Emiria's known works. The proportions of the figure are anatomically correct and correspond closely to Spies's photograph. Similarly, the modeling conveys the figure's solidity and closely follows the chiaroscuro effect of the black and white photograph that was almost certainly shot in natural lighting. For example, the brow, cheek, nose, lips, and chin in both the painting and the photograph are all lighter in shade, highlighted against the darker tones of the eye sockets, jawline, and neck, which are shrouded in shadow. The gently rounded arch of the shoulder is given prominence in the photograph by its relative size within the image and its evenly pale tone. In the painting, a light-colored highlight along the top of the otherwise darker shoulder draws our eyes upwards to the man's lips, which Emiria has made longer than they are in the photograph, and highlighted in a lurid crimson red.

The addition of color in Emiria's painting allows her to transform, subtly yet significantly, the appearance of the anonymous subject as he appears in Spies's photograph. This is citation with explicit differentiation, and its art-historical function is to highlight a peculiarity (or misrepresentation) in Spies' image. The red of the man's lips in *Pucuk Layu (Wilting Stamen)*, which is carefully applied to convey their moist fullness, corresponds exactly to the red of the two hibiscus flowers, one of which is placed behind the man's right ear and one atop his *udeng* headdress. In the same vibrant scarlet color, Emiria has also added long, delicate stamens to each of these flowers. These stamens are entirely absent in Spies's photograph. In her discussion of this painting, Arbuckle asserts that "the placement of the two flowers upon [the *udeng*] is peculiar."[73] Because she was unaware of the Spies photograph that Emiria's painting was based on, Arbuckle's claim relies on an assumption about what she calls "customary rules" in "Balinese culture."[74] She does not distinguish between different villages or regions within Bali.[75] And she does not explain how "customary rules" in "Balinese culture" were shifting and changing during the period in which Emiria was working, with writers such as G. N. M. Wirjasutha having advocated profound transformations in social structure, such as an overhaul of the caste system.

Knowing that the painting is made in direct response to Spies's photograph, it is possible that this citation with differentiation was actually intended to augment or correct the "misrepresentation" in Spies's image. Arbuckle claims that the stamens in the flowers in Emiria's painting are "unusually limp" as "Balinese men wear hibiscus flowers with stamens that are firm and erect to symbolise their *kewibawaan* or masculine authority."[76] While this generalization is doubtless based in rigorous observations and oral testimonies gathered during Arbuckle's pioneering research, it is nevertheless not supported by the photographic evidence.[77] On the contrary, in Spies's photograph, the flowers have no stamens at all. Arbuckle proposes that "Emiria's style was expressive, not a representation of reality as it existed," and suggests that her depiction of the "unusually limp" hibiscus stamens is "a calculated 'misrepresentation.'"[78] Yet the stamens in Emiria's painting also have a compositional function: their lines accentuate the curves in the man's face and headdress.[79]

The composition of Spies's photograph emphasizes his attraction to its anonymous subject, consistent with his queerness, which Emiria would almost certainly have known about. By the 1940s, when Emiria began professionally exhibiting, it would have been difficult for her to overlook this aspect of Spies's life; his sexuality was subjected to very public scrutiny in a series of colonial crackdowns on deviant sexualities in 1938 and 1939, leading to his arrest.[80] Moreover, Spies's queerness is visible in many of his photographs; the scholar Eng-Beng Lim argues that in Spies's "ethnophotography" he "stages the languid gaze, entranced posture, and wry smile of both Spies and 'the boys,' who appear to be in on the joke about their queer masquerade."[81] Spies's attraction to the young man in the photograph published in Goris's book is evident in its composition: the human figure fills the frame from edge to edge, leaving no room for any sense of the setting to encroach in the background. The play of light and shadow on the man's handsome features dominates the image, which Spies appears to have photographed using a soft-focus lens, imbuing the figure with a dreamy quality that approximates the experience of being overcome with desire while gazing at the man.[82]

We can also deduce Spies's attraction to the man by viewing the photograph in relation to his biography and his photography practice more broadly. He wrote, of the Balinese (and Javanese and Sundanese), that "the people . . . are so incredibly beautiful, so delicately built, brown and aristocratic, that everyone who is not one of them should be ashamed."[83] The amorous and physical attraction implicit in Spies's work is downplayed, however, in Roelof Goris's book where it is published (despite Goris's own queerness).[84] There, Spies's photograph is accompanied by a caption that describes the image as depicting a "South Balinese with precious kris, of which the upper part of the scabbard consists of ivory; the golden hilt is set with precious stones."[85] Consistent with Goris's anthropological approach in the guidebook, the caption emphasizes the observable qualities of the kris but says nothing of the anonymous human subject. Yet despite this framing within the publication, when composing the photograph, Spies seems to have been drawn to the man himself, rather than to his decorated dagger.

A similar starry-eyed infatuation is conspicuous in Emiria's painting too, suggesting that Emiria was energized by and deliberately emphasizing her own (aesthetic and/or perhaps sexual) attraction to the man. This is seen in her use of gem-like colors to highlight the man's lips, eyes, and various bodily adornments.

We may speculatively interpret this as Emiria's implicit allegiance to the embattled Spies, or as her visual assertion of her own desires, or perhaps some combination of the two. Arbuckle suggests that Emiria was "able to explore fluid representations of native male sexuality."[86] Yet it is also possible that the artist may have been expressing her own sexuality as a woman and an artist. Emiria's enchantment with and desire for the man in *Pucuk Layu (Wilting Stamen)* is palpable. She uses the same shade of scarlet red on the man's kris, his lips, the flowers he wears, and on her own signature, which has the effect of unifying the painting and linking the man's radiant beauty with that of his decorative weapon, his floral ornamentation, and the artist's own individuated identity, as represented by her signature.[87] Similarly, she uses the same rich Prussian blue in the jewels of the kris, and in the iris of the man's eyes. It appears that for Emiria, the man himself is as beautiful, alluring, and luminous as his precious dagger.

This sets Emiria's work apart from that of her European contemporaries, who also painted depictions of Balinese men wearing *udeng*, and suggests that in this painting, she is not only directly citing Spies, but also indirectly referring to several other male Western artists who worked in Bali in the period. Arbuckle compares *Pucuk Layu (Wilting Stamen)* to a painting by the Dutch artist Willem Gerard Hofker (1902–1981), titled *Njoman Pegug* (1938). In it, a flash of crimson red paint is also used, yet in Hofker's painting, it appears only on the hilt of the kris, and not in the man's facial features. The apparently heterosexual Hofker's use of color to focus attention on the kris rather than the man is consistent with Goris's captioning of Spies's photograph to emphasize the qualities of the dagger rather than the figure. By contrast, Emiria's integrated distribution of accent colors throughout her composition seems to make clear her attraction to the man, as well as to his finery; through its citation with differentiation, her approach defies the colonial fascination with objects rather than human subjects, even as it relies on Spies's photograph.

Compared to *Pucuk Layu (Wilting Stamen)*, the brushwork in *Tari Kebyar (Balinese Dancer)* is much looser and the style is less naturalistic, yet the composition of the painting is also based closely on a photograph by Walter Spies that was published in 1938 in *Dance and Drama in Bali*, a book written by Beryl de Zoete.[88] Emiria's painting and Spies's photograph both depict the dancer and choreographer Gusti Raka performing the *kebyar* dance, making her art-historical citation explicit and obvious to anyone familiar with the source image. In both images, the figure fills the frame with his outstretched posture, flowing garb, and distinctive props. The dancer's opened folding fan, held in his right hand, stops just short of the top and left corner of both pictures; the fold of cloth covering his folded legs almost reaches the lower edge of the frames, while its extremity is slightly cropped on their right sides; and Gusti

Raka's elegantly poised fingers stretch nearly to the right edge of both pictures. Describing Gusti Raka, de Zoete rhapsodizes that "his hands are dazzlingly beautiful. His long nails elongate them fantastically."[89] The delicately pointed shape is clearly visible in Spies's photograph while their dimensions are further exaggerated in Emiria's painting. Moreover, in both the painting and photograph, the dancer's arms are brightly illuminated by the sunlight directly above: a line of lighter color highlights the upper side of his deltoid, bicep, and forearm muscles, while a sharply outlined shadow is cast crisply on the ground beneath.

Most strikingly, in both the painting and photograph, Gusti Raka's startlingly wide-open eyes dominate as a principal feature of the image; by compositionally highlighting this detail, Emiria emphasizes its significance and rarity. Emiria visually underscores Gusti Raka's eyes through her use of chalky white, which stands out in distinct contrast from the more subdued and darker colors that fill the rest of the canvas. Yet the shape of the eyes is consistent in both the painting and photograph: an arched semicircle of white envelops the pupil and iris, which de Zoete describes as "blazing eyes and gestures of defiance" as if "scared by a vision, imagining some fear." This is quite at odds with her characterization of Gusti Raka's face as "rather hard and inexpressive in dancing."[90] Images capturing this disarming moment of a *kebyar* dancer's eyes opened wide enough to reveal the sclera (or white of the eyes) are rare. Many contemporaneous photographs of *kebyar* dancers show dancers with impassive faces. Spies's ability to photographically document the precise moment of Gusti Raka's astonishingly open eyes—especially given that, in de Zoete's words, "in *Kebyar* everything is fleeting"[91]—may reflect his long-term residency in Bali and his deep familiarity with the dance. Through its citing, Emiria's painting reveals this special quality in Spies's work.

Emiria's use of color and composition to highlight this feature suggests a deeper, perhaps even allegorical fascination with the dancer's wide-open eyes. In another painting made several years later, titled *Penari Bali (Balinese Dancer)* (1957), the dancer's sclera are again emphasized; the whites of the eyes are almost the only use of white in the entire composition.[92] This repeated depiction of the ocular expressiveness of Balinese dance suggests that the intermedial citation—in which the painting refers to the performers as well as to Spies's photograph—was deeply inspiring for Emiria.

A final feature that recurs in both Spies's photograph and Emiria's painting is the *gamelan* orchestra visible behind the dancer. This serves to visually convey the unity between choreography and the music, which is essential in the *kebyar* dance, and which amplifies the painting's intermedial impact. In these ways, the *gamelan* orchestra underscores Emiria's art-historical emphasis on intersections between different artistic media. In the photograph, the sinewy frames of individual musicians playing the *trompong* are clearly visible; in the painting, these men's features are no longer visible, as their forms have been simplified to become solid shapes of dark brown (in the background, at the center and to the left of the dancer) and deep red (to the right of the dancer), but the gongs of the *trompong* instruments they play remain distinct and easily distinguishable. De Zoete notes that "only a fine musician can become a fine dancer of *Kebyar*" and cites Mario's statement that "no one is qualified to dance *Kebyar* who cannot play every instrument in the gamelan." She moreover notes that Gusti Raka's interpretation of the dance differs from his teacher Mario's in its relationship to the music. Gusti Raka "interprets its dynamics in much greater detail, with ingenious accents of arms and hands."[93] So too, Emiria interprets the dynamics of the *gamelan* in general and of Gusti Raka's rendition of the *kebyar* in particular. Her paintings after photographs are already animated by the tensions and slippages between these two image-making media and by her ability to rely on Spies's images while also transforming them. In *Tari Kebyar (Balinese Dancer)*, the intermediality is extended from two-dimensional pictures into four-dimensional dance and musical performances. The painting vibrates and resonates like a gong.

After sustained viewing of the two paintings I have discussed in this chapter in relation to the Walter Spies photographs that they are responding to, it becomes clear that there is one final differentiation at work in Emiria's citation of these source images; her use of paint to focus our attentions is important, much like the lens and aperture of a camera may sharpen or soften a mechanically reproduced image. In *Pucuk Layu (Wilting Stamen)*, she has taken a blurry, soft-focus photograph and sharpened it, rendering the image as a crisp and relatively naturalistic painting, with several pronounced highlights, such as the man's crimson red lips and sparkling blue eyes. By contrast, in *Tari Kebyar (Balinese Dancer)*, she has taken a very tightly focused photograph—one that precisely captures a fleeting moment in which Gusti Raka's eyes are opened extraordinarily wide under the bright midday sun, which casts a clear shadow beneath him—and she has softened it, rendering the image blurred and indistinct through her use of loose, visible brushstrokes. What can we make of Emiria's painterly twisting of Spies's photographic vision, and how might it have been received by her contemporaries?

Writing in 1946, Sudjojono—Emiria's colleague in Persagi, who as cofounder of that collective was also one of the most prodigious writers among the artists of the period—had the following to say about Emiria's work:

> Emiria, even though a woman, [is] more macho than other people. Her style is primitive, honest like a small child. Her heartfelt emotion

> springs like a boil on a virgin's lips. Unbridled, unaccountable, whether we like it or not it appears suddenly in overlooked places. Plenty of people do not understand her art, because Emiria's aesthetic is very peculiar. However, to those who understand, Emiria continues to be sympathetic in her impulsiveness.[94]

This short but dense statement contains several insights as well as several revealing misconceptions couched in highly gendered terms. The suggestion that Emiria's work is "honest" and characterized by its "impulsiveness" seems to rest on a stereotype of femininity and suggests that Sudjojono was unaware of her paintings made after photographs, in which a kind of carefully planned deliberation is required. Similarly, the notion that Emiria's work is "unbridled" seems blind to the rather meticulous reworking of compositions from Spies's photographs in the paintings. In calling Emiria "macho," Sudjojono was very likely unaware of the heterosexual feminine desire for the Balinese man that is suggested in *Pucuk Layu (Wilting Stamen)*, and in calling her style "primitive" and her aesthetic "peculiar" he is apparently ignorant of her depiction of a distinctly modern and wildly popular dance, the *kebyar*, in *Tari Kebyar (Balinese Dancer)*. There are many misapprehensions and sexist assumptions about her work. So where is the insight?

In comparing Emiria's work to "a boil on a virgin's lips," Sudjojono seems to have hit on its indescribably special quality, and the quality that makes her paintings not only take time to see but also to reward sustained study: that is, their *weirdness*. To imagine "a boil on a virgin's lips" is to imagine a flaw, even an ugly blemish, yet one that it is impossible to look away from. For Sudjojono, we may presume, a "virgin" is tacitly desirable and implicitly available for his possession. A boil may cast into question that desirability, and Emiria's work seems to resist acquisitive domination. The imagined boil may be compared to what literary scholar Thomas H. Ford calls the "weirdness" in a text. Inherent in the weirdness (as in the imagined, metaphorical boil) is "an element of surprise," something "unfamiliar, alien, and unexpected" (much like a blemish on a virgin's lips) yet also "familiar and foreign at the same time," what is "predestined" and thus "determines, in condensed form, the fatality of all the other parts of the text, awarding them the necessary organization just as they are." Perhaps this is what Sudjojono means when he says "Emiria's aesthetic is very peculiar." More than merely eccentric, weirdness is (in Ford's terms) "some element that is at once different from the rest of the text and yet wholly representative of it." It is something that feels "both unavoidable and unaccountable."[95] The "peculiar" qualities in Emiria's paintings are not merely quirks but are fundamental to their impact.

Unaccountable; this is also a word Sudjojono uses to describe Emiria's work. He also says it "appears suddenly," as if with what Ford calls "an element of surprise." Perhaps what Sudjojono is identifying in Emiria's work is its weirdness. That weirdness is amplified by her practice of citing: the strangeness of her paintings stands in contrast not only to the paintings of her peers but also to the photographs by Spies, whose compositions she relies on even while she also defies them through her many changes and differentiations. Just "like a boil on a virgin's lips," once we have seen Emiria's reliance on and defiance of Spies's photographs, we cannot unsee these qualities. Once we have noticed her sharpening of a previously soft-focus image and her softening of a previously crisp one, these features become "unavoidable." As unavoidable, perhaps, as "a boil on a virgin's lips" is impossible to look away from. Perhaps the purportedly promiscuous Spies is the virgin, and Emiria is the boil. Or perhaps Bali is the boil, or Gusti Raka, or the *kebyar* dance; the Balinese word *kebiar*, after all, refers to "a sudden outburst of flames" or a "flash." It may be compared "to the bursting open of a flower."[96]

The weirdness in Emiria's work is an important resource in the quest for what Flores calls "art-historical alterity," and it suggests ways in which artistic art histories can enrich and expand the discourse and offer inspiration for scholars as well.[97] Just as Emiria is able to impose her own individuated artistic approach when citing Spies's photographs while revealing aspects of his work that are special and unique, so too can scholars follow Flores's lead in developing new and weird ways of doing and making art histories, including approaches that are (in Elkins's terms) eccentric.[98]

In recent decades in the context of the postcolonial turn, it has become increasingly common for scholars to point to the Southeast Asian origins or inspirations for canonical Western artists; however, relatively scant attention has been paid to Southeast Asian artists' quotations of contemporaneous artworks by their peers in the region. We know, for example, that Balinese music inspired the acclaimed American composer Philip Glass (b. 1937), and that he was introduced to the form by the work of Spies's friend, the musicologist Colin McPhee.[99] Such stories are important reminders of the transcendent power of Southeast Asia's arts and culture, but they may also unintentionally reinforce the assumption that Southeast Asia offers a source of inspiration for artists who are necessarily located elsewhere in cosmopolitan centers. We know little of what artists working in Southeast Asia during the 1940s thought of each other's work, for example. By focusing attention on how a Southeast Asian artist like Emiria cites contemporaneous artworks made within this region (a form of "inter-Asia referencing" within artistic practice), we can simultaneously provincialize the West and deprovincialize Southeast Asia.[100]

Several scholars have referred to artworks as "citational paintings," yet the meanings and implications of the concept have not been elaborated in detail or in relation to a decolonial agenda. Although one scholar has argued that "the practice of citation was well theorized" in China during the Song period (960–1279), the term has been chiefly deployed in relation to Western art.[101] For example, Linda Hutcheon uses the term to describe in general terms some parodic tendencies in Western representational art.[102] Perhaps Emiria's appropriation of Spies's queer gaze might be considered parodic in some ways. More specifically, Miwon Kwon writes of "citational paintings of various [Western] genres, including abstraction, still-life, portrait and landscape."[103] Perhaps Emiria's taking of Spies's photographs from an anthropology book and a book on dance might be considered an implicit commentary on the genre-like conventions of different academic disciplines and of photography as art.[104] Most recently, Emmelyn Butterfield-Rosen has called Édouard Manet's 1860s works "citational paintings," drawing on Aby Warburg's "art-historical insights about the repetition-structure of gestural language in European art," among other ideas.[105] Butterfield-Rosen's usage comes closest to my own, as she contends that Manet's (and other artists') works themselves communicate ideas about art history. As she discusses almost exclusively European art, however, the implications of Butterfield-Rosen's argument on the (de)colonial politics of art history are not elaborated.

Reliance and Defiance

For Emiria to make citational paintings in the context of colonial and decolonizing Indonesia is an act of defiance. It is an assertion of her right and ability to cite from a European artist's work. Implied in this citational practice is a theory of art—in terms of both production and reception—as enabling exchange and engagement that transcends the colonizer/colonized binary opposition and decenters the colonial encounter through its process of inter-Asia referencing within Southeast Asia. Emiria's citational paintings contain an intelligence and are an example of what Mieke Bal calls "image-thinking."[106] They raise questions that scholars are also engaged with, such as how "different cultures approach the issue of citation" and how technology (in this case, photography) may change "the way we think about the practices of repetition."[107] They may also be considered to perform "lateral citation," a term that has recently been proposed to describe the practice (common in examples of autotheory) of "cit[ing] one's peers, friends, cohort, or colleagues instead of citing only upward—established philosophers, scholars with tenure, and so on."[108] For Emiria—subjugated as a woman and a colonized subject—to laterally cite Spies (who was born the year after her) is a sign of her daring and decolonizing attitude of subversion and epistemic resistance.

We have seen that in Claire Holt's published writing she was tepid in her appreciation for Emiria's work and emphasized her biography; in her unpublished notes, she also underestimated the extent of the artist's engagement with her peers. If we follow Spong's approach in *The painter-tailor*, as discussed in chapter 1, and look to Holt's unpublished archives, we will find that Holt wrote of her "impression that Emiria just looks down on other Indonesian painters," even though she also listed a few whose work the artist had told her she appreciated.[109] Yet there is ample evidence to suggest that Emiria engaged actively with her artist peers. In addition to her paintings citing the photographs of Walter Spies—as well as the paintings of other Western artists like Hofker—there are also several discussions of other artists in Emiria's unpublished letters, demonstrating her sustained interest in her peers throughout the 1940s and early 1950s. She mentions several artists by name, and in 1954 also composed a poem of seven stanzas and almost sixty lines addressed to her fellow artists in Indonesia. The poem opens with a lament for the hardship suffered by artists who must endure the laziness of uninformed collectors and publics.

> What do you care about honor
> Oh painter by profession
> If your work is admired only by
> a flock of ducks
> even though it was wrought through
> suffering
> and struggle
> that touched your very soul
> only to be sold
> to these ducks in such a lazy fashion?[110]

As well as suggesting her critical empathy for her fellow artists, the poem indicates the basic fact that Emiria was deeply and continuously concerned with what her peers were doing. The "flashes of power and originality" that Holt reluctantly identified in Emiria's works are inherently dialogic, reflexive, and embedded in their art-historical moment, which was a moment of heated anticolonial sentiment and hotly modern dance.[111] To understand Emiria's works as citing enables us to construct an art-historical narrative that does not depend on notions of succession and influence, and it also does not dispense with careful observation of formal and aesthetic qualities. Emiria draws from and reflects her art-historical context, and she develops a sophisticated analysis and shares this within her work. As art historians of Southeast Asia's modern and contemporary art working to develop new methods and lexicons and to epistemically and aesthetically decolonize the discipline, we may do well not only to study these citational paintings but also to learn from the reliance and defiance of their approach.

3

STAGING

"My name is Sanh, I was born in 1944 to Vietnamese and Khmer parents," says the narrator of Thao Nguyen Phan's artwork titled *First Rain, Brise Soleil* (2021–ongoing).[1] "Seeing no future being a farmer in the Mekong Delta, at 19, I ventured to Saigon to be a construction worker," Sanh continues. The first chapter of the three-channel "evolving moving image" artwork is titled "Memory of a Construction Worker," and Sanh's words—conveyed in subtitled text rather than in speech—read much like the transcript of an oral history interview with a laborer whose career took place at the height of the Second Indochina War, better known in Vietnam as the American War. As well as revealing demographic shifts from agricultural to urban labor, Sanh's testimony goes on to illuminate aspects of Southeast Asia's modernist architectural history that are usually elided or invisible in scholarly accounts.

Yet despite the resemblance to oral history, Sanh's words were, in fact, written by the artist; Sanh is Phan's speculative invention, a made-up character she is staging in her work, and not an actual historical figure.[2] Oral history interviews with construction workers in Southeast Asia during the twentieth century are extremely rare; such sources may not even exist at all for sites like wartime Saigon. Sanh's invented textual testimony as a fictional construction worker, however, in *First Rain, Brise Soleil* is juxtaposed against the artist's footage of a real building that still stands today, the General Sciences Library in Ho Chi Minh City (designed by Nguyen Huu Thien and Bui Quang Hanh) (fig. 3.1).[3] This is one of Phan's many favorite modernist structures. It was built during the period of the American War. The artist's camera tracks

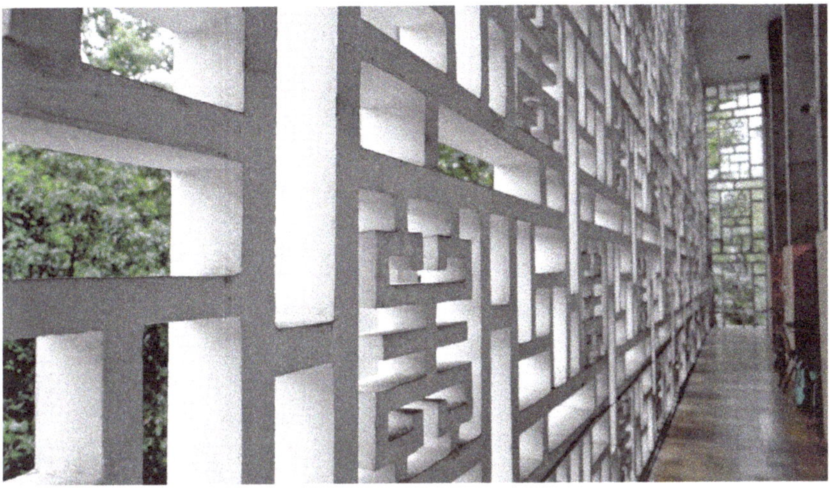

FIGURE 3.1. Thao Nguyen Phan, *First Rain, Brise Soleil*, 2021–ongoing. Three-channel video with sound, 16 mins 7 secs. Digital still from one channel. © Thao Nguyen Phan, courtesy of the artist.

affectionately across the building's distinctive perforated screen walls, constructed in finely fashioned concrete. Gradually, we realize that Sanh's imagined account aims, at least in part, to enable the staging of a kind of architectural history from below for these exquisite breeze blocks, also known as brise-soleils, which are evocatively emblematic of Saigon in particular and of tropical Southeast Asia in general. Later in *First Rain, Brise Soleil*, we see similarly lingering, loving footage of brise-soleils on architecturally significant modernist buildings in Hue (designed by Ngo Viet Thu) and Phnom Penh (designed by Vann Molyvann).[4]

This chapter is about *staging* in artistic art histories in Southeast Asia. I understand staging as a speculative and creative contemporary strategy for recovering and resurfacing aspects of the modern past (and the art, architecture, and visual culture of the modern past) that may otherwise have been lost due to limitations in archival or other sources. I also use the concept of staging to describe contemporary artists' critical conjecturing about the legacies of under-studied modernisms within present-day art and culture. Although it takes diverse forms, in essence, staging is art-historical speculating. While I see the provisional and continuous activity of staging in artistic art histories as related to the "speculative turn" in global anglophone literature—which has had a significant impact in this region—I also see staging as a response to specifically Southeast Asian art-historiographical circumstances of records often being dispersed, incomplete, and/or inaccessible.[5] Moreover, staging in artistic practice draws not only on architectural histories and formalist art histories but also on sound studies, urban studies, and other adjacent disciplines. Staging is a generative and generous word-image, which I elaborate as being at once dramatic, heterochronic, experimental, and contingent. I address each of these four inter-related qualities in more detail in this chapter.

I discuss Thao Nguyen Phan's *First Rain, Brise Soleil*, which stages speculations about modernist architecture, and also works by Fyerool Darma (1987–) and Hilmi Johandi (1987–), which speculate about the afterlives of images and sounds from both colonial archives and objects. The three artists—who are approximately the same age, and all exhibit their work both within Southeast Asia and beyond—share an interest in transnational practices in the region's modernisms. By moving from a close reading of Phan's work, to Fyerool's, and then Hilmi's, I show different facets of the speculating they are doing. Phan invents missing historical sources, while Fyerool invents missing historical narratives, and Hilmi fills a gap in scholarship. The tendency for all these artists to reuse imagery from the art of the past links these practices of staging to the citing I discussed in chapter 2; this is particularly clear in the case of Hilmi's work, which I also discussed briefly in chapter 2. Moreover, the affection and reverence seen in their works (particularly in Phan's attitude to modernist architecture) links them to the honoring I discussed in chapter 1. Yet whereas the previous chapters addressed artists' engagements with art histories to which they were personally proximal or even related, this chapter involves an expanding scope of reference. The works discussed in this chapter encompass research, thinking, and theorizing that goes beyond artists' immediate personal or family and kinship connections, stretching farther back in time, including into distant or obscure, sometimes (formerly) colonial archives.

The strategy of artistic art histories I call staging centers on the recovery of lost narratives and the bringing together of disparate modes of knowledge (including multisensory, embodied ways of knowing) and storytelling (including speculations and educated guesses); this is demonstrated in Phan's invention of a construction worker. By inventing the laborer named Sanh for *First Rain, Brise Soleil*, Phan is staging stories about modernism that are missing from the archival record. More specifically, she is speculating about hitherto overlooked microhistories of this region's modernist tropical architecture, built during the decades of political decolonization, which was often—particularly in Vietnam—won through a prolonged and violent struggle.[6]

With this line of inquiry, the artist is building on and drawing together two fields of scholarship that have otherwise rarely, if ever, intersected. The first comprises studies of modernist architecture in Southeast Asia; these have typically focused on a small number of locally celebrated architects and their interactions with prominent political (and sometimes royal) figures.[7] The perspectives of construction workers and less well-known architects, as well as other microhistorical narratives of construction, have been largely disregarded within this first field of scholarship.[8] A second field that I see as related to Phan's work consists of oral histories, which are increasingly prized by scholars of modernist architecture and art history in general.[9] Southeast Asia, however, has largely been disregarded within this second field of scholarship, possibly due to a scarcity of sources, particularly for places within the region that have been ravaged by war and other upheavals. Phan's *First Rain, Brise Soleil* is staging a novel intersection between these two areas of study—Southeast Asian modernist architecture and oral microhistories. And by speculatively bringing these fields together, she is proposing the possibility for a poetic art-historical alterity in how the past is known and imagined.

By interweaving Sanh's fictional stories with other, seemingly more factual tales that she has taken from research in various scholarly sources, Phan is also staging an encounter between history and speculation. Scholars may also occasionally turn to judiciously framed speculative claims—I have tried to do this in my own research on modernist architecture in Cambodia, when I used family photographs from a private collection to imagine the experience of living in a 1960s apartment complex—yet rarely if ever with the delicate sophistication and daring ambiguousness that Phan and other artists accomplish.[10] Artistic art histories may offer possibilities that build on and also extend beyond what scholars can typically achieve.

Staging as Dramatic, Heterochronic, Experimental, and Contingent

The example of Sanh's imagined oral history in Phan's *First Rain, Brise Soleil* embodies the polysemous quality of *staging* as I understand it: staging is dramatic, heterochronic, experimental, and contingent. First, the encounter between history and speculation that Phan presents in this artwork is theatrical, performative, and cinematic (it is staged like a play or a scene from a movie). Second, it is temporally rich and complexly layered (encompassing several stages in the historical record). Third, this encounter has the quality of a test or demonstration (it is staged like an experiment). And fourth, it is necessarily provisional and subject to revision and change (resembling a temporary structure, like staging).[11] By scaffolding over gaps in the historical record—gaps that result from colonial and other forms of historical violence, including war—Phan and other artists like her are critically repositioning these absences not as shortcomings but as fertile sites for artistic and art-historical reimagination across time.

While the term staging is quite widely used by contemporary artists, its meanings and implications are not always elucidated. Sometimes, it may simply mean presenting or making public, typically through an exhibition, performance, publication, or similar means. Often, the term may be used in a way that encompasses some but not all the polysemous qualities I have described previously. By focusing on staging as dramatic, heterochronic, experimental, and contingent, I do not intend to prescriptively suggest that the concept must always include all these aspects. Rather, in this chapter, I focus on artworks that, despite their differences, share these qualities in common.

These four interdependent understandings of staging—as dramatic, heterochronic, experimental, and contingent—can all be seen in *First Rain, Brise Soleil*. First, the artwork is dramatically presented like a theatrical stage. Phan's simple arrangement of the three screens together at one side of a squarish room with seating facing it easily recalls a theater or cinema, as do scenes set in domestic environments that have been filmed using medium shots that emphasize the resemblance between a home and a film set. Second, it is heterochronic. The artwork brings together several stages of history and multiple moments in time. The artwork features some footage that is recognizably from the present-day, as well as some stories about the American War period in Vietnam and Cambodia during the 1960s and early 1970s, some about the 1980s Vietnam-backed regime in Cambodia, and even one account of an ancient mythological tale about a durian and an apocryphal love affair. Third, it is experimental. The artwork proposes speculative historical accounts like it is staging an epistemological experiment. It tests the plausibility of Sanh's invented testimony against "real" historical facts derived from research in reputable scholarly sources. And fourth, the artwork is contingent and announces its provisional nature like the staging on which future iterations of the artwork will continue to be built. In its title screens, Phan calls *First Rain, Brise Soleil* an "evolving moving image," signaling its changing nature and the likelihood of continuing modifications in the artwork.

Before discussing the concept of staging in more detail and then turning to examine artworks by Phan, Hilmi and Fyerool, it may be helpful to note that many artists in Southeast Asia and its diasporas, as elsewhere, have adopted a similar strategy to address historical narratives unrelated to art. This phenomenon has been studied by the curator June Yap, who suggests that "histories have been appropriated by artists in Singapore and Malaysia," with many works relying on viewers being familiar with the "historical backstory."[12] Similarly, the art historian Jane Blocker has observed "the hypersensitivity toward and awareness of the past" that she argues characterizes the contemporary.[13] Although a wider consideration of artists engaging with histories in general (beyond art histories) is beyond the scope of this book, I hope that the concept of staging—although it emerges from my study of artistic art histories—may also be useful for future studies more broadly.

Theorizing Staging in Southeast Asia

By inventing the fictional construction worker named Sanh, Thao Nguyen Phan is orchestrating an encounter between informed research and intuitive guesswork. This delicate balancing act is familiar in the practices of many artists for whom staging is an important strategy for doing and making artistic art histories. The care and consideration involved sets these works apart from fiction, but the creative and fictitious quality of the work also sets it apart from conventional art-historical writing, which is usually more evidence-based. I understand staging as a mode of practice that is at once deeply concerned with the past—often with recovering stories about lesser-known artistic figures, about whom there are scant archival sources—but also tightly interwoven with the concerns of the present.

My understanding and articulation of staging as a theoretical concept is inspired by and departs from three key sources in Southeast Asia. These are: first, the artist Hilmi Johandi's deployment of the terms staging and stagecraft in his unpublished writings and in the titles of his artworks that depict sites in Singapore and Malaysia; second, the scholar meLê yamomo's elaboration of staging in his book on the sonic qualities of modernity in Manila; and third, the prevalence of puppetry-based performing arts throughout this region. These performing art forms are generally considered ancient but are regularly reworked in contemporary settings and cited in modern and contemporary visual art and other cultural settings.[14] I elaborate each of these three sources in turn. All of them suggest a multisensory and embodied approach to art-historical knowledge. In this chapter, my discussion of Hilmi will focus on his articulation of staging. I will turn to another example of his practice later in the chapter in order to expand the range of speculations that staging can encompass.

For Hilmi, staging and stagecraft are poetic turns of phrase that enable him to entwine several different kinds of space and spectatorship. In his 2019 solo exhibition, titled *Stagecraft: Landscapes and Paradise*, a series of paintings and a stop-motion video animation collude to combine the recognizably real but very obviously constructed spaces of theaters, theme parks (known in Merdeka-era Singapore as "worlds"), hotels, and resorts with illusory and often physically impossible imagined spaces within the works. This compositional strategy is briefly discussed in an essay in the exhibition catalog. The writer, Lawrence Chin, describes "a carefully balanced tension between what is possible and what is not," noting that "spatial relations reference real-life experiences in one instance but dissolve into absurdity in defiance of physical laws in others."[15] This is seen, for example, in a painting titled *Landscapes & Paradise (I)* (2019) (fig. 3.2).

For me, the experience of looking at this painting is one of zooming in on a spatially coherent scene, then zooming out to an increasing sense of impossibility and theatricality. Near the center of the painting, three figures stand knee-deep in water and toss a ball to one another. Below this scene, nearer to the viewer in the pictorial space, a gradated strip of sand-colored paint suggests the beach from which this trio has presumably wandered into the sea. In isolation, this vista is idyllic, as if staged. Yet the palm tree that overlooks this beach setting does not grow out from the sand along the coastline but instead appears to be a two-dimensional cutout protruding from an offstage space obscured by a vertical plane on the left of the canvas, painted in the same sandy hues as the shore; it seems to be a stage prop. The realization that the three figures and the sea depicted here are not to be understood as real but instead as part of a stage set is confirmed by the presence of red curtains to the right of the image—a recurring motif in Hilmi's paintings—and what appears to be a stage light near the bottom edge of the canvas in the foreground of the space of the stage. Yet, just as I begin to feel confident that I am looking at a representation of a stage rather than a beach, I begin to notice inconsistencies. The space of the stage itself has also been distorted; the artist's disobeying of the conventions of linear perspective is underscored by his inclusion of numerous diverging diagonal lines and planes running vertically and horizontally across the picture.

I understand these compositional strategies as Hilmi's reminder of his own role in staging what I am looking at. In an unpublished dissertation, titled "Staging Illusion," Hilmi picks at what he terms "the constructedness of the illusion," citing art historians such as Rosalind Krauss and Jonathan Crary.[16] On my regular visits to his studio over the past eight years, I have slowly begun to realize that the complex spatial ambiguities and unlikely juxtapositions he achieves in his paintings and moving image works are the result of an iterative process of collaging fragments of images cut out from disparate archival sources, chiefly derived from postcards from Singapore in the twentieth century. The "constructedness" that Hilmi repeatedly refers to in his dissertation and in conversations is not only pictorial and spatial but also encompasses "strong ideological [and] conceivably political tendencies, which incline towards the sociopolitical agendas of the state." For Hilmi, the "constructedness" of real spaces in Singapore "mediates the strategy of power" and deliberately invokes the "pleasures of consumption."[17] What Chin calls the "unsettling" and "challenging" affective experience of viewing paintings like *Landscapes & Paradise (I)* may be derived not only from the artist's ability to stage spatial conundrums, but perhaps also from a recognition of his staging of strategies to induce desires usually managed (in the Singapore context) by the state.[18]

Staging, for Hilmi, is primarily spatial, but it uses pictorial space to surface usually subliminal or invisible forces of coercion and control that may be historical, political, and affective in nature. His implicit suggestion that an artist's staging of desire in spatial terms may be related to or even complicit with the state's stage-managing of aspects of Singapore's image is heightened for me when I slowly realize that the space depicted in *Landscapes & Paradise (I)* also resembles the gallery space in which his exhibition is held (fig. 3.3). The exposed trusses visible at the top edge of the canvas are similar to those supporting the vaulted ceiling in the main exhibition hall; this is visible also in photographic documentation published on his gallery's website.[19] When I ask Hilmi about this, he claims that it is an accident, a coincidence, not part of his plan. But knowing that the gallery is housed in a building that was originally used as a military barracks during Singapore's colonial era, which is now leased by a government agency as part of a centrally-planned arts precinct, I cannot help but wonder whether Hilmi's obsessive focus on "constructedness" in staging is making me hypersensitive to the structures that frame my encounters with artworks, including with artistic art histories. These structures are spatial and architectural, to be sure, but they also conceptually and imaginatively (and perhaps ideologically) ensnare my body in contested histories and complex present-day dynamics.

For yamomo, by contrast, staging is primarily temporal, and he emphasizes the theatrical cadences of the term to underscore the performative nature of the colonial and other histories that Hilmi also considers. A scholar who also practices as an artist and curator, yamomo uses the term staging to affirm Southeast Asia's agency in the cocreation of modernities during colonial rule, arguing that "Manila was the staging site of the different modernist aspirations."[20] Rather than being imposed from a colonial elsewhere, modernities are created—performed—within colonial sites like Manila, and the context sets the stage, playing a role just as important as the (colonial) historical actors or ideas who

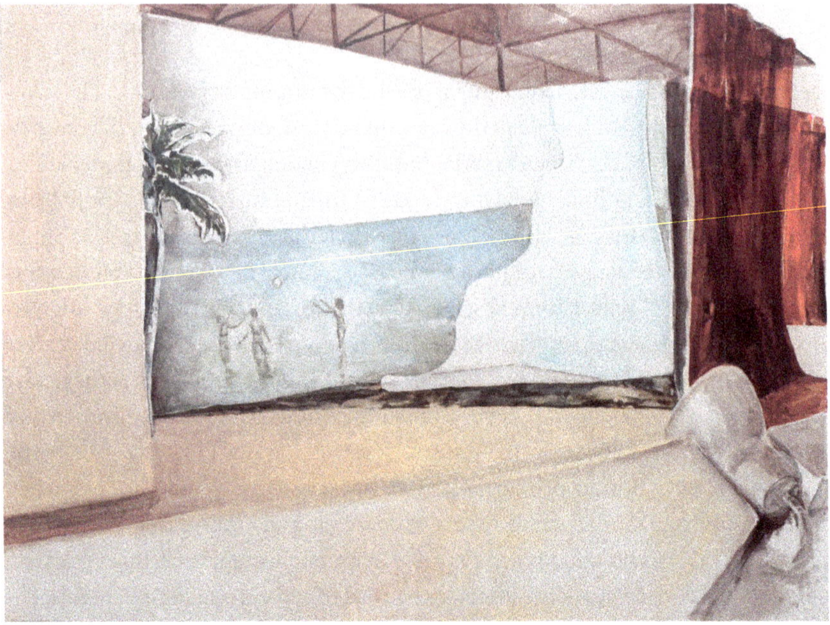

FIGURE 3.2. Hilmi Johandi, *Landscapes & Paradise (I)*, 2019. Oil on linen, 109.2 × 150 cm. Private collection. © Hilmi Johandi, courtesy of the artist and Ota Fine Arts.

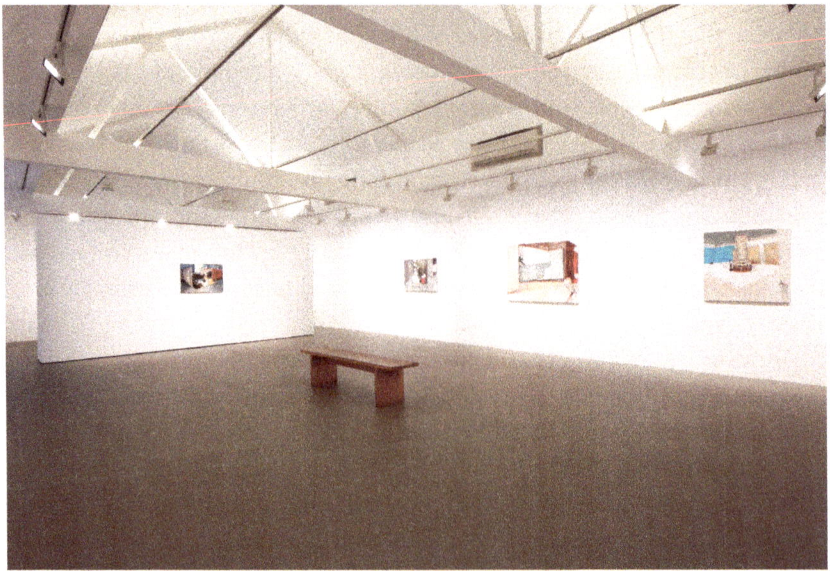

FIGURE 3.3. Hilmi Johandi, installation view of *Stagecraft: Landscapes and Paradise*, 2019. Ota Fine Arts Singapore. © Hilmi Johandi, courtesy of the artist and Ota Fine Arts.

have arrived from foreign shores. Like many other historians of the nineteenth century, yamomo also highlights the importance of "translocal" interactions as a result of improvements in "transcontinental travel and worldwide communication" in reconfiguring the modern capitalist order to a new phase he terms the "staging of globalisation."[21] The repeated recourse to "the performative metaphor of 'stagings' (of globalisation), rather than 'stages' or 'phases' of a linear progressive taxonomy" is explained as yamomo's way to describe and theorize the "systematic imagining of the world's globality and how this is embodied and performed."[22] History does not move in a straight line, but it happens (and is staged) multiply, iteratively, and concurrently across and between many places. That is, for yamomo, staging is a process that enacts the entanglement of the planet.

Spatial and temporal staging are also entangled. Yamomo's articulation recalls historian Rebecca E. Karl's *Staging the World*, a book about a 1904 opera performed in Shanghai, which she argues performed Chinese nationalist ideas. Karl proposes that the opera's "staging of the world" encompassed both "its literal containment of the world on the stage as well as . . . its metaphorical reference to the world as China's stage."[23] The sense of both conceptually condensed and spatially compressed "containment" that Karl describes here helps me grasp the pregnant sense of possibility in Hilmi Johandi's paintings, such as *Landscapes & Paradise (I)*. His construction and deconstruction of pictorial space is also a playing or performing of historical time. To understand staging as both a "staging of the world" (as Karl proposes) and a "staging of globalisation" (as yamomo suggests) links the temporal or historical aspect of the term, emphasized by yamomo, to its spatial facets, as foregrounded by Hilmi.

These understandings of staging also rest on a rich sense of contingency, an experimental and almost improvisational quality, which is also present in the staging of puppet shows in various Southeast Asian theatrical traditions. Although performances of *wayang* in Indonesia and the Malay world, like performances of *nang yai* in Thailand and *lkhon sbek* in Cambodia, often center on well-known stories such as those of the Ramayana, each iteration—each staging—is always at least somewhat unique, if only because it is performed live. Many versions of puppet-based performances across the region also incorporate extensive improvisation, often related to topical events involving politicians, celebrities, or members of local communities. The scholar Jan Mrázek notes that "*wayang* and other arts that are central in their world are marginal in art history."[24] The ephemeral, chimeric nature of the performing arts may be one reason for this. Offering a "parable" and provocation, Mrázek generously suggests that "art historians . . . should learn from puppeteers . . . rather than subjecting *wayang* to a standard gaze."[25]

My concept of *staging*—as dramatic, heterochronic, experimental, and contingent—draws on the articulations of the concept in the works of Hilmi, yamomo and puppetry, and seeks to follow Mrázek's lead in avoiding a standard gaze. Just as art historians may have much to learn from puppeteers, so too may we gain from following the lead taken by artists in their staging of art-historical encounters that are as speculative as they are rigorous.

In the next section, I return to the invented construction worker in Thao Nguyen Phan's work, with which this chapter began, to further elaborate the kind of staging I perceive in her continuing and provisional practice of artistic art histories.

First Rain, Brise Soleil by Thao Nguyen Phan: Staging History and Fiction

Sanh's fictional account of working on the construction of modernist buildings is accompanied, as I have mentioned already, by moving images of real architecture. As is often the case in Phan's work, the video footage is also interwoven with animations. Made alongside the moving images are paintings; in one (titled *On Illusion*) (2022) (fig. 3.4), the rhyming, rectilinear, and receding stairwells at Vann Molyvann's Institute of Foreign Languages in Phnom Penh, completed in 1971, are overlaid and interwoven with the curvaceous, bamboo-like brise-soleil at Ngo Viet Thu's Independence Palace in Saigon, completed in 1966 (fig. 3.5).[26] Phan's enchantment with the aesthetic qualities and spatial experience of these buildings is palpable.

By staging the paintings and moving images together, Phan is poetically drawing attention to the stories of the people who made these buildings: not the heroic architects, but the anonymous construction workers whose labor and creative contributions are so often forgotten by the writers of (architectural and other) histories. "I am from Ha Tien, a small town near the largest cement factory in South Vietnam, which was established in 1964," the fictional Sanh says. Unlike the fictional narrator, this cement factory is not imagined, and indeed it still stands today.[27] Historians note that it was first established with "a low-interest, five-year credit of 60 million francs ($12 million)" given by France, who during the 1960s also funded (through loans and grants) various other industrial facilities as well as practical training.[28] This so-called "aid" was given in the context of the Second Indochina War. A hotly contested and violent conflict enacted within the context of the Cold War, the war in Vietnam and neighboring countries also involved extensive monetary intervention from the invading United States and from the former colonial power, France. Connecting this geopolitical macroeconomics with the individual experience of life at the time, Phan imagines the microhistorical impact of the war and financial aid on a young man like Sanh. When he moved to Saigon around 1963 in search of work, Sanh recounts, "Saigon was at its peak of American intervention, but it was a vibrant time." His imagined memory aligns with recent accounts by political historians, who offer archival evidence that wartime Saigon "was a politically vibrant city" with a "vibrant press."[29]

Sanh is a fictional character, but the world he describes is one based in historical record, drawing on the artist's research as well as her lifelong habit of listening to the memories of her elders. The narrative in *First Rain, Brise Soleil* shifts between the make-believe and the real. It imaginatively stitches these two realms together, making them appear coextensive and conjoined. Phan herself writes of the "boundaries between real time and fictional time, real space and fantastical space."[30] Seemingly following the artist's lead, the art historian Nora A. Taylor suggests that Phan's work "explores this magical place between fiction and reality," while the curator Zoe Butt contends that Phan's work questions "the ambiguity of how we determine fact from fiction."[31] If we think of *First Rain, Brise Soleil* as a kind of staging in which varying kinds of imagined narrative and historical research come together—a realm that is theatrical but also experimental and provisional—we may see the possibility for artistic art histories to move beyond the usual (Western, colonial) understanding of reality as securely separate from fiction.

Phan's intermittent interleaving of invented stories and historical facts is delicate and porous, like the cross-hatched weaving of the dried leaves of the attap tree used to construct the walls of wooden houses in the Mekong Delta and throughout Southeast Asia. These thatched walls, dappled in soft sunlight, appear gorgeously in *First Rain, Brise Soleil* along with Sanh's words (fig. 3.6). In these woven attap walls, the warp and weft are indistinguishable, having been folded together by hand from the same ubiquitous and miraculous organic material; so too do historical fact and imagined fiction become interchangeable elements in Phan's woven narrative constructions. The kind of "modest wooden stilt house" in which attap is used is, as Sanh says, "vernacular and folkloric." The construction of walls from the woven leaves of the dried palm tree is practical but also poetic. It enables easy ventilation, necessary in the tropics, while also providing an opportunity for aesthetic playfulness in the patterning of light and shadow. Similarly, Phan's commingling of real and invented stories has various narrative functions and enables many visual pleasures. To be clear, my aim here is not to call into question the truth of historical claims or to suggest that this is what the artist's works are doing. Instead, my central concern is to begin to find words to make sense of the artist's interest in the weaving

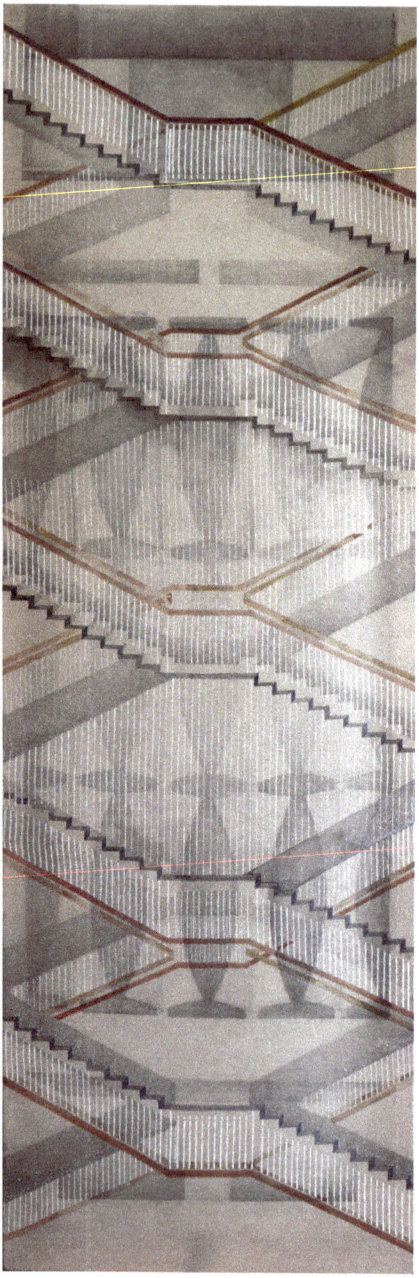

FIGURE 3.4. Thao Nguyen Phan, *On Illusion*, 2022. Watercolor and pigment on natural silk, 226 × 75 × 8 cm. © Thao Nguyen Phan, courtesy of the artist.

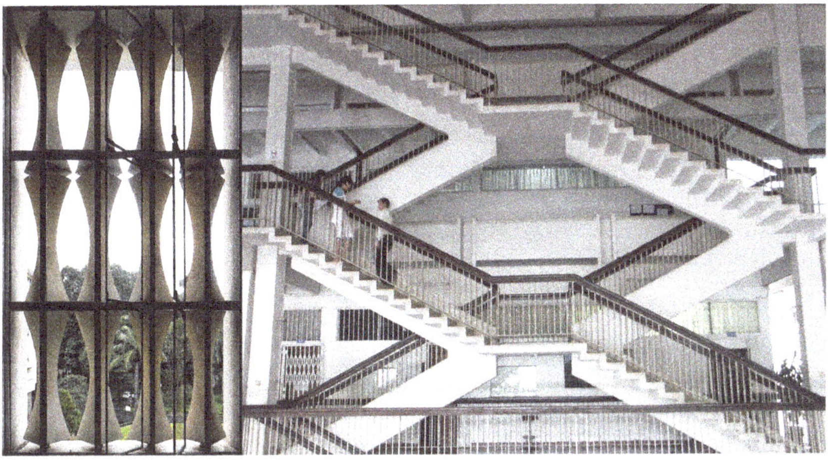

FIGURE 3.5. Left: Vann Molyvann (architect), Institute of Foreign Languages, Phnom Penh, completed 1971. Photograph by Pen Sereypagna. © Pen Sereypagna, courtesy of the artist. Right: Nguyen Van The (designer), *brise-soleil* at Independence Palace, Saigon (Ngo Viet Thu, architect), completed 1966. Photograph by Carlos Twose, cropped, reproduced under CC licensing (https://creativecommons.org/licenses/by-nd/2.0/).

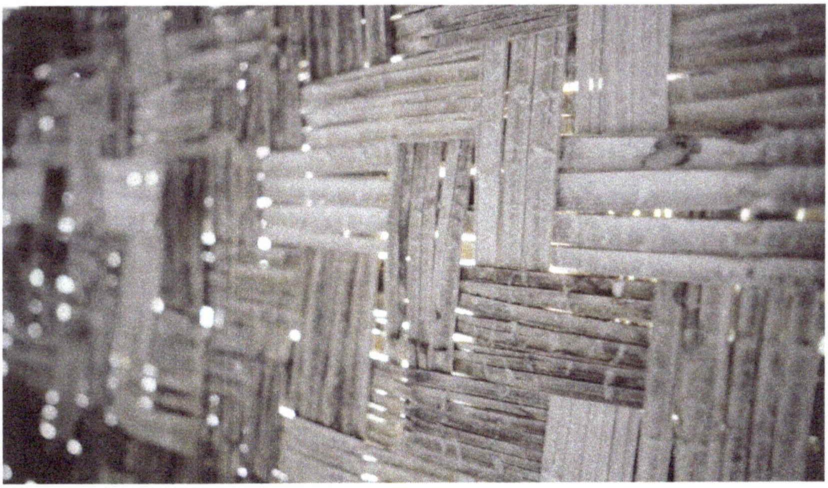

FIGURE 3.6. Thao Nguyen Phan, *First Rain, Brise Soleil*, 2021–ongoing. Three-channel video with sound, 16 mins 7 secs. Digital still. © Thao Nguyen Phan, courtesy of the artist.

together of historical records and imagined stories—staging them together—which has been an increasingly prominent facet of her work.

Phan's sources include several scholarly works as well as her own observations and inventions; a viewer familiar with the history and architecture of the region will easily detect several specific historical and aesthetic references in the film. The first and most obvious is the political context. I have already mentioned the veracity with which Saigon during the Second Indochina War is evoked. Moreover, Sanh describes his experience working in Phnom Penh "in the '80s and '90s," a period he calls "the Vietnamese's involvement in Cambodia." Specifically, he recalls his involvement in the accidental fire that engulfed the Preah Suramarit National Theatre in 1994. The historian David Chandler notes that with the 1979 Vietnamese invasion of Cambodia liberating the country from the genocidal Khmer Rouge, "for the first time since the 1950s, Cambodia was controlled by a foreign power." He also records that the Vietnam-backed regime of the 1980s "was unable to engender widespread trust among what remained of Cambodia's educated elite."[32] It was in this context of political unease that the Preah Suramarit National Theatre was all but destroyed in a fire in 1994, when a worker left a blowtorch unattended during a lunch break.[33] Phan was certainly familiar with Helen Grant Ross and Darryl Leon Collins's widely-cited account *Building Cambodia: 'New Khmer Architecture,' 1953–70*, and in her imagination, as articulated by Sanh, the fire "happened when we were using welders to fix the steel frame of the ceiling." Sanh specifically mentions that he was "lucky not to be filed with a lawsuit, as the building was not insured." Again, the detail seems to have been drawn from Ross and Collins's foundational publication, which records that "neither the agency funding the renovation work nor the contractor was insured."[34]

Not only historical information, but even poetic images in Phan's artwork are adapted from scholarly sources. For example, when describing the remarkable brise-soleil that adorned the Preah Suramarit National Theatre, Sanh says they "were of a very smart design, built from many connected concrete three-winged shapes, like fish scales," that he astutely suggests were "probably a symbolic reference to the aquatic life of the Mekong," referring to the river that flows through Cambodia to Vietnam. Sanh's invented account of Molyvann's design for the Preah Suramarit National Theatre conforms closely with scholarly sources. Ross and Collins also describe the building as having "ventilated walls resembling fish scales" and note that, in its triangular shape, the overall structure of the theatre "is evocative of a ship steaming down the river."[35] Echoing this lyrical suggestion, Phan juxtaposes her drawings of the building with footage of children crossing a river on a bridge, staging a visual interplay between the water and the fish-like, boat-like building (fig. 3.7). As Phan notes, "images are sometimes much richer than words."[36]

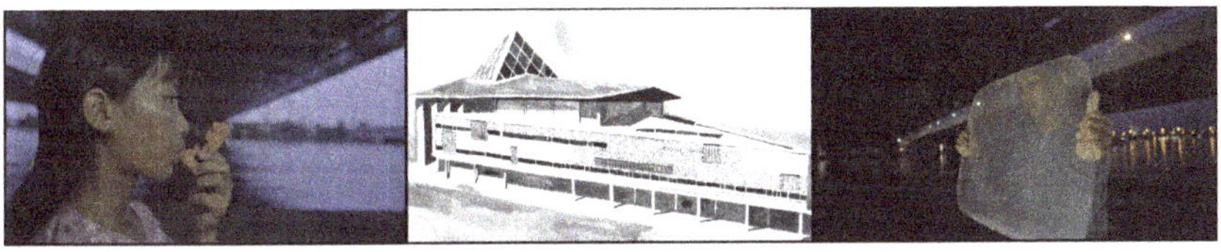

FIGURE 3.7. Thao Nguyen Phan, *First Rain, Brise Soleil*, 2021–ongoing. Three-channel video with sound, 16 mins 7 secs. Digital still. © Thao Nguyen Phan, courtesy of the artist.

Phan is not the first person to have sensed the symbolic significance of the fire that burned the theater in Phnom Penh. The writer and journalist Robert Turnbull noted that the "burned-out theater" was seen by many (including diasporic Cambodians) as emblematic of the "demoralized" state of the performing arts in Cambodia during the 1990s and early 2000s.[37] The filmmaker Rithy Panh eulogized the site in his 2005 feature-length docudrama, titled *The Burnt Theatre*, or *Les Artistes du Théâtre Brûlé*.[38] Although the distinctive architectural features of the theater are key to Phan's interest in the building, it is clear that the artist is also concerned with ensuring a degree of accuracy in her evocation of its history, and that her fascination is fueled, at least in part, by her awareness of previous scholarly and artistic work on the subject.

First Rain, Brise Soleil by Thao Nguyen Phan: Staging *Parafabulation*?

Phan's staging of history and fiction within the space of a single artwork places her approach in proximity to a constellation of related practices that have been described in varied ways. I see her work as similar to but different from the kind of contemporary art that is often called *parafiction*, and I see her drawing on a narrative strategy that is similar to but different from the kind of historical writing that has been called *critical fabulations*. I now briefly examine these and some other relevant terms before proposing the neologism *parafabulation* in an effort to characterize Phan's approach to staging in artistic art histories.

In recent years, the term parafiction has often been used to characterize artworks in which "real and/or imaginary personages and stories intersect with the world as it is being lived."[39] The art historian Carrie Lambert-Beatty, who popularized the term in the discourse of (mostly Euro-American) contemporary art, suggests that "parafictioneers produce and manage plausibility," which she describes as conditional and subjective; "plausibility (as opposed to accuracy) is not an attribute of a story or image but of its encounter with viewers."[40]

The art historians Nora A. Taylor and Karin Zitzewitz propose that artists in South and Southeast Asia "approach history as a 'figure of thought'" and "adopt or imagine new rhetorical forms with which to approach the past."[41] Phan is also interested in the conditions of encounter—what Lambert-Beatty calls the viewers' "various configurations of knowledge and 'horizons of expectation'"—and indeed the artist speaks often of the material conditions that shape these, such as her own experience of "the education I received growing up in Vietnam," in which only "the narrow official version" of the nation's history was taught.[42] Coming of age as an artist, including through formal training in Vietnam, Singapore, and the US, Phan's practice has certainly been informed by the kinds of practice that have been called parafiction.

Yet Phan's approach also differs from the parafictional; while the artist's works do toy with what is and is not believable, this is not their main contribution or importance. Rather, Phan's creations of what the artist calls "a half-real and half-fictitious visual experience" are affectively weaving imagination into history, exploring the limits and lacunae in historical accounts of the decolonizing world or Global South, most often centered on Southeast Asia and Vietnam.[43] This blending of the real and the invented is a strategy shared across the region. The literary scholar Joanne Leow proposes that the staging of a theatrical play-within-a-play about history in Singapore "opens up an alternative space in the mode of the self-conscious, sometimes melodramatic historical reenactment."[44]

Through fictive inventions, Phan embroiders factual records of the past as if she were darning the holes in an old and worn cloth. She approaches absences and imperfections not as lamentable lacks but rather as opportunities for flourishing embellishment. Neither Phan nor I nor any scholar I know has ever found or heard of any oral histories that record the experience of construction workers in Saigon in the 1960s or in Phnom Penh in the 1980s and 1990s. The artist's invented version, quoted in part previously, may or may not be plausible, but this seems somewhat beside the point. More important, I think, is that Phan's invention of Sanh is insightful in its suggestion of the possibility that intimate, individual ties—like the life of an "unimportant worker," as Sanh describes himself—may bind together these two important historical moments in these two cities, which, after all, are separated by just two decades and just a few hours' drive. Whereas parafictions are, according to Lambert-Beatty, "related to but not quite a member of the category of fiction as established in literary and dramatic art," Phan's practice is related to but not quite the same as a historical account as established in academic disciplines, such as history, art history, and architectural history.[45] Few if any scholars have yet managed to articulate the connected histories and complex relationships between 1960s

Saigon under American rule and 1980s Phnom Penh under Vietnamese rule. Phan's invented link between these time-spaces in the figure of Sanh offers the possibility for imagining other, deeper affinities.

Phan is not, however, attempting to play the role of artist as historian. In conversation, she often says that she values the "freedom" and "openness" of "artistic research" as distinct from so-called scholarly "rigor." Phan shares with other artists an interest in trying, in the words of art historian Mark Godfrey, to "represent stories about the past, and often previously unacknowledged ones" while simultaneously "subjecting conventional modes of narrative and historiography to critical scrutiny."[46] But clearly this does not make her a historian, even if she affirms that *First Rain, Brise Soleil* "was partly inspired by a conversation I had with my uncle about his experiences as a young man during the Cambodian-Vietnamese war in 1979."[47] The artist describes her method of borrowing from literary and other sources in aesthetic rather than hermeneutic terms as "appropriat[ing]" and "borrow[ing]."[48] She freely admits that "the way I read is intuitive, as I did not have any training in philosophy or writing."[49] She is palpably fascinated by the past and by the ways stories of the past are written as histories, but her own practice seeks something else less governed by rules and conventions than the discipline of history with a capital H. The artist declares, "I question the obligation to classify and denominate genres, segregating poetry, fictions, history, documents, and the visual arts."[50]

Just as Phan's practice seems related to but distinct from the parafictional approach as articulated by Lambert-Beatty or from the artist-as-historian approach as proposed by Godfrey, so too it resonates with yet diverges from the kind of storytelling known as *speculative history*, which is also often called *alternate history*. Increasingly popular in literary, televisual, and filmic works made in recent decades, speculative or alternate history proceeds from a "counterfactual historical speculation," for example, by imagining what the world today might have been like if the Nazis had won World War II.[51] Phan came closest to this mode of thought in the 2017 two-channel moving image work titled *Tropical Siesta*. The narrative begins by setting the scene: "Vietnam. The Present." Almost immediately, however, it becomes clear that this is not the country as we know it, but rather an alternate version. The narrative continues: "After years of independence and performing seclusion policy, the government has successfully realized agriculture as central to the nation's economy. Everyone is a farmer." In reality, fewer Vietnamese people work in agriculture today than ever before.[52]

Despite this attempt to speculatively reimagine what an alternate version of the present day may have been like had history unfolded differently, the *Poetic Amnesia* project, of which *Tropical Siesta* is one component, is primarily concerned with how stories of the past might be told differently or enlarged and embellished. Accompanying the *Tropical Siesta* video are nearly 100 paintings on paper, titled *Voyage de Rhodes*. The watercolor images are painted on pages from a book published by the seventeenth-century missionary Alexandre de Rhodes. As Taylor astutely observes, the artist's "watery pigments are laid softly onto the paper, allowing the print to seep in and out of the drawings," and in some instances, "Phan seems to extrapolate on De Rhodes' words."[53] In *Tropical Siesta*, the artist plays with the possibility of speculating on an alternate present, yet in *Voyage de Rhodes*, her primary concern remains firmly with the past, with the traces it leaves behind, and with the stories that are missing from or obscured within those documents. That the film and paintings were exhibited together under the title *Poetic Amnesia* is telling of Phan's central preoccupation with looking back on the past rather than speculating about an alternate present.

Phan's interest in speculation, being concerned with addressing gaps within the historical record, often comes close to the critical fabulation proposed by the historian Saidiya Hartman in her efforts to understand aspects of the experience of slavery that are not found in historical records. Hartman declares her desire "to displace the received or authorized account, and to imagine what might have happened or might have been said or might have been done."[54] A special significance of Hartman's approach is its ability to give voice to figures otherwise marginalized from historical accounts, including women and enslaved people. Hartman's interest in "what might have happened" trains our focus on the past, and in this way it differs from the kind of speculative or alternate history described previously, which is concerned with how the present might have been different if past events had unfolded differently. For Hartman, images and texts from the past have a vital power; "documents and images and fragments arrive with a certain force. They are not inert or de-animated."[55] More than bringing the past back to life, archives are perhaps immortal, or even undead.

Phan has a similar sense of the vivacious energy and fertility of historical traces and of images as being always already alive. She writes of her "faith in the visual language and its capacity to acknowledge the past."[56] Her works attempt a recuperation of stories from the past that have been lost to the passage of time and the violence of colonial encounters, such as the contributions of construction workers like the fictive Sanh. Hartman asserts that "critical fabulation is not in service of the colonial project . . . I came to critical fabulation in recognition of the violence that has made certain kinds of knowing, certain forms of telling, and certain ways of proceeding impossible." In her attempt to "break open and transform the archival encounter," Hartman in her scholarly writing offers one model for what Phan in her artistic practice calls "a sense of dreadful optimism."[57]

If there is a kind of oxymoronic contradiction in Phan's dreadful optimism—a kind of impossibility, ambiguity, and instability—then in those very qualities of wobbliness and difficulty, the term may begin to get at the essence of what the artist is doing with her work, which is an approach I propose we call *parafabulation*. I suggest we think of *First Rain, Brise Soleil* as a parafabulation because it is adjacent, but not identical or equivalent, to Hartman's critical fabulation. It is motivated by a similar instinct and politics: to redress historical damage and loss through the possibility of sensitive and historically informed fiction and speculation. Yet, as a practice that is not primarily archival and that is not at all scholarly, Phan's art also occupies a space that is clearly outside of and distinct from Hartman's concept. In suggesting this alterity-yet-adjacency, I draw on Lambert-Beatty's concept of parafiction as a strategy that "remains a bit outside" fiction, "like a paramedic as opposed to a medical doctor."[58]

In her practice, Phan repeatedly invents stories, but these fictions are not exactly lies (or fabulations) any more than they are real histories. Phan's artworks have a different form and function than the historical narratives offered by Hartman or any other scholar. As Lambert-Beatty observes, "the paramedic, after all, doesn't attempt to heal the patient. She resuscitates him, she staunches his bleeding. She keeps pressure on his wounds."[59] Parafabulation is a form of staging. Phan's works may be considered parafabulations in their refusal to be only either fictions or histories, but instead to stage encounters between both that transcend either. The works make us sensible to the violence of historical omissions without pretending to try to heal these scarring injuries.

When recalling the fire that destroyed the Preah Suramarit National Theatre, Sanh, the fictional narrator in *First Rain, Brise Soleil*, laments, "I came to Phnom Penh with enthusiasm and I left Cambodia in guilt." He continues, "I was half Khmer and I mourned the loss. I imagined it was traumatic for the Khmer performing artists, whose beloved theatre became debris in just one morning." He does not mention the other, larger traumas that predate this event, traumas of colonial domination, violence, genocide. Those are perhaps indescribable. But in his fictional memories of history, Sanh keeps pressure on the wounds.

Fyerool Darma and Erik Flower: Multisensory, Embodied Staging

Fyerool Darma's artworks titled *Pathfinder* (2023) (fig. 3.8) and *P4thfind3rzZ* (2023–24) (fig. 3.9) are engaged with histories of art that are so fragmented, uncertain, and lost that they can be difficult to specify or name. They cannot

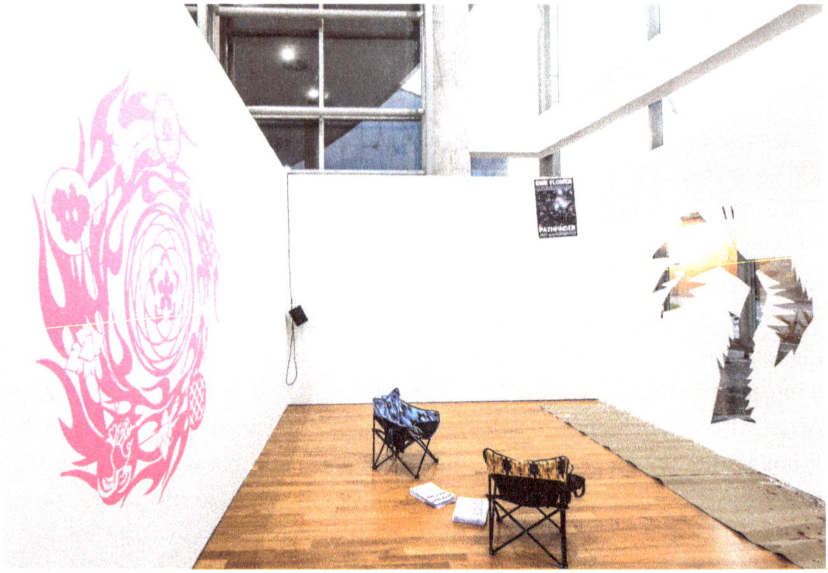

FIGURE 3.8. Fyerool Darma, with Aleezon, Sharmini Aphrodite, berukera featuring Erik Flower, *Pathfinder*, 2023. Shaped plywood, vinyl acrylic (Vinylfarbe; Lefranc & Bourgeois), printed polycotton on reupholstered camping chairs with pigments and coating (Samurai2K), 7mil polyester film, sound, 13 mins. Installation view at NTU ADM Gallery, Singapore. Image courtesy of NTU ADM Gallery. © Fyerool Darma, courtesy of the artist.

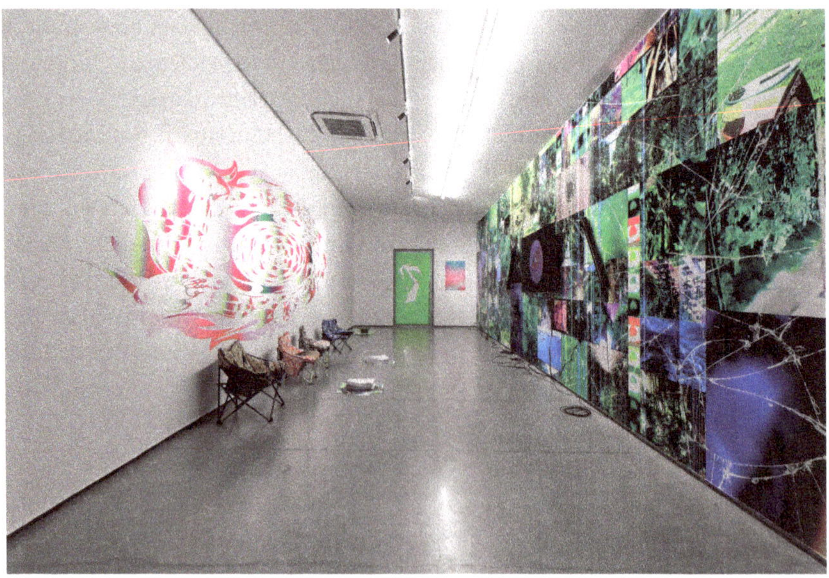

FIGURE 3.9. Fyerool Darma, with Aleezon, Sharmini Aphrodite, berukera and Erik Flower, *P4thfind3rzZ*, 2023. Printed polycotton on reupholstered camping chairs, polyvinyl on concrete, video, color with stereo, 17 mins 19 sec. Installation view at MAIIAM Contemporary Art Museum. Photographer Karin Mongkonphan, image courtesy of MAIIAM Contemporary Art Museum. © Fyerool Darma, courtesy of the artist.

be known only by looking—indeed, they can never be wholly known in any way. And so Fyerool's works enact an embodied form of staging that brings the art of the past into multisensory and speculative contact with the present. Like Phan's *First Rain, Brise Soleil*, Fyerool's works are dramatic, heterochronic, experimental, and contingent. *Pathfinder* features a screenplay and *P4thfind-3rzZ* a narrative video work, making the space of both installations theatrical, like a stage. Both works examine archival materials from 1917 with a very contemporary attitude and aesthetic; they entangle several stages of history. The works are not polished but rather improvisatory, as if staged like experiments. And they are ephemeral and impermanent installations, which, like scaffolding or staging, are to be destroyed at the end of their exhibition period. In these ways, the works epitomize the qualities of staging in artistic art histories. But whereas Phan's staging involves inventing missing historical sources, Fyerool's involves inventing the story of a man (who may have been an artist) who was all but forgotten by history.

The starting point for both *Pathfinder* and *P4thfind3rzZ* was Fyerool's discovery, while reading a 2021 essay by the scholar meLê yamomo, of a man named Muhamed bin Hadji Abdurrahim, who was born around 1890 in Johor and later took the name Erik Flower. The Berlin Sound Archive holds several recordings of Flower orating poetry and performing music, according to yamomo, that were made when he was a 27-year-old prisoner of war in a German internment camp during the First World War. These recordings consist of Flower reading poetry in the Malay *pantun* verse form (popularized by Charles Baudelaire and others under the misspelling, *pantoum*), as well as singing and playing "a traditional song (generally labeled *lagu*) on a European violin." While the recordings are not made publicly accessible by the archive "due to ethical concerns," the descriptions provided by the archive and explicated by yamomo suggest that Flower was a cosmopolitan figure with an artistic temperament and a special interest in literature and music.[60] Nothing more is known about Flower, other than this fragment offered by yamomo in the context of a larger discussion concerned with early sound recordings from Nusantara, as well as with (formerly) colonial archives and the beginnings of ethnomusicology as a field of study. No known images of Flower survive, only sound recordings.

Fyerool was fascinated by this fragmentary trace of Flower for many reasons, mostly arising from his fanciful staging of this sonic relic in dynamic dialogue with the artist's concerns in the present. In its tantalizing brevity and unavoidable incompleteness, yamomo's account of Flower and his poetic and musical arts enabled an array of questions to arise in Fyerool's mind, which he began to work through intuitively in his artistic practice.[61] With each of these questions, Fyerool was imaginatively staging not only Flower's forgotten history but also his possible relevance to and resonance with the contemporary art of the present day. Fyerool was bringing Flower back to life.

Fyerool wondered, was Erik Flower an "artist" in the contemporary sense of the word? What did he think of life in Berlin, a city now synonymous (for Fyerool) with global contemporary art and electronic music? Was it possible that Flower might have chosen to migrate to Europe (as many artists in Southeast Asia continue to do today) rather than being forcibly shipped there as a colonial subject in the context of the First World War? Might imagining this possibility of a deliberately diasporic shift rather than a forced and subjugated transfer somehow reinvest Flower with an agency he loses when he is remembered only as colonized body and a prisoner of war? Why did Muhamed bin Hadji Abdurrahim take the name Erik Flower? Or why was it given to him? What might this choice, if indeed it was a choice, say about the character of this man, if indeed he did identify as a man in terms of gender identity or sexual orientation? What moments of joy might Flower have felt? Which part of Johor might Flower have hailed from? Fyerool wondered, might Flower have once lived near to Fyerool's collaborator, the writer Sharmini Aphrodite, in Johor Bahru? What was it about Flower that so captivated Fyerool's imagination, the latter wondered? Was it Flower's performance of *pantun*, a verse form that has fascinated Fyerool for many years and which has appeared in several of his previous artworks?[62] Or was it Flower's evasive and chimeric near-invisibility?[63] When, where, and how had Flower died? Did he turn into a flower? Or does he live on, as a ghost or spirit or energy, making his presence known through occasional disruptions in the electrical currents that Fyerool relies on to use his computer and make his artworks?

These and related questions about the enigma of Erik Flower inspire and animate *Pathfinder* and *P4thfind3rzZ*, which together I understand as Fyerool's efforts toward staging an encounter between the historical Erik Flower, whose traces languish in the Berlin Sound Archive, and the imagined and flourishing Erik Flower, invented by Fyerool to amplify his nearly-forgotten voice. Both artworks are room-sized installations, and despite their differences they share several elements in common. Both comprise vinyl wallpaper designed by the artist, which is his most frequently recurring medium since 2020; he writes that "polyvinyl decals are a heritage of the present."[64] The material gained prominence in contemporary art only during the second decade of the twenty-first century. The use of this unmistakably present-day aesthetic foregrounds the distinctly contemporary staging of Flower's story in Fyerool's work. *Pathfinder* centers on a sound piece that follows the archival recording of Flower by featuring a European violin. The work also includes a screenplay, written in collaboration with the Johor-resident Sharmini. The text—which, blurring historical fact and speculative fiction, is staging an intervention into the record of Flower's life and practice—is presented on A4 paper in multiple copies. Visitors are invited to read and take it with them in a gesture of generosity and openness sharply at odds with the tight access controls imposed by the Berlin Sound Archive. In place of a standalone sound piece, *P4thfind3rzZ* centers on a video that imagines Flower as having been reincarnated in the form of a robot dog, the kind used in present-day Singapore to assist with policing and other surveillance tasks.[65] All of these components, in both works, may be considered Fyerool's efforts toward speculatively staging possible pathways for the spirit of Erik Flower to enter the imaginative space of the contemporary (and contemporary art) a century after he recorded his poems and songs in Berlin.

Both *Pathfinder* and *P4thfind3rzZ* also include chairs that serve as both functional and sculptural elements within the installations, inviting the possibility for visitors to spend time with the works and experience Fyerool's staging of Flower in the present day as an embodied and theatrical experience. More specifically, they are folding camping chairs, which are affordable, portable, and available almost anywhere, signifying the artist's interest in shared cultural phenomena. Yet they are upholstered in custom-made covers featuring designs commonly associated with Malay cultures, signifying the artist's interest in specific aesthetic differences within shared cultures. The presence of the chairs is inspired, in part, by Fyerool's engagement with the ideas of the scholar, artist, and curator Mieke Bal, who writes that "seating, benches or chairs, participate in the image-thinking endeavour, and become material 'thought-images', just as did the dark stage." She continues that the "(physical) element of comfort and time is . . . intellectual, political and artistic all at once."[66] Fyerool's interest in Bal was prompted by her inclusion in the same exhibitions—which I curated in Singapore and Chiang Mai—for which he had been commissioned to make *Pathfinder* and *P4thfind3rzZ*.

While his works share Bal's sense of the importance of seating to facilitate deep and thoughtful engagement, they may also be understood as subtle, implicit, and respectful critiques of the potential for ocular centrism in Bal's concept of "image-thinking."[67] After all, as I have already mentioned, there are no known surviving images of Erik Flower or his works; the only traces of his life and practice are sonic rather than visual. Fyerool wondered, could Bal's concept of image-thinking be extended to sound-thinking?

The chairs in Fyerool's installations are not only intellectually engaging objects but also encourage aesthetic enjoyment. They are adorned with a fabric that is analogous in its use of materials to the shifting archival format of Flower's sound recordings. In the archives, audio has been transferred from archaic analogue technologies (including shellac discs and wax cylinders) to easily transferrable digital files.[68] Similarly, the upholstery on the chairs—sewn by Fyerool's collaborator, Aleezon—uses commercially mass-produced fabric, the design of which transfers the appearance of laboriously hand-woven (or "analogue") *songket* textiles into easily reproducible digitally printed patterns. This kind of cheaply printed fabric, which is readily available in markets in places such as Johor, makes the labor-intensive and expensive *songket* designs accessible to wider publics, including both Malay people and others. Digitization of the obscure analogue recordings could also make Flower's poems and songs accessible to wider publics, again enabling transcultural sharing.

The Berlin Sound Archive's refusal to grant ready access to the recordings—regardless of their good intentions for withholding that access—perpetuates the German institution's colonial control over Flower's art and memory. By staging an alignment between the open-source, digitally-printed *songket* fabric and the speculative reimagining of Flower's story and songs, Fyerool invites visitors to consider these differing attitudes to access and generous sharing. Importantly, this thinking is done not only by looking at the images printed on the fabrics or other visual elements in the installation, but also by feeling them and even sitting on them, staging a full, corporeal interaction with these materials. This embodied thinking learns from and builds on but may also extend or diverge from Bal's image-thinking.

Fyerool's multisensory staging of embodied encounters with Flower enlarges standard approaches to speculative art histories, which tend to privilege the visual and/or the philosophical rather than corporeal and auditory forms of situated knowledge. One scholar notes that the Latin root of the English word speculate is *specularia*, which means "to look," or "window"—emphasizing visuality—and proposes that many approaches to speculative art histories are driven by an interest in "the possibilities the so-called speculative turn in [European] continental philosophy holds for art history and art theory."[69] Sjoerd van Tuinen seeks "alternatives to the contemporary complementarity of the philosophy of art (including aesthetics) and art history," which he argues are "often based on mutual recognition and critical limitation rather than imaginative crossover."[70] Yet even this cautious and critical approach of skepticism about the usefulness of philosophy for art history retains the discipline's usual reliance on visual knowledge and assumes Western terms of reference. Because Fyerool's speculative staging of encounters with Flower begins from a decolonial and Southeast Asian stance, he is better able to imbue other senses and ways of knowing in his approach.

While I consider Fyerool's work on Flower an example of staging in artistic art histories, I also recognize that these projects stretch the usual definitions of art and art histories. It remains debatable whether Flower can or should be considered an "artist," and whether the recordings of his poems and songs can or should be considered "art." This uncertainty arises not only from the paucity of information known about Flower but also from the murky circumstances in which his recordings were made. While, like Fyerool, I may not agree with the Berlin Sound Archive's decision to restrict access to these recordings "due to ethical concerns," I recognize that the ethical questions raised by these materials are challenging, messy, and perhaps irresolvable. Flower's recordings might easily be considered documents of political history—surfacing the colonial violence of Southeast Asian soldiers being interned as prisoners of war in the First World War—but to approach them within the realm of art history (and thereby to treat them, at least in part, as aesthetic objects) is an unexpected provocation and complication.

This provocation, as well as being speculative and relying on the staging of Flower's archival materials in dialogue with Fyerool's contemporary concerns, is also decolonizing in its aspirations. It makes visible—or, rather, audible and bodily palpable—the Western and colonial concepts that structure usual understandings of art and therefore art histories. In asking whether Erik Flower was an artist, Fyerool is not only questioning the unknown (and probably unknowable) aspects of Flower's biography, he is also interrogating the uncomfortably colonial origins of modern conceptions of what an artist is.

By speculatively staging the possibility of a dramatic, heterochronic, experimental, and contingent contemporary encounter with Flower's 1917 sound recordings, Fyerool gently and poetically prospects the possibility of a more comfortable and decolonial approach to these historical materials. It is comfortable because it offers aesthetic pleasure and is embodied and embraced within the soft furnishing of the artist's carefully upholstered chairs. It is also comfortable because it is speculative, staging possibilities for play and imagination rather than only certainty and control. In this way, the work fulfils Kuan-Hsing Chen's aspiration "to be humble about our knowledge claims."[71] And it is comfortable because it is an encounter in which Fyerool and the visitors engaging with his artwork are collaboratively setting the terms of engagement rather than having them imposed by some well-meaning (formerly) colonial archive in a distant land.

One of the most striking aspects of Fyerool's *Pathfinder* is the work's use of wordplay in staging comic confrontations between the German and Malay languages and between the differing knowledge systems epitomized by the archives on one hand and the artists on the other. The Malay word *laut*, meaning "sea," seems unexpectedly to appear in the Berlin Sound Archives, because the German word *laut* refers to "sound." Neither Fyerool nor his collaborator Sharmini Aphrodite know German, yet both know the Malay language.

The screenplay in *Pathfinder* includes the words, "The Berlin Sound Archives are also known as the *lautarchiv*—if you know what *laut* is, you know what we are trying to say." This line makes subtly but decisively clear that the artwork is addressed directly and perhaps primarily to Malay speakers. It also speculatively reimagines the archive's claim to be an archive of sounds (*laut*) insofar as the archive holds recordings of Malay people from seafaring communities, such as coastal Johor, it may also be an archive of the sea (*laut*). The screenplay continues: "Erik Flower we who have no power release you." This line can be understood in at least two ways. It may be an admission that Fyerool and his collaborators have no power over life, death, and the spirit world; they have "no power to release" Flower from death or from whatever spirit realm he inhabits. They can bring him back to life only in their art and imagination. The line may also be a registration of Fyerool's and Sharmini's powerlessness to access the sound recording of Flower, blocked by the well-meaning but nevertheless paternalistic (and perhaps colonial) rules of the Berlin Sound Archives. While Fyerool and Sharmini were likely frustrated by this prohibition, they nevertheless maintained the possibility that Erik Flower—when he lived or as he now lives on as a ghost or spirit—preferred to be in Berlin rather than Johor.

It is notable that both possible readings of this line take for granted that the artist and his collaborator are addressing Flower directly, thereby assuming the possibility for some kind of communication with the dead or some way to bring him back to life. The screenplay continues: "Erik Flower we are calling you to come home/Erik Flower we are calling you to stay there if you wish." Just as the artwork speculatively imagines the possibility of Flower (like many contemporary artists) having chosen Berlin has his home rather than having it forced on him as a colonial subject and prisoner of war, so too the screenplay is staging both possibilities: the dream of Flower returning to the *laut* (sea) in Johor and the hope that he may also be able to remain in the archive of *laut* (sounds) in Berlin, if he prefers.

By speculating in these ways and staging these multiple and seemingly contradictory understandings of the archival materials as simultaneous possibilities, Fyerool's work on Flower draws on multiple knowledge systems, languages, and ethics of care to contribute to the ongoing work of decolonizing in his artistic art histories. This provisional and continuous decolonizing impulse—which is embedded in the multisensory, embodied, and speculative nature of Fyerool's work—addresses not only European archives but also Southeast Asian ways of thinking about and critically responding to these collections. It offers pleasure and also discomfort, and these affects both feel needed and nourishing for a poetics of inclusion in which the desire and curiosity of contemporary artists in Southeast Asia are centered and celebrated.

Hilmi Johandi: Staging (and Circumventing) the Picturesque

I have suggested that speculatively inventing historical figures like the construction worker named Sanh is Thao Nguyen Phan's way to address gaps in archives of modernist architecture in Vietnam and Cambodia, and that playfully speculating about fragmentary traces in archives is Fyerool Darma's way to reclaim the agency of near-forgotten figures like Erik Flower. Despite their differences, both artists make works that are dramatic, heterochronic, experimental, and contingent, and their artistic art histories use strategies of staging that are embodied and multisensory. They poetically enlarge the range of stories that art histories can include, accommodate, and learn from, and in these ways, they bring the past back to life and into proximity with their own lives.

Similar qualities are evident in Hilmi Johandi's *Stagecraft: Landscaped Grounds* (2023–24), a public installation that is sited in popular parklands in the Wessex Estate in Singapore and is the artist's largest artwork realized to date (fig. 3.10). Like Phan's and Fyerool's projects of staging, Hilmi's work is also theatrical (playing with imagery of a theatrical stage), concerned at once with the past and the present (engaged in multiple stages of history), testing out new ideas and techniques (staged like an experiment), and temporary (its structure repurposing materials used in scaffolding or staging). Moreover, the work is made to be perceived not only from a single or static viewing position but, rather, temporally and "in the round," while the visitor passes through and circumambulates around the space in which the installation's seven distinct components are sited. In this way, Hilmi's installation also invites an embodied encounter, activating not only the visitor's sense of sight but also the feeling of movement through time and through an environment that is constantly changing with the permutations of the tropical climate.

In its title, *Stagecraft: Landscaped Grounds* draws attention to its stage-like components and to its environmental context. The installation comprises seven metal structures of varying sizes, which display panels of soft, almost pastel colors that have been cut out to form organic shapes and silhouettes resembling recognizable elements from the environment, such as hills, clouds, trees, and shrubs. In two structures, fragments of text appear; the words "Come to Malaya" are discernible, written in an old-fashioned typeface that mimics calligraphic handwriting. These varying components of the artwork are dispersed across a grassy clearing dotted with trees, which is flanked on one side by a cluster of colonial-era buildings and on the other side by a park sited along a former railway. The structures are made from steel scaffolding, the kind

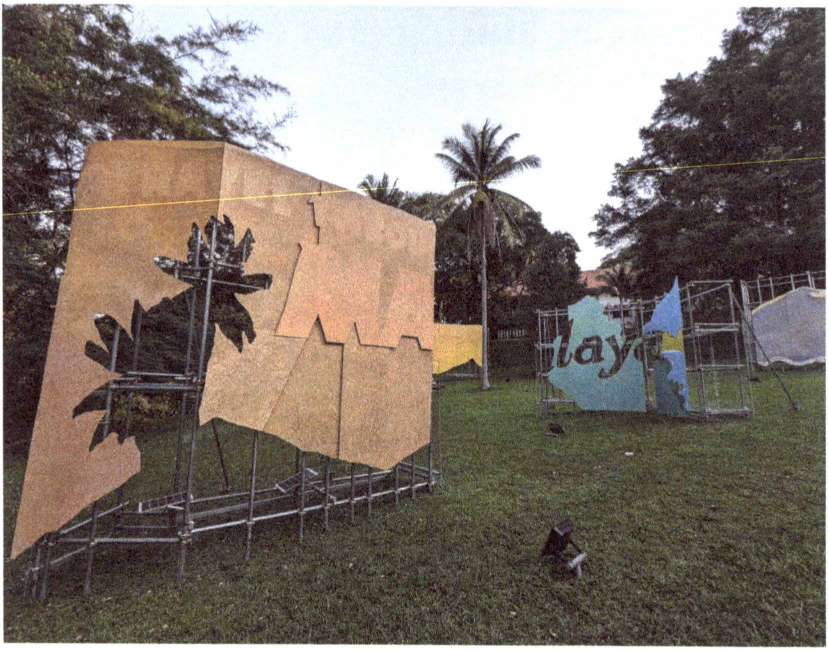

FIGURE 3.10. Hilmi Johandi, *Stagecraft: Landscaped Grounds*, 2023–24. Public installation, Wessex Estate, Singapore. Photograph by the author. © Hilmi Johandi, courtesy of the artist and Ota Fine Arts.

usually seen on theatrical stage sets and construction sites, onto which large flat sheets of metal printed with weatherproof color pigments have been attached to form large images resembling stage backdrops that are then angled to face slightly different directions. From some viewing positions, these images align and appear to overlap, while from other viewing positions they appear separate and distinct.

The artwork is conceived to be viewed while passing through the site, which is commonly used as a thoroughfare.[72] In this respect, it is an experimental staging of an enlarged, outdoor version of the installations Hilmi has been constructing within interior exhibition spaces since 2018, when he first presented his artwork at the Singapore Art Museum (in an exhibition I curated).[73] *Stagecraft: Landscaped Grounds* was also commissioned by the Singapore Art Museum, and for this project Hilmi worked closely with curator Selene Yap in the conceptualization and realization of the work.[74] I visited the artist's studio several times during the year-long process of developing the project, and I spoke regularly with both Hilmi and Yap before, during, and after the public launch of the artwork in 2023.

Two key ideas underpin my thinking about the way that Hilmi's installation contributes to artistic art histories: the first idea is related to the *picturesque*, and the second to *circumvention*. First, I see the work as revealing that the picturesque aesthetics prominent in colonial-era images of Southeast Asia in general and Malaya (now Malaysia and Singapore) in particular also remain present in present-day built environments. Hilmi's work is citing 1930s posters advertising the Federated Malay States Railways, as I will show later on, and these posters typify the use of picturesque conventions in the composition of images and in the arrangement of spaces. An expansive category, as an aesthetic concept (distinct from its everyday usage), picturesqueness essentially involves what one scholar terms "appropriation of nature and the environment as aesthetic objects."[75] That is, the picturesque is more than simply pretty; it is an aesthetic expression of the cultivation and domination of the natural world. Various conventions around the composition of images and spaces govern picturesque expressions of this control over nature. The enduring prevalence of picturesque aesthetics in Singapore and other Southeast Asian cities is in large part a result of colonial-era urban planning, which deployed picturesque aesthetic conventions familiar from British built environments. Picturesque urban planning, like other manifestations of colonialism, continues to cast a long shadow, which Hilmi (like many contemporary artists) seeks to illuminate in his practice.

Second, I see Hilmi's installation as circumventing a direct critique of enduring coloniality, or a direct exposition of picturesque aesthetics in contemporary environments. Instead of explicitly confronting these historical and art-historical phenomena, Hilmi chooses to instead stage a roundabout, indirect response. In a discussion of Singaporean literary and cinematic works contemporaneous with Hilmi's artistic practice, the scholar Joanne Leow argues that circumvention or "acts of overreaching, outwitting, and making the circuit, or finding a way around" have been crucial both as aesthetic strategies and as tactics for evading censorship and other forms of state control.[76] When I ask Hilmi if his work is in part "about coloniality," he responds affirmatively, without hesitation. But when I then ask him if he would ever articulate this explicitly or publicly, he responds again without hesitation: "not so directly."[77] That indirectness, which seems akin to what Leow terms circumvention, is vital to Hilmi's artistic sensibility. He seems to be staging a considered, even covert response to colonial legacies.

Like much of Hilmi's practice, *Stagecraft: Landscaped Grounds* teeters between abstraction and representation, largely resulting from the artist's compositional strategy, which centers on citing and reconfiguring fragments of found images. For this work, these found images are almost exclusively posters from the early twentieth century, promoting the Federated Malay States Railways, a colonial organization founded in the late nineteenth century. These posters typically depict idyllic rural environments, reflecting the colonial imagination of Malaya as a land of abundant natural resources. The literary scholar Siti Nuraishah Ahmad argues that Malaya was represented "as an abundant garden" in both British and European colonial-era literature, and she "highlights the importance of representations of space in shaping the British creative imagination on Malaysia, where previous research focused on representations of its peoples and cultures."[78]

It is precisely these representations of space that have captured Hilmi's attention, although he studies them with particular attention to visual and spatial (rather than literary) qualities within the context of his artistic art histories. Although some of the colonial-era posters that Hilmi examined portray mountainous terrains (such as one designed by Hugh Murton Le Fleming, dated 1933) (fig. 3.11) and others present views of fertile plains (such as one designed

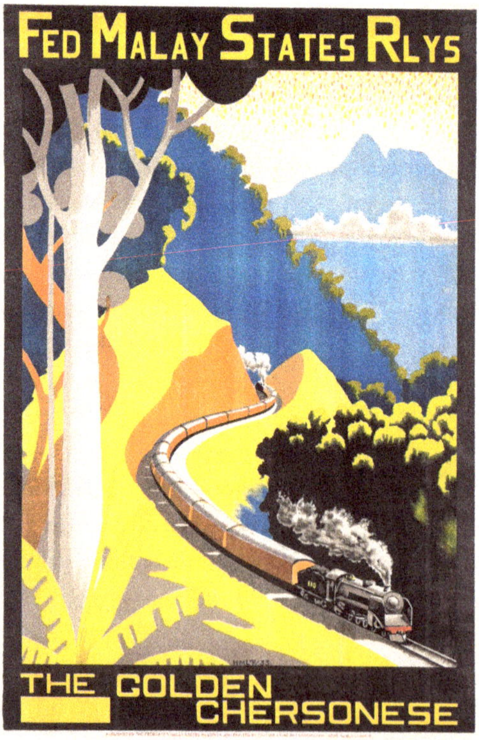

FIGURE 3.11. Hugh Murton Le Fleming, poster, 1933. Collection of National Museum of Singapore. Image courtesy of National Heritage Board, Singapore.

by J.R. Charton, dated circa 1930), all of them share a particular fascination with the depiction of palm trees.[79] More than simply a way of recording the ubiquitous vegetation of the tropics, these palm trees play an important compositional function in the poster designs, serving as framing devices to add graphic impact to the images while also working to align the tropical scenery with the ideals of the European aesthetic convention of the picturesque. In Le Fleming's correspondence (which Hilmi had not seen when making his work), the colonial poster artist frequently described the scenery of Malaya as "picturesque" and his wife, Rosalind Le Fleming, also remarked that "the palms [were] as usual exquisite."[80]

Like other examples of citing that I discussed in chapter 2, Hilmi's references to these colonial-era posters involve both a reliance on their images and a defiance of their colonial authority. After viewing a range of posters available online and in publications, Hilmi decided to focus his attention on examples available within Singapore's National Collection, which therefore belong, at least in some abstract legal sense, to all Singaporeans, and thus also to him. He decided to refrain from doing in-depth research about the British artists who designed these posters to instead focus his energy on studying their compositions and other formal qualities. Yap was able to facilitate a visit for Hilmi to see the original prints, held in secure storage at Singapore's Heritage Conservation Centre. During this visit, Hilmi was fascinated by the textures of the colors achieved during the lithographic printing process, visible under a magnifying glass but difficult or impossible to perceive without magnification.

Hilmi himself had been staging experiments with lithography in recent years prior to taking on this project; he explained that "I find the idea of layers in printmaking is quite interesting." The grainy, uneven planes of color on the commercially printed sheets of metal in *Stagecraft: Landscaped Grounds* derive their uneven pigmentation and appearance of texture from Hilmi's experiments staged by significantly enlarging the original lithographically printed posters. This aspect of his installation not only provides visual interest and suggests the presence of the artist's hand in developing the designs, which were later manufactured by a machine. It also hints at Hilmi's attitude to citing, demonstrating that he claims his right to focus on whichever aspects of the colonial-era images capture his attention without feeling obliged to share the credit with the British artists who had designed these posters to share their colonial fantasies of Malaya and promote colonial extraction from this land.

Crucial to understanding the importance of Hilmi's work is perceiving its relationship to its spatial context. The Wessex Estate comprises small and medium buildings dating to the late colonial era that were originally built as military barracks and military housing.[81] They have been maintained in their original architectural form, including the continued use of distinctive black and white paint, which was popular in the period. Now managed by a government agency, the buildings in Wessex Estate are today variously used as rental housing (overwhelmingly occupied by foreigners, mostly white people) as well as restaurants, cafes, and other small businesses.[82] The area is adjacent to a long, narrow linear park known as the Rail Corridor, built along the now decommissioned railway line that once connected Singapore to peninsular Malaysia, which was particularly important during the colonial period, when the two countries together formed the Federated Malay States, or Malaya. The architectural historian Lai Chee Kien notes that "train lines and systems were built, primarily to serve the colonial economy."[83] While the Rail Corridor has undergone regular changes in its landscaping, the Wessex Estate area today remains very similar in its appearance as it was when it was built during the colonial era. Like many open spaces built in Singapore in the colonial era, the Wessex Estate's balancing of built environments and stage-managed nature displays strongly picturesque overtones. As the art historian Maggie M. Cao notes, "both landscape painting and actual landscapes" may share common aesthetic qualities.[84]

Many scholars have observed the varied ways in which picturesque aesthetics—characterized by an appreciation for cultivated (and thereby controlled) views of nature—have developed from their origins in eighteenth century English philosophy to now influence many aspects of life far from England, including urban planning. Through various permutations of Western modernist urban planning in the twentieth century, a persistent desire for "walkability" led to many advocates for a picturesque approach to designing cities.[85] In an account of utopian impulses in the planning of Bangkok, the architectural historian Lawrence Chua argues that "the naturalizing of urban conditions through the conventions of the picturesque reduced the city and its economic functions to a natural phenomenon."[86] In an expansive study of Singapore's parks, the scholar of landscape architecture, Raffaella Sini, argues that the postcolonial nation-state's approach to shared green spaces has consistently created "picturesque environments" with the aim of "fostering social interaction and encouraging community bonding" and even "nation building."[87] She notes that diverse elements of park planning—including public sculpture—contribute to this aim, and that Singapore's built environments are "dynamic and evolutionary" because of the city-state's "demolish and re-build philosophy."[88]

While many urban scholars have identified the enduring impact of the picturesque, few have offered fine-grained, close readings that identify specific motifs that serve to perpetuate picturesque aesthetics through colonial and postcolonial eras. Moreover, few have offered an embodied or experiential account of the lived experience of navigating post-picturesque spaces in contemporary urban environments. These kinds of analysis are more familiar in art and architectural histories, yet relatively few scholars working within these disciplines have addressed Singapore's contemporary handling of colonial-era environments, or the twenty-first century reworking of picturesque aesthetics.

This is where Hilmi's work comes in, filling a gap in scholarship, by revealing insights that are perhaps most effectively conveyed through artistic art histories. By staging his artworks in direct spatial dialogue with the historic Wessex Estate area, he can imbue the experience of walking through this space with a theatrical quality while also heightening awareness of the heterochronic convergence of the past and the present in the design of the built environment, particularly in the controlled domination over nature. Hilmi chooses to circumvent direct confrontation with the enduring presence of colonial and picturesque aesthetics in today's built environments, particularly in the present day management of trees and other elements of nature, while still drawing attention to these phenomena. This staging of an indirect critique—a circumvention—allows the possibility of simultaneous pleasure (I enjoy walking through these spaces) and discomfort (I recognize the imprint of coloniality on these spaces).

This circumvention therefore enables a decolonizing of knowledge. I can understand these spaces in several ways, both as tied to their colonial past and as delinked from that past in the embodied, multisensory experience of walking through the area in the present day. Moreover, Hilmi chooses to reproduce the picturesque aesthetics of the posters but in a fragmented form. This staging of an indirect picturesqueness—another circumvention—shows me that the physical environments built and landscaped by British colonists were three-dimensional versions of the picturesque fantasies they depicted in their posters. Yet it also allows me the possibility of shifting my attention away from this colonial legacy to instead focus on the beauty of the palm trees themselves.

From certain positions, as I walk through the Wessex Estate, I see a real palm tree align perfectly with the silhouette of a palm tree in Hilmi's installation. The effect is extraordinary and arresting: at once beautiful and uncanny. *Stagecraft: Landscaped Grounds* epitomizes the special efficacy of artistic art histories in staging embodied encounters that bring both pleasure and discomfort.

Staging a Widening and Multisensory Field

The artworks discussed in this chapter represent an enlarged and widening field of vision, hearing, and embodied experience. Whereas the artists discussed in previous chapters addressed their artistic art histories to subjects in close physical, temporal, or familial proximity to them, those discussed in this chapter turn their attention outward to more distant and unfamiliar subjects. Phan, Fyerool, and Hilmi are staging multisensory encounters with artworks made by people who they never met and to whom they have no prior personal connection.

The next chapter continues this expansion of reference, as it discusses artists whose practices go beyond the art-historical to embrace the autotheoretical. At the same time, the next chapter also represents a return to the personal. Whereas my theorizing of staging draws on Hilmi, yamomo, and puppetry—all sources rooted in Southeast Asia—my approach to autotheorizing in the next chapter places the region in dialogue with critical discourses further afield.

4

AUTOTHEORIZING

In a book titled *I Am An Artist (He Said)*, originally published in Thai in 2005, the artist, writer, and educator Araya Rasdjarmrearnsook (1957–) declares:

> The satisfaction derived from artmaking—the entire process from conceptualisation to execution, with revision in between and after the work is finished, as well as the acknowledgement of other people's views—doesn't seem to be any different from the satisfaction one could derive from other kinds of work, and so I'm not sure why I have to talk about it.[1]

Like many statements in Araya's uncategorizable book of essays—is this art history? art theory? memoir? gossip? fiction?—these lines are tantalizingly multivalent. On one hand, this passage is consistent with Araya's repeated diminishment of the perceived specialness and high status of art and artists. Her use of the somewhat unusual and inelegant term *artmakers* (in Thai, *khon tham ngan silpa*) instead of the more usual (and more high-minded) term *artists* (*silapin*) reflects this undermining attitude and casts the production of art in a banal light.[2] On the other hand, this passage also contradicts Araya's suggestions elsewhere in the same book that if "*something* is not useful in real life . . . it's more fitting as material for writing or artmaking," and even that perhaps "the intention of artmaking is to find truth, to serve society, or even to find stress relief."[3]

At times, Araya's book (and several of her other works) seem to be disdainful of art and "artmaking," while in other moments these seem to be a source of deep and life-sustaining comfort—"nourishments [that] help this woman artist 'get by'"—in the face of the multiple and intersectional challenges that Araya has faced in the male-dominated Thai artworld.[4] She has been exhibiting her art in Thailand since 1979 and internationally since 1980; she has won numerous national prizes in Thailand and shown at many of the world's most prestigious exhibitions, including documenta and numerous biennales such as Venice, Johannesburg, and Sydney. She is best-known for a series of videos, made between 1997 and 2005, that depict real human corpses, which the artist interacts with. Her impressive achievements reflect her dedication to artistic practice. Elsewhere, Araya has written that "I often wish I could reach that ultimate state of self-realization: individuality through the process of making art."[5] Yet in *I Am An Artist (He Said)*, she also undermines this possibility by creating multiple personas. The book is narrated in the first-person by masculine and feminine narrators (rendered in the English translation as "He Said" and "She Said"), both of whom are Araya.

Araya's book—which could even be considered an artwork—is an example of *autotheorizing* as art history.[6] Despite being originally written as regular columns for a mass-circulation newspaper magazine, the book does not hesitate to educate its readers about both the art of the recent and distant past. It includes detailed accounts of Araya's own experiences as an artist—including travels to historic exhibitions abroad—as well as extensive discussions of the works of other artists from Thailand, Southeast Asia, and beyond. Araya muses on self-portraits by Otto Dix, Max Beckmann, Yves Klein, Bruce Nauman, and others.[7] Reflecting her imbrication in a network of other artists, she gossips about the origins of the iconic *Pink Man* series by the Bangkok-based artist Manit Sriwanichpoom (1961–) and about the behavior of Singapore-based artist Charles Lim (1973–) during his visit to Chiang Mai soon after his work was exhibited at documenta 11 in 2002.[8] She imagines conversations between canonical Thai modernists, such as Misiem Yipintsoi (1906–88) and Khien Yimsiri (1922–71), whose works are rarely discussed in relation to each other.[9]

In all of these and other ways, her writing could be considered art history, and yet it is a decidedly subjective version, one in which Araya herself is always explicitly present in the telling by writing as either "He Said" or as "She Said." She reflexively remarks on the differences between her accounts of art and those in "art history classes," quipping that "if art history was full of these kinds of stories, I in my He mode would have been disturbed."[10] In some moments, it's clear that Araya loves art and its histories; at other times, she seems sick of it all, when other aspects of life intrude. In short, Araya's art-historical writing is also a kind of autobiographical exercise, yet one in which larger concepts about art and life feature prominently; this is what I mean by proposing that it is autotheorizing as art history.

The many contradictions and inconsistencies in Araya's attitude toward art, art history, and artmaking—as something hardly worth talking about, yet also as something of profound value and importance—are emblematic of the chimeric, shapeshifting qualities she ascribes to herself (or her selves) as the narrating "I" in her book and also in many of her artworks. While Araya insists on her ability to draw on her own lived experiences as a source of knowledge able to generate highly theoretical insights, she nevertheless refuses to allow her sense of self to be confined to a single, fixed, or stable persona. She states with beguiling directness: "one day I found that truth as we know it changes."[11] Through my ongoing attempts at reckoning with this slippery evasiveness of Araya's performance of her artistic and literary self, or rather her multiple selves, I find myself turning not only to Araya's practice as an artist-writer-educator but also to ideas around autotheory.

In a recent study, the scholar Lauren Fournier describes autotheory as a practice rather than a genre: a kind of "performative life-thinking" with which artists, writers, scholars, and others are "aligning theory and the self, discourse and life." In a manner akin to some forms of feminist life writing and écriture féminine, Fournier suggests, "autotheoretical works move between theory and philosophy . . . and the experiential and embodied." This way of working, Fournier claims, raises questions about whether "theory and the personal [are] opposed, or are they inextricably enmeshed."[12] Central to the importance of autotheory, in this view, is its potential to enlarge the parameters of "critical legitimacy" and continue the ongoing shift away from the old view that "for one's work to be considered intellectual and critical . . . one had to have an air of objective authority."[13]

While some artists, writers, and scholars have described themselves as autotheorizing, the term can also be used to characterize a wider range of practices; someone may be working autotheoretically even if they never describe themselves in this way or use the term at all. The concept enables a revisionist reappraisal of art, writing, scholarship, and other practices from the past and the present. Autotheory is part of a larger shift toward recognizing and valuing the partial, subjective, and situated nature of all knowledge and thinking and unthinking the Western binary splitting the body from the mind.

Whereas autotheoretical practices are typically valued for challenging or enlarging usual understandings of theory, I see the autotheoretical works of Araya and other artists working in or affiliated with Southeast Asia as also placing productive pressure on usual understandings of the auto or self, illuminating the capacity of the authorial "I" to shift and swerve in exciting ways. By doing and making artistic art histories in which their own practices are central, these artists are playing at least two roles: they are artists, and they are commentators (or even historians) addressing their own work. For many artists, numerous other personas also accrue alongside these roles, either in the imagination or because of biographical exigencies (or both). The auto or self—the "I" who writes or speaks or makes art that draws together lived experience with theoretical work—may be productively unstable and is usually generatively plural. There is often no single "I" in the autotheorizing that many artists do and make.

This chapter is about autotheorizing as a tendency within artistic art histories in Southeast Asia. I argue that autotheoretical work enlarges and complicates our understandings of artists' selves and sensibilities and their relationship to the art worlds in which they work, emphasizing the possibility for transformation in an artist's life and sense of self. The first part of the chapter comprises a historiographical consideration of the interdisciplinary exchanges between art history and anthropology that enable a kind of autotheorizing in some scholarly writing on Southeast Asia's art. After this, I discuss paintings and writings done during the 1990s and 2000s in Phnom Penh by the self-taught artist Svay Ken (1933–2008). His works are artistic art histories about himself, historicizing his own life as an artist and autotheorizing about his reliance on a network of interlocutors and supporters. The chapter concludes with a return to Araya. While her book is clearly both autotheorizing and doing art history, the presence of art-historical ideas in her artworks is less clear; it is as if she has metabolized art history, and the distinction between her art and the art of the past (her own and that of other artists) becomes indistinct.

Svay Ken and Araya Rasdjarmrearnsook: Directness and Evasiveness

Discussing Araya and Svay Ken together in this chapter is an unexpected yet deliberate gesture to indicate the breadth of practices and life stories in Southeast Asia's contemporary art. Although they never met and their works are very different in style and technique, both Araya and Svay Ken are credited with heralding a new kind of artistic practice that has come to be called "contemporary," and both were among the first generation in their respective home countries to be exhibited in new, transnational networks of biennales and museums surveying the art of the world, including the Global South. Araya's path to contemporary art included studying at top art schools in Thailand and Germany between 1974 and 1990, whereas Svay Ken took up painting in 1993 at the age of sixty with no formal training.

That the two artists had vastly differing educational and life experiences is reflected in their works. A typical example of Svay Ken's autotheorizing is *I Showed Guests at the Swimming Pool My Paintings* (2001) (fig. 4.1). The work is

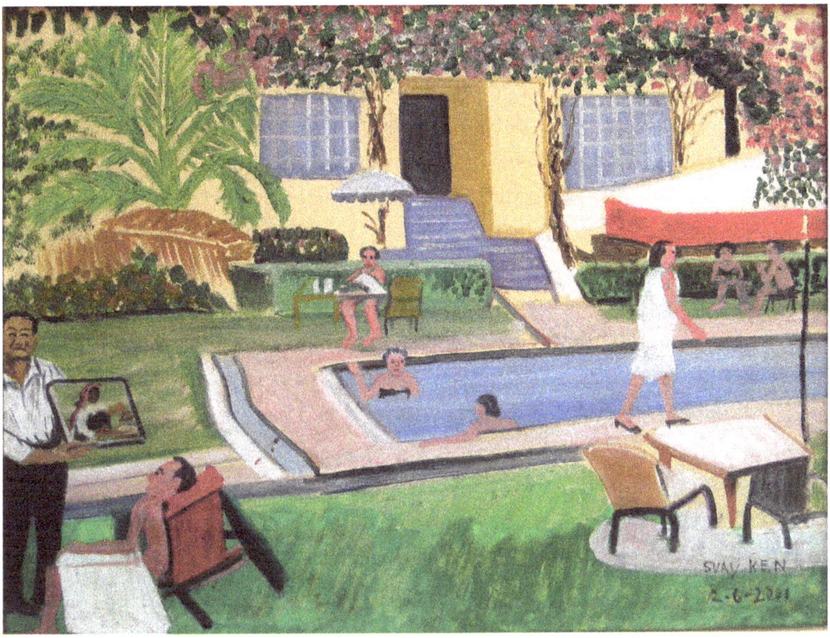

FIGURE 4.1. Svay Ken, *I Showed Guests at the Swimming Pool My Paintings*, 2001. Oil on canvas. Private collection. Reproduced with kind permission from Svay Pisith. © Svay Ken.

done in a charmingly unaffected manner befitting the artist's self-taught status. It portrays the artist himself, neatly dressed in a white collared shirt, holding up a painting for inspection by a pink-skinned man, dressed only in a towel, who reclines on a lounge by the pool of the exclusive Phnom Penh hotel where Svay Ken worked for most of his life. In the background of this exchange, several other pink-skinned people, presumably guests in the hotel, lounge in and around the hotel pool. Svay Ken situates himself at the extreme periphery of the scene; his ear and upper body are partly obscured, cropped by the left edge of the canvas. This compositionally spatializes the hard-working artist's feelings of being socially and economically marginalized in this environment of luxury and relaxation. In a lengthy autobiographical text, he recalls situations like the one depicted in the painting.

> When foreign guests came now and then to swim in the pool of the Hotel, I would take my pictures and try to show them to them. Some guests were annoyed and didn't want to look, but others who loved art looked at my paintings and smiled, praising the pictures.[14]

It is unclear, in *I Showed Guests at the Swimming Pool My Paintings*, whether the towel-clad man on the pool lounge is one of the annoyed or praising ones, but it is certain that Svay Ken, with his neat attire and his impassive, deeply lined face, is resolute in his determination to "get some money to support my wife and children" by selling paintings, despite "beginning to feel my age."[15] The artwork constitutes a fairly straightforward and direct record of a key moment early in Svay Ken's artistic career. It draws on his lived experience to think and theorize about artistic labor as a pursuit that is both noble and difficult. For Svay Ken, being an artist placed him in uncomfortable situations. Yet it was made worthwhile for him when he brought home the profits from his sales, and his "wife was very happy."[16] After her passing, he continued to paint into his old age "in order to have money and be able to give offerings and do good deeds."[17]

A typical example of Araya's autotheorizing is *Prostitute's Room* (1993) (fig. 4.2); the artwork makes clear how different her approach is, when compared with Svay Ken's, and that her work has metabolized art history to a degree that makes it also quite different from other examples of artistic art histories discussed in this book. Like Svay Ken's painting, Araya's installation may also be considered a kind of self-portrait, albeit in a much less direct and more allegorical mode. Instead of depicting her likeness, the work indirectly, abstractly, and conceptually reflects her experience as an artist and as a Thai woman. Araya writes,

> Self-portraits that are more than a personification of an artist as a human being are those that relate to the social situation of the places where an artist lived, and sometimes the grave situations that brought severe hardships.[18]

The piece was made when Araya was living in Germany and encountering the hardships experienced by many Thai sex workers there. It is an installation made with dark cloth curtains, arranged to form a small enclosure, in which bowls filled with dried blood rest on the floor. While each of these materials are familiar, like the setting depicted in Svay Ken's painting, Araya's intentions in arranging them as an installation are not immediately clear. This defamiliarizes these everyday materials. The uncomfortable narrowness of the space demarcated by the curtains is emphasized by their extravagantly great height, suspended from the ceiling.

The blood, for its part, recalls both violence and menstruation; paired with the title, it suggests that the artwork is best understood as Araya's response to the treatment of sex workers in Germany. During an earlier period of study there, the artist had conducted interviews with and befriended Thai women

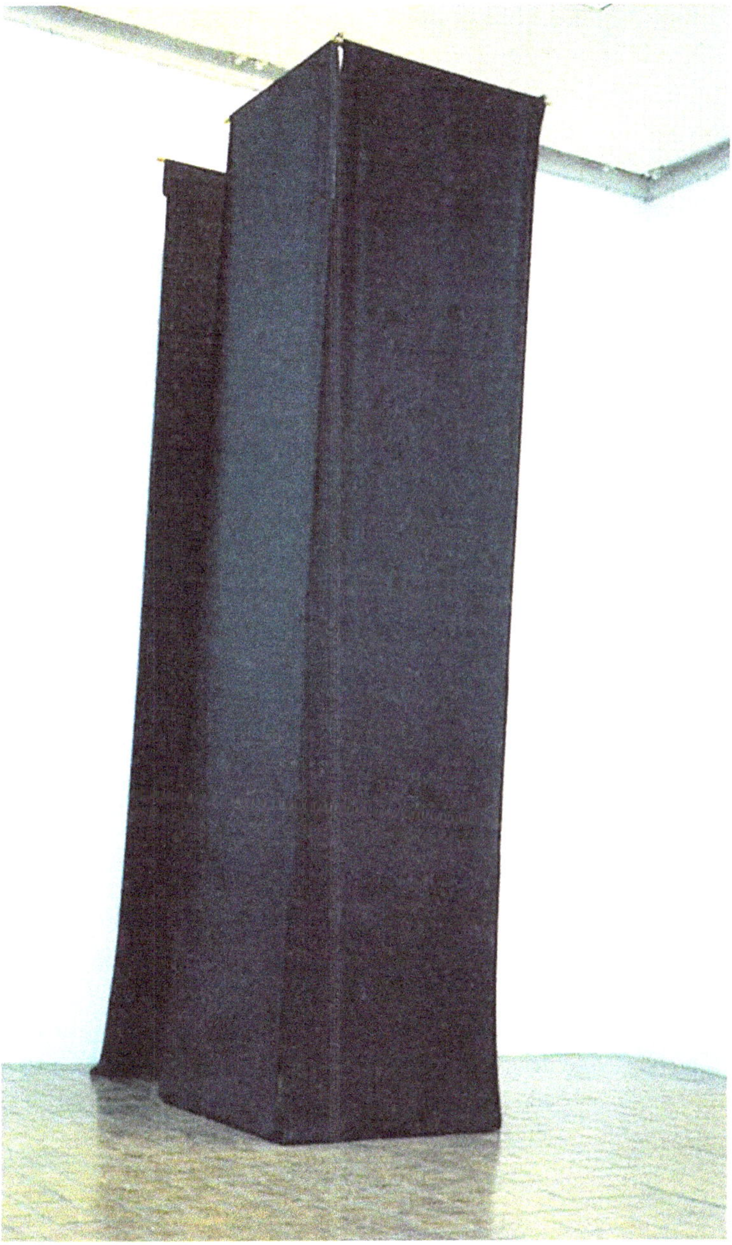

FIGURE 4.2. Araya Rasdjarmrearnsook, *Prostitute's Room*, 1993. Installation view at 1st Johannesburg Biennale, 1995. Collection of the artist.

working in Germany "as housewives, waitresses, masseurs and sex workers."[19] Her works, including *Prostitute's Room*, may be at once reflections on the hardships faced by these more subaltern women, reflections on their difference or alterity from Araya's more privileged experience as an artist, and also reflections on the similarities and shared experiences that bonded the artist and other Thai women in Germany despite those differences.

When *Prostitute's Room* was exhibited in the 1st Johannesburg Biennale, it was reviewed by the acclaimed South African artist Candice Breitz, who linked the work to larger, cultural differences. Breitz describes the "tiny, curtained-off rooms [as] symbolic of the confinement of Asian women within patriarchal, western stereotypes."[20] She further proposes that "the installation reflected on the consumption and degradation of women through sexual abuse, pointing at the same time, towards the cultural dominance which certain cultures exert over others."[21] As well as being a kind of social commentary, *Prostitute's Room* is also Araya's response to a mode of artmaking she encountered during her travels far from Thailand, which she also writes about in *I Am An Artist (He Said)*. After describing a 1975 performance by Shigeko Kubota in which the New York-based Japanese artist utilizes her own menstrual blood, Araya feels seized by a "cultural divide: the prim, prudish attitude of Thai artists versus the nakedness and provocation of *farang* [foreign or non-Thai] artists."

Prostitute's Room is Araya's autotheoretical attempt to navigate a middle path through this cultural divide, finding a position for her own artistic practice that transcends the binary of Thai versus foreign and proper versus provocative. It takes up subject matter—sex work—that has been prevalent throughout Western art history, from Édouard Manet to Nan Goldin, yet was relatively novel within Thai art at the time.[22] Just as Svay Ken makes palpable his own social discomfort in *I Showed Guests at the Swimming Pool My Paintings*, the narrow space of *Prostitute's Room* highlights the feelings of constraint Araya has experienced as an artist. The key difference in these two artworks, which are both artistic art histories and both autotheorizing, is in the directness of Svay Ken's work and the evasiveness and difficulty of Araya's.

By discussing the works of Araya and Svay Ken together in this chapter, I show that, despite their differences, both Araya and Svay Ken share a special interest in using their work to reflexively examine their own practices in relation to the (very different) art worlds in which they have circulated. In Araya's words, "we never really make choices directly and completely independently because we cannot cut loose from these socio-cultural conditions."[23] In the 1990s and early 2000s, before the solidification of the "global contemporary" in institutions and circuits that are familiar today, many other kinds of art worlds proliferated; Svay Ken's included the lobbies and poolside areas of the Phnom

Penh hotel where he worked, while Araya's included exhibitions and universities in northern Thailand, Johannesburg, West Germany, and beyond. In her later works, such as *Two Planets* (2008) and *Village and Elsewhere* (2011), Araya stages humorous and poignant encounters between Thai villagers and canonical images from Western art history, thereby dramatizing the disconnect between cultures, including between different art worlds.

In this chapter, I examine these artists' practices in dialogue with scholarly discussions of autotheory by Fournier and others. I suggest that artists, including Svay Ken and Araya, are not only often more comfortable with autotheorizing than art historians and other scholars are—despite the recent "autotheoretical turn" in the humanities—but they are also often able to do autotheorizing in more sophisticated and sensitive ways while sharing artistic art histories that involve their own lives and practices. This offers a potentially rich resource for the discipline of art history more broadly, which is particularly valuable for art historians working on and in Southeast Asia. Many of these scholars have been influenced by or work across art history, anthropology, and area studies, and therefore they may be more likely to embrace autotheorizing as a method of research and writing alongside other, more conventional techniques. Although many of the key figures Fournier cites are white, Western artists and writers (for example, Maggie Nelson is cited as foundational), she also affirms the need to study other antecedents and articulations of autotheory beyond the North and the West. This chapter is a contribution to this ongoing project of pluralizing and decolonizing autotheory as a tool for art-historical doing and making, even as the concept remains emergent and continues to come into focus.

Scholarly Art Histories, Anthropology, and Area Studies in Southeast Asia

Before examining autotheoretical tendencies in Southeast Asia's art histories, it may be productive to consider the nature of the field more broadly. As I have said, art history as it is practiced in and for this region is often distinctly different from the art history that may be familiar in other parts of the world. From its inception in the mid-twentieth century, modern and contemporary art history as a scholarly discipline has always been particularly porous in Southeast Asia. A great deal of important and influential scholarly writing on the modern and contemporary art of the region has been done in area studies, anthropology, and across these (and other) disciplines. Neither of the first books to discuss the region's modern art—Marco Hsü's 1963 *Brief History of Malayan Art* in Chinese and Claire Holt's 1967 *Art in Indonesia* in English—were written by professional art historians. As well as being an artist, Hsü worked as the principal of a primary school in Singapore, while Holt studied art, journalism and law before moving to Indonesia in 1930.[24] Despite, or perhaps because of, their unorthodox and interdisciplinary approaches, Hsü's and Holt's books remain widely read and frequently cited today.[25]

Neither Hsü nor Holt are particularly autotheoretical in their work—despite both having close, personal connections with many of the artists they wrote about—but many art historians working in and on Southeast Asia have drawn on anthropology to enable a kind of self-reflexive writing and thinking of themselves into their work.[26] The anthropologist Kenneth M. George, for example, recalls traveling "to centers of art activity" in the US as "escort and sidekick" to the Bandung-based artist A. D. Pirous (1932–2023), where he learned for the first time "about Euro-American art history, a field in which I had no background or experience . . . through the eyes and experience of someone from Asia." Moving from this lived experience to a larger and more theoretical insight, George proposes that, through this encounter, he and Pirous were "reversing the patterns of authority and learning that we associate with imperialism."[27] I will discuss some other examples of anthropological autotheorizing in scholarly art histories later on.

In the decades since Holt and Hsü were writing, anthropology and area studies (and interdisciplinarity more generally) have continued to have a substantial impact on art-historical research and writing in and on Southeast Asia. This is partly due to clearly systemic and institutional factors, and it is perhaps also a result of other phenomena that are less easy to specify. From Hsü's and Holt's pioneering publications onwards, Southeast Asia's art histories have developed in the shadow of the Cold War—which was violently fought in much of the region—and the concomitant rise of area studies, particularly in American universities, to serve national political interests (as well as scholarly ones).[28] As Nora A. Taylor observes, "due to universities' area-studies requirement that students learn a local language, art historians of Southeast Asia are also area specialists." One corollary of this is that most "specialize in individual countries," thereby galvanizing the nation as the dominant frame for art-historical work on Southeast Asia.[29] In this way, the methodological underpinnings of art-historical studies of Southeast Asia's art have been shaped, at least in part, by the geopolitical circumstances of the Cold War.

A result of all this, as Taylor drily notes, is that "Asian art history as an academic discipline is still very much an unfinished project."[30] Writing over a decade later, and based at a university in Singapore rather than the US, David Teh concurs with Taylor, calling art history "a discipline that has yet to flourish in Asia."[31] Teh's lament is directed at the intellectual substance of art history in

Asia, but it echoes Sabapathy's complaint about the discipline's longstanding inability to secure a strong institutional base for teaching in any of Singapore's universities.[32] Arguably, as I proposed in the introduction, this situation has begun to change in Singapore and elsewhere in the region, with growing interest in and varied forms of support for art-historical work since about 2010. And arguably, the "unfinished" nature of art history as a discipline that Taylor identifies may be not a shortcoming so much as an opportunity, including for artistic art histories, to continue to imaginatively enlarge and decolonize thinking and writing on art.

While art history in Southeast Asia may be "unfinished" or "yet to flourish," the discipline has been remarkably open to anthropological ways of working, whereas outside the region, art history and anthropology are typically seen as being at odds with one another. In his *History of Art History*, Christopher S. Wood neatly encapsulates anthropology's "point of view" as being "that art is continuous with other forms of symbolic behavior."[33] By contrast, Wood describes art historians' attitude to art as "engagement with the painting or drawing as art, and not just as a supplement to scripture or as display of wealth."[34] Whereas anthropologists are concerned with an entire culture as a "system of symbol exchanges," art historians in their special focus on art must be especially alive to "the pleasure in art that figures felicity in life," which Wood calls "an ambiguous appeal."[35] He argues somewhat rhapsodically that art-historical work necessitates a poetic orientation to ambiguous uncertainty:

> Recognition and misrecognition, questioning and disappointment, prompts and restagings of desire. Enswirled in this pleasure you swim upstream and enter into the interplay of the collective and the individual, into the conditions of life, now repeated and intensified. The artwork forces you to adjust to the alterities thrown up by history.[36]

In this conception of the discipline, art history is concerned with art as both a product and producer of particularly complex currents of culture and history; "art is not just an object but an event," one emerging from "conditions of life" that are geographically and temporally specific.[37] For anthropologists, by contrast, art is typically not understood as a special or separate realm of activity but instead as intimately connected to the wider culture, which often matters more for interpretation than the art itself. As such, a scholar like Taylor—who adopts what she calls an "ethnographic approach" to "combine art history and anthropology"—can assert: "It was the artist as a person that mattered in Vietnam more than his or her work. Or rather, the work mattered because of the artist and if the artist mattered, so did the work." [38] The contrast with Wood's characterization of art-historical work is stark. The decentering of artworks within art histories, to instead focus on (for Taylor) artists or (for many other scholars) social, political, and other historical contexts, infuses many of Southeast Asia's art histories with attitudes that may be more familiar in anthropology and area studies.

Wood proposes that "art history managed by artists keeps art in the foreground,"[39] and many artistic art histories do indeed center artworks, even while celebrating artists' own subjective perceptions and lived experiences, which is arguably also a kind of autotheory. Examples discussed in previous chapters demonstrate this. For instance, the lavish and plentiful lingering close-up and wide-angle shots of I Gusti Made Rundu's painting in Sriwhana Spong's video, discussed in chapter 1, foreground Spong's visual appreciation for the artwork. At the same time, Spong's video also unambiguously situates the painting in the (spatial and kinship) context of her ancestral home in Bali and discusses it from the highly subjective (and autotheoretical) viewpoints of Gusti Rundu's son and Spong herself. Similarly, Emiria Sunassa's paintings, discussed in chapter 2, emphasize the primacy of Walter Spies's photographs of Balinese people as their compositional source, even while implicitly asserting Emiria's own agency in subjectively changing aspects of their appearance in her paintings. In chapter 3, I discussed Hilmi Johandi's decision to focus on the imagery of colonial-era posters depicting Malaya without examining the biography of the British artists who designed them. I also described Thao Nguyen Phan's extensive footage of the brise-soleil façades of modernist buildings in Cambodia and Vietnam that, like Spong's lingering shots of Gusti Rundu's painting, foreground the artist's fascination with the aesthetic qualities of the architecture, even while staging her own speculations about its histories.

While each of these various examples of artistic art histories "keeps art in the foreground," they all also draw on methods and sensibilities from anthropology and area studies, which are often autotheoretical in their approach. Spong and Phan both use interviews (and conversations) extensively. This is what Taylor calls an "ethnographic approach," which outside Southeast Asia may be more common in anthropology than in art history. This is overlaid with playful first-person speculations. Hilmi and Emiria both focus their attention on images that may be more comfortably considered "visual culture" than art; these photographs of local people and posters advertising colonial tourism are the kinds of images that area studies scholars may be more likely to study than art historians.[40] This infuses their works with a distinctly personal sensibility.

As these examples make clear, artistic art histories integrate the conventional art-historical focus on artwork (identified by Wood) with the conventional anthropological and area studies focus on wider cultural systems, and they thereby resist any binary understanding of these disciplines as being counterposed. Just as Taylor aims to "combine art history and anthropology," so too do the artists discussed in previous chapters reflect both disciplines' attitudes toward art as articulated by Wood; art is viewed as special (an attitude typical of art historians), while it is also viewed as part of and continuous with a larger cultural context (in the manner of anthropologists and area studies scholars).

In this respect, artistic art histories follow a path taken by many scholarly accounts of Southeast Asia's modern and contemporary art, a path that frequently crisscrosses with adjacent disciplines and often adopts autotheoretical methods along the way. Astri Wright characterizes the development of scholarship on Indonesian art in recent decades as defined by several kinds of expansion, broadening and deepening the field until it becomes like "some pulsing rainbow, surrounded by creative and fascinating cohorts."[41] It was not always so. Elsewhere, Wright reveals that her initial proposal to research Indonesia's modern art at the doctoral level was discouraged by her advisor and rejected by funding agencies. Writing in the first-person and unafraid of exposing her vulnerabilities, Wright admits that she "had to learn on my own, an alternative mode to the traditional masculine-academic style encountered in different variations throughout my university studies."[42]

This crisscrossing between art history, anthropology, area studies, and other disciplines contributes greatly to the quirkiness and flexibility of forms found in many accounts of modern and contemporary art in Southeast Asia, which opens a space of possibility for autotheoretical work.

Autotheorizing in Scholarly Art Histories in Southeast Asia

Wright's frequent use of first-person narrative, disclosure of personal experiences, and emphasis on the subjective and partial nature of her knowledge—not to mention the refreshing eccentricity of her prose—are all qualities associated with autotheory. Although (to my knowledge) Wright does not describe herself in this way, it may be productive to consider her work as autotheoretical. Fournier describes autotheory as a capacious and accommodating concept and impulse, and she suggests that "even though it is a recent term, only really taking off in the late 2010s . . . 'autotheory' embodies centuries-long problems within philosophy." She proposes that "a tendency toward working autotheoretically" can be observed in the work of such diverse thinkers as Immanuel Kant, Karl Marx, Sigmund Freud, and Frantz Fanon.[43] I find this revisionist reappraisal of canonical scholarship exciting, because it enables a rethinking of the (often undisclosed) relationship between personal life and theoretical insight. Even scholars who write with an impersonal third-person style are often drawing from their subjective, lived experiences. More recent forms of autotheoretical writing simply make this explicit.

Although it remains a marginal (or, at least, less common) practice within most academic art histories, Wright is far from alone in autotheorizing in her scholarly writing on Southeast Asia's modern and contemporary art. Like Wright, however, other scholar-practitioners of autotheoretical art history also do not describe themselves in these terms. The feminist art historian Wulan Dirgantoro recounts that when conducting "fieldwork" in Indonesia "during the second trimester of my pregnancy, both male and female artists warmed up to my presence and became more open to discussing their works and personal lives."[44] This personal experience yields a theoretical insight about common Indonesian attitudes toward feminisms and feminists. Việt Lê, a self-described "researcher at a North American university, independent international curator, boat refugee, conceptual artist, and queer male," intersperses his discussions of contemporary art and critical theory with startling first-person accounts of his memories of "my midnight raft escape from Sài Gòn with my mom at age three."[45] This personal experience yields a theoretical insight about the recursive nature of memory and trauma. And T. K. Sabapathy, in his 2010 account of the decline and longstanding paucity of art history teaching in Singapore, shares his own educational experience ("I began the study of history of art in 1958 in the then University of Malaya") in order to demonstrate the effect of the local university's failure to implement an art history program. When the head of the history department urged Sabapathy to "consider studying art history at the graduate level" the then-student was left wondering, "How should I develop such studies, though?" since there were no professors of art history in Singapore at the time.[46] Sabapathy's personal experience engenders his theoretical insight about the repeated prioritizing of the exhibitionary display of art over educational training in art's histories. This too can be understood as autotheorizing, even though Sabapathy never employs the term.

Dirgantoro, Lê, and Sabapathy—like Wright, George, and others—are all drawing on anthropology, area studies, and other forms of interdisciplinarity in their art histories, and this creates a space for their occasional autotheorizing. Dirgantoro cites numerous area studies scholars and draws on her first-hand familiarity with Indonesian cultural contexts in describing the interactions between artists and their publics. Lê declares his debt to the "self-reflexivity" and "thick description" prized by anthropology while also registering his dissatisfaction with "traditional ethnographic divides between home and research abroad" enshrined in the notion of "fieldwork."[47] Sabapathy studied history at the undergraduate level in Singapore, and he has often called for greater attention to archaeological and other historical accounts of Southeast Asia's premodern cultures.[48] It is largely because of their interdisciplinary approach to art histories—their aliveness to the openness of the field in Southeast Asia—that these and other scholars are able to adopt autotheorizing strategies in their writing.

These examples can all be considered autotheoretical (even though none of these writers describe themselves in this way) because they bring together lived experience and theoretical insight. Despite their differences in topic and tone, Dirgantoro, Lê, and Sabapathy all reflexively foreground their own subjective positions and encounters and draw on these to generate larger ideas. They are, in Alex Brostoff and Lauren Fournier's terms, "mov[ing] between 'theory' and 'practice,' between 'living,' 'thinking,' and 'making.'"[49] Their meandering back and forth from art history to adjacent fields allows their work to also turn inward at times.

Yet my understanding of autotheorizing as it appears in these works goes beyond this bridging of the self and the theoretical to involve a significant questioning of the stability or coherence of the self-identity of the writer. In all three examples cited previously, the scholar's narrating self or "I" undergoes a significant transition or transformation. For Dirgantoro, this is pregnancy, a state that is not only inherently temporary but also constantly changing. Lê, for his part, describes a repeated back-and-forth in his adult life between living in the present day (as a scholar, artist, and so on) and the past (as a "boat refugee"). And for Sabapathy, his own need to travel abroad to pursue his education in art history offers both opportunities for new experiences and discoveries and cause for lament about the shortcomings he perceives in the local university system.

This potential of autotheory—to not only put pressure on normative understandings of theory, but also to challenge the assumed stability or singularity of the auto or self—has been underexplored in anglophone scholarly literature on the subject. Brostoff and Fournier insightfully note that many practitioners of autotheory "conscientiously work against the self-containment of the 'auto' [and] cast light and shadow on multiple vectors of identity as they intersect with others."[50] Yet their elaboration of this point is directed chiefly toward autotheoretical citation practices. This leaves room for more thinking about how autotheorizing can reveal a mutable authorial "I," which is multiple and contingent, and with these qualities, brings theory back to life.

I have suggested that the autotheorizing done in the previously mentioned scholarly art histories involves a substantial emphasis on the self as being in a state of flux: either because of a process of change and transition (such as pregnancy or educational experience) or because of more existential instability (such as recurring memories of trauma). In this regard, these scholars are akin to many artists who work autotheoretically and whose practices productively problematize the nature of the artistic self.

Autotheorizing and the Beginnings of "Southeast Asian Contemporary Art"

As we have seen, Araya Rasdjarmrearnsook and Svay Ken are very different artists in many ways. Aesthetically, Araya's artworks take diverse forms and shift from printmaking (from the 1970s to early 1990s), to sculpture and installation (from the early to late 1990s), to video and moving image (from the late 1990s onwards), to a return to sculpture and installation, often incorporating moving image (from the 2010s onwards). Svay Ken, by contrast, worked exclusively with oil on canvas and maintained a consistent aesthetic approach from when he took up painting in 1993 until his death in 2008.

In terms of subject matter, Araya's works are wide-ranging. After an early interest in melancholic landscapes, in the 1990s she turned to address women's bodies and social positions. From 1997, she began working with human corpses. From the mid-2000s, she began interacting with dogs and other non-human animals in her works and considering cross-cultural experiences of canonical Western artworks. These shifts in subject matter all encompass the artist's lifelong interest in death, loss, and related affects. Araya's works are frequently allegorical, abstract, or conceptual, and their subject matter is often elusive and takes time to apprehend.

Svay Ken's works, by contrast, are typically straightforward and direct in their narrative approach, depicting in a literal and clear way his lived experiences, such as memories of important events in his life (both personal and in the nation's political history), as well as people, places, and objects of personal significance. The experience of looking at Svay Ken's paintings is also relatively straightforward; they feel like a window into his memories of his life. The experience of engaging with Araya's artworks can be much more complex and difficult; they often feel like evasive games, demanding sustained attention and work to make sense of their layered meanings.

Undergirding these differences in their artworks, Araya and Svay Ken have also led very different lives, both defined by many shifts and changes. Araya has travelled extensively and studied art in Thailand and twice in Germany, whereas Svay Ken was self-taught as an artist and worked for most of his life in a hotel in Phnom Penh. While Araya's life has been marked by personal tragedies, including the early death of her mother, Thailand has prospered for most of her adult life. Svay Ken, by contrast, lived through numerous violent regime changes in Cambodia, from French and Japanese colonial rule, through independence and a US-backed coup, to the genocidal Khmer Rouge regime, then occupation by Vietnam and then the United Nations, and finally Hun Sen's oligarchy.

Despite these manifold differences, however, Araya and Svay Ken share several significant characteristics. For both artists, writing has been an important practice alongside making art. Araya has authored numerous books, while Svay Ken has written two substantial autobiographical texts to accompany exhibitions, one more than 40 pages long. In both Thailand and Cambodia, it is somewhat unusual for artists to write so extensively or, at least, to publish their writings. Moreover, both Araya and Svay Ken have been quite open in reflecting on the economics of their artistic practice. Araya freely admits to relying on her salary as an educator at Chiang Mai University to support herself—despite this being looked down on by other artists—while Svay Ken freely discloses the prices his paintings have fetched, and his pride at being able to support his family through sales of his artworks alongside his salary as a hotel worker.[51]

Both Araya and Svay Ken have been historicized as being among the first generation of artists from Southeast Asia marking the shift from a (national) modern art to a (transnational or global) contemporary art. The scholar Arnika Fuhrmann notes insightfully that "Araya opposes herself to current neotraditionalist trends in art that recuperate [Thai] national or religious symbols." By "oppos[ing] a certain opportunist use of Thainess and Buddhism in art" and by adopting "cosmopolitan and global references and media" and participating in transnational networks for the study and exhibition of art, Araya aligns herself with a new generation of (global) contemporary artists, distancing herself from an earlier generation of (Thai, national) modern artists.[52] Similarly, the art historian Pamela N. Corey notes that although "it is tempting to place Svay Ken . . . as 'modernist' . . . [he] is credited by many in the Phnom Penh community as the father of contemporary art" as a result of his "artistic productivity, experimentation, and development in subject matter."[53] Cambodia's art-historical trajectory is starkly different from Thailand's because of the Khmer Rouge genocide, which wiped out a vast majority of artists practicing before 1975, and because of the decades of economic precarity and diplomatic isolation that followed. Yet the sense that the hallmarks of contemporary (as distinct from modern) art include participation in transnational exhibitions and a dedication to ongoing experimentation is shared in the two countries. This means that despite their differences, Araya and Svay Ken are both considered pioneers of the contemporary.

Moreover—and most significantly, in the context of this chapter—both Araya and Svay Ken have worked extensively to historicize their own practices, making artistic art histories in which they are the central protagonists. As with other aspects of their work, the stylistic and conceptual approach taken by each artist has differed, with Svay Ken's account of his artistic practice told in a straightforward, autobiographical manner, whereas Araya's narrating of her own trajectory as an artist is characterized by many twists and turns and a kind of metabolizing of the art-historical within her artworks. Yet both Araya and Svay Ken have returned repeatedly to making artistic art histories of their own practices, historicizing themselves in their writing and in their artwork. More than being simply autobiographical, Araya's and Svay Ken's narration of their lives as artists is also theoretical; as well as being a turn inward, it also encompasses a turn outward through thinking and theorizing about the role and social position of contemporary artists in the context of Southeast Asia at the turn of the twenty-first century. In this way, both artists are autotheorizing as they make artistic art histories about themselves.

For Araya, autotheorizing enables a kind of serious yet playful trickery in which an ever-expanding array of personas—many Arayas—emerge as if in a proverbial hall of mirrors. For Svay Ken, by contrast, autotheorizing facilitates a sensitive emplacement of what Araya calls "artmaking" within the wider context of life, in particular, a life pulled in drastically different directions by the unusually and tragically tumultuous turns of Cambodia's modern history. With both Araya's and Svay Ken's works, I find the concept of autotheorizing useful for making sense of the relationship between the individual artists and the art worlds in which they moved.

Both Araya and Svay Ken may have found the need for autotheorizing, and more generally for making artistic art histories about themselves, because they felt that no one else was writing historical accounts of them and their work. Araya, at least, was included in several exhibitions and essays curated and written by Apinan Poshyananda, a Cornell-trained art historian (and sometime artist) and her peer. Svay Ken, on the other hand, first began painting at a time when there were no scholars of modern and contemporary art working in or on Cambodia. For both artists, the need to write (and artistically make) their own art histories may have at first felt like a necessity, but it also became an opportunity for them to think and theorize in ways that enlarged their art.

Svay Ken: Autotheorizing About Art's Place in Life and the Artist's Reliance on Others

The painting *I Showed Guests at the Swimming Pool My Paintings* is one of several works in which Svay Ken narrates the history of his own life as an artist.

In addition to a large number of individual self-portraits depicting the artist at his easel, two major series narrate Svay Ken's life and practice. These artistic art histories are aesthetically straightforward and direct, as is typical of the artist's style, but they are also autotheorizing in complex, conceptual ways.

This understanding of Svay Ken's practice—as being thoughtful and theoretical—makes it available for close reading on par with other contemporary practices that are considered artistic research. As Kamini Vellodi has shown, discourse around "artistic research" emerged in specific locations, far from Cambodia, in order "to assess and evaluate artistic production within academia."[54] The circumstances in Cambodia during the 1990s and early 2000s were so radically different than those in, say, the UK and Scandinavia that it can be hard for practices like Svay Ken's to be accommodated within the concept of artistic research. Indeed, during his lifetime Svay Ken's paintings were at least once exhibited as "outsider art."[55] He was not an art-world insider in any conventional sense.

Svay Ken's works about himself as an artist can be categorized as belonging to two main groups: first, paintings concerned with the significance of art within Svay Ken's tumultuous life and second, works about his relationships with professional and creative networks. The first group of works—several of which are gathered in a series called *Painted Stories* (2001)—emphasizes the importance of painting as a way for the artist to support his family and earn money for the Buddhist practice of making merit by giving donations. Yet this body of work also stresses that being an artist came late in Svay Ken's life—beginning at the age of 60 in 1993—and that in this sense it is just one small part of a much larger story. The second group of works, gathered in a series called *A Good Friend is Hard to Find* (2005), shows that although Svay Ken worked alone as a painter, he understands artistic practice as being part of a larger network and ecology. These works emphasize the importance of collaboration and support in making Svay Ken legible as an artist to wider art worlds beyond Phnom Penh. I discuss each of these two main bodies of work in turn.

The artist's first major foray into historicizing his own artistic practice came in 2001, the year after the death of his wife, Tith Yun. Svay Ken was commissioned by the Reyum Institute of Arts and Culture—Phnom Penh's most important center for contemporary art at the time, which had opened in 1998—to make a series of paintings to accompany a lengthy text he had written about his own life to commemorate Tith Yun's passing. The series comprises 117 works, each illustrating moments in the life of Svay Ken and his late wife. These paintings are reproduced in a publication titled *Painted Stories: The Life of a Cambodian Family from 1941 to the Present* alongside an English translation of Svay Ken's text.

Svay Ken's key aims with *Painted Stories* appear twofold: to celebrate his late wife and to record the many twists and turns that their lives together had taken. These include their move from the countryside to the city, their temporary return to the countryside during the genocidal Khmer Rouge regime's evacuation of Phnom Penh from 1975 to 1979, and their enmeshment in Cambodia's violently turbulent history during their lifetime. In keeping with the artist's desire to pay tribute to his late wife, the written narrative opens not with Svay Ken's own childhood and background but instead with an account of Tith Yun's family, and the first sixteen paintings in the series depict moments in her life before she met her future husband. These paintings, in tandem with the text, record Tith Yun's difficult childhood in the Cambodian countryside after the death of her mother as well as her diligence as a student and worker, both before and after her shift to the capital.

Among the 117 works in the *Painted Stories* series, only five directly depict the artist at work, which reflects both the fullness of his life and his belated adoption of painting; it autotheoretically emplaces Svay Ken's artistic practice within the larger context of the many turns taken in his life. Before the first of these—number 103 in the series—we see Svay Ken and his wife earning income in a range of other ways, such as selling food, working at the hotel, and even gathering newspapers to sell. The frequent turns to new ways of making a living are indicative of the economic hardships that Cambodia faced during Svay Ken's lifetime.

Interviews with Svay Ken confirm that he saw being an artist as chiefly a way for him to support his family and that, far from being something to be embarrassed about, this approach to painting was a source of pride. "I was under a lot of pressure to find an alternative way to earn a living," he explained in 2008, "in order to support my family and so that my children could continue their studies."[56] It was because of this Svay Ken "decided to learn how to make paintings." Despite his lack of training, he "was eager to become an artist and had the passion to do so," he affirmed. He bought some supplies and simply "started painting." Svay Ken was palpably proud of his ability to earn income from his paintings, saying "I could sell 50 paintings in a single day." Yet he also viewed his artistic practice as a way "to instruct people about subjects such as education through artwork," including taking concepts "from Buddhist theories." For Svay Ken, making paintings was one in a long series of activities he worked hard at to improve life for himself and his family.

Among the five works in the *Painted Stories* series that directly depict Svay Ken as an artist, the message is clear and consistent: for Svay Ken, making paintings was only a meaningful and valuable activity because of the artist's relationship to others. Were it not for various kinds of support from people in his network, Svay Ken would not have enjoyed the success that he did, and he would not have been recognized as an artist, first in Cambodia, then in the region, and then beyond.[57] The five works in *Painted Stories* that show the artist at work reveal how this view is expressed through his visual autotheorizing.

All five of these paintings depict Svay Ken in relation his network, emphasizing his inter-reliance on his art world and larger community ties. Three of the five paintings show the artist with other people: one with a patron, one with his wife and some monks, and one with the couple who organized the *Painted Stories* exhibition and book. Two others show him alone but in the presence of gallery signboards that suggest an active invitation to wider publics. With these works, Svay Ken autheoretically emphasizes the relationship between the artist and his interlocutors and supporters.

The three paintings depicting the artist with other people are all accompanied by text in which Svay Ken expresses his gratitude for their support. The first of these depicts Svay Ken and a taller white man, who the text describes as "a Canadian journalist named Ed Fitzgerald [who] came and offered to make a business with me." In the artist's account, Fitzgerald and his daughter provided financial support, including paying Svay Ken's son Pisith's way through school. "I would like to thank them again for helping me," the artist writes.[58] A second painting depicts Svay Ken and his wife making offerings of food and drinks to three monks; the caption explains that "we offered food to the monks in front of our gallery every morning."[59] This indicates that for a devout Buddhist like the artist, giving thanks to people who have offered material support for his artistic practice and making offerings to the Buddhist *sangha* (community of monks) were alike, which is consistent with his statements, such as the one quoted previously, about using his art to share Buddhist concepts. The third painting in the *Painted Stories* series that depicts the artist with other people shows him and his wife seated happily with Ly Daravuth and Ingrid Muan. By establishing and operating the Reyum Institute of Arts and Culture, they supported Svay Ken in both direct and indirect ways. They commissioned him to make the paintings in *Painted Stories*, and they also organized other exhibitions that inspired him as he developed his practice. All five of these paintings show the artist at ease, central in the composition, in clear contrast to his discomfort in the margins of *I Showed Guests at the Swimming Pool My Paintings*. The works are expressing Svay Ken's happy reliance on his networks.

Taken together, the works in *Painted Stories* are autotheorizing about Svay Ken's confidence to make a public declaration of his profession as an artist—despite having had no formal training and a difficult life working many jobs—as being gratefully indebted to his networks and community. The two paintings in the series that depict Svay Ken alone both prominently feature gallery signboards, as clear indications of the public-facing nature of his artistic practice. It was showing his paintings in these galleries that made him legible as an artist. Thus, even though the paintings depict Svay Ken alone, the implication is that the success of which he is so palpably proud is owed not only to his own labor but also to the support of others.

Four years after *Painted Stories*, Svay Ken devoted the entirety of the series titled *A Good Friend is Hard to Find* (2005) to examining his relationship as an artist with the art historian and curator (and sometime artist) Ingrid Muan. Whereas *Painted Stories* reflects the fullness of Svay Ken's life, emplacing art-making in the context of many other vocations with which he supported his family before becoming an artist, by contrast, the works in *A Good Friend* focus only on the few years in which the artist knew and worked with Muan from 1998 until her death (from an infection resulting from a dog bite) in 2005. Thus, *A Good Friend* in its entirety is an example of artistic art histories, whereas only five of the works in *Painted Stories* can be considered in this way. While the historical scope and focus of *A Good Friend* is thus notably different from the expansive *Painted Stories*, the two series nevertheless share an autotheoretical emphasis on the networked nature of artistic practice and Svay Ken's happy reliance on other people to achieve legibility and prominence as a contemporary artist in the Cambodian context. In both series, the paintings are best understood in relation to the accompanying text authored by the artist.

Most of the works in *A Good Friend* depict Svay Ken and Muan together in a tribute to their close relationship of friendship and collaboration. The series is also an example of honoring, a mode of practice discussed in chapter 1. Several paintings depict the two seated together at a table; in one of these, a fresh coconut with a straw sits in the space between them (fig. 4.3), while in two others, a white paper document occupies this position (fig. 4.4). In all of these works, the table is the same blue color; seen together, the works are autotheorizing about the easy intertwining of the pair's friendship (as signified by the taking of drinks together) and professional collaborations (represented by the paperwork, likely a document Muan helped to type or translate for Svay Ken). This enmeshing of work and pleasure is also reflected in the wide smiles seen in most works in the series, particularly in the works that also depict Svay Ken's late wife, Tith Yun. As the artist writes in the text accompanying the series, Muan "got to know not only my work, but also my wife and children."[60] Muan appears equally comfortable at a Buddhist ceremony and at Tith Yun's funeral as she does working on documents about international exhibitions of Svay Ken's work or photographing his paintings.

The artist's admiration for Muan's constancy in both personal and professional settings is emphasized by his decision to portray her in identical attire in

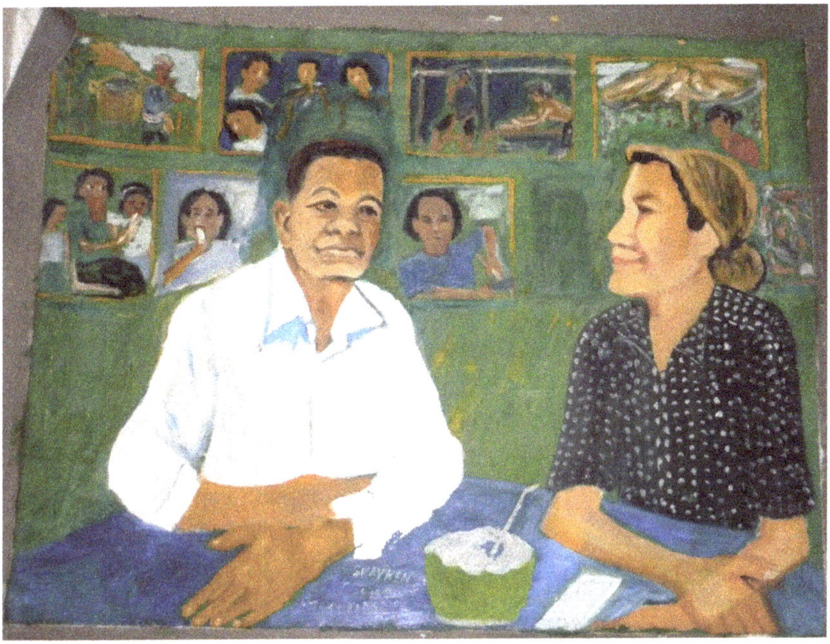

FIGURE 4.3. Svay Ken, from the series *A Good Friend is Hard to Find*, 2005. Oil on canvas. Private collection. Reproduced with kind permission from Svay Pisith. © Svay Ken.

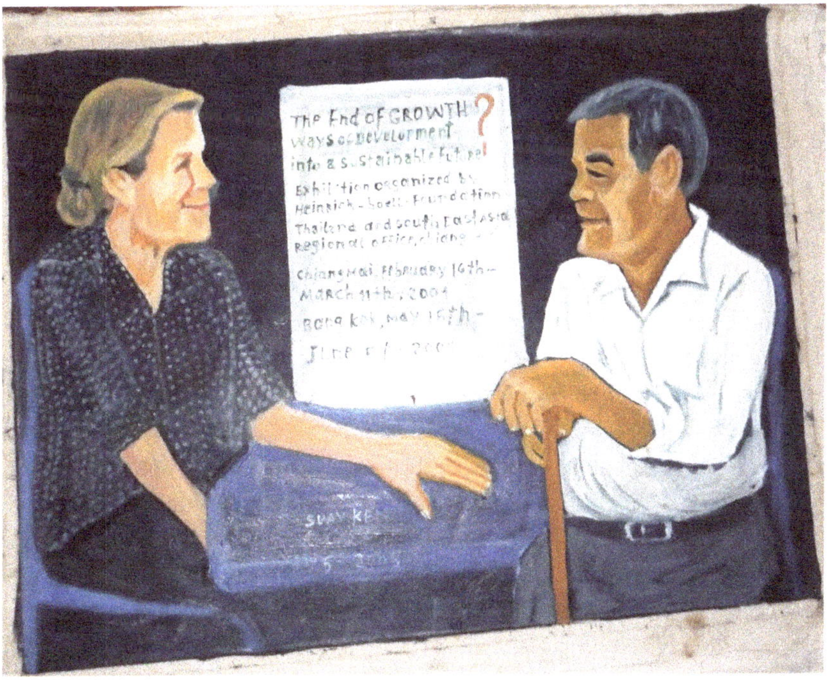

FIGURE 4.4. Svay Ken, from the series *A Good Friend is Hard to Find*, 2005. Oil on canvas. Private collection. Reproduced with kind permission from Svay Pisith. © Svay Ken.

every painting, even those depicting events several years apart. He writes that Muan "dressed plainly, liking to wear long black pants made from a soft cotton and a dark shirt with white spots like gecko eggs" and that she "always dressed like this, at a ceremony or in her daily life."[61] By maintaining the same physical appearance for Muan, regardless of the context, Svay Ken underscores his perception of her as humble and hardworking, drawing from his own lived experience of interacting with her as a friend and colleague.

Many of the professional roles that Muan played with Svay Ken, which today would be called curatorial, were new in the Cambodian context at the time but have become common since art has come to be considered contemporary. Corey notes that "perceptions of the 'contemporary' in Cambodian art have been produced through an exchange of local and international criteria; it remains an amorphous conception."[62] When the Reyum Institute of Art and Culture opened in 1998 (under its short-lived original name, Situations), it was the first gallery dedicated to contemporary art in the country.[63] In a similarly momentous "first," when Svay Ken was invited to exhibit his paintings in the 1st Asian Art Triennale, held in 1999 at the Fukuoka Asian Art Museum, he became the first artist from Cambodia to be exhibited in any international biennale since 1959.[64] When the Fukuoka curators visited Phnom Penh in 1998 as research for their exhibition, this was probably the first time Cambodia had been included on the itinerary of the emerging class of international curators in Asia. In the years since then—and especially from the end of the 2000s or the early 2010s onwards—Phnom Penh has become a regular stop for curators doing research trips in the region.

Each of these unfamiliar experiences are reflected in *A Good Friend*, and the series constitutes an invaluable and autotheoretical account of the emergence of new ways of working that are now commonly associated with contemporary art. The dominant affective response to these developments, for Svay Ken, seems to have been discomfort. In paintings that portray the visit from the Fukuoka curators, Svay Ken looks anxious and withdrawn, and he depicts his emotional and professional distance from the visitors in starkly spatial terms. One painting shows Svay Ken and his wife impassively looking on while two curators intently photograph his paintings that hang on the wall in the background of the scene (fig. 4.5). The artist and his wife are standing close together, so their bodies overlap in the picture; this is a compositional indicator of familiarity and intimacy that appears often in Svay Ken's paintings. By contrast, the two curators stand at some distance from the pair, with the one nearest to Tith Yun pointing his elbow toward her as he lifts his arms to use his camera. Neither curator is looking at the artist, and their backs are turned to us as viewers of the painting as well, indicating clearly that they had little if any concern for

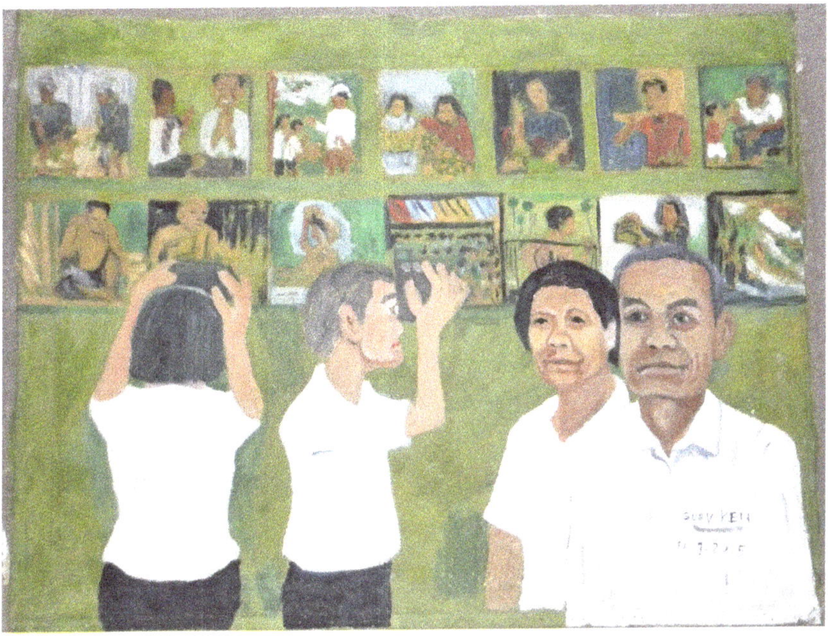

FIGURE 4.5. Svay Ken, from the series *A Good Friend is Hard to Find*, 2005. Oil on canvas. Reproduced with kind permission from Svay Pisith. © Svay Ken.

Svay Ken and were interested only in his paintings. In another painting, the artist is joined by Muan, on the left side of the painting, while four visitors stand together on the right side (fig. 4.6).[65] Again, the artist's closeness to Muan is reflected in their proximity in the composition, and the visitors also appear to be a tight-knit group, their bodies overlapping as well. Between these two groups, however, lies a substantial distance, almost as wide as one of the people. Filling this literal but also clearly allegorical space, Muan's hand is outstretched toward the visitors, and above her hand, Svay Ken has inscribed the word *silpakar*, a Khmer term for "artist." The implication here is that Muan is serving as Svay Ken's translator, both in a linguistic sense and also in larger and more conceptual ways.

The word *silpakar*, which fills the void between Svay Ken and Muan on one side and the visitors on the other side, functions both to keep the two groups separate and also to link them, or bridge the various kinds of distance that separate them. With this inclusion of extra-diegetic text in the image, Svay Ken seems to be autotheorizing about his complex or perhaps even somewhat conflicted attitude toward his participation in international contemporary art exhibitions. He seems to revel in this opportunity but also to feel uneasy about

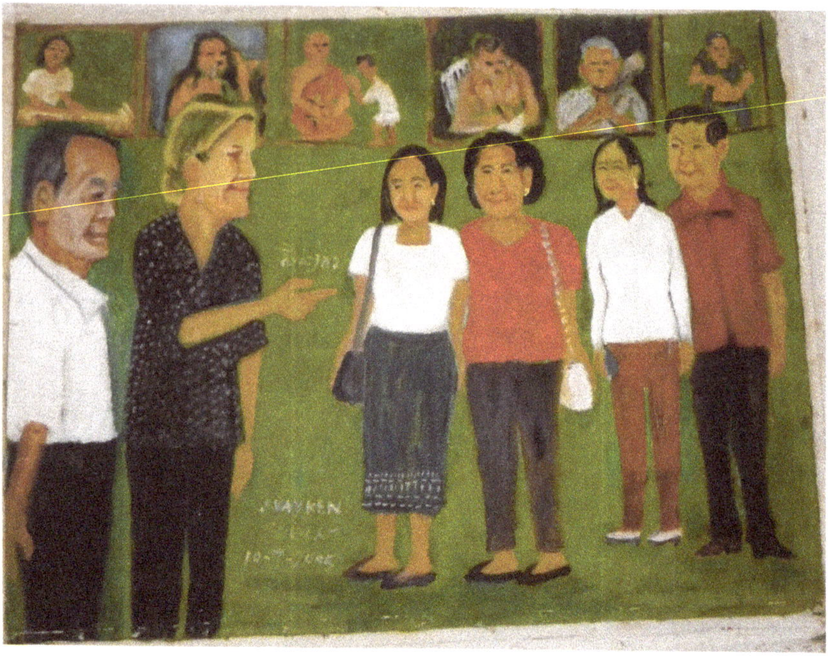

FIGURE 4.6. Svay Ken, from the series *A Good Friend is Hard to Find*, 2005. Oil on canvas. Reproduced with kind permission from Svay Pisith. © Svay Ken.

the process. Being written in Khmer, the word *silpakar* would be unintelligible to most non-Cambodian viewers of the artwork. This language barrier was a repeated cause of stress for the artist, as is evidenced in another painting from the series that shows his anguished face upon receiving a letter from Fukuoka requesting an artist's statement and other text in a short period of time. But despite this language barrier separating them, Svay Ken and the visiting curators had a shared interest in making sense of his practice as being legible as the work of an *artist*, not merely "a person who makes paintings" (in Khmer, a *jāng gumnuu*) or "a modern Cambodian painter" (*vicitrakar*) but an *artist*. It is this word—*silpakar*—that has come to be most commonly used by contemporary artists to describe themselves.

As well as being stressed by the visiting curators and their subsequent long letters in English, Svay Ken was also immensely proud of being included in the Fukuoka exhibition and of all his other international achievements. "In 1999 my name was known throughout Asian art circles," he boasts in the text accompanying *A Good Friend*.[66] He gratefully admits that he owes his fame and success to Muan's assistance, writing that he was "publicized throughout Japan . . .

due to the efforts of Ingrid Muan, who helped me with all her heart and soul with no regard for reward – not even a single cent."[67] As with his repeated expressions of humble gratitude throughout *Painted Stories*, this is a clear indication of Svay Ken's view that his success and wellbeing were due not only to his own labor but also his interdependence with his networks and community.

Moreover, the artist's expressions of gratitude to Muan and his inclusion of the Khmer word *silpakar* in the painting are also signs that Svay Ken was perhaps only able to recognize himself as an artist and be recognized in this way by others because of his connection to an emerging infrastructure of contemporary art. There is a quantum leap from *Painted Stories*, where Svay Ken appears with a single painting in two self-portrait works, to *A Good Friend*, in which as many as ten paintings can be seen hanging on the walls in the background of some works, and in which two scenes of exhibitions show a large and diverse crowd gathered to celebrate Svay Ken's paintings. In the four years between *Painted Stories* and *A Good Friend*, Svay Ken's reputation has advanced to the point of seeing his name known far and wide as an artist.

Svay Ken's paintings offer one of the only substantial visual records of the emergence of contemporary art in Cambodia. Few images of Ingrid Muan circulate in the public realm, and the story of the Reyum Institute of Art and Culture has been addressed only in a small number of scholarly articles.[68] The significance of the 1st Asian Art Triennale in 1999 for the expansion of contemporary art networks through Southeast Asia has been under-explored in scholarship; few exhibition histories of Southeast Asia's art have been attempted by scholars to date.[69] Thus, like other examples of artistic art histories discussed in this book, Svay Ken's autotheoretical accounts of his own participation in this moment are not mere addendums to augment conventional, scholarly versions of these events; rather, they are the first steps toward this history being better known and available for further study.

There is one final way in which Svay Ken's paintings align with other works discussed in this book: his *A Good Friend* exhibition was a kind of offering in tribute to Muan's passing. In this way, the project recalls the examples of honoring in chapter 1. The paintings are dated between March and June 2005, meaning that he began work within two months of Muan's passing on January 29 of that year. But the exhibition opened on January 29, 2006, exactly one year after her death. The printed publication accompanying the exhibition includes a dedication in Khmer and English: ". . . for Ingrid, with love . . ." while the Reyum website declares that "today, we present these paintings as an 'offering.'"[70] More than simply a heartfelt personal and professional tribute to Muan, this offering is also religious and spiritual in nature; in Cambodia, the one-year anniversary of a death is typically marked with special rituals, in keeping with the ancestor worship that prevails in Cambodian practices of Buddhism.[71] Again, this framing of the exhibition as an offering originates not with Svay Ken or any other single individual but rather in the collective and collaborative efforts of the artistic network and community. The Reyum website conveys this through use of the first-person plural, "us" and "we," in the statement: "As for us at Reyum, we are still struggling to find words. Through this exhibition, we wish to say our continuing love for her."[72]

Svay Ken certainly did not think of himself as an art historian and would have been wholly unfamiliar with the concept of autotheorizing, but in his works that I understand in these terms, he clearly had a strong sense of the importance and impact of love and its role in the remembering of the past. If other artistic art histories can be understood as enabling a poetics of inclusion, then Svay Ken's historicizing of his own practice and of the importance of others—chiefly Muan—in enabling it may also be considered a poetics of affection, gratitude, honoring, and love.

Araya Rasdjarmrearnsook: Autotheorizing and Metabolizing Art Histories

I have already mentioned that Araya's uncategorizable 2005 book, *I Am An Artist (He Said)*, could be considered an artwork. "The text *is* an artwork in itself: the process of writing it is also a process of artmaking, the laborious nuts and bolts of which is scrutinised by the writer herself throughout the book." This is the provocation, or speculation, offered by the writer Kong Rithdee, who translated the work.[73] Understood in this way, it is conceivable that there may be no distinction between Araya's artworks and her literary efforts.

Certainly, Araya has taken steps to bring her practices of artmaking and writing closer together. This is particularly clear since her 2018 to 2019 solo exhibition, *An Artist is Trying to Return to 'Being a Writer'*, held at 100 Tonson in Bangkok. Over the course of its six-month run, the exhibition gradually accrued objects in the gallery space; at first, it was almost empty. Araya used the exhibition's duration as a deadline for completing a novel (her longest to date). A review of the exhibition affirmed that it was "a perfect interweaving of her conceptual art and literature" since "Araya's writing and art are intricately knitted together and virtually indistinguishable from one another."[74] In a subsequent solo exhibition held at Tyler Rollins Fine Art in New York, titled *A Novel in Necessity's Rhythm* (2020), Araya affixed to the wall dozens of pages of the incomplete translation of the novel she had written during the 100 Tonson exhibition. She also showed large digital prints on canvas, in which extracts of

FIGURE 4.7. Araya Rasdjarmrearnsook, *Potpourri* (detail), 2019. Digital C print on canvas. Collection of the artist. © Araya Rasdjarmrearnsook, courtesy of the artist.

the text from this translation are layered over each other until they become illegible (fig. 4.7). These works may be a return to some of her earlier and smaller pieces, such as *Writing Has Begun Now* (1991), in which fragments of Thai text emerge from a dense palimpsest of textures and colors (fig. 4.8).

Such works may be considered "asemic writing," which the writer and scholar Peter Schwenger describes as a practice that shows us that "writing is already an image, even if we tend not to recognize it as such." The text in her images offers not "'explanation' but rather something that calls for explanation—that is, a stimulus to thought."[75] Moving from still to moving images, Araya frequently reads from texts in her video pieces, as in her earliest moving image work, *Reading Inaow for Female Corpse* (1997) (fig. 4.9). She also often includes her own writing in the catalogs for her exhibitions. These entanglements of Araya's literary and artistic practices support Kong's suggestion that *I Am An Artist (He Said)* might be an artwork even while it is also a book.

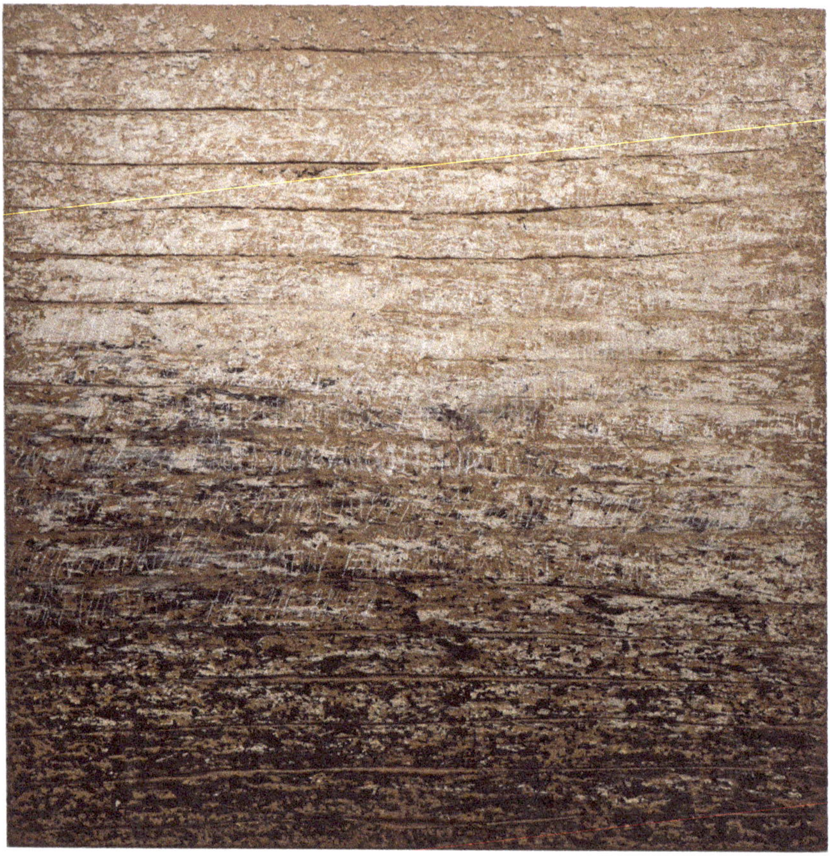

FIGURE 4.8. Araya Rasdjarmrearnsook, *Writing Has Begun Now*, 1991. Tempera sand on wood, 185 x 182 cm. Private collection. © Araya Rasdjarmrearnsook, courtesy of the artist.

Yet this is not the usual understanding of Araya's writing, which is typically considered a practice that is separate from her artmaking even though the two are closely related. Scholars, including David Teh, have noted that she seems better known as a writer than as an artist within Thailand.[76] Indeed, for the reviewer to be able to say that "Araya's writing and art are intricately knitted together" relies on an understanding that they are, in fact, two distinct and separate entities, otherwise they could not be "knitted together." As the same reviewer admitted, they are not totally united but rather only "*virtually* indistinguishable from one another."[77] Similarly, the impact of Araya's artworks that bring her writing into the realm of her artworks—such as those incorporating text into images—relies on an apprehension that artmaking and writing are

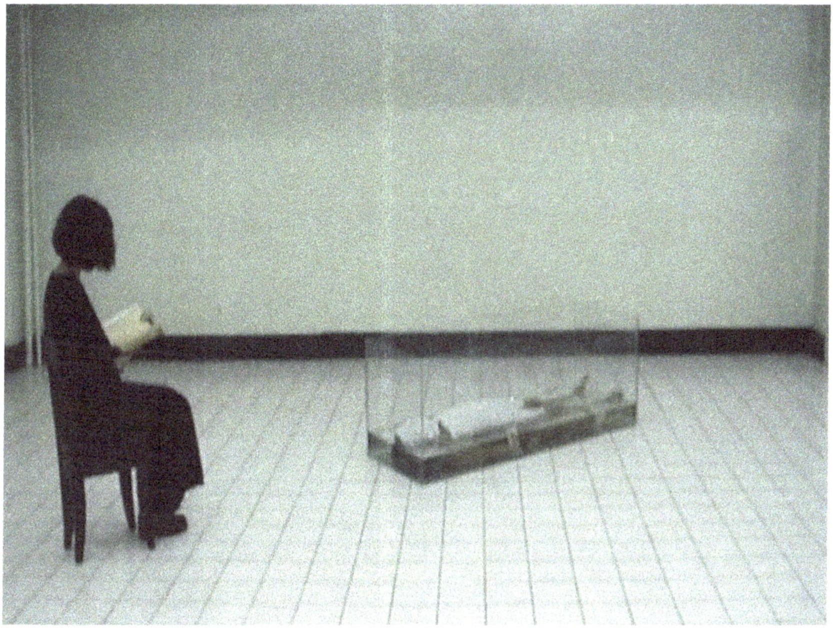

FIGURE 4.9. Araya Rasdjarmrearnsook. *Reading Inaow for Female Corpse*, 1997. Single-channel video with sound, 6 mins 56 secs. Digital still. Collection of National Gallery Singapore. Image courtesy of National Heritage Board, Singapore.

two kinds of practice even though for Araya they are also closely related in form, concept, subject matter, and sensibility.

One area in which the difference between Araya's artmaking and her writing can be most clearly perceived is in the legibility of art history within these practices. Whereas various kinds of art histories—including autobiographical accounts of Araya's own artistic career, as well as accounts of her contemporaries in Thailand and Southeast Asia, and ruminations on historical artists in the region and beyond—are clearly written about in Araya's book and thus can be definitely seen and cited in her artworks, they are less readily recognizable.

Many of Araya's artworks could arguably be considered art-historical insofar as they frequently engage with and rework her own earlier artworks. For example, a case could be made that the layered text prints shown in *A Novel in Necessity's Rhythm* are art-historically engaged with the layered text prints she made three decades earlier, such as *Writing Has Begun Now*. Similarly, a case could be made that the recurring presence of forms resembling coffins or corpses, appearing in works in diverse media across her oeuvre, reflects a kind

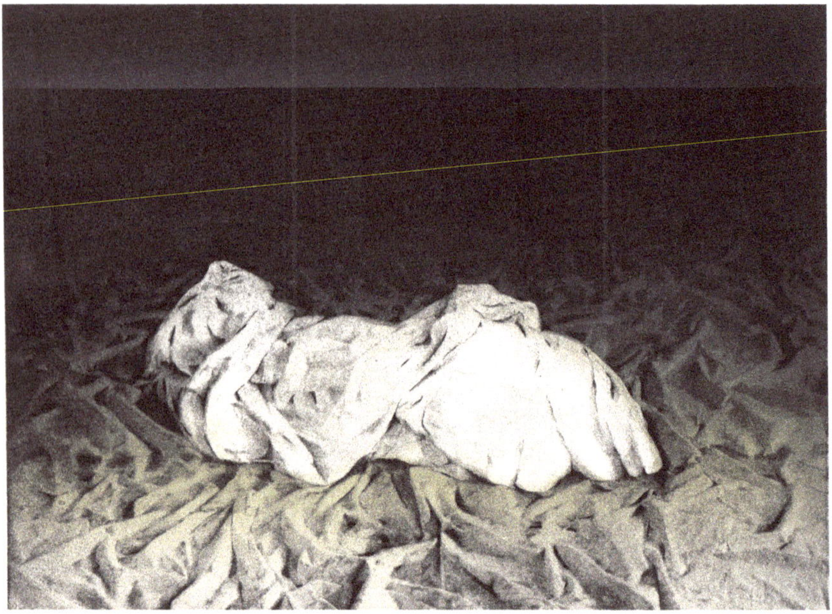

FIGURE 4.10. Araya Rasdjarmrearnsook, *Thinking of Grandmother*, 1987. Intaglio print. © Araya Rasdjarmrearnsook, courtesy of the artist.

of art-historical reworking of this image and form. Coffins and corpses appear or are invoked in works ranging from Araya's earliest intaglio prints, such as *Thinking of Grandmother* (1987) (fig. 4.10), to her sculptural installations, like *Buang (Trap)* (1995), to her videos made with corpses between 1997 and 2005, and many other works besides. Similarly, a case could be made that these works are also thinking and theorizing about artworks by other artists. For example, Araya's integration of text and image could be considered a response to mural paintings in Thai Buddhist temples that depict scenes from the Thai telling of the Ramayana and from the Jataka tales. Her fascination with the depiction and invocation of dead bodies could also be considered a response to Buddhist depictions of suffering or to Western art's tradition of portraiture.

But while all these claims about how Araya's artworks are engaged with art histories may be compelling in different ways, they do not overcome the stubborn, almost "asemic" illegibility of art history within her practice. This makes Araya's artworks quite different from her book. Whereas most readers could quite confidently and easily identify the moments in *I Am An Artist (He Said)* at which Araya is writing about or doing or making art history—such as the examples mentioned earlier in this chapter, which reflect her reliance on a network of peers—it would be difficult or impossible for many viewers to point to the art-historical elements in her artworks. The previous claims about Araya's art being engaged with art histories may be compelling, but they are also confusing and seem to stretch the conceptual category of art history so much that it is at risk of becoming almost meaningless.

Art history is recognizable as art history in works like those I have discussed throughout this book in much the same way that a figure is discernible because of its ground. Art historians discuss figure and ground as mutually constitutive elements in the composition of many images. Distinguishing figure from ground is an important part of the visual perception of a recognizable, nameable shape or form. Figure-ground tests have even been used by psychologists. Images like Edgar Rubin's canonical "figure-ground vase," which depicts the stem of a vase that also appears like the silhouette of two human faces, visually represent the cognitive processes involved in figure-ground perception. Art history in Araya's artworks may be like these silhouettes of the human faces in the image of a vase. Just as it makes its presence known and becomes recognizable as art history—remembering that art histories in Southeast Asia are not the same as versions developed in the North and the West—then, just as quickly, it recedes from view, becoming indistinguishable from the rich and fertile mass of other ideas, references, and forms in her artworks.

Art histories, even histories of Araya's own practice, are elusive in her artworks because they have been metabolized. The figure is no longer separable from the ground—the art histories from the artworks—because they have melted into each other or, perhaps, devoured each other. They have become one, as lovers are said to do, or perhaps they have returned to each other, like the proverbial ashes to ashes, dust to dust. (This sentence, which entwines sex and death with a measure of cliché, is my own attempt at metabolizing Araya's literary aesthetic and sensibility. Just as she spends a good deal of time with art histories, I spend a lot of time with her and her work.) Araya's lifelong preoccupation with art history—with the art of the past and accounts of this art, whether that art is by herself, her peers, or strangers living in distant times and places—is so all-consuming that it has consumed her artistic practice, or her artistic practice has consumed art history. The art historian David Joselit uses the metaphor of metabolism to describe the ability of artworks to "metabolize" concepts (such as Bauman's "liquid modernity") as well as materials (such as food) and transform them into art.[78] This is particularly significant for Joselit because of "the mid-twentieth-century fascination with a collapse or near-collapse of art into life."[79] But whereas artworks made with food may still be recognized as food, Araya's metabolizing of art histories in her works may render them no longer nameable as art histories.

If the elusiveness of the metabolized art histories in Araya's artworks marks the difference between her artistic practice and her book, then the two have in common a devotion to autotheorizing. Just as Araya uses (and plays with) first-person pronouns liberally in *I Am An Artist (He Said)*, so too does she appear in many of her own artworks. For example, in *Reading Inaow with Female Corpse*, her lively presence makes the deadness of the corpse at once haunting in its alterity and comforting in its familiarity. Her melancholy, as she intones a sad-sounding love poem in sing-song Thai (which is presented without subtitles and, in its archaic poetic language, is also difficult for many Thai native speakers to fully grasp), invites imaginative speculation and projection about the mood that might inhere in the otherwise inert dead body. Araya's practice is also autotheorizing in its more oblique references to her own body. The slender, feminine-looking legs carved from heavy, solid timber in *Buang (Trap)*, her largest sculptural installation to date, resemble her own limbs and bring to mind her account of her own experience of being prohibited from pursuing sculpture. She writes:

> When I was 20, I wanted to learn sculpture. The teacher said, 'A woman cannot learn this medium, the work is too difficult for her.'
>
> When I grew up and when I was close to the end of girlhood . . . many of the adult boys said, 'A woman should be worried if she is not married.'
>
> I learnt to be concerned about these two things together. If I could make sculpture, I wouldn't get married or, rather, because for the moment I was not married, I was therefore able to make sculpture.[80]

Viewed in light of this anecdote, the sculptural components in *Buang (Trap)* may be understood not only as Araya's complaint and lament that, as she says, "most women fall into a trap set for them by society," but these same elements may also be her celebration of her own escape from this "trap."[81] This is autotheorizing, to be sure. But is it artistic art histories? Or has the metabolizing of art histories in Araya's art brought us to a new place?

Art history's susceptibility to dissolution—into art, for Araya, but also into curatorial practice in other cases—has been well noted. T. K. Sabapathy observes that in the foreword to an exhibition inaugurating the new National Gallery Singapore (NGS), the museum's director, Eugene Tan, rhetorically collapses the study of the art of the past into the display of that art. "The exhibition is art history and the history of art is the exhibition," Sabapathy says with more than a hint of concern about the slippage he observes in Tan's formulation.[82] NGS opened in 2015, boasting the world's largest public collection of Southeast Asia's modern and contemporary art. One worry might be that if NGS exhibitions are understood to substitute for (or be the same as) art history, then this art history will necessarily privilege artists whose artworks are available for loan, or ideally acquisition, and then display.[83]

If museums metabolize art histories in the way that artists like Araya can, then will curators be invested with too much power to decide not just which practices are deemed worthy of display and study but also which practices are legible as artmaking? I end this chapter with some brief comments about what we might learn from autotheorizing in artistic art histories about who gets to count as an artist.

Autotheorizing in Artistic Art Histories: Who is an Artist?

Svay Ken quite suddenly picked up a brush and started painting at the age of 60. He had no formal training, and he had spent much of his lifetime working in a hotel and supporting his family through other forms of semi-skilled labor. Within six years, he became Cambodia's most internationally celebrated artist, and he remains today by far the most well-known of his generation. Araya Rasdjarmrearnsook is also one of the most internationally exhibited artists of her generation in Thailand, overcoming the sexism she experienced, even the startlingly casual violence of being told: "Well, if she wants to die, she can."[84]

The biographies of both artists defy societal expectations about who can be an artist and what kind of artist a person from the wrong class, background, or gender can be. Moreover, in their artworks and writings, Araya and Svay Ken are autotheorizing about the experience of becoming and being an artist despite all the challenges and obstacles they each faced. Svay Ken's *Painted Stories* shares tales of his successes after initially being mocked for his paintings. Araya's *Buang (Trap)* rejects paternalistic advice cautioning her against making sculpture because it was unwomanly to do so.

Araya's and Svay Ken's life stories and artistic art histories also reveal that a person—even an artist—does not have to live only one life or have only one mind. Painting was one in a long list of professions Svay Ken took up to earn money to support his family and do good deeds. Sculpture is one in a succession of mediums Araya has worked with, and the social position of women is one in a series of topics she has taken up as subject matter in her works. Svay Ken's response to receiving visits and invitations from Japanese curators, as recorded in *A Good Friend*, shows that he could be both stressed and delighted by these encounters. Araya's shifting between masculine and feminine narrating voices, in *I Am An Artist (He Said)*, shows that she could choose what role to play, what persona to publicly adopt.

The two artists suggest that being an artist is not a solitary activity but rather one intimately connected to a fertile network and buzzingly social community of interlocutors, translators, mediators, curators, and friends. Araya's book toggles between accounts of her own life and artmaking and discussions of her peers in Thailand and Southeast Asia, artists of different generations and canonical figures from art history. Svay Ken's works express his gratitude to his supporters and his reliance on figures, such as Ingrid Muan, to make his practice legible as that of an artist in the contemporary sense. Despite their radically divergent life stories and aesthetic approaches, perhaps one thing these two artists have in common—which may be shared by all makers of artistic art histories—is a sustained and sustaining concern with other artists, and other people, as cocreators of their artworks and of the stories that keep them alive.

EPILOGUE

Teaching

In the final scene of *Reincarnations of Shadows*, the "evolving moving-image-poem" Thao Nguyen Phan made "as a tribute to artist Diem Phung Thi" that I discussed in the introduction, the contemporary artist shifts from speculatively narrating specific episodes from the modernist sculptor's life to musing on larger aspects of her attitudes and experiences. Text onscreen declares the contemporary artist Phan's attitude toward the late Diem:

> She is a traditional character,
> a contemporary character,
> historical, fictional,
> for there is this slippage all the time.[1]

In this succinct and poetic statement, Phan is thinking, theorizing, and teaching all at once about the multivalences of artistic sensibility and (post)colonial positionality. Shortly after this, Phan offers her vision of Diem's "way of thinking." The contemporary artist imagines her modernist forebear to "find beauty not in the thing itself but in the patterns of shadows, the light and the darkness, that one thing against another creates." These words are superimposed as subtitles over a tableau of Diem's sculptures, moodily lit from one side, and viewed through a veil of silk that renders them hazy, indistinct, and seductive (fig. E.1). This imagery invites a literal interpretation of Phan-as-Diem's words about "patterns of shadows," but an allegorical reading is also possible, which views these "shadows" not only as the result of light but also as an effect of interactions between different artists and artworks. In this video, and in Phan's

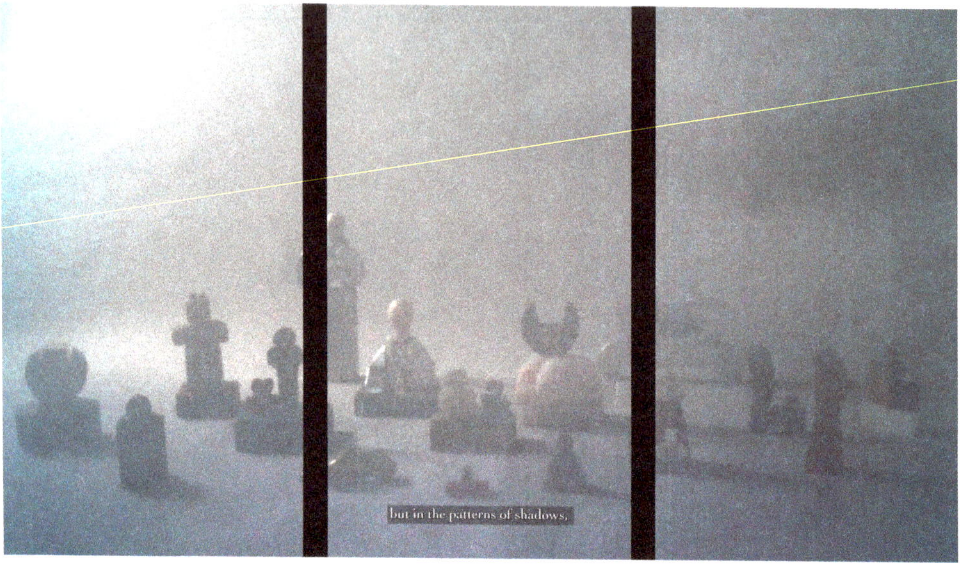

FIGURE E.1. Thao Nguyen Phan, *Reincarnations of Shadows*, 2023–ongoing. Three-channel video with sound, 16 mins, 50 seconds. Digital still. © Thao Nguyen Phan, courtesy of the artist.

other projects and writings about Diem Phung Thi, Phan appears interested not only in the modernist sculptor's artwork as a "thing itself" but also as a source of illumination and insight into her own practice, which spans different media and epitomizes a distinctly contemporary sensibility.

In this book, I have also been alive to and concerned with the effects of interactions between contemporary artists and their modernist forebears, which Phan terms "the light and the darkness, that one thing against another creates." More specifically, in this book I have approached artistic art histories as a mode of practice chiefly concerned not only with research but also with thinking and theorizing about the art of the past and thereby about the possibilities for decolonizing art-historical knowledge.

Yet while artists are thinking and theorizing within their artistic art histories, in these works, they are also *teaching*. In this epilogue, I turn my attention to the teaching that happens within these practices and examine this phenomenon in relation to the pedagogical turn within contemporary art (in which Southeast Asia's artists and collectives have played a particularly prominent role). I discuss the early work of Singapore-based artist Ho Tzu Nyen (1976–) while also returning to the work of Araya Rasdjarmrearnsook. By using the term *teaching* in place of its various alternatives, I am not intending to "privilege the theme of teaching over that of learning" or to suggest a hierarchy like "the adult/child distinction."[2] Rather, I see all teaching as being always already a process of learning and necessarily grounded in practice and research. As in the rest of this book, I use the present participle verb, teaching, to emphasize that this is a provisional and continuous process, including in its contributions to always ongoing efforts of epistemic decolonizing.

In what follows, I show that artistic art histories offer some inspiring examples of individual artists being highly effective educators within their artworks. By focusing on education within the practices of individual artists, I offer a counterpoint to the recent emphasis on collective pedagogy in Southeast Asia. This has been most prominent in the practices of the Jakarta-based collectives ruangrupa (est. 2000) and Gudskul (est. 2018), both of which reached their largest and most international publics at documenta 15, which ruangrupa curated in 2022. Other education-focused groups in Indonesia include Kunci Study Forum & Collective, based in Yogyakarta, who initiated the School of Improper Education as "a long-term collective learning process" in 2016.[3] The project functions, in part, to critique "the unspoken competitive culture in universities" and "the feudal-style structure [that] is entrenched in the education process."[4] These and other projects in Indonesia echo the emphasis on "knowledge sharing and learning together" at other collective-run education spaces elsewhere in Southeast Asia, such as at Sa Sa Art Projects (2010–2024) in Phnom Penh.[5] In the Indonesian context, artists' collectives known as *sanggar* are one important precursor of these contemporary teaching projects.[6] Elsewhere, an earlier manifestation of a similar sensibility is the series of events known as Midnight University, organized by artists including Mit Jai Inn as part of the Chiang Mai Social Installation festivals held during the late 1990s.[7] Taken together, these initiatives all indicate the prominence of collective learning among artists in Southeast Asia; by contrast, the educational activities of individual artists in the region have been less well-studied.

In this epilogue, I propose that art history as a scholarly discipline may be a site of epistemic injustice that may be best addressed through an intersectionality that is necessarily as political as it is poetic in its sensibility. With these latter comments, I speculatively conclude the book by pointing to the larger implications of the concept of artistic art histories, beyond the specific practices in Southeast Asia that I have discussed, suggesting that thinking, theorizing, and teaching are always ways of learning and knowing. Thus, I end this book by returning to its beginning: specifically, to my intention to contribute to the ongoing task of deprovincializing Southeast Asia's art and art histories as part of both decolonizing the discipline and bringing the art of the past back to life.

Ho Tzu Nyen: Teaching on Television

In 2005, the Arts Central subset of the Central channel (a nationwide free-to-air television broadcaster in Singapore) aired a four-part series by the artist Ho Tzu Nyen. Titled *4x4: Episodes of Singapore Art*, the series comprises four segments that blur the distinction between video art, documentary television, conceptual art, and pedagogy. Each twenty-three-minute episode concentrates on a single artwork by a different Singapore artist, ranging from *Tropical Life* (1959), a well-known painting by Cheong Soo Pieng (1917–1983), to a little-known, unrealized conceptual proposal by Lim Tzay Chuen (1972–) titled *Alter #11* (2002). In a recent interview, Ho describes *4x4* as "infiltrating" Singapore's state-dominated television infrastructure "and us[ing] its outreach to extend my work beyond the gallery."[8] He is not alone in perceiving television to be a fertile site for cultural contestation. In Indonesia, for example, the writer Veven Sp. Wardhana (1959–2013) dedicated extensive works of journalism and experimental fiction to "the social role and impact of television."[9] A widespread, sustained, and artistically sophisticated interest in television across Southeast Asia may in part be explained by a sense that "the distinction between popular culture and high culture is less evident in everyday life" in urban centers across the region.[10]

Ho's *4x4: Episodes of Singapore Art* epitomizes the doing and making of artistic art histories in Southeast Asia, perhaps more clearly, unequivocally, and unambiguously than any other artwork I have discussed in this book. Each episode features research, thinking, and theorizing about the art of the past. Most episodes include footage from archives, lingering close-up shots of artworks, and other techniques typical of most art-historical work. The series is clearly made in dialogue with scholarly art historians; ideas and information in at least one episode predate the publication of a scholarly article on a related topic by Kevin Chua, an art historian working in an American university (and Ho's friend and frequent interlocutor).[11] Two years after the series aired, Ho completed a master's dissertation on a canonical event in Singapore's modern art history, suggesting that the research done for the artwork may have been linked to research done for academic purposes.[12] In a contemporaneous review of the *4x4* series, the curator Russell Storer observed that "with a few key exceptions, art historical research in Singapore has largely been borne by artists themselves, documenting, archiving and writing about the practices of their peers."[13] While Ho's was probably the first artwork to take the form of a national television broadcast in Singapore, the artist's interest in art-historical research was evidently carrying on an established tradition among artists in the country and across the region.

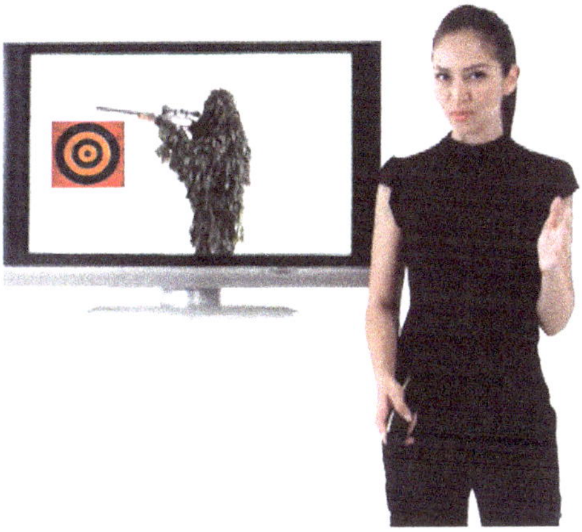

FIGURE E.2. Ho Tzu Nyen, *4x4 - Episodes of Singapore Art: Episode 4: Lim Tzay Chuen - The Invisible Artwork*, 2005, HD Video, 23 min. © Ho Tzu Nyen, image courtesy of the artist and Kiang Malingue.

As well as being a particularly clear exemplar of the mode of practice I call artistic art histories, Ho's *4x4* is also centrally concerned with teaching. The episodes center on actors who are filmed alongside screens displaying images and/or text, directly addressing the audience via the camera (fig. E.2). This format is familiar from many educational talk show programs on TV but also recalls the setup of a typical classroom, in which a teacher or professor directly addresses the students. More specifically, the display of images on the screen recalls the projection of slides in an art history class. Whereas most classrooms are led by a single instructor, each of the *4x4* episodes feature two actors—one man, one woman—who take turns to describe and analyze the artwork. They frequently differ in their interpretations and, at times, even interrupt each other. Disagreements are met with further, more vehement disagreements; questions are answered with other questions. This feels less like the kind of debate I am familiar with from TV talk shows and more like the kind of discussion I hope for in my art history seminars and tutorials.

Ho's interest in teaching may also have been informed by the time he spent in classrooms immediately prior to beginning work on *4x4*. Throughout 2004—the year before making the TV series—Ho had been a regular fixture in Singapore secondary schools and junior colleges, delivering performance lectures about Singapore's early history. This pedagogical program was adapted from the artist's installation, titled *Utama – Every Name in History is I* (2003). From this teaching experience, as well as from his own studies in Singapore and his dialogues with artists, curators, and scholars, Ho would have been acutely aware of the near-total absence of art history in school curricula in Singapore at the time. Ho made *4x4* during a period of what T. K. Sabapathy would later term "an entrenched, unyielding, systematic refusal to recognize the study of art as an academic discipline."[14] Ho's decision to not only make art history the subject of his artwork but also to make the teaching of art history central to his aim in *4x4* is best understood as the artist's intervention in this context. The anthropologist Michael M. J. Fischer proposes that "artists have the initial advantage [because] they are allowed to present unfinished, enigmatic, and unexplained works."[15] Considering Ho's success in teaching Singapore's art histories when almost no schools or universities were doing so, I would add that artists may also have an advantage over scholars because they are often able to sidestep (or, in Joanne Leow's terms, "circumvent"[16]) educational bureaucracies and communicate with publics through other channels.

The format of the teaching in *4x4* is also significant; by featuring two hosts who frequently disagree with each other, Ho is insisting on the possibility for multiple and conflicting understandings of a work of art. Although this may seem obvious, the notion that there can be many right answers to a question about a work of art may not always be so readily accepted in the context of the Singapore education system, which has been characterized as having "considerable rigidities caused by tracking at the secondary level."[17] According to another report, "pupils with poorer grades are streamed into the 'arts stream.'"[18] In the context of this apparent disdain for arts-related education, the violence with which *4x4*'s male host disagrees with the female host throughout the series—culminating in a grotesque blood-stained megaphone in one horror-style scene in the final episode—suggests a hostility to the basic idea that art can be understood in widely differing ways. Although the Singapore education system has changed and improved substantially in the years since Ho made *4x4*, this was the prevailing discourse when the work aired on national TV. A dialogue, such as the one Ho choreographs between the two hosts in each of the *4x4* episodes, often functions to cultivate a receptiveness to the open-ended quality of art. In a 2012 interview, Ho agreed with the suggestion that the "perpetually arguing" actors in *4x4* are "an attempt to dialectically open up interpretations of the artworks in question."[19] This echoed the artist's suggestion, almost a decade earlier in 2005, that "the two hosts form an almost dialectical pair."[20]

The fact that the dialogues in *4x4* are always between a man and a woman has led to some criticisms of the work. Both Storer and the critic Lee Weng Choy have described the format of the episodes as a "binary structure," with Storer noting that "this aspect attracted some criticism as essentialist."[21] Regrettably, the substance of that criticism has not been documented. What has been well recorded, however, are the artist's intentions in setting up what he calls an "oscillating 'hosts' system." In a text published around the same time as the *4x4* broadcast, Ho explains:

> I try to create a system whereby the authority of the 'host' is constantly questioned. First, I split the 'host' into two (or more) figures, perpetually in conflict with each other. It is through their exchanges that they provide information to the viewers . . .
>
> At any one time, only one of the hosts appears. They never appear together. For example, when the male addresses the absent female host, he directs his addresses to the camera. By implication, the viewer will sense that the female host is on the other side of the camera, which is to say – in the space of the viewer. By addressing the camera, the male host therefore simultaneously addresses the viewer and the female host. When the female host appears on screen and speaks, she likewise addresses the camera directly – and the viewer's position then oscillates into that of the male host.[22]

Informed by this account, I understand the effect of the *4x4* episodes being structured as a series of disagreements or dialogues as not to construct a "binary" but rather to strengthen the teaching aims of the series by destabilizing the authority of the host-as-teacher, instead emphasizing the agency of the audience-as-student. Whereas a binary solidifies and stresses differences between two positions, the "oscillating" system, as Ho explains it, seeks instead to constantly undermine the power of *both* hosts to determine the meaning of artworks and to repeatedly remind the viewers of their own ability to actively and critically engage with the claims made by both hosts.

Another feature of *4x4*'s "oscillating 'hosts' system" that further destabilizes the authority of the two hosts as educators is their mutation throughout the series. Despite recurring in all four episodes and being recognizable and well-known TV actors who appear in the same attire throughout, neither of the two hosts are consistent in their personality or in their attitude or approach to the artworks presented in *4x4*. In some moments, the woman performs a stereotypically feminine role, offering a more emotionally informed analysis while the man performs a supposedly masculine role, offering a more cerebral interpretation. But at other times, and just as often, their roles switch, and the man becomes hysterical while the woman calmly offers facts and historical context. This dissolving of the distinctions between the two hosts further guards against the danger of the structure becoming binary in nature and reinforces the potential of *4x4* for effective teaching.

Araya Rasdjarmrearnsook: Teaching the Dead

Ho's interest in undermining the perceived masculine/feminine binary and the authority of the host-teachers in *4x4* echoes the approach taken by Araya Rasdjarmrearnsook in her book *I Am An Artist (He Said)*, which was published in Thailand in the same year that Ho's series screened in Singapore. As I discussed in chapter 4, I *Am An Artist (He Said)* is structured as a dialogue between masculine and feminine narrators—rendered in English as "He Said" and "She Said"—who are just as chimerical and unstable as the two hosts in Ho's episodes. Their personalities seem to infect each other and switch and sometimes perhaps even merge.[23] Although they are never named and are always identified by the same pair of gendered personal pronouns, Araya's narrators seem to number not just two but many. The ambiguity here—when reading Araya's book, I am often uncertain which persona is narrating at any given moment—heightens the sense of dissolution and guards against the danger of a binaristic reading. This further curtails the perceived power of Araya's narrators, shifting the agency instead to the reader. Similarly, Ho varies the actors who appear in different episodes of *4x4*, further diminishing their aura of authority. The various hosts all speak with a similar accent and affect that is recognizably distinctive to TV actors in Singapore. This underscores their artifice: they are clearly actors playing the role of teachers, and as such, viewers may feel reluctant to wholly defer to their views and feel more empowered to cultivate their own opinions.

Araya and Ho were unaware of each other's projects, yet I understand both to offer generative theoretical and educational models for how to think beyond the easy assumption of a binary whenever two interlocutors are involved, especially if these roles are cast as masculine and feminine, with actors or narrators playing the role of teachers. Araya's book appeared in 2005 in Thai (a language Ho does not read) while Ho's series was broadcast on Singapore national television (and thus inaccessible to Araya in Thailand). Yet the structural similarities and atmospheric resonances between Araya's and Ho's projects are striking. Both artists seem aware that teaching often requires a kind of back-and-forth dialogue between two positions or two speakers. This awareness may be informed by both artists' classroom experiences: Ho's during lecture performances at schools across Singapore in 2004 and Araya's as a professor at Chiang Mai University. Rather than separating their teaching from their artworks, Araya in *I Am An Artist (He Said)* and Ho in *4x4* seem to be exploring possibilities for teaching *within* their practices, specifically within artistic art histories. This may be a precursor to more recent teaching projects initiated by art collectives elsewhere in Southeast Asia.

Araya writes extensively about education in her book; she even suggests that "the only place left to talk about art is in the art class."[24] This pithy statement is elaborated as a challenge to the tendency for the market to reduce art to numbers and for museums or institutions to reduce art to logistics. But for Ho, who in 2005 wanted not just to talk about art but rather to talk specifically about art history, there were very few classrooms available in which the subject could be discussed. His turn to artistic art histories and his embrace of teaching in *4x4* thus poetically and polemically creates a space for critical discussion of the art of Singapore's past. Since, as Sabapathy has argued, histories of art in Southeast Asia are entwined with efforts at self-determination and decolonization, Ho's creation of a televisual art history classroom is also engendering a zone of epistemic decolonization, in which new interpretations of canonical artworks like Cheong Soo Pieng's can emphasize the artist's imbrication in the rapidly changing social context of Singapore during the period leading up to and following independence from colonial rule.[25]

As individual artists who are teaching within their works, both Araya and Ho grapple with the danger of seeming overly authoritative. This is less of a risk in the collective educational projects mentioned above, which emphasize nonhierarchical sharing and collaboration. Ho and Araya contend with this challenge head-on by proposing ways of teaching that are open and dialogic even though embedded within a single artist's practice. The repeated undermining of the stability and authority of the hosts-as-teachers in Ho's *4x4* and the narrators-as-teachers in Araya's *I Am An Artist (He Said)* are joined by other rhetorical devices and techniques that further modulate the artists' claims to pedagogical authority.

As well as staging a seemingly endless cascade of questions and disagreements between the two hosts in *4x4*, another way in which Ho decenters his own pedagogical authority is by diffusing and dispersing the project across several different formats and media. Alongside the broadcast, another component of *4x4* took the form of a live public event. Concurrent with the series screening on national television, the artist organized a forum and accompanying exhibition at the Substation, a prominent Singapore art and theater space.[26] Describing the event, Storer proposes that "it was perhaps with a tongue in his cheek that Ho put together the forum consisting of art historians, critics and curators . . . this was a humorous gesture, performed in the Substation's theatre, with the participants acting out their roles as Ho directed from above."[27] While Storer's account emphasizes the theatrical qualities of the event, the presence of several professors among its lineup also gave the forum a distinctly educational quality. In the absence of many art history classrooms in Singapore at the time, Ho was repurposing an arts and theater venue into a space for teaching and learning with artistic art histories. Yet instead of then assuming the role of teacher (as he had in his *Utama* lecture performances), Ho invited several educators to share the stage.

Araya, for her part, appears in many of her video artworks in roles that recall her off-screen position as professor. In several of the videos featuring corpses, made between 1997 and 2005, she reads to dead bodies; the artist appears in a seated position (and sometimes standing or pacing) while the corpse or corpses are lain on the floor or on a trolley. The setup resembles a teacher reading to students in a classroom in some works, and in others, a parent at a child's bedside: scenarios in which it is usual to encounter one person actively speaking and/or reading while others listen (or don't listen) silently and inertly. Araya's interest in simulating educational environments culminated in her videos featuring corpses that were presented at the 2005 Venice Biennale, which include *The Class* (2005) (fig. E.3). In these works, the artist fully embraces the classroom connotations of the situation she orchestrates and appears in front of a blackboard, explicitly "teaching" the nameless corpses who are positioned like students.

Araya's videos made with corpses facilitate a kind of conversation beyond the grave. This radically extends the tendency of both Ho and Araya to structure the teaching in their artworks around a dialogue and exchange of ideas, belying their status as individual artists (rather than collectives). Much of the humor of Araya's videos made with corpses—particularly in *The Class*—is derived from the silence of the corpses: their inability to participate in the discussion. Feminist art historians Jacqueline Millner and Catriona Moore characterize Araya's works as a "form of ironic pedagogy" which, unlike "conventional pedagogical methods," successfully avoid "imposing strictures on the capacity to think imaginatively."[28] The irony, of course, is that Araya teaching corpses is also actually Araya literally talking to herself. This may also be an instance of her self-sufficiency as an individual artist often ostracized by the male-dominated Thai art world.[29]

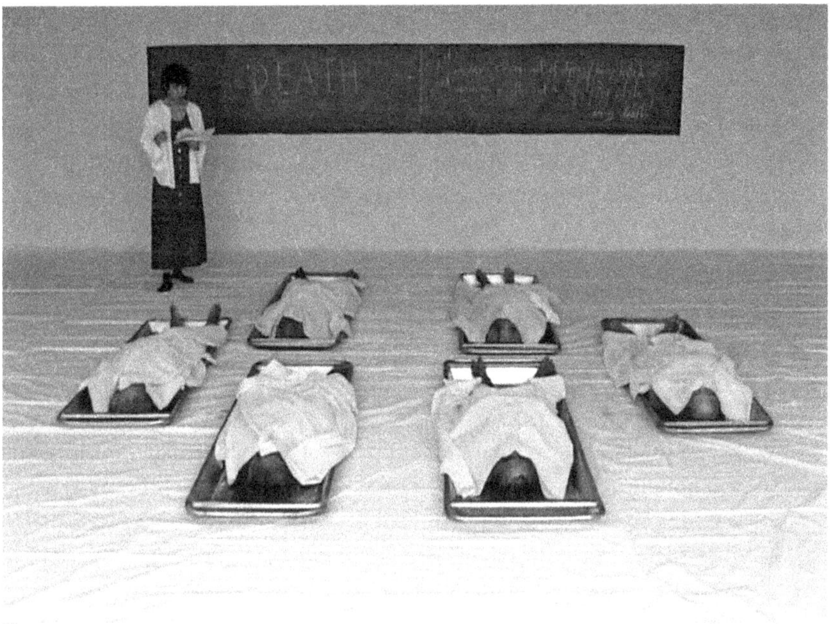

FIGURE E.3. Araya Rasdjarmrearnsook, *The Class*, 2005. Single-channel video with sound, 16 mins 30 secs. © Araya Rasdjarmrearnsook, courtesy of the artist.

Yet Araya also enlarges the scope of the teaching in her works to encompass other knowledge systems that exceed the rational understandings that usually dominate formalized education. She maintains that the corpses in her videos are communicating with her in some deeper and nonverbal way; the artist claims to have felt, at some bodily level, the participation of the dead bodies in her videos. Araya learned from them, she says. When asked in a 2007 interview about her role as a teacher, Araya's response was: "I think that this job could develop people."[30] An obvious reading of this statement would be that the artist thinks that her students are "developing" through the experience of learning. But with Araya's insistence that even dead bodies can communicate, I reread her claim as encompassing her own development through the experience of teaching. Araya thinks that the job of teaching can "develop people", including not only her students but also herself as a teacher and an artist.

This conception of artistic teaching as a process of learning may be self-evident, but it is also highly significant. Most educators would readily agree that they have learned from their students or from the experience of preparing and delivering lessons, even about subjects that may be very familiar to them. This is an experience I have enjoyed, particularly when I teach material that is closely related to my research. When as educators we feel that we are learning while teaching, the time spent in a classroom takes on an added value beyond being a job that enables us to do our research. Artists also often speak of practice as a journey of discovery. What Araya calls "artmaking" is also a way of learning.

Teaching, Learning, and Knowing (As Honoring, Citing, Staging, and Autotheorizing)

At the beginning of this epilogue, I proposed that when artists are thinking and theorizing in their artistic art histories, they are also teaching. When artists are learning by doing various kinds of art-historical research (with methods ranging from conventional to experimental), they are learning about the art of the past and also teaching by sharing their discoveries and insights by making their artworks. This becomes self-evident only when these artworks are made accessible by appearing in exhibitions, publications, or other settings for the socializing of artistic practice with publics. All these activities and processes—thinking, theorizing, learning, teaching, and sharing with publics—are essential to the process of reanimating and subjectivizing the art of the past, bringing it back to life. In other words, contemporary artists making artworks about the under-studied modernisms of Southeast Asia are always already teaching, even while they are also honoring, citing, staging, and autotheorizing.

Honoring, citing, staging, and autotheorizing—the partial and provisional list of continuous and contingent strategies in artistic art histories that I discussed in this book—are all ways of researching, thinking, and theorizing. The creatively critical, playfully political, and poetically inclusive ways in which artists do art-historical work in Southeast Asia draws on the discipline's unique history here. As I have argued, art histories and creative practices have always been tightly entwined in Southeast Asia, ever since the first books on modern art appeared in the 1960s, both of which were written by artists. In the decades since, artists and curators have continued to write important and influential texts. Artistic art histories—within artworks, rather than writings—are nourished by this tradition of the discipline in Southeast Asia; they grow from this regional way of working and, in turn, contribute to the continuation of art-historical work that is quirky, queer, and often refreshingly unconcerned with the disciplinary norms of the North and the West. While studying and learning, artists doing and making art histories by honoring, citing, staging, and autotheorizing (and in other ways as well) are also teaching and imagining new possibilities for the forms their work may take.

All these activities and processes of doing and making are also forms of decolonial, feminist, and queer knowing. I could propose that artistic art histories produce knowledge, but I prefer to say that they enable and enact knowing; they reveal knowing to be a provisional and continuous practice rather than a fixed or final state. This conception of knowledge and knowing as gradual and tentative, fragmentary and partial is aligned with both decolonial and feminist conceptions of epistemology. Scholars of decolonial theory have noted that knowledges from Asia and other parts of the decolonizing world or Global South have been "disparaged by Western authority" and "channeled as religious or mystic [and] cast away as eternally peripheral."[31] In an influential study, others propose that "to decolonize knowledge and the methodologies by which it is produced" requires "decolonizing both the knowledge of the colonized and the knowledge of the colonizer."[32] This leads to an understanding of "ecologies of knowledges" that encompass different ways of knowing.[33] Similarly, the feminist scholar Lorraine Code advocates "facing uncertainty, approaching the world with blurred vision," as these are necessary for the difficult process of "rethinking the epistemic basis" and "breaking out of embedded categories and labeling practices."[34] Code performs a Derridean deconstruction of the binary between objective and subjective knowledges. Like Donna Haraway, she understands knowledge as situated and partial.[35] Code rejects the idea that objectivity and subjectivity are "dichotomous, polarized [and] fixed and rigid," instead proposing the "possibilities of reciprocal interaction between and among such constructs."[36] Despite their differences, I see these and other articulations of decolonial and feminist theories of knowledge as related in their resistance to a colonial and patriarchal idea of knowledge as singular, fixed, and final. Knowing is always situated, always ongoing, and perpetually subject to revision and reimagination.

By enacting ways of knowing that are provisional and continuous, artistic art histories enable contemporary artists in Southeast Asia and its diasporas to revisit and reimagine the art of the past, perceiving it as being present in their own lives and pertinent to their present-day worldviews. This brings the art of the past back to life—making it lively and relating it to lived experience—and it also holds space for a kind of epistemic loosening, or perhaps even liberation. Colonial ways of knowing are tight, limited, and oppressive; colonized subjects are "prevented by dominant knowledge from representing the world as one's own and in one's own terms." This is because "the Eurocentric epistemological North [is conceived] as the only source of valid knowledge . . . the only valid understanding of the world is the Western understanding of the world."[37] Artistic art histories in Southeast Asia—and my approach to analyzing these practices throughout this book—typically follow a path "of partially engaging with Western theory to subvert Western theory's position of authority."[38] The scholar May Adadol Ingawanij similarly advocates "liv[ing] artistically with theories of whatever provenance."[39]

Yet by entwining theory with practice—knowing by doing and making—artistic art histories also enable a divergence from or even transcendence of this path. Writing in 1986, the artist and critic Nguyễn Quân used the conjoined term "art theory-criticism" (*lý luận-phê bình* in Vietnamese) and stated that "people usually complain that art theory-criticism in our country always lags behind artistic creation."[40] In these practices, the art theory and criticism that Nguyễn Quân already conjoins are also attached to practice, or what he calls "artistic creation." This means that as well as "theory-criticism [being] considered nourishment for the artistic mind," the "artistic mind"—which I characterize as knowing by doing and making—can also be nourishing for "theory-criticism."[41] In other words, artistic art histories conjoin artmaking with thinking, theorizing, and historicizing about art. These artworks are also art histories, as art histories can also be artworks. They are like *art-art-history-theory-criticism-pedagogy.*

As well as being a source of nourishment and aesthetic inspiration, the thinking, theorizing, teaching, and especially knowing in art is also political. Its politics are inseparable from its poetics, including its intimation of a poetics of inclusion. There are at least two aspects to this politics. The first I have already mentioned: valuing artistic practice as a way of knowing is a challenge to colonial and patriarchal epistemologies, a refusal to understand knowledge as singular and certain. The second aspect is larger and more abstract and thus may encompass the first.

Valuing artists as a source of art-historical insight counters the risks of epistemic injustice in art history as a discipline—or in academia and museums more generally—which may view artists as objects to be studied rather than as subjects who offer their own methods and theories for research. Epistemic injustice is a term used to describe "a wrong done to someone specifically in their capacity as a knower." The philosopher Miranda Fricker proposes two main kinds of epistemic injustice: testimonial injustice, which "occurs when prejudice causes a hearer to give a deflated level of credibility to a speaker's word," and hermeneutical injustice, which "puts someone at an unfair disadvantage when it comes to making sense of their social experiences."[42] Although he does not use the term, the historian Theara Thun addresses epistemic injustice when he advocates that scholars take seriously the vernacular-language chronicles and other manuscript sources that have been typically overlooked in Western history writing. "Western notions of history never entirely displaced the premodern indigenous conceptions of the past," he argues.[43] Often, colonial and patriarchal prejudices like racism and sexism are at fault, but epistemic injustices are not solely caused by these bigotries and can also arise from a host of other biases. The concept emerged as part of philosophy and theory's ethical turn.[44]

Bringing these philosophical ideas into lively contact with contemporary art and discourses prompts me to ask: what disciplinary norms within scholarly art history and museums might perpetuate epistemic injustice by discounting, disregarding, or derogating artists as sources of art-historical thinking, theorizing, teaching, and knowing? How might art history also participate in an ethical turn while retaining its poetics?

Responding to epistemic injustice may rely on forms of intersectionality. Although the term intersectionality is typically attributed to the Black feminist scholar Kimberlé Crenshaw, the concept significantly predates her scholarly work.[45] The Black feminist scholar Patricia Hill Collins insists on "the importance of intersectionality *before* its academic discovery" and argues that an over-emphasis on Crenshaw's role "assigns value to intersectionality when it became an academic commodity," thereby disregarding the concept's importance to "social movements," including "desegregating of colleges and universities."[46] Collins cautions against intersectionality being reduced to a "buzzword" because this perpetuates "testimonial quieting and smothering dissent" by delegitimizing politicized knowledge.[47] For me, the salience of Collins's critique of academic discourse around intersectionality is that she reveals that an over-investment in an idea as an "academic commodity" (divorced from ways of knowing outside academia) also contributes to an epistemic injustice that downplays some forms of knowledge—and some knowers—as less valuable than others.

With this in mind, I want to be clear in acknowledging that I did not invent artistic art histories, and I am not the first to recognize the importance of artists in thinking, theorizing, teaching, and knowing about Southeast Asia's modern and contemporary art. Although I may have coined the term artistic art histories, these kinds of artistic practice existed long before I named them, both in Southeast Asia and beyond. Just as it is important to recognize intersectional activist practices before Crenshaw's academic work, so too do I affirm that artists were making artistic art histories—and thinking and theorizing within and about these practices—long before I wrote this book.

My aim in explicating artistic art histories and in writing this book has been to amplify the voices of artists in Southeast Asia and center their insights and ways of thinking and theorizing. I hope this helps contribute to the ongoing decolonizing of art-historical work by resisting institutional and discursive structures that may quieten artists' testimonies. I understand artists' testimonies to include what has been called "representing the world as one's own and in one's own terms."[48] What artists say and do—including within their artworks—matters, as it can be an expression of individual, cultural, and collective self-determination. It also matters because of its aesthetic form, enabling a poetics of inclusion. What artists say and do in their artworks matters because practice and research are interrelated, and sometimes even indistinguishable.

In affirming that art history as it is practiced in and for Southeast Asia differs from the art history of the North and the West, I recognize that many (perhaps most) of the foundational scholars of Southeast Asia's modern and contemporary art have also been artists. These include Marco Hsü (author of the first book on the subject, published in Chinese in 1963), Ingrid Muan (founder of the Reyum Institute of Arts and Culture in Phnom Penh, discussed in chapter 4), meLê yamomo (theorist of staging, discussed in chapter 3), and many others. Other key scholars have also practiced as curators. These include T. K. Sabapathy and Patrick D. Flores, whose ideas have been ever-present guides throughout this book. While focusing on the forms of practice I call artistic art histories, my work here has also been enabled by the creativity, eccentricity, and liveliness I find in the work of many scholarly art historians, including those who also practice as artists or curators.

Back to Life

I end this book by returning to its beginning: revisiting three images that have guided me, provisionally and continuously, and that reorient us back to life. This reanimation and subjectivization is also an intersectional process and practice, and in its intersectionality, it is poetic and political.

As I mentioned in the introduction, when Vann Molyvann affirmed his aspiration to "bring tradition and heritage *back to life*" he was not only advocating a new way to imagine a "modernity" that was not "inspired superficially by Western ideas that destroy all traces of the past."[49] He was also calling for concrete action in the realms of both pedagogy and research. In 1965—just over a decade after Cambodia's independence—Molyvann oversaw the transformation of the École des arts cambodgiens (School of Cambodian Arts), established under colonial rule, into the Sākalavidyālăy Bhūmind Vicitr Silpà (Royal University of Fine Arts). Alongside the establishment of faculties and teaching curricula, he announced the formation of a new research institute. "Research teams are at present being sent into the provinces for the purpose of taking photographs, films and tape-recordings of everything of artistic interest," Molyvann explained, "with priority accorded to that part of the Khmer artistic heritage which is in danger of being lost," including studying "mural paintings in bad condition [and] stories and legends hitherto passed down by word of mouth." He described this task as having "importance . . . only exceeded by its urgency."[50] The liveliness of the art of the past, for Molyvann, lay in its relevance to research, practice, and teaching, and to the intersections between these ways of doing and making.

When Sara Ahmed declared her desire "to bring theory *back to life*," she was calling for a renewed recognition that "the personal is theoretical," as I also mentioned in the introduction.[51] Theory and lived experience are not separate; the presence of the past in the present is also instructive and inspiring. Liveliness lies in the interactions between these different modalities of time and ways of knowing. As Ahmed writes, "intersectionality can bring us back to life because it is full of life."[52] Artistic art histories may be considered a kind of aesthetic and epistemic intersectionality. In bringing together embodied, multisensory, and other ways of decolonial and feminist knowing, thinking, and theorizing, these practices are teaching us about the liveliness of the art of the past.

Finally, Thao Nguyen Phan's *Reincarnations of Shadows* is also teaching us that Diem Phung Thi's sculptures are not dead but alive. When Phan filmed herself presenting a joss stick as an offering to a sculpture by Diem, her gesture recalled funerary customs. Yet in this video, we see that the large, outdoor sculpture is made of stone that is home to lush, lively, green vegetation, while we see a smaller work can be invaginated within the fleshy and vital cavity of a ripe papaya (Fig. Int.1 and Int.2). It is poetic and significant that in the final scene of *Reincarnations of Shadows*, which I discussed at the beginning of the epilogue, Phan only allows us to see Diem's sculptures through a screen of silk: a material Phan uses in her own artwork that Diem never used in hers. In this way, Phan quietly but insistently reminds viewers of her video that we are only seeing and knowing Diem's sculptures through the lens, prism, and veil of Phan's contemporary practice. I have studied Diem's artworks independently, but after watching Phan's video, I now feel that I am seeing them anew, as if through Phan's eyes.

Artistic art histories are not only bringing the art of the past back to life but are also teaching us that this art was already living. The art of the past was always alive, as it is here with us now; although it comes from history, art always belongs to the present, to artists, and to us all.

Acknowledgments

We all know that creative and critical work is collaborative, thinking and writing are sustained by intellectual friendships, and ideas are shared in both formal and informal settings. Artists are sometimes better than scholars at recognizing and acknowledging the range of interlocutors and inspirations that enable and nourish their work. For example, the credits that conclude Thao Nguyen Phan's *Reincarnations of Shadows*—the artwork I discuss in this book's introduction and epilogue—name not only various technical assistants and research informants but also "the air, the trees, the river, the mountains, and the spirits."

This book is dedicated to the artists whose work it discusses. Their practices have given me not only extraordinary objects to look at and think with and about but also novel ways of thinking and learning as well as new possibilities for knowing. These artworks are "the air" and "the spirits" that have nourished my writing here. I thank each of these artists for being so generous with their work, their time, their insights, their clarifications, and their provision of images. I also thank Iskandar Waworuntu for kind permission to reproduce images of the late Emiria Sunassa's work and Svay Pisith for kind permission to reproduce images of the late Svay Ken's work.

Many other artists have also inspired and guided my thinking in this book, even if space has not allowed me to discuss their work within its pages. They are too numerous to name here, but in particular, I thank Albert Samreth, Cheong Kah Kit, Chulayarnnon Siriphol, Citra Sasmita, Clare McCracken, Enzo Camacho and Ami Lien, Guo-Liang Tan, Heman Chong, Hoo Fanchon, Hyphen –, Ian Tee, Ian Woo, Jacqueline Hoang Nguyen, Jeremy Sharma, Kanitha Tith, Khvay Samnang, Leila Shirazi, Nguyen Thi Thanh Mai, Nontawat Numbenchapol, Orawan Arunrak, Pech Song, Pen Sereypagna, Rushdi Anwar, Savanhdary Vongpoothorn, Tada Hengsapkul, Tan Zi Hao, The Vann Molyvann Project, Womanifesto, Yee I-Lann, Zarina Muhammad, Zulkhairi Zulkiflee, and many others.

Central concerns in this book are the intertwining of art-historical and creative practices and the value of a regional approach to art and to knowledge about it. Among the many scholars who exemplify these qualities, I gratefully acknowledge that I could not have written this book without the guiding inspiration of the art historian-curators Patrick D. Flores and T. K. Sabapathy. I thank them both for their tireless dedication to thinking imaginatively, playfully, and provocatively with the art of this region and for their patient, generous, and keenly critical engagement with my work. I also thank Kanaga and Patrick for the warmth of their friendship and mentorship over many years, which I treasure deeply.

Several scholars and friends were generous enough to read early drafts of chapters and proposals and offered invaluable and constructive comments on my work; for this, I thank Chanon Kenji Praepipatmongkol, C. J. Wee Wan-ling, David Chandler, Lawrence Chua, Li Qi Peh, Mieke Bal, and Simon Soon. I especially thank Brianne Cohen and Patrick D. Flores, who both read the entire manuscript and whose empathic and astute mind-expanding annotations and suggestions helped hone the book's final form. I also thank Saloni Mathur, whose clear-sighted insights revealed a path forward through my revisions and encouraged me to embrace that which is peculiar to this region.

Among the many other scholars and friends who have been important interlocutors for my thinking or generously supported me in other ways, I thank Adrian Vickers, Alex Burchmore, Anthony Gardner, Ashley Thompson, Chairat Polmuk, Chaitanya Sambrani, David Teh, Edwin Jurriëns, Iftikhar Dadi, Jeannine Tang, Jiat-Hwee Chang, John Clark, Kevin Chua, Kunci Study Forum & Collective, Kwok Kian Woon, Lee Weng Choy, Maggie Jack, Mark Bradley, Mark Ledbury, May Adadol Ingawanij, Michelle Antoinette, Nikos Papastergiadis, Nora A. Taylor, Pamela N. Corey, Priya M. Jaradi, Sayan Daengklom, Simon Soon, Thanavi Chotpradit, Theara Thun, Viet Le, Wulan Dirgantoro, Yin Ker, Yvonne Low, and others too numerous to name here. I also thank all my wonderful colleagues in the Department of Art History and the School of Humanities at Nanyang Technological University, including C. J. Wee Wan-ling, Karin G. Oen, Michael Walsh, Michelle Lim, Neil Murphy, and many others.

Curatorial thinking and making, which exceeds the textual even as it embraces it, has been another important source for this book. Alongside the artists and scholars already named, many curators and friends have enriched, supported, and enabled my work here in various ways, and I offer thanks to Adele Tan, Anca Rujoiu, Bill Nguyen, Carlos Quijon Jr, Charmaine Toh, Chelsea Chua, Cheng Jia Yun, Chum Chanveasna, Erin Gleeson, Grace Samboh, Gridthiya Gaweewong, Hyunjin Kim, June Yap, Kathleen Ditzig, Kittima Chareeprasit, Le Thuan Uyen, Low Sze Wee, Lynda Tay, Marcella Lista, Nathalie Johnston, Philippe Pirotte, Rahel Joseph, Riksa Afiaty, Russell Storer, Sa Sa Art Projects, Selene Yap, Seng Yu Jin, Shabbir Hussain Mustafa, Siddharta Perez, Sohrab Mohebbi, Stuart Comer, Ute Meta Bauer, Vera Mey, Wong Binghao, Zoe Butt, and many others. I particularly thank Ryan Inouye for his early affirmation that artistic art histories could be "a thing" and the Hyphen – collective for opening multiple pathways connecting curatorial and other modes of research and practice.

Bridging artistic, curatorial, scholarly, and other ways of thinking and working, I offer special thanks to my colleagues and friends from *Southeast of Now: Directions in Contemporary and Modern Art in Asia*. This peer-reviewed scholarly journal—still the only one focused on the art of this region—was first conceived with the brilliant Vera Mey amidst the magical detritus of two empires in Siem Reap in 2013, and it has been published since 2017 by the stellar team at NUS Press. The open access journal has grown to become not only a forum for innovative work on the region's art but also a community for thinking freely beyond geographical, disciplinary, and institutional borders. I thank all past and present members of the editorial collective and advisory board, as well as Peter Schoppert and Lena Qua; together with you all, I look forward to the journal's next decade.

Several institutions have offered nurturing environments that enabled the research and writing of this book. I thank Nanyang Technological University (NTU) in Singapore for a postdoctoral fellowship from 2017 to 2019, when the seeds of the project were planted, and for research leave in 2025, when it was shaped into its final form. I gratefully acknowledge that this research is generously funded by a Start-Up Grant (number 03INS001578C420) from NTU. I also gratefully acknowledge that this research is generously funded by the Ministry of Education, Singapore, under its Academic Research Fund Tier 1 (RS05/22 and RG65/25). It is this funding which has allowed the book to be available via Open Access, and for this I am particularly thankful. Any opinions, findings and conclusions or recommendations expressed in this material are those of the author and do not reflect the views of the Ministry of Education, Singapore. I thank my wonderfully supportive colleagues at NTU (particularly C. J. Wee Wan-ling for his wise and generous guidance through the institution) and at National Gallery Singapore, where I worked as a curator from 2019 to 2022, before returning to NTU as assistant professor in 2022. I am grateful to the Australian National University for awarding me a Sir William Dobell Visiting Fellowship in 2025, during which I completed work on the book. I also thank the organizers and audiences of invited talks, lectures, and presentations in which I presented work in progress from the book and received helpful questions and feedback at venues including the Association for Art History annual conference, the Australian National University, the College Art Association annual conferences, Cornell University's Gatty Lecture Series, Jameel Arts Centre in Dubai, the Museum of Modern Art in New York, the National Taipei University of Education, NUS Museum at the National University of Singapore, the Outpost Art Organisation in Hanoi, the University of Colorado Boulder, the University of Melbourne, the University of Sydney, and others.

My work has also been ably supported by exceptional research assistance from Nurul Kaiyisah (Kai) Latip, who is an outstanding researcher herself, with a bright future and much to offer. I thank her and my other graduate and undergraduate students for being sources of endless energy. I am also grateful for support from librarians, which is invaluable even while it often remains invisible. I particularly thank the library staff at NTU, Asia Art Archive, Cambridge University, and National Gallery Singapore (especially Szan Tan and Andy Koh).

Cornell University Press has offered impeccable support throughout the project. I thank my editor, Sarah Grossman, for her patience and guidance, as well as all other staff involved in bringing the book into being. I am also very grateful to the two anonymous peer reviewers, whose astute comments greatly improved my work. I also thank Rachel Lyon for her work on the index. All remaining errors and shortcomings are, of course, mine alone.

This book has engendered several other projects that have allowed me an opportunity to pursue lines of inquiry that sometimes align with and sometimes diverge from artistic art histories. One such project is an edited volume on Emiria Sunassa, which is forthcoming with Leiden University Press; I thank my coeditors Anissa Rahadiningtyas and Marije Plomp and all the contributors to that book. A second was a two-part survey retrospective exhibition on Araya Rasdjarmrearnsook, titled *The Bouquet and the Wreath*, presented from 2025 to 2026 at MAIIAM Contemporary Art Museum in Chiang Mai and Jameel Arts Centre in Dubai, as well as an accompanying publication. I thank Ajarn Araya, as well as my cocurator, Kittima Chareeprasit, and all the project's contributors and collaborators, particularly Giacomo Lamborizio, Lucas Morin, and Nora Razian. A third offshoot from this book was a traveling exhibition titled *The Unfaithful Octopus*, which I curated at NTU ADM Gallery in Singapore in 2023 and at MAIIAM in Chiang Mai in 2024. I thank all the contributors and support staff and particularly the artists who participated in that project: Araya Rasjdarmrearnsook, CAMP, Chulayarnnon Siriphol, Diem Phung Thi remade by Thao Nguyen Phan, Fyerool Darma, Ian Tee, Mieke Bal, and the late Ricardo de Baños and Alberto Marro. The exhibition's title was borrowed from the words of Mieke Bal, which have been a constant companion while I wrote this book.

Some parts of chapters 2 and 3 have appeared in an earlier form in previous publications. These are acknowledged in the relevant sections of those chapters.

Friends and family have sustained my work in more ways than I can say. Several of them are writers working in other genres. I thank Anna Cordner, Brandon Chua, Daniel Mattes, Daryl Qilin Yam, Geoffrey O'Connor, Jessica Venables, and Samuel Lee (and Andrew Yang Ming). I also thank Georgia, Myrina, Danni, Chris, Dom, Sidd, Vera, Pam, Ed, and especially Liz, my keenest reader of all, who first introduced me to art and writing and the miraculous worlds they open. Finally, I thank Guo-Liang for everything.

Notes

INTRODUCTION

1. The work is titled *Reincarnations of Shadows* and subtitled "an evolving moving-image-poem as a tribute to artist Diem Phung Thi." It was first exhibited in 2023 at HangarBicocca in Milan. A revised version was subsequently shown at Art Basel Hong Kong in 2024, at National Gallery Singapore in 2025, and elsewhere.

2. The man's name is Phan Dinh Hoi, and he was the personal assistant of Diem Phung Thi from 1993 until her death in 2002.

3. Thao Nguyen Phan, "Thao Nguyen Phan on Diem Phung Thi: The Metamorphosis of Signs," Artists on Artists et al. vol 2, *Cobo Social*, January 18, 2021; Diem Phung Thi is not discussed in foundational studies by art historians Nora A. Taylor (on modern art in Vietnam) or John Clark (on modern art in Asia), nor in any exhibitions or catalogues surveying Southeast Asia's modern art that have been produced by National Gallery Singapore, Singapore Art Museum, or Fukuoka Asian Art Museum, the museums most actively involved in studying and exhibiting the region's modern art. This is not a failure or simple oversight; rather, there are specific reasons for this omission, which I discuss in greater detail in a forthcoming article. Taylor, for example, focuses on artists in the northern capital city of Hanoi, whereas Diem worked in the smaller city of Hue in central Vietnam.

4. Patrick D. Flores, "Art-Historical Alterity in the Post-Colony," in *Art History and Emergency: Crises in the Visual Arts and Humanities*, ed. David Breslin and Darby English (Sterling and Francine Clark Institute and Yale University Press, 2016), 95; Patrick D. Flores, "Address of Art: Vicinity of Region, Horizon of History," in *Charting Thoughts: Essays on Art in Southeast Asia*, ed. Low Sze Wee and Patrick D. Flores (National Gallery Singapore, 2017), 12.

5. Thao Nguyen Phan, quoted in Aaina Bhargava, "Vietnamese artist Thao Nguyen Phan is reviving the legacies of forgotten female artists and exploring her homeland's heritage," *Tatler Asia*, January 1, 2024, https://www.tatlerasia.com/lifestyle/arts/thao-nguyen-phan-interview.

6. Thao Nguyen Phan, in conversation with the author, 2022.

7. Claire Bishop, "Information Overload," *Artforum* 61, no. 8 (April 2023) https://www.artforum.com/features/claire-bishop-on-the-superabundance-of-research-based-art-252571/.

8. T. K. Sabapathy, "The Nanyang Artists: Some General Remarks" (1979), in *Writing the Modern: Selected Texts on Art & Art History in Singapore, Malaysia & Southeast Asia, 1973–2015*, ed. Ahmad Mashadi, Susie Lingham, Peter Schoppert, and Joyce Toh (Singapore Art Museum, 2018), 345. Emphasis added.

9. Mieke Bal, *Quoting Caravaggio: Contemporary Art, Preposterous History* (University of Chicago Press, 1999), 21–22.

10. Tamara Loos, "Reading *Gender Trouble* in Southeast Asia," *The Journal of Asian Studies* 79, no. 4 (2020): 928.

11. Patrick D. Flores, "A Possible Coordinate," in *South by Southeast*, ed. Patrick Flores and Anca Verona Mihuleţ (Osage Art Foundation, 2016), 6.

12. The concept of the "geopoetic" is indebted to Patrick D. Flores. See, for example, "'There, hapless state . . .': The Geopoetic of Co-Suffering," in *Interlaced Journeys: Diaspora and the Contemporary in Southeast Asian Art*, ed. Patrick D. Flores and Loredana Pazzini-Paracciani (Osage Publications, 2020), 7–15.

13. Patrick D. Flores, "Address of Art: Vicinity of Region, Horizon of History," in *Charting Thoughts: Essays on Art in Southeast Asia*, ed. Low Sze Wee and Patrick D. Flores (National Gallery Singapore, 2017), 18.

14. Michelle Antoinette, *Reworlding Art History: Encounters with Contemporary Southeast Asian Art After 1990* (Rodopi, 2014), xliv.

15. Marco C. F. Hsü, *A Brief History of Malayan Art*, trans. Lai Chee Kien (Millennium Books, 1999); Claire Holt, *Art in Indonesia: Continuities and Change* (Cornell University Press, 1967).

16. That is, much of the writing on these artists is curatorial or journalistic rather than academic in nature.

17. I thank Ashley Thompson for her insights on the false dichotomy of mainland and maritime Southeast Asia.

18. Kevin Chua, "Exhibiting Modern Asian Art in Southeast Asia," *Yishu: Journal of Contemporary Chinese Art* 13, no. 2 (2014): 111.

19. David Teh, *Thai Art: Currencies of the Contemporary* (MIT Press, 2017), 2. Emphasis added.

20. T. K. Sabapathy, "Intersecting Histories: Thoughts on the Contemporary and History in Southeast Asian Art," in *Intersecting Histories: Contemporary Turns in Southeast Asian Art*, ed. T. K. Sabapathy (School of Art, Design and Media, Nanyang Technological University, 2012), 39.

21. June Yap, *Retrospective: A Historiographical Aesthetic in Contemporary Singapore and Malaysia* (Strategic Information and Research Development Centre, 2016), 6.

22. Eva Kernbauer, *Art, History, and Anachronic Interventions Since 1990* (Routledge, 2022), 1.

23. Antoinette, *Reworlding Art History*, 313.

24. Antoinette, *Reworlding Art History*, 495.

25. Antoinette, *Reworlding Art History*, 497.

26. Danny Butt, "The Promise of Artistic Research in the Asia Pacific," *Manusya: Journal of the Humanities* 23 (2020): 330–331.

27. Butt, "The Promise of Artistic Research," 330. Another study of the phenomenon is Caroline Ha Thuc, *Research-Based Art Practices in Southeast Asia: The Artist as Producer of Knowledge* (Palgrave Macmillan, 2022).

28. Tom Holert, *Knowledge Beside Itself: Contemporary Art's Epistemic Politics* (Sternberg Press, 2020), 7. Emphasis in original.

29. Kamini Vellodi, "Thought Beyond Research: A Deleuzian Critique of Artistic Research," in *Aberrant Nuptials: Deleuze and Artistic Research 2*, ed. Paulo de Assis and Paolo Giudici (Leuven University Press, 2019), 215–219.

30. Holert, *Knowledge Beside Itself*, 11. For an account that extends beyond contemporary art, see Harald Klinke, ed., *Art Theory as Visual Epistemology* (Cambridge Scholars Publishing, 2014).

31. Hsü, *Brief History of Malayan Art*. Holt, *Art in Indonesia*. Accounts from the 1990s and 2000s include: Apinan Poshyananda, *Modern Art in Thailand: Nineteenth and Twentieth Centuries* (Oxford University Press, 1992); Patrick D. Flores, *Painting History: Revisions in Philippine Colonial Art* (Office of Research Coordination, University of the Philippines and National Commission for Culture and the Arts, 1998); Nora A. Taylor, *Painters in Hanoi: An Ethnography of Vietnamese Art*, 2nd ed. (NUS Press, 2009).

32. T. K. Sabapathy, "Developing Regionalist Perspectives in Southeast Asian Art Historiography" [1996], in *Contemporary Art in Asia: A Critical Reader*, ed. Benjamin Genocchio and Melissa Chiu (MIT Press, 2011), 47–61. Sabapathy (and others) had called for a regional approach earlier (since the 1980s) but had not yet put it into practice in the discussion of specific artists and works.

33. For example, most of the region's major art-historical archives (such as Indonesian Visual Art Archive in Yogyakarta, Malaysia Design Archive in Kuala Lumpur, National Gallery Singapore Library & Archive in Singapore, and Bophana Audiovisual Resource Center in Phnom Penh) are independent of universities.

34. James Elkins, *The End of Diversity in Art Historical Writing: North Atlantic Art History and Its Alternatives* (De Gruyter, 2021), 8.

35. Patrick D. Flores, *Painting History: Revisions in Philippine Colonial Art* (Office of Research Coordination, University of the Philippines and National Commission for Culture and the Arts, 1998), 3.

36. Simon Soon, "What is Left of Art? The Spatio-Visual Practice of Political Art in Indonesia, Singapore, Thailand, and the Philippines, 1950s–1970s," unpub. PhD diss., University of Sydney, 2015, 21, 25, 30.

37. T. K. Sabapathy, "Premises for Critical Studies of Modern Art in Southeast Asia" (1982), in *The Modern in Southeast Asian Art: A Reader*, vol. 1., ed. T. K. Sabapathy and Patrick D. Flores (National Gallery Singapore and NTU Centre for Contemporary Art Singapore, 2023), 75.

38. Phan, quoted in Bhargava, "Vietnamese artist."

39. T. K. Sabapathy, "Introduction to Intersecting Histories: Contemporary Turns in Southeast Asian Art" (2012), reprinted in T. K. Sabapathy, *Writing the Modern: Selected Texts on Art and Art History in Singapore, Malaysia and Southeast Asia*, ed. Ahmad Mashadi, Susie Lingham, Peter Schoppert, and Joyce Toh (Singapore Art Museum, 2018), 318.

40. Patrick D. Flores, *Past Peripheral: Curation in Southeast Asia* (NUS Museum, 2008).

41. Patrick D. Flores, "First Person Plural: Manifestos of the 1970s in Southeast Asia," in *Global Studies: Mapping Contemporary Art and Culture*, ed. Hans Belting, Jacob Birken, Andrea Buddensieg, and Peter Weibel (Hatje Cantz, 2011), 224–271.

42. Roger Nelson, "Curating as (Expanded) Art History in Southeast Asia: Recent Independent Projects in Ho Chi Minh City, Luang Prabang and Phnom Penh," *ARTMargins* 9, no. 2 (2020): 33–60.

43. As noted, the very first book to address modern art in the region was written in Chinese and first published in 1963 by an artist: Hsü, *A Brief History of Malayan Art*, trans. Lai Chee Kien (Millennium Books, 1999). Subsequent artist-writers include men like Rod. Paras-Perez (1934–2011) in the Philippines, Redza Piyadasa (1939–2007) in Malaysia, Apinan Poshyananda (1956–) in Thailand, and Ca Le Thang (1949–) in Vietnam, as well as women like Siti Adiyati (1951–) in Indonesia, Imelda Cajipe Endaya (1949–) in the Philippines, Ma Thanegi (1946–) in Myanmar, and Araya Rasdjarmrearnsook (1957–) in Thailand. In Singapore, the prominent contemporary artist-curator Ho Tzu Nyen (1976–) and artist-educator Wang Ruobing (1975–) have both produced influential art-historical writings.

44. Patrick D. Flores, "Moments of the Modern in Southeast Asia: Art, Region, Art History," in *Shaping the History of Art in Southeast Asia*, ed. Patrick D. Flores and Kenji Kajiya (Japan Foundation Art Center, 2017), 8.

45. Christopher S. Wood, *A History of Art History* (Princeton University Press, 2019), 54 and 84. Early accounts of art histories are not always reliable. One study has argued that a seventeenth century book by the Chinese artist Zhang Taijie fabricated paintings

and texts. J. P. Park, "Art-Historical Fiction or Fictional Art History?: Zhang Taijie, Dong Qichang, and the Literary Making of the Past in Early Modern China," *Archives of Asian Art* 72, no. 2 (October 2022): 181–219.

46. Saloni Mathur, "A Retake of Sher-Gil's *Self-Portrait as Tahitian*," *Critical Inquiry* 37, no. 3 (Spring 2011): 520–521; Saloni Mathur, *A Fragile Inheritance: Radical Stakes in Contemporary Indian Art* (Duke University Press, 2019); Richard Bartholomew, *Richard Bartholomew, the Art Critic*, ed. Rati Bartholomew, Carmen Kagal, and Pablo Bartholomew (BART, 2012).

47. Yuki Kihara in dialogue with Patrick Flores, as part of the symposium, "Worlds Apart, Strangers Together," public program at National Gallery Singapore, March 23, 2024.

48. Mbembe's comments on deprovincializing are précised in Paul Gilroy, "Transcript: In Conversation with Achille Mbembe," Sarah Parker Remond Centre, University College London, June 17, 2020, accessed September 2024, https://www.ucl.ac.uk/racism-racialisation/transcript-conversation-achille-mbembe; See also Sabelo J. Ndlovu-Gatsheni, "Provincializing Europe and Deprovincialising Africa: Prospects for Decolonizing the Humanities," *Présence Africaine* 197 (2018): 342, 347. I have elaborated my concept of deprovincializing elsewhere. See Roger Nelson, "'My World is Modern': Deprovincialising Chen Cheng Mei and You Khin, Artists from Southeast Asia Who Traversed the Global South," *Southeast of Now: Directions in Contemporary and Modern Art in Asia* 5, no. 1–2 (October 2021): 205–249; Roger Nelson, "Two Tales of Two Cities: Contemporary Art, Southeast Asia, Divergent Approaches," *Art Journal* 81, no. 4 (2022): 146–149. The latter is a review of books by Pamela N. Corey and Việt Lê.

49. Dipesh Chakrabarty, *Provincializing Europe: Postcolonial Thought and Historical Difference* (New Edition) (Princeton University Press, 2000).

50. To conceive of deprovincializing as an option draws on the proposal that decoloniality be conceived as an "option" rather than a "mission" because to conceive of "imperatives in abstract" is to "assume the universality of your own imperatives." Walter D. Mignolo, "Decoloniality is an Option, Not a Mission," in Walter D. Mignolo and Catherine E. Walsh, *On Decoloniality: Concepts, Analytics, Praxis* (Duke University Press, 2018), 224.

51. To grasp this perpetual state of becoming, I turn to A. L. Becker's suggestion that we "try thinking . . . that there is no such thing as Language, only continual languaging." A. L. Becker, "Language and Languaging," *Language & Communication* 11, no. 1/2 (1991): 34.

52. Pramoedya Ananda Toer, *This Earth of Mankind*, part 1 of *The Buru Quartet*, trans. Max Lane (Penguin, 1996 [1981]), 321.

53. Linda Tuhiwai Smith, *Decolonizing Methodologies: Research and Indigenous Peoples*, 3rd ed. (Zed Books and Bloomsbury Publishing, 2021), xii.

54. Dia al-Azzawi, Ismail Fattah, Saleh al-Jumaie, Muhammad Muhraddin, Rafa al-Nasiri and Hashem Samarji, "Manifesto: Towards a New Vision (1969)," trans. Anneke Lenssen, Sarah Rogers, Nada Shabout, in *Modern Art in the Arab World: Primary Documents*, ed. Anneke Lenssen, Sarah Rogers, and Nada Shabout (Museum of Modern Art, 2018), 309. Emphasis added.

55. Cara L. Lewis, *Dynamic Form: How Intermediality Made Modernism* (Cornell University Press, 2020), 16. Emphasis in original.

56. Jennifer C. Nash, *How We Write Now: Living with Black Feminist Theory* (Duke University Press, 2024), 13.

57. Mieke Bal, "Citational Aesthetics: For Intermediality as Interrelation," in *The Palgrave Handbook of Intermediality*, ed. Jørgen Bruhn, Asun López-Varela Azcárate, and Miriam de Paiva Vieira (Palgrave Macmillan, 2024), 479.

58. Bal, "Citational Aesthetics," 469.

59. Nelson, "Curating as (Expanded) Art History."

60. Vann Molyvann, quoted in Helen Grant Ross and Darryl Leon Collins, *Building Cambodia: 'New Khmer Architecture' 1953–1970* (Key Publisher, 2006), 205. Emphasis added.

61. See Roger Nelson, "Locating the Domestic in Vann Molyvann's National Sports Complex," *ABE Journal: Architecture Beyond Europe*, special issue "Paradoxical Southeast Asia," 11 (2017): 1–25. See also Ross and Collins, *Building Cambodia*, especially 200–237.

62. Marshall Berman, *All That is Solid Melts into Air*, revised edition (Penguin, 1988 [1982]), 68.

63. Alice G. Guillermo, "The Institutions of the Modern Art World in the Philippines," in *Modernity in Asian Art*, ed. John Clark (Wild Peony, 1993), 126.

64. See, for example, Partha Mitter, "Decentering Modernism: Art History and Avant-Garde from the Periphery," *The Art Bulletin* 90, no. 4 (2008): 531–548; Chika Okeke-Agulu, *Postcolonial Modernism: Art and Decolonization in Twentieth-Century Nigeria* (Duke University Press, 2015); Keith Moxey, "Is Modernity Multiple?" in *Visual Time: The Image in History* (Duke University Press, 2013), 11–22; Joan Kee, *The Geometries of Afro Asia: Art Beyond Solidarity* (University of California Press, 2023); Iftikhar Dadi, *Modernism and the Art of Muslim South Asia* (University of North Carolina Press, 2010).

65. Sara Ahmed, *Living a Feminist Life* (Duke University Press, 2017), 10. Emphasis added.

66. These include the Nguyen Art Foundation and the Quang San Museum in Ho Chi Minh City and The Outpost in Hanoi. The latter held a small exhibition dedicated to the artist in 2024, titled *The Curious Adventure of the Modules – a visual essay on Điềm Phùng Thị.*

67. Catherine Grant, *A Time of One's Own: Histories of Feminism in Contemporary Art* (Duke University Press), 21.

68. Araya Rasdjarmrearnsook, *I Am An Artist (He Said)*, trans. Kong Rithdee (National Gallery Singapore, 2022), 199.

69. I thank Patrick D. Flores for his insights on this topic, in conversation in November 2023.

70. Grant, *A Time of One's Own*, 74.

71. Grant, *A Time of One's Own*, 24.

72. Lydia Vasko, "Going for Gold: National Gallery Singapore Approaches Final Stages of Construction," *The Straits Times*, August 9, 2014, accessed September 2024, https://www.straitstimes.com/singapore/going-for-gold-national-gallery-singapore-approaches-final-stages-of-construction. The figure is in Singapore dollars. Here and throughout this paragraph, data on population size and GDP is taken from the International Monetary Fund.

73. Although the budget is not released publicly, its scale can be deduced from the list of artwork acquisitions that are published in the Annual Reports of National Gallery Singapore, which are available at: https://www.nationalgallery.sg/about/about-the-gallery/annual-reports.

74. See, for example, Julia Jacobs and Tom Mashberg, "U.S. Returns 30 Looted Antiquities to Cambodia," *The New York Times*, August 8, 2022, https://www.nytimes.com/2022/08/08/arts/us-cambodia-looted-antiquities.html. See also Louise Tythacott and Panggah Ardiyansyah, eds., *Returning Southeast Asia's Past: Objects, Museums, and Restitution* (NUS Press, 2021).

75. Anadolu Agency, "British Museum to Display Ottoman Master's $7.4M 'Young Woman Reading' Painting in London," *Daily Sabah*, October 4, 2019, https://www.dailysabah.com/arts-culture/2019/10/04/british-museum-to-display-ottoman-masters-74m-young-woman-reading-painting-in-london.

76. At NTU, the first art historian was awarded this scholarship (known as HIPS) in 2022 and commenced studies in 2023.

77. T. K. Sabapathy, *Road to Nowhere: The Quick Rise and Long Fall of Art History in Singapore* (The Art Gallery at the National Institute of Education, 2010), 37.

78. "About Us," *Malaysia Design Archive*, accessed September 2024, https://www.malaysiadesignarchive.org/aboutus/.

79. "About Bophana Center," *Bophana*, accessed September 2024, https://bophana.org/about/.

80. The nonprofit organization succeeded the Cemeti Art Foundation, which operated with a similar mission from 1995 to 2007. Asia-Europe Foundation, "Digital Archive of Indonesian Visual Art," *Culture 360*, September 6, 2010, https://culture360.asef.org/resources/indonesian-visual-art-archive-ivaa/.

81. "Preserving Local Culture Through Films," *Save Myanmar Film*, https://www.savemyanmarfilm.org/.

82. "About Us," *Hyphen –*, accessed September 2024, https://hyphen.web.id/about-us/. The group's name includes the word Hyphen and the en dash.

83. Francesca Aton, "LaToya Ruby Frazier Wins 2022 Carnegie International's Top Prize," *ARTnews*, September 26, 2022, https://www.artnews.com/art-news/news/latoya-ruby-frazier-malcolm-peacock-hyphen-collective-win-58th-carnegie-international-prizes-1234640515/. I served on the Carnegie Museum of Art's international jury to select the prize-winners.

84. "Roung Kon Project," *Roung Kon Project*, accessed September 2024, https://www.roungkonproject.com/about; Nelson, "Curating as (Expanded) Art History."

85. "About," *Spirit of Friendship*, accessed September 2024, https://web.archive.org/web/20181225123916/http://spiritoffriendship.org/, December 2018 version; Nelson, "Curating as (Expanded) Art History."

86. Sabapathy, "Premises," 75.

87. Among the vast scholarly literature on the significance of reflexive situatedness in anthropology and in other disciplines, I take particular inspiration from the refreshing and sometimes startling first-person writing in a recent book on contemporary art in Cambodia and Vietnam, written by an art historian who is also an artist, a curator, and a poet. See Việt Lê, *Return Engagements: Contemporary Art's Traumas of Modernity and History in Sài Gòn and Phnom Penh* (Duke University Press, 2021).

88. Lauren Fournier, *Autotheory as Feminist Practice in Art, Writing and Criticism* (MIT Press, 2021), 5; Tuhiwai Smith, *Decolonizing Methodologies*, 2.

89. Many of my classmates at school in Naarm/Melbourne, Australia, were migrants or refugees from or with ties to Southeast Asia. My early fascination with the region was also encouraged by family friends like John Legge, a respected scholar of Southeast Asia and its histories (and, like me, also a white man without familial connection to the region), who would regale my mother (also a historian) and me with tales of his encounters with the leading minds of the decolonizing decades in this part of the world. I later undertook a PhD on the region's modern and contemporary art histories as well as several years of language classes.

90. Since 2012, I have curated exhibitions and other projects in various galleries, museums, and other settings in Cambodia, Malaysia, Singapore, Thailand, Vietnam, and elsewhere. From 2019 to 2022, I worked as curator at National Gallery Singapore, where, in addition to organizing exhibitions, I contributed to the acquisition of artworks for the world's largest public collection of Southeast Asian modern art. I have taught at the National University of Singapore and Nanyang Technological University.

91. Some artists may define themselves by their nationality, others as Southeast Asian. Some may be comfortable with both ways of self-identifying and some with

neither. These self-identifications may shift over time. I have noticed that younger artists tend to be more comfortable to describe themselves as Southeast Asian in more recent years.

92. Ho Tzu Nyen, "About," *The Critical Dictionary of Southeast Asia*, 2012–ongoing, https://cdosea.org/#about/b.

93. Ahmad Mashadi, "Regionalist Perspectives on Southeast Asian Art: Editorial Overview," in T. K. Sabapathy, *Writing the Modern: Selected Texts on Art and Art History in Singapore, Malaysia and Southeast Asia*, ed. Ahmad Mashadi, Susie Lingham, Peter Schoppert, and Joyce Toh (Singapore Art Museum, 2018), 332.

94. Holly High, "An Introduction to Stone Masters," in *Stone Masters: Power Encounters in Mainland Southeast Asia*, ed. Holly High (NUS Press, 2022), 6.

95. Elmo Gonzaga, "Regionalism as Anti-colonialism: Imaginaries of Area in South East Asian Omnibus Film and Database Art," *South East Asia Research* 32, no. 2 (2024): 125–141.

96. Yve-Alain Bois, Denis Hollier, Rosalind Krauss, and Hubert Damisch, "A Conversation with Hubert Damisch," *October* 85 (Summer 1998): 3–17. The concept is deployed in Bal's various works, including in Mieke Bal, *Image-Thinking: Artmaking as Cultural Analysis* (Edinburgh University Press, 2022).

97. Sabapathy, "The Nanyang Artists," 345.

98. Yap, *Retrospective*, 325. Emphasis in original.

99. Kuan-Hsing Chen, *Asia as Method: Toward Deimperialization* (Duke University Press, 2010), 3.

100. Chen, *Asia as Method*, 3.

101. The phrase is adapted from a very different context. Anne Middleton Wagner, *Three Artists (Three Women): Modernism and the Art of Hesse, Krasner and O'Keeffe* (University of California Press, 1996), 2.

102. Chairat Polmuk, "Affect: Notes from Southeast Asian Visual Culture," in *Routledge Handbook of Contemporary Buddhism*, ed. Stephen C. Berkwitz and Ashley Thompson (Routledge, 2022), 327–342.

103. Tobias Werron, Jelena Brankovic and Leopold Ringel, "Theorizing Together," *Distinktion: Journal of Social Theory* 25, no. 2 (2024): 231.

104. Ashley Thompson, *Engendering the Buddhist State: Territory, Sovereignty and Sexual Difference in the Inventions of Angkor* (Routledge, 2016), 31, 45.

105. Araya Rasdjarmrearnsook, *I Am An Artist (He Said)*, trans. Kong Rithdee (National Gallery Singapore, 2022), 99.

1. HONORING

1. The event described took place early one morning in December 2022.

2. "Prumsodun Ok & Natyarasa," *Prumsodun Ok*, accessed September 2024, https://www.prumsodun.com/natyarasa.

3. Prumsodun Ok, in conversation with the author, December 2022.

4. Jennifer C. Nash, *How We Write Now: Living with Black Feminist Theory* (Duke University Press, 2024), 11.

5. Nash, *How We Write Now*, 22.

6. Nash, *How We Write Now*, 45.

7. Prumsodun Ok, *The Serpent's Tail: A Brief History of Khmer Classical Dance* (self-published, 2018), 5–6, accessed September 2024, https://www.serpentstail.info/; page numbers refer to the PDF version: https://www.academia.edu/36957739/THE_SERPENTS_TAIL_A_BRIEF_HISTORY_OF_KHMER_CLASSICAL_DANCE.

8. Prumsodun, *The Serpent's Tail*, 174. Emphasis added.

9. Prumsodun, *The Serpent's Tail*, 176. Emphasis added.

10. Prumsodun, *The Serpent's Tail*, 176.

11. Toni Shapiro-Phim, "Cambodia's Seasons of Migration," *Dance Research Journal* 40, no. 2 (Winter 2008): 61.

12. Shapiro-Phim, "Cambodia's *Seasons of Migration*," 61.

13. C. Pierce Salguero, "Honoring the Teachers, Constructing the Lineage: A *Wai Khru* Ritual among Healers in Chiang Mai, Thailand," in *Translating the Body: Medical Education in Southeast Asia*, eds. Hans Pols, C. Michele Thompson, and John Harley Warner (NUS Press, 2017), 295–318.

14. Quoted in Prumsodun, *The Serpent's Tail*, 135.

15. Toni Shapiro, "Dance and the Spirit of Cambodia," unpub. PhD diss., Cornell University, 1994, 46.

16. Andreas Huyssen, *Memory Art in the Contemporary World: Confronting Violence in the Global South* (Lund Humphries, 2022), 13.

17. Toni Shapiro, "Mediating Cambodian History, the Sacred, and the Earth," in *The Routledge Dance Studies Reader*, third edition, eds. Jens Richard Giersdorf and Yutian Wong (Routledge, 2019), 266.

18. Shapiro, "Dance and the Spirit of Cambodia," 46–47.

19. The national newspaper in Cambodia even reported "threats of violence" that Prumsodun has received. Cristina Maza, "All-male, All-gay Dance Troupe Stages its Cambodian Debut," *The Phnom Penh Post*, August 12, 2016, https://www.phnompenhpost.com/post-weekend/all-male-all-gay-dance-troupe-stages-its-cambodian-debut.

20. Salguero, "Honoring the Teachers," 300.

21. The scholar Ashley Thompson notes that "the 'passing of the *babil*' sequence of any ceremony serves explicitly to demarcate the sacred space around the individual(s) or object(s) for which the ceremony is performed, and to assemble the *bralịṅ* ["vital spirits" or "souls"] in the person(s) or object(s) in question." Thus, by passing the *babil* candle holder when attending a *sampeah kru*, we are not only embodying art-historical lessons about the *kru* or lineage, but also participating in the ritual "calling of the souls." Ashley Thompson, *Engendering the Buddhist State: Territory, Sovereignty and Sexual Difference in the Inventions of Angkor* (Routledge, 2016), 151; see also 150–161.

22. I am grateful to Vera Mey for introducing this work to me. The artist prefers that the title appear in sentence case, rather than with each word capitalized.

23. Sarah Farrar, "Costume for a Mourner," *Museum of New Zealand Te Papa Tongarewa*, undated [circa 2017–2018], accessed September 2024, https://collections.tepapa.govt.nz/object/1045146.

24. Sriwhana Spong, "*Scirinz* (A Running Sore): Particular and Ecstatic Scripts of the Body by Mystic Women in the Middle Ages and Early Modern Europe," unpub. Doctor of Fine Arts thesis, University of Auckland, Aotearoa New Zealand, 2021, i.

25. Sriwhana Spong in conversation with Tendai John Mutumbu, "Sriwhana Spong" *Ocula Magazine*, July 6, 2018, https://ocula.com/magazine/conversations/sriwhana-spong/.

26. Spong, "*Scirinz*," 42.

27. Spong, "*Scirinz*," 43.

28. I thank Vera Mey for this insight.

29. Adrian Vickers, *Balinese Art: Paintings and Drawings of Bali 1800–2010* (Tuttle Publishing, 2012), 27. Vickers refers to the artist as I Gusti Putu Rundu. While variations in Balinese names are common, this instance is somewhat puzzling. As the scholar Hildred Geertz explains: "The birth-order name gives the relation of the person to his or her siblings. First-born people are called Wayan or Putu, second-born Nyoman, third-born Madé, and fourth-born Ketut." Hildred Geertz, *Images of Power: Balinese Paintings Made for Gregory Bateson and Margaret Mead* (University of Hawai'i Press,

1994), ix. Vickers clarified (in correspondence with the author, in July 2023) that Putu can also refer to someone born while their grandfather is still alive, so it is possible to be called both Putu and Made.

30. Sriwhana Spong, in conversation with the author, May 2023. Unless otherwise noted, all other quotes and information from the artist are derived from conversations with the author during 2023.

31. Claire Holt, *Art in Indonesia: Continuities and Change* (Cornell University Press, 1967).

32. *The Virtual Museum of Balinese Painting*, a digital resource initiated by Vickers among others, offers images of eight works by Gusti Rundu, while stating that 56 works are known. It also provides some additional citations on the artist. "I Gusti Made Rundu, born 1918, died 1993, 56 works," accessed September 2024, https://bit.ly/3NnLBLP; see also https://heurist.sydney.edu.au/heurist/?db=balipaintings&website&id=40124#.

33. Noting the increasing international visibility of contemporary artists affiliated with the region, Taylor notes that "the list of artists from Southeast Asia who have gained the attention of curators worldwide is growing every day." Nora A. Taylor, "Art without History? Southeast Asian Artists and Their Communities in the Face of Geography," *Art Journal* 70, no. 2 (Summer 2011): 11.

34. Information in this paragraph is derived from the website of the artist's Auckland gallery, Michael Lett: https://michaellett.com/artist/sriwhana-spong/ (accessed September 2024).

35. Spong, "*Scirinz*," 72.

36. Wong Binghao, "No Models: Sriwhana Spong's *Instruments*," *Southeast of Now: Directions in Contemporary and Modern Art in Asia* 6, no. 1 (March 2022): 113.

37. Alice Te Punga Somerville, "relative," in *Always Italicise: How to Write While Colonised* (Auckland: Auckland University Press, 2022), 31.

38. Sawako Nakayasu, *Say Translation is Art* (Ugly Duckling Presse, 2020), 2. With thanks to Tan Zi Hao.

39. Nakayasu, *Say Translation is Art*, 8.

40. Jack Halberstam, *The Queer Art of Failure* (Duke University Press, 2011).

41. Patrick D. Flores, "Towards a Lexicon of Inclinations: Words Forming Worlds in Southeast Asia," *Asian Diasporic Visual Cultures and the Americas* 3 (2017): 41–2. In the latter quote, he refers specifically to the Indonesian phrase *jiwa ketok* ("visible soul"), which is attributed to the artist S. Sudjojono.

42. On the limits and potentials of cameras attached to animals, see Donna Haraway, *When Species Meet* (University of Minnesota Press, 2008). With thanks to Brianne Cohen.

43. For example, see Nicholas Bourriaud, "Coactivity: Between the Human and Nonhuman," *Flash Art* 326 (June–August 2019), accessed September 2024, available online: https://flash—art.com/article/coactivity-between-the-human-and-nonhuman/.

44. "I Gusti Made Rundu," *The Virtual Museum of Balinese Painting*; Lucinda Bennett, "Secret Languages, Stranger's Houses, Snakes," *The Pantograph Punch* (June 2018): unpaginated.

45. Originally trained as a dancer, Spong occasionally makes performances. In 2021, she collaborated with Ki Sujarwo Joko Prehatin and Aris Daryono for a 20-minute performance titled *The Poem is a Temple*, presented at The Roberts Institute of Art, London.

46. Jerome Robbins Dance Division, The New York Public Library, "Gusti Rundu and son Sanuan, November 25, 1956; Arie Smit and members of Gusti Rundu family," *New York Public Library Digital Collections*, accessed September 2024, https://digitalcollections.nypl.org/items/510d47dc-4a72-a3d9-e040-e00a18064a99.

47. The Virtual Museum of Balinese Paintings is available at https://heuristnetwork.org/bali-paintings/ (accessed September 2024).

48. Nora A. Taylor, *Painters in Hanoi: An Ethnography of Vietnamese Art*, 2nd ed. (NUS Press, 2009), 3.

49. I have suggested elsewhere that "scholars of the region's art might also choose to look elsewhere for textual documents which illuminate and elucidate paintings and other images. If, as Taylor claims, 'art history records are rare,' then perhaps a more bountiful source of inspiration might be found in the chimeric forms of literature." Roger Nelson, "Behind the Painting, A Pantoum: Literature and Art and Southeast Asia," in *The Routledge Companion to Art and Literature*, ed. Neil Murphy, W. Michelle Wang, and Cheryl Julia Lee (Routledge, 2024), 456.

50. Teagan Bradway and Elizabeth Freeman, "Introduction: Kincoherence/Kinaesthetics/Kinematics," in *Queer Kinship: Race, Sex, Belonging, Form* (Duke University Press, 2022), 1.

51. Bradway and Freeman, "Introduction," 3.

52. Bradway and Freeman, "Introduction," 4. Emphasis in original.

53. Spong, "*Scirinz*," 61.

54. Spong in "Sriwhana Spong."

55. Emphasis added. Archival records indicate that the first public screening of a film made by a Cambodian was in 1960, but that the king, and later head of state, Norodom Sihanouk made films privately before this. For an introduction to Cambodian cinema history, see Jessica Austin, "Gender and the Nation in Popular Cambodian Heritage Cinema," unpub. Masters thesis, University of Hawai'i, Mānoa, 2014.

56. Davy Chou, "Interview," in the press kit for *Golden Slumbers,* 2011, http://anthologyfilmarchives.org/uploads/press_pdf/GoldenSlumbersDP-7.pdf.

57. Davy Chou, "Interview."

58. Van Chann died in 1969. Davy Chou, "ANA Grants 2010 Full Proposal: Documentary Film *Golden Slumbers*," *Arts Network Asia*, 2010, http://artsnetworkasia.org/content/proposals/ChouDavy.html.

59. "About Us," *KonKhmerKounKhmer*, undated [circa 2010], accessed September 2024, https://konkhmerkounkhmer.wordpress.com/about/.

60. "Bodeng Sar (White Building)," *La Biennale di Venezia*, 2021, https://www.labiennale.org/en/cinema/2021/lineup/orizzonti/bodeng-sar-white-building.

61. Chou, "ANA Grants 2010 Full Proposal."

62. Shapiro, "Dance and the Spirit of Cambodia," 8.

63. Shapiro, "Dance and the Spirit of Cambodia," 10.

64. Roger Nelson, "'The Work the Nation Depends On': Landscapes and Women in the Paintings of Nhek Dim," in *Ambitious Alignments: New Histories of Southeast Asian Art, 1945–1990*, eds. Stephen H. Whiteman, Sarena Abdullah, Yvonne Low, and Phoebe Scott (Power Publications and National Gallery Singapore, 2018), 19–48.

65. Yin Ker, "Śāntiniketan and Modern Southeast Asian Art: From Rabindranath Tagore to Bagyi Aung Soe and Beyond," *Artl@s Bulletin* 5, no. 2 (2016): 18.

66. Sherry Buchanan, *Tran Trung Tin: Paintings and Poems from Vietnam* (Asia Ink, 2002).

67. "Kanitha Tith–How Heavy is Time? (2020)," *Casco Art Institute: Working for the Commons*, June 16, 2020, YouTube, accessed September 2024, https://www.youtube.com/watch?v=vs0e05Bc_Tc.

68. In 2024, Anti-Archive moved its offices into a building formerly occupied by the now-defunct artist-run space, Sa Sa Art Projects.

69. Leslie Barnes, "*Un cinéma sans image*: Palimpsestic Memory and the Lost History of Cambodian Film," in Post-Migratory Cultures in Postcolonial France, eds.

Kathryn Kleppinger and Laura Reeck (Liverpool University Press, 2018), 79. This section also draws on Chou's conversations with the author since 2012.

70. Barnes, "*Un cinéma sans image*," 80.

71. As well as Barnes' essay, cited previously, see Marie Krämer, "In Search of a Lost Cinema: Cinephilia and Multidirectional Moving Image Memory in *Golden Slumbers* (Davy Chou, 2012)," *Alphaville: Journal of Film and Screen Media* 21 (2021): 72–88.

72. See Giulia Palladini and Marco Pustianaz, *Lexicon for an Affective Archive* (Live Art Development Agency and Intellect, 2018).

73. For more on Sihanouk's films, see Eliza Romey, "King, Politician, Artist: The Films of Norodom Sihanouk," unpub. Master of Arts thesis, La Trobe University, Melbourne, 1998.

74. David Chandler, *The Tragedy of Cambodian History: Politics, War, and Revolution Since 1945* (Yale University Press, 1991), 153; Milton Osborne, "The Passions of a Prince," in *Before Kampuchea: Preludes to a Tragedy* (Allen & Unwin, 1979), 44–58. Osborne describes theater doors being locked to trap cinema-goers inside during some screenings of Sihanouk's films.

75. Roung Kon Project, "Lux Cinema."

76. Roger Nelson, "Curating as (Expanded) Art History in Southeast Asia: Recent Independent Projects in Ho Chi Minh City, Luang Prabang and Phnom Penh," *ARTMargins* 9, no. 2 (2020): 52–53.

77. Margaret Jack, *Media Ruins: Cambodian Postwar Media Reconstruction and the Geopolitics of Technology* (MIT Press, 2023), 111.

78. Jack, *Media Ruins*, 111.

79. Roung Kon Project, "A Brief Introduction of Cambodian Cinema," *Roung Kon Project*, undated (circa 2020), accessed September 2024, https://www.roungkonproject.com/about.

80. The Capitol Cinema in Phnom Penh, now demolished, has special significance because it was the only cinema designed by Vann Molyvann (1926–2017), Cambodia's most celebrated modernist architect. Constructed in 1955 and renovated after a fire in 1967, the Capitol was also featured on the cover of the German architecture magazine, *Arch+*, in a 2021 special issue titled "Contested Modernities: Postcolonial Architecture and Identity Construction in Southeast Asia." The image was also used in an article by the architect and independent research Hun Sokagna, who is also a member of the Roung Kon Project. Helen Grant Ross and Darryl Leon Collins, *Building Cambodia: 'New Khmer Architecture' 1953–1970* (Key Publisher, 2006), 279; "Contested Modernities–Postkoloniale Architektur und Identitätskonstruktion in Südostasien," *Arch+* 243 (April 2021). See https://archplus.net/de/archiv/ausgabe/243/ (accessed September 2024).

81. Barnes, "*Un cinéma sans image*," 84.

82. Savunthara Seng, one of many younger filmmakers inspired and supported by Chou—and employed part-time by the Anti-Archive film production company Chou cofounded—made "traces" the theme of a transnational Southeast Asian cinema magazine he initiated. "Traces gesture, shock, defy, and aspire toward a greater truth," he writes, noting the "generative power of traces." Savunthara Seng, Alyssandra Maxine, and Duong Manh Hung, "Welcome to Issue 2 of Marg1n Magazine: Traces," *Marg1n* 2 (2025): 4.

83. Davy Chou, "Interview."

84. Alexander Supartono and Alexandra Moschovi, "Contesting Colonial (Hi)stories: (Post)colonial Imaginings of Southeast Asia," *Journal of Southeast Asian Studies* 51, no. 3 (September 2020): 345.

85. Clare Veal, "Nostalgia and Nationalism: Facebook 'Archives' and the Constitution of Thai Photographic Histories," *Journal of Southeast Asian Studies* 51, no. 3 (September 2020): 2.

86. Veal, "Nostalgia and Nationalism," 25.

87. Mieke Bal, *Quoting Caravaggio: Contemporary Art, Preposterous History* (University of Chicago Press, 1999), 1. Emphasis added.

2. CITING

1. On "epistemic politics" see: Tom Holert, *Knowledge Beside Itself: Contemporary Art's Epistemic Politics* (Sternberg Press, 2020).

2. Hilmi Johandi, quoted in The Artling Team, "An Interview with Hilmi Johandi," *The Artling*, June 18, 2014, accessed September 2024, https://theartling.com/en/artzine/interview-helm-johandi/.

3. For discussion of this issue, see Alfian Sa'at, Faris Joraimi and Sai Siew Min, eds., *Raffles Renounced: Towards a Merdeka History* (Ethos Books, 2021).

4. Hilmi Johandi, quoted in Roger Nelson, "Immersion, Fragmentation, and the Insidious Spectacle: Interview with Hilmi Johandi," in *President's Young Talents 2018*, ed. Joyce Toh (Singapore Art Museum, 2018), 103. My discussion of Hilmi draws in part on my experience curating his work for this exhibition.

5. Andrew Ranard, *Burmese Painting: A Linear and Lateral History* (Silkworm Books, 2009), 76–82.

6. Su Lin Lewis, *Cities in Motion: Urban Life and Cosmopolitanism in Southeast Asia, 1920–1940* (Cambridge University Press, 2016), 164.

7. There are numerous examples in Peter Lee, ed., *Amek Gambar–Taking Pictures: Peranakans and Photography* (Asian Civilisations Museum, 2020), 98, 155, 177.

8. Oil on canvas, 60 × 76cm, National Gallery Singapore. I thank Simon Soon for his insights during our conversations about this painting, which I helped acquire for the collection of National Gallery Singapore.

9. On dogs as pets in colonial Southeast Asia and their appearance in photo portraits, see Timothy P. Barnard, *Imperial Creatures: Humans and Other Animals in Colonial Singapore, 1819–1942* (NUS Press, 2019), 68–73.

10. Kim Lim, quoted in Joleen Loh, "Relocating Kim Lim: A Cosmopolitan Perspective," *Southeast of Now: Directions in Contemporary and Modern Art in Asia* 2, no. 2 (October 2018): 42–43.

11. Kim Lim in a 1988 letter, quoted in Hammad Nasar, "Notes from the Field: Navigating the Afterlife of 'The Other Story,'" in *Field Notes 4* (Hong Kong: Asia Art Archive, 2015), 57–58.

12. Kim Lim, photograph of Çavdarhisar, Turkey, 1996. Collection of the Estate of Kim Lim. © Estate of Kim Lim. Photo: Kim Lim; Kim Lim, *Kudah*, 1989, rose aurora marble, 112.4 × 42.5 × 27.3 cm, private collection © Estate of Kim Lim; Photo: Kim Lim. Published in: Joleen Loh, "The Photographs of Kim Lim: A Visual Essay," *Art History* 44, no. 3 (June 2021): 539 and 551.

13. For more on the relationship between these media, see Sarah Hamill and Megan R. Luke, eds., *Photography and Sculpture: The Art Object in Reproduction* (The Getty Research Institute, 2017).

14. Loet Leydesdorff, "Theories of Citation?," *Scientometrics* 43, no. 1 (1998): 5.

15. With thanks to Anissa Rahadiningtyas, Hilmi Johandi, and Simon Soon. There is little, if any, distinction between citing and quoting in Indonesian, Khmer, and several other Southeast Asian languages. For more on terminologies, see Chotpradit et al., "Terminologies of 'Modern' and 'Contemporary' 'Art' in Southeast Asia's Vernacular Languages: Indonesian, Javanese, Khmer, Lao, Malay, Myanmar/Burmese, Tagalog/Filipino, Thai and Vietnamese," *Southeast of Now: Directions in Contemporary and Modern Art in Asia* 2, no. 2 (October 2018): 65–195.

16. When the artist Ho Tzu Nyen, whose work I discuss in the epilogue, cocurated (with Hsu Chia-Wei) the 2019 Asia Art Biennial at the National Taiwan Museum of

Fine Arts, a room for "footnotes" was included, allowing several of the exhibited artists to present research materials related to their artworks.

17. T.K. Sabapathy, "Developing Regionalist Perspectives in Southeast Asian Art Historiography," in *Contemporary Art in Asia: A Critical Reader*, ed. Melissa Chiu and Benjamin Genocchio (MIT Press, 2011), 51.

18. James Elkins, *The End of Diversity in Art Historical Writing: North Atlantic Art History and Its Alternatives* (De Gruyter, 2021), 8.

19. Elkins, *The End of Diversity*, 11.

20. Björn Hellqvist, "Referencing in the Humanities and its Implications for Citation Analysis," *Journal of the American Society for Information Science and Technology* 61, no 2 (2010): 310–318.

21. Semsar Siahaan's painting is titled *Olympia, Identitas Ibu dan Anak* (*Olympia, Identity with Mother and Child*) (1987), oil on canvas, 140.5 x 290 cm, National Gallery Singapore. Yee I-Lann's work is titled *Wherein one cultivates cultural codes, the noble endeavours of mankind and thereby puts them in their place* (2013), giclee print on paper, 63 x 180 cm, Minneapolis Institute of Art. Art historian Aminudin T. H. Siregar has emphasized how Semsar's work "represents actual problems in social, political and [economic] spheres experienced by Indonesia at that time," focusing on the historical rather than art-historical connotations of the painting. See Aminudin T. H. Siregar, "He Who Comes as an Invalid and Wounded," in *Semsar Siahaan: Art, Liberation*, ed. T. K. Sabapathy (Gajah Gallery, 2017), 29. Discussing Yee's work, the scholars Alexander Supartono and Alexandra Moschovi recognize the artist's "ironic visual responses to . . . pictorial clichés" in nineteenth-century photography, yet emphasize that her work prompts viewers to "re-examine colonial relations and stereotypes" rather than to consider the politics of the reuse of a found image. Alexander Supartono and Alexandra Moschovi, "Contesting Colonial (Hi)stories: (Post)colonial Imaginings of Southeast Asia," *Journal of Southeast Asian Studies* 51, no. 3 (September 2020): 361.

22. John Clark, *Modern Asian Art* (University of Hawai'i Press and Craftsman House, 1998), 246.

23. Thanks to the artist Fyerool Darma for his extensive insights on this topic, in conversations since 2020.

24. Ingrid Muan, "Citing Angkor: The 'Cambodian Arts' in the Age of Restoration 1918–2000," unpub. PhD diss., Columbia University, New York, 2001.

25. Apinan Poshyananda, *Modern Art in Thailand: Nineteenth and Twentieth Centuries* (Oxford University Press, 1992).

26. Citation analysis, also sometimes called scientometrics or bibliometrics, is a scholarly field within the sciences (and to a lesser extent, social sciences) that relies largely on quantitative methods. See Leydesdorff, "Theories of Citation." See also Hellqvist, "Referencing in the Humanities."

27. Leo Steinberg, "Introduction: The Glorious Company," in Jean Lipman and Richard Marshall, *Art About Art* (E. P. Dutton and Whitney Museum of American Art, 1978), 21–22.

28. Steinberg, "Introduction," 22.

29. Steinberg, "Introduction," 23.

30. Steinberg, "Introduction," 25.

31. Steinberg, "Introduction," 25.

32. Partha Mitter, "Decentering Modernism: Art History and Avant-Garde from the Periphery," *The Art Bulletin* 90, no. 4, 2008, 531–548.

33. This chapter, and especially this section, is a substantially revised and expanded adaptation of Roger Nelson, "Emiria Sunassa's Citational Paintings: 'Like a Boil on a Virgin's Lips,'" *Oxford Art Journal* 46, no. 3 (2023): 407–426. I thank Adrian Vickers

and two anonymous peer reviewers for their insightful comments on an earlier draft of that essay.

34. Persagi is an abbreviation of *Persatuan Ahli Gambar Indonesia*, meaning Union of Indonesian Painters or, literally, Union of Indonesian Picture-Makers. See Claire Holt, *Art in Indonesia: Continuities and Change* (Cornell University Press, 1967), 197. For an introductory account of Persagi's importance in the context of regional modernist movements, see Masahiro Ushiroshoji, "The Birth of 'Fine Art' in Southeast Asia, 1900–1945," in *Charting Thoughts: Essays on Art in Southeast Asia*, ed. Low Sze Wee and Patrick D. Flores (National Gallery Singapore, 2017), 130–139.

Most of the other women exhibiting as artists in this period were "expatriates," often married to colonial officers. See Yvonne Low, "A 'Forgotten' Art World: The Singapore Art Club and its Colonial Women Artists," in *Charting Thoughts: Essays on Art in Southeast Asia*, ed. Low Sze Wee and Patrick D. Flores (Singapore: National Gallery Singapore, 2017), 104–119.

35. Unknown, "Emiria Sunassa: How She Came To Be a Painter," *Indonesian Affairs* (April–May 1952): 54.

36. Holt, *Art in Indonesia*, 252.

37. Holt, *Art in Indonesia*, 252.

38. Working for the CIA in the context of the Cold War likely encouraged Holt to privilege life experiences and identity categories over formal concerns. See Deena Burton, *Sitting at the Feet of Gurus: The Life and Dance Ethnography of Claire Holt* (Xlibris US, 2009), 98.

Wulan Dirgantoro, *Feminisms and Contemporary Art in Indonesia: Defining Experiences* (Amsterdam University Press, 2017), 81, 90.

39. Heidi Arbuckle, "Performing Emiria Sunassa: Reframing the Female Subject in Post/colonial Indonesia," unpub. PhD thesis, University of Melbourne, 2011. Arbuckle notes that Emiria was also known as Emiria Soenassa Wama'na Poetri Al'alam Mahkota Tidore, a noble appellation (6).

40. Tilman Seebass, "Change in Balinese Musical Life: 'Kebiar' in the 1920s and 1930s," in *Being Modern in Bali: Image and Change*, ed. Adrian Vickers (Yale University Southeast Asian Studies, 1996), 71–91. *Kebiar* refers both to the musical form and to the seated dance form.

41. Seebass, "Change," 71.

42. Adrian Vickers, *Bali: A Paradise Created* (Periplus Editions, 1989), 132, 172.

43. Henk Schulte Nordholt, "Localizing Modernity in Colonial Bali during the 1930s," *Journal of Southeast Asian Studies* 31, no. 1 (March 2000): 105.

44. Emiria Sunassa, typed letter to Prof. Dr. G. F. Pijper, dated November 7, 1947, translated by Zena Vollenberg-Jenkins, from the Guilaume Frédéric Pijper archive and collection, Leiden University Libraries.

45. Adrian Vickers, *Balinese Art: Paintings and Drawings of Bali, 1800–2010* (Tuttle, 2012), 125–8.

46. Vickers, *Balinese Art*, 126.

47. Vickers, *Balinese Art*, 113.

48. On McPhee and Spies, see Geffrey Corbett Green, "Walter Spies, Tourist Art and Balinese Art in Inter-war Colonial Bali," unpub. PhD thesis, Sheffield Hallam University, 2002, 122 n. 5. On photography and anthropology, see Ira Jacknis, "Margaret Mead and Gregory Bateson in Bali: Their Use of Photography and Film," *Cultural Anthropology* 3, no. 2 (1988): 160–77. See also Tara Blake and Janet Harbord, "Typewriters, Cameras and Love Affairs: The Fateful Haunting of Margaret Mead," *Journal of Media Practice* 9, no. 3 (2018): 215–27.

49. Hildred Geertz, *Images of Power: Balinese Paintings Made for Gregory Bateson and Margaret Mead* (University of Hawai'i Press, 1994).

50. Eng-Beng Lim, *Brown Boys and Rice Queens: Spellbinding Performances in the Asias* (New York University Press, 2013), 72.

51. Vickers, *Bali,* 183.

52. Arbuckle, "Performing Emiria Sunassa."

53. Yvonne Low, "Women Artists: Becoming Professional in Singapore, Malaya and Indonesia," unpub. PhD thesis, University of Sydney, 2014, 30–31, 107–111, 124, 177.

54. Carla Bianpoen, ed., *Indonesian Women Artists: The Curtain Opens* (Indonesian Arts Foundation, 2007), 103–108.

55. In Dirgantoro's study, for example, none of Emiria's paintings are discussed for more than half a page.

56. Shabbir Hussain Mustafa, ed., *Tropical: Stories from Southeast Asia and Latin America* (National Gallery Singapore, 2023); Riksa Afiaty and Charles Esche, eds., *Power & Other Things: Indonesia & Art, 1835–Now* (Snoeck, 2017); Sarah Lee and Sara Siew, eds., *Reframing Modernism: Painting from Southeast Asia, Europe and Beyond* (National Gallery Singapore, 2016); Phoebe Scott, *Familiar Others: Emiria Sunassa, Eduardo Masferré and Yeh Chi Wei, 1940s–1970s* (National Gallery Singapore, 2022).

57. I had the privilege of viewing Emiria's works in person during my time working as a curator at National Gallery Singapore (from 2019–2022) and during a research trip to Yogyakarta in 2023, including at the home of Iskandar Waworuntu, who oversees the artist's estate, as well as in several private collections with the generous assistance and collaboration of Grace Samboh. I am currently coediting (with Anissa Rahadiningtyas and Marije Plomp) a volume on Emiria, which will include new translations of a recently uncovered and previously unstudied trove of her letters as well as newly commissioned essays. It is forthcoming with Leiden University Press.

58. Dirgantoro, *Feminisms,* 95.

59. Udeido Collective, interview with Dicky Takndare, Betty Adii, and Michael Yan Devis, trans. Anissa Rahadiningtyas, in Scott, *Familiar Others,* 55.

60. See, for example, *Wanita Sulawesi (Sulawesi Woman),* 1958, Oil on canvas, 66 × 47 cm, Collection of Oei Hong Djien Museum, Magelang. The work is reproduced in Dirgantoro, *Feminisms,* 85.

61. Examples include paintings by S. Sudjojono, held in the collection of the Galeri Nasional Indonesia, and works by Agus and Otto Djaya, held at the Stedelijk Museum.

62. Writing in Indonesian in 1974, the art historian Sudarmaji noted the "dark colours" in Emiria's work, attributing her "discard the technique" style to her having been a "student of Sudjojono." Quoted in translation in Arbuckle, "Performing Emiria Sunassa," 85.

63. Basuki Resobowo, untitled letter to Oesman Effendi, dated October 19, 1949 and sent from Jakarta. Translated by Katherine Bruhn. Basuki Resobowo and Oesman Effendi, "The Development of New Indonesian Painting: A Correspondence between Two Painters," in *The Modern in Southeast Asian Art: A Reader,* vol. 1., ed. T. K. Sabapathy and Patrick D. Flores (National Gallery Singapore and NTU Centre for Contemporary Art Singapore, 2023), 382.

64. Quoted in translation in I Nyoman Darma Putra, "From Balinese to Indonesian; Poetry from the Colonial and National Revolution Periods," in *A Literary Mirror: Balinese Reflections on Modernity and Identity in the Twentieth Century* (KITLV Press, 2011), 94–5.

65. See Patrick D. Flores, "Towards a Lexicon of Inclinations: Words Forming Worlds in Southeast Asia," *Asian Diasporic Visual Cultures and the Americas* 3, no. 1–2 (2017): 35–53.

66. Arbuckle, "Performing Emiria Sunassa," 232–3.

67. On Cephas's significance in a global context, see Christine Barthe, ed., *Photographs 1842–1896: An Early Album of the World* (Kaph Books, 2019), 165.

68. Susie Protschky, *Photographic Subjects: Monarchy, Photography and the Making of Colonial Citizens* (Manchester University Press, 2019).

69. Protschky, *Photographic Subjects*, 46, 52 n. 65.

70. On photography's debt to Western traditions of painting, see David Bate, *Photography: The Key Concepts* (Berg, 2009). See also Aaron Scharf, *Art and Photography*, revised ed. (Penguin, 1974).

71. Roelof Goris, *Bali: Godsdienst en Ceremoniën* [Bali: Religion and Ceremonies] (Batavia: Druk G. Kolff & Co., 1930). I thank Charmaine Toh and Andy Koh for their kind assistance with my research on this book.

72. Vickers, *Bali*, 153; Arbuckle, "Performing Emiria Sunassa," 5.

73. Arbuckle, "Performing Emiria Sunassa," 238.

74. Arbuckle, "Performing Emiria Sunassa," 237.

75. By contrast, the dance scholar Beryl de Zoete notes substantial differences between the *kebyar* dance as it is performed in the north and south of the island. Beryl de Zoete and Walter Spies, *Dance and Drama in Bali* (Harper and Brothers Publishers, 1938), 232–241.

76. Arbuckle, "Performing Emiria Sunassa," 238.

77. Arbuckle cites a conversation with Pak Cok, "a descendent of the royal family in Pejeng and a Brahman who is often requested to conduct ceremonies." Arbuckle, "Performing Emiria Sunassa," 235, 238.

78. Arbuckle, "Performing Emiria Sunassa," 238.

79. I thank Adrian Vickers for this observation.

80. Emiria first exhibited in 1940, according to Arbuckle, "Performing Emiria Sunassa," 5. On Spies's sexuality, see Green, "Walter Spies," 129–134.

81. Lim, *Brown Boys*, 18.

82. The original Spies photograph has not been located. It is possible that the soft-focus quality was enhanced in the process of its reproduction in Goris's book.

83. Quoted in Lim, *Brown Boys*, 72.

84. Vickers, *Bali*, 184. Vickers has also suggested (in personal communications with the author, September 2022) that the commercial nature of Goris's publication would have necessitated this downplaying of the sexual overtones in Spies's photography.

85. "Zuid-Baliër met kostbare kris, waarvan het bovendeel der schede uit ivoor bestaat; het gevest uit goud, is met edelgesteenten bezet."

86. Arbuckle, "Performing Emiria Sunassa," 238.

87. Arbuckle also claims that the kris and flowers are unusual when worn in combination with the *udeng*. Arbuckle, "Performing Emiria Sunassa," 237.

88. The book comprises 343 pages of text and 112 photographic illustrations, of which 110 are works by Spies.

89. De Zoete, *Dance and Drama in Bali*, 235.

90. De Zoete, *Dance and Drama in Bali*, 235. De Zoete does not describe the Balinese receptions of Gusti Raka or of the *kebyar* dance; Vickers (in personal communications, September 2022) suggests that the wide eyes (*mata dedeling*) may also have been understood as shock or amazement at the dancers' unusual loss of control over their emotions.

91. De Zoete, *Dance and Drama in Bali*, 234.

92. The painting is reproduced in Nelson, "Emiria Sunassa's Citational Paintings," 423.

93. De Zoete, *Dance and Drama in Bali*, 235.

94. S. Sudjojono, *Seni Lukis, Kesenian, Seniman* [Painting, Art, Artist], quoted in translation in Dirgantoro, *Feminisms*, 82–83.

95. Thomas H. Ford, *How to Read a Poem: Seven Steps* (Routledge, 2021), 75–77. With thanks to Marion Campbell. Ford's development of the concept is indebted to Adorno's "riddle-character."

96. Seebass, "Kebiar," 79.

97. Patrick D. Flores, "Art-Historical Alterity in the Post-Colony," in *Art History and Emergency: Crises in the Visual Arts and Humanities*, ed. David Breslin and Darby English (Sterling and Francine Clark Institute and Yale University Press, 2016), 95.

98. James Elkins, *The End of Diversity in Art Historical Writing: North Atlantic Art History and Its Alternatives* (De Gruyter, 2021), 164.

99. Vickers, *Bali*, 160.

100. See Chua Beng Huat, "Inter-Referencing Southeast Asia: Absence, Resonance and Provocation," in *Methodology and Research Practice in Southeast Asian Studies*, ed. Mikko Huotari, Jürgen Rüland, and Judith Schlehe (Palgrave Macmillan), 273–288. See also Kuan-Hsing Chen, *Asia as Method: Toward Deimperialization* (Duke University Press, 2010).

101. Martin Powers, "The Art-Historical Art of Song China: Citation and Historicism in *Tao Yuanming Returning to Seclusion*," *Ars Orientalis* 49 (2019): 23.

102. Linda Hutcheon, *A Theory of Parody: The Teachings of Twentieth-Century Art Forms* (University of Illinois Press, 2000), 42.

103. Miwon Kwon, "Promiscuity of Space: Some Thoughts on Jessica Stockholder's Scenographic Compositions," *Grey Room* 18 (Winter 2004): 56. Kwon is describing Gerhard Richter's paintings.

104. "Unlike [Margaret] Mead's approach, Spies's visualization of Bali is much less interested in the purchase of a scientific façade. Rather, it veered toward art" (Lim, *Brown Boys*, 46).

105. Emmelyn Butterfield-Rosen, *Modern Art and the Remaking of Human Disposition* (University of Chicago Press, 2021), 18–19.

106. Mieke Bal, *Image-Thinking: Artmaking as Cultural Analysis* (Edinburgh University Press, 2022).

107. Paul Duro, "Why Imitation, and Why Global?" in *Theorizing Imitation in the Visual Arts: Global Contexts*, ed. Paul Duro (Wiley Blackwell, 2015), 11.

108. Lauren Fournier, *Autotheory as Feminist Practice in Art, Writing and Criticism* (MIT Press, 2021), 154.

109. Claire Holt, unpublished field note headed "Emiria to HBS," dated February 23, 1956; Claire Holt papers, 1927–1970, Collection Number: 14-27-2648, Cornell University Library. A scanned record of these archival papers was kindly provided by Adrian Vickers.

110. Emiria Sunassa, typed letter to Prof. Dr. G. F. Pijper, dated May 6, 1954, translated by Zena Vollenberg-Jenkins, from the Guilaume Frédéric Pijper archive and collection, Leiden University Libraries.

111. Holt, *Art in Indonesia*, 252.

3. STAGING

1. The three-channel video is dated by the artist as 2021–ongoing. It was first shown at the artist's solo exhibition at Tate St Ives in 2022 and again in *The Milk of Dreams* at the 59th Venice Biennale in the same year. Some parts of my discussion of this artwork have been substantially revised and expanded from an exhibition catalogue essay: Roger Nelson, "Thao Nguyen Phan's Parafabulations: Thinking Alongside *First Rain,*

Brise-Soleil," in *Thao Nguyen Phan: Reincarnations of Shadows*, eds. Lucia Aspesi and Fiammetta Griccioli (Pirelli HangarBicocca and Marsilio Editori, 2023), 125–142.

2. Unless otherwise cited, information about Thao Nguyen Phan's artwork is drawn from my conversations with the artist since 2013 and an interview conducted at her studio in Saigon (Ho Chi Minh City) in April 2023.

3. Their names with diacritics: Nguyễn Hữu Thiện and Bùi Quang Hanh. For more on the design, see Andrew Cruse, "Tropical Comforts in Vietnam," *ABE Journal: Architecture Beyond Europe* 19 (2021), accessed June 2025, https://doi.org/10.4000/abe.12515. For a more general overview of modern architecture in the country, which draws on several Vietnamese-language sources, see Mel Schenck, *Southern Vietnamese Modernist Architecture: Mid-Century Vernacular Modernism* (Architecture Vietnam Books, 2020).

4. Brise-soleils are found far beyond Southeast Asia, of course; Phan recounts the experience of visiting the Bangladesh National Parliament in Dhaka in early 2020 as one inspiration for her work. See "Architecture is the Painting of Making Space: Pen Sereypagna in conversation with Thao Nguyen Phan," in *Thao Nguyen Phan*, eds. Anne Barlow and Giles Jackson (Tate, 2022), 50.

5. For an account of speculative fiction in Southeast Asia, see Ng Yi-Sheng, "A Gate of Dragon's Teeth: A Decolonial Approach to Writing Precolonial Historical Fiction in Singapore," unpub. PhD diss., Nanyang Technological University, Singapore, 2021. Ng affirms that "it is not magical realism that kept the folkloric tradition alive in an age of deracinating modernity, but popular speculative fiction" (68).

6. On tropical modernist architecture in Southeast Asia, see Jiat-Hwee Chang, *A Genealogy of Tropical Architecture: Colonial Networks, Nature and Technoscience* (Routledge, 2016).

7. See, for example, Helen Grant Ross and Darryl Leon Collins, *Building Cambodia: 'New Khmer Architecture' 1953–1970* (Key Publisher 2006).

8. There are exceptions. For a significant example of scholarship that redirects attention away from celebrated architects, see Jiat-Hwee Chang, Justin Zhuang, and Darren Soh, *Everyday Modernism: Architecture & Society in Singapore* (Ridge Books and NUS Press, 2023).

9. Matthew Partington and Linda Sandino, eds., *Oral History in the Visual Arts* (Bloomsbury, 2013); Janina Gosseye, Naomi Stead, and Deborah van der Plaat, eds., *Speaking of Buildings: Oral History in Architectural Research* (Princeton Architectural Press, 2019).

10. Roger Nelson, "Locating the Domestic in Vann Molyvann's National Sports Complex," *ABE Journal: Architecture Beyond Europe* 11 (2017): par. 25, 26, 38.

11. Some of my comments on the four facets of staging have been substantially revised and expanded from "Staging: Notes on Hotels and Hospitality in the Work of Svay Ken and Hilmi Johandi," an essay I contributed to the forthcoming catalogue for the exhibition *Guest Relations*, held at Jameel Arts Centre in Dubai in 2023. I thank the curators of that exhibition, Murtaza Vali and Lucas Morin, for their comments.

12. June Yap, *Retrospective: A Historiographical Aesthetic in Contemporary Singapore and Malaysia* (Strategic Information and Research Development Centre, 2016), 5.

13. Jane Blocker, *Becoming Past: History in Contemporary Art* (University of Minnesota Press, 2016), 13.

14. They include water puppets called *múa rối nước* in Vietnam, as well as various kinds of shadow puppets, including those called *wayang* in the Malay world (an archipelagic and peninsular zone also known as Nusantara, which encompasses Indonesia, Singapore, and Malaysia), others called *lkhon nang sbek* in Cambodia, and *nang yai* in Thailand.

15. Lawrence Chin, "The Value of Almost: Some Thoughts on Paintings by Hilmi Johandi," in *Stagecraft: Landscapes and Paradise* (Ota Fine Arts, 2019), unpaginated.

16. Hilmi Johandi, "Staging Illusion: Seeing Void," unpub. Master's (Fine Arts) diss., Lasalle College of the Arts, Singapore, 2018, 5.

17. Hilmi, "Staging Illusion," 37.

18. Chin, "The Value of Almost," unpaginated.

19. "Hilmi Johandi | Stagecraft: Landscapes and Paradise," *Ota Fine Arts*, 2019, accessed September 2024, https://www.otafinearts.com/exhibitions/67-hilmi-johandi-stagecraft-landscapes-and-paradise-hilmi-johandi/.

20. meLê yamomo, *Theatre and Music in Manila and the Asia Pacific, 1869-1946: Sounding Modernities* (Palgrave Macmillan, 2018), 6.

21. yamomo, *Theatre and Music*, 33.

22. yamomo, *Theatre and Music*, 59.

23. Rebecca E. Karl, *Staging the World: Chinese Nationalism at the Turn of the Twentieth Century* (Duke University Press, 2002), 28.

24. Jan Mrázek, "Ways of Experiencing Art: Art History, Television, and Javanese Wayang," in *What's the Use of Art? Asian Visual and Material Culture in Context*, eds. Jan Mrázek and Morgan Pitelka (University of Hawai'i Press, 2008), 293.

25. Mrázek, "Ways of Experiencing Art," 299.

26. Although Thu (Ngô Viết Thụ) is credited as the architect of the building, the unique brise-soleil at the Independence Palace was designed in collaboration with the sculptor Nguyen Van The (Nguyễn Văn Thế). Cruse, "Tropical Comforts in Vietnam."

27. The factory is now called Vicem, the Vietnamese Cement Industry Corporation, which operates twelve plants and is described as the country's "major established cement manufacturer." Peter Edwards, "Cement in Vietnam," *Global Cement Magazine*, April 19, 2012, https://www.globalcement.com/magazine/articles/687-cement-in-vietnam.

28. Stanley Robert Larsen and James Lawton Collins, Jr, *Vietnam Studies: Allied Participation in Vietnam* (Department of the Army, 1975), 166.

29. Heather Marie Stur, *Saigon at War: South Vietnam and the Global Sixties* (Cambridge University Press, 2020), 2, 31. See also Andrew J. Gawthorpe, *To Build As Well as Destroy: American Nation Building in South Vietnam* (Cornell University Press, 2018).

30. Phan Thao Nguyen, "Artist Statement," in *Poetic Amnesia*, ed. Zoe Butt (The Factory Contemporary Art Centre, 2017), 13.

31. Nora A. Taylor, "(Tran)scribed History: Thảo Nguyên Phan's Palimpsest Visions of Colonialism and Conversion," *Afterall* 47 (Spring/Summer 2019), accessed September 2024, https://www.afterall.org/articles/transcribed-history-thao-nguyen-phans-palimpsest-visions-of-colonialism-and-conversion/; Zoe Butt, "Poetic Amnesia," in *Poetic Amnesia*, 35.

32. David Chandler, *A History of Cambodia*, fourth edition (Westview Press, 2008), 277, 281.

33. Ross and Collins, *Building Cambodia*, 26–27.

34. Ross and Collins, *Building Cambodia*, 27.

35. Ross and Collins, *Building Cambodia*, 27.

36. Phan, quoted in "Architecture is the Painting of Making Space," 48.

37. Robert Turnbull, "A Burned-out Theater: The State of Cambodia's Performing Arts," in *Expressions of Cambodia: The Politics of Tradition, Identity, and Change*, eds. Leakthina Chau-Pech Ollier and Tim Winter (Routledge, 2006), 137.

38. See Boreth Ly, "Screening the Crisis of Monetary Masculinity in Rithy Panh's *One Night After the War* and *Burnt Theatre*," in *Film in Contemporary Southeast Asia*, eds. David C. L. Lim and Hiroyuki Yamamoto (Routledge, 2012), 53–72.

39. Carrie Lambert-Beatty, "Make-Believe: Parafiction and Plausibility," *October* 129 (Summer 2009): 54.

40. Lambert-Beatty, "Make-Believe," 72–73. Lambert-Beatty later states: "We have the responsibility—and feel the pressure—to be ever more inclusive and transnational in our narratives. But, as this paper's Euro-American focus itself demonstrates, few of us have the languages, the cultural knowledge, or the local art-historical background to properly master a fraction of what we would like to think, teach, and write about" (84).

41. Nora A. Taylor and Karin Zitzewitz, "History as Figure of Thought in Contemporary Art in South and Southeast Asia," *Art Journal* 77, no. 4 (Winter 2018): 46.

42. Lambert-Beatty, "Make-Believe," 73; Phan, quoted in "Empathy not Erasure," *Tate Etc.* 54 (Spring 2022), April 26, 2022, accessed September 2024, https://www.tate.org.uk/tate-etc/issue-54-spring-2022/empathy-not-erasure.

43. Phan, "Artist Statement," in *Poetic Amnesia*, 13. Phan's repeated reference to histories from other parts of Southeast Asia and from other regions in the world (for example, her citing of Indian and Japanese literature in *Mute Grain*) is relatively unusual among her peers.

44. Joanne Leow, "Confabulation as Decolonial Pedagogy in Singapore Literature," in *Decolonizing the English Literary Curriculum*, eds. Ato Quayson and Ankhi Mukherjee (Cambridge University Press, 2024), 178.

45. Lambert-Beatty, "Make-Believe: Parafiction and Plausibility": 54.

46. Mark Godfrey, "The Artist as Historian," *October* 120 (Spring 2007): 170.

47. Phan, quoted in "Empathy Not Erasure."

48. Phan, quoted in "Imprinting Parallel Histories: Thao Nguyen Phan in conversation with Zoe Butt," *Fondazione In Between Art Film*, 2021, accessed September 2024, https://still.inbetweenartfilm.com/en/imprinting-parallel-histories/.

49. Phan, quoted in "Imprinting Parallel Histories."

50. Phan, "Artist Statement," in *Poetic Amnesia*, 14.

51. Gavriel Rosenfeld, "Why Do We Ask 'What If?' Reflections on the Function of Alternate History," *History and Theory* 41, no. 4 (December 2002): 90.

52. "Agriculture and Fishing," *OpenDevelopment Vietnam*, May 14, 2020, accessed September 2024, https://vietnam.opendevelopmentmekong.net/topics/agriculture-and-fishing/#ref-3846269-16.

53. Taylor, "(Tran)scribed History."

54. Saidiya Hartman, "Venus in Two Acts," *Small Axe* 12, no. 2 (2008): 11. Quoted in Daniela Rosner, *Critical Fabulations: Reworking the Methods and Margins of Design* (MIT Press, 2018), 1.

55. Hartman, quoted in Huey Copeland, Leah Dickerman, and Pamela M. Lee, "Between Visual *Scenes* and Beautiful *Lives*: A Conversation with Saidiya Hartman," *October* 180 (Spring 2022): 90.

56. Phan, "Artist Statement," in *Poetic Amnesia*, 14.

57. Hartman quoted in Copeland, Dickerman and Lee, "Between," 100–01. Phan, "Artist Statement," in *Poetic Amnesia*, 14.

58. Lambert-Beatty, "Make-Believe," 54. Pamela Nguyen Corey proposed the concept of "parahistory" in an unpublished seminar presented at Nanyang Technological University, Singapore, in April 2023, titled "The Purpose of Parahistory in Late Socialist Vietnam."

59. Lambert-Beatty, "Make-Believe," 82.

60. meLê yamomo, "Acoustic Epistemologies and Early Sound Recordings in the Nusantara Region: Phonography, Archive, and the Birth of Ethnomusicology," in *Made in Nusantara: Studies in Popular Music*, eds. Adil Johan and Mayco A. Santaella (Routledge, 2021), 78.

61. This paragraph, and my subsequent discussion of this artwork, draws on my regular conversations and correspondences with Fyerool Darma throughout 2023 and 2024, in Singapore, Chiang Mai, and online. During this period, I served as the curator commissioning the artist's works on Flower for exhibitions I organized—both titled *The Unfaithful Octopus*—at Nanyang Technological University in Singapore (in 2023) and at MAIIAM Contemporary Art Museum in Chiang Mai (in 2024).

62. Roger Nelson, "Behind the Painting, A Pantoum: Literature and Art and Southeast Asia," in *Routledge Companion to Literature and Art*, eds. Neil Murphy, W. Michelle Wang, and Cheryl Julia Lee (Routledge, 2024), 452–466.

63. This liminal and potentially liberatory state is one that some contemporary artists, like Fyerool (who is a member of Singapore's minoritized Malay community), may struggle to attain in the twenty-first century (in the context of Singapore's Chinese majority population).

64. Fyerool Darma, "Polymerized Heritage," *Future Anterior* 19, no. 1 (Summer 2022): 101.

65. Kenny Chee, "Robot Dog Spot Finds New Work: Scanning Worksites, Sending Results Over 5G," *The Straits Times*, October 19, 2021, https://www.straitstimes.com/tech/tech-news/robot-dog-spot-finds-new-work-scanning-worksites-sending-results-over-5g.

66. Mieke Bal, *Image-Thinking: Artmaking as Cultural Analysis* (Edinburgh University Press, 2022), 7.

67. In fact, Bal's articulation of "image-thinking" is already expansive, encompassing not only visual artefacts but also works of literature, theory, and cinema, among others.

68. yamomo, "Acoustic Epistemologies," 78.

69. Samuel Saelemakers, "Foreword," in *Speculative Art Histories: Analysis at the Limits*, ed. Sjoerd van Tuinen (Edinburgh University Press, 2017), 9.

70. Sjoerd van Tuinen, "Introduction," in *Speculative Art Histories: Analysis at the Limits*, ed. Sjoerd van Tuinen (Edinburgh University Press, 2017), 11.

71. Kuan Hsing Chen, *Asia as Method: Toward Deimperialization* (Duke University Press, 2010), 3.

72. In mid-2024, the artwork was relocated from its original site to a similar clearing nearby. Here, I discuss its original iteration. I will address its relocation in a forthcoming journal article.

73. Roger Nelson, "Immersion, Fragmentation, and the Insidious Spectacle: Interview with Hilmi Johandi," in *President's Young Talents 2018*, ed. Joyce Toh (Singapore Art Museum, 2018), 101–109.

74. Hilmi's project was part of a larger series of public art commissions, curated by Selene Yap with her colleagues, titled *Singapore Deviation*. For more information, see "Singapore Deviation: Wander with Art through the Rail Corridor," *The Everyday Museum*, Singapore Art Museum, 2023, https://www.theeverydaymuseum.sg/project/singapore-deviation/.

75. Dabney Townsend, "The Picturesque," *The Journal of Aesthetics and Art Criticism* 55, no. 4 (Autumn 1997): 368.

76. Joanne Leow, "Circumventing the Archive: *The Art of Charlie Chan Hock Chye* and *To Singapore, with Love*," *Verge: Studies in Global Asias* 6, no. 1 (Spring 2020): 60.

77. Quotes from Hilmi Johandi are mostly derived from a recorded interview and informal conversation with the artist and Selene Yap, held at Hilmi's studio, in March 2024. I also draw on conversations and regular studio visits since 2017.

78. Siti Nuraishah Ahmad, "Malaysia as the Archetypal Garden in the British Creative Imagination," *Southeast Asian Studies* 3, no. 1 (April 2014): 49-50.

79. Both Le Fleming's and Charton's works can be viewed online. "Malaysian Golden Chersonese Malay States Railway Travel Poster," Roots, National Heritage Board, undated, accessed September 2024, https://www.roots.gov.sg/en/collection%20landing/listing/1392905; "'Travel Through Malaya by FMS Railways' poster (Mount Ophir, Johor)," Roots, National Heritage Board, undated, accessed September 2024, https://www.roots.gov.sg/Collection-Landing/listing/1132482.

80. Letter from Rosalind Le Fleming to her mother, dated March 11, 1930, in Hugh Morton Le Fleming, "Transcript of Le Fleming's Letters to Florence Le Fleming," typed by Steven Fleming. Cambridge University Library, Hugh Le Fleming Collection, GBR/0115/RCS/RCMS 371/2.

81. For more on this history, see Rodolphe De Koninck, "Wessex Estate: Recollections of British Military and Imperial History in the Heart of Singapore," *Asian Journal of Social Science* 31, no. 3 (2003): 435–451.

82. In our interview, Selene Yap speculated that 80 to 90 percent of the Wessex Estate residents she interacted with during the development and installation of Hilmi's project were white foreigners.

83. Lai Chee Kien, "The Enigma of Departure: Remembering Singapore's Railway Lines and Stations," *BiblioAsia* (October–December 2011), unpaginated, accessed September 2024, https://biblioasia.nlb.gov.sg/vol-7/issue-3/oct-dec-2011/singapore-railway-lines/.

84. Maggie M. Cao, *The End of Landscape in Nineteenth-century America* (University of California Press, 2018), 4.

85. Raymond Isaacs, "The Urban Picturesque: An Aesthetic Experience of Urban Pedestrian Places," *Journal of Urban Design* 5, no. 2 (2000): 150–154.

86. Lawrence Chua, *Bangkok Utopia: Modern Architecture and Buddhist Felicities, 1910–1973* (University of Hawai'i Press, 2021), 64.

87. Raffaella Sini, *Singapore's Park System Master Planning: A Nation Building Tool to Construct Narratives in Post-Colonial Countries* (Springer, 2020), 173.

88. Sini, *Singapore's Park System*, 341.

4. AUTOTHEORIZING

1. Araya Rasdjarmrearnsook, *I Am An Artist (He Said)*, trans. Kong Rithdee, ed. Roger Nelson and Chanon Kenji Praepipatmongkol (National Gallery Singapore, 2022), 354.

2. Kong Rithdee, translator of Araya's book to English, notes of the term "artmaker" that "Araya deliberately uses it throughout the book to signify a more casual, perhaps more mundane association than 'artist'." Kong Rithdee, endnotes to "Introduction," in Araya, *I Am An Artist (He Said)*, 18 n. 1.

3. Araya, *I Am An Artist (He Said)*, 8, 100. Emphasis in original.

4. Araya, *I Am An Artist (He Said)*, 160.

5. Araya Rasdjarmrearnsook, quoted in Susie Wong, "Araya Rasdjarmrearnsook," in *Southeast Asian Art Today*, ed. Joyce van Fenema (Singapore: Roeder Publications, 1996), 234.

6. The suggestion that the book may also be an artwork is from Kong Rithdee, "Translator's Note," in Araya, *I Am An Artist (He Said)*, 417.

7. Araya, *I Am An Artist (He Said)*, 339–52.

8. Araya, *I Am An Artist (He Said)*, 124–25, 296–300.

9. Araya, *I Am An Artist (He Said)*, 385–87.

10. Araya, *I Am An Artist (He Said)*, 339, 345.

11. Araya, quoted in Wong, "Araya Rasdjarmrearnsook," 234.

12. Lauren Fournier, *Autotheory as Feminist Practice in Art, Writing, and Criticism* (MIT Press, 2021), 14.

13. Fournier, *Autotheory*, 14, 47.

14. Svay Ken, *Painted Stories: The Life of a Cambodian Family from 1941 to the Present*, ed. Ly Daravuth and Ingrid Muan (Reyum Institute of Art and Culture, 2001), 40.

15. Svay Ken, *Painted Stories*, 39.

16. Svay Ken, *Painted Stories*, 40.

17. Svay Ken, *Painted Stories*, 47.

18. Araya, *I Am An Artist (He Said)*, 340.

19. Clare Veal, "Water is Never Still: Araya Rasdjarmrearnsook's Sculptural and Installation Practice," *Afterall* 47, no. 1 (Spring/Summer 2019): 93.

20. Candice Breitz, "The First Johannesburg Biennale: Work in Progress," *Third Text* 9, no. 31 (1995): 92–3.

21. Breitz, "The First Johannesburg Biennale," 93.

22. Observing a growing trend in the 1990s and early 2000s, Araya jokingly calls sex work "one sexy topic," quoting an (unnamed) "man who believes he knows women inside out" as saying that "if women artists want to be famous in Thailand, they must tackle the topic of prostitution." Araya, *I Am An Artist (He Said)*, 160.

23. Araya, quoted in Wong, "Araya Rasdjarmrearnsook," 234.

24. On Hsü: Lai Chee Kien, "Translator's Notes," in Marco C.F. Hsü, *A Brief History of Malayan Art*, trans. Lai Chee Kien (Millennium Books, 1999), xii. On Holt, see Deena Burton, *Sitting at the Feet of Gurus: The Life and Dance Ethnography of Claire Holt* (Xlibris, 2009), 3.

25. Hsü's book was the subject of an exhibition at the NUS Museum, running from 2013 to 2015, titled *Between Here and Nanyang: Marco Hsu's Brief History of Malayan Art*. Holt's photographs were exhibited as part of an exhibition at the Latvian Centre for Contemporary Art, in 2018, titled *Shared History*. Her archives are also held at the New York Public Library and Cornell University.

26. Holt exhibited alongside several of the artists she wrote about in 1956. This is documented in Dan Soewarjono, "Dikitar Pelukis Dan Pengartja Wanita" [Around women painters and sculptors], *Budaya Jaya* (January 1957): 26–54. Thanks to Grace Samboh for introducing this source to me and for arranging its translation.

27. Kenneth M. George, *Picturing Islam: Art and Ethics in a Muslim Lifeworld* (Wiley-Blackwell, 2010), 7.

28. Bruce Cumings, "Biting the Hand That Feeds You: Why the 'Intelligence Function' of American Foundation Support for Area Studies Remains Hidden in Plain Sight," *Global Society* 28, no. 1 (2014): 70–89.

29. Nora A. Taylor, "Introduction: Who Speaks for Southeast Asian Art?," in *Modern and Contemporary Southeast Asian Art: An Anthology*, ed. Nora A. Taylor and Boreth Ly (Cornell Southeast Asia Program Publications, 2012), 4.

30. Taylor, "Introduction: Who Speaks for Southeast Asian Art?," 4.

31. David Teh, "The City in Time: Contemporary Art and Urban Form in Vietnam and Cambodia" [book review], *Journal of Asian Studies* 83, no. 2 (2024): 497.

32. T. K. Sabapathy, *Road to Nowhere: The Quick Rise and Long Fall of Art History in Singapore* (The Art Gallery at the National Institute of Education, 2010).

33. Christopher S. Wood, *A History of Art History* (Princeton University Press, 2019), 288.

34. Wood, *A History of Art History*, 5.

35. Wood, *A History of Art History*, 27, 5.

36. Wood, *A History of Art History*, 5.

37. Wood, *A History of Art History*, 22.

38. Nora A. Taylor, *Painters in Hanoi: An Ethnography of Vietnamese Art*, 2nd ed. (NUS Press, 2009), 4–5; Nora A. Taylor, "The Southeast Asian Art Historian as Ethnographer?" *Third Text* 25, no. 4 (2011): 485.

39. Wood, *A History of Art History*, 26.

40. This is another way in which the discipline of Art History in Southeast Asia has developed differently from in the North and West. Most museums and scholarly art historians here focus on works considered "fine art." The turn to "visual culture," particularly in the North American academy, has had surprisingly little impact in the region.

41. Astri Wright, "The Arc of My Field is a Rainbow with an Expanding Twist and All Kinds of Creatures Dancing: The Growing Inclusivity of Indonesian Art History," in *Producing Indonesia: The State of the Field of Indonesian Studies*, ed. Eric Tagliacozzo (Cornell Southeast Asia Program Publications, 2014), 126.

42. Astri Wright, "Self-Taught All the Way: Three Contemporary Women Artists in Indonesia," in *Women Imaging Women: Home, Body, Memory: Papers from the Conference on Artists from Indonesia, Philippines, Thailand and Vietnam*, ed. Flaudette May V. Datuin and Patrick D. Flores (Ford Foundation, Art Studies Foundation, Cultural Center of the Philippines, 1999), 118.

43. Fournier, *Autotheory*, 36.

44. Wulan Dirgantoro, *Feminisms and Contemporary Art in Indonesia: Defining Experiences* (Amsterdam University Press, 2017), 31

45. Việt Lê, *Return Engagements: Contemporary Art's Traumas of Modernity and History in Sài Gòn and Phnom Penh* (Duke University Press, 2021), xiv, xi.

46. Sabapathy, *Road to Nowhere*, 4, 16.

47. Lê, *Return Engagements*, 39.

48. T. K. Sabapathy, "Developing Regionalist Perspectives in Southeast Asian Art Historiography" [1996], in *Contemporary Art in Asia: A Critical Reader*, ed. Benjamin Genocchio and Melissa Chiu (MIT Press, 2011), 47–61.

49. Alex Brostoff and Lauren Fournier, "Introduction: Autotheory ASAP! Academia, Decoloniality, and 'I,'" *ASAP/Journal* 6, no. 3 (2021): 490.

50. Brostoff and Fournier, "Introduction: Autotheory ASAP!" 498–9.

51. Araya, *I Am An Artist (He Said)*, 71–73.

52. Arnika Fuhrmann, *Ghostly Desires: Queer Sexuality and Vernacular Buddhism in Contemporary Thai Cinema* (Duke University Press, 2016), 164–65.

53. Pamela N. Corey, "The 'First' Cambodian Contemporary Artist," *Udaya: Journal of Khmer Studies* 12 (2014): 78–79.

54. Kamini Vellodi, "Thought Beyond Research: A Deleuzian Critique of Artistic Research," in *Aberrant Nuptials: Deleuze and Artistic Research 2*, ed. Paulo de Assis and Paolo Giudici (Leuven University Press, 2019), 215.

55. "Svay Ken and Chath Piersath: Outsider Art," *Java Creative Café*, April–May, 2003, accessed September 2024, https://javacreativecafe.com/gallery/outsider-art-2003/.

56. Quotes from Svay Ken in this paragraph are from: Nico Mesterharm (director), Lach Chantha and Meta House, "Svay Ken Talks (2008)," YouTube, May 9, 2023, video, 41:09, accessed September 2024, https://www.youtube.com/watch?v=Wo87N13d_WU.

57. Svay Ken was clearly aware of his regional and international successes; in his writing and in interviews, he refers to *New York Times* coverage and other accolades.

58. Svay Ken, *Painted Stories*, 41.

59. Svay Ken, *Painted Stories*, 43.

60. Svay Ken, *A Good Friend is Hard to Find: An Homage to Ingrid by Painter Svay Ken*, trans. Helen Jarvis (Reyum Publishing, 2006), 8.

61. Svay Ken, *A Good Friend is Hard to Find*, 7.

62. Corey, "The 'First' Cambodian Contemporary Artist," 62.

63. Other spaces, like the New Art Gallery where Svay Ken had held his first exhibition (as depicted in *Painted Stories*), were essentially shops selling frames, paintings,

and prints. By contrast, Reyum commissioned artists to make works for themed exhibitions, organized events, and published books on a range of topics related to art and culture.

64. For more on the art-historical significance of this inclusion, see Roger Nelson, "The Gap Which Separates: Simultaneity, Disparity, and Audiovisual Linking Technologies in 'Southeast Asian Contemporary Art,'" *positions: asia critique* 33, no. 1 (2025): 161–191.

65. It is unclear if these visitors are also the Fukuoka curators or an unrelated group.

66. Svay Ken, *A Good Friend is Hard to Find*, 9.

67. Svay Ken, *A Good Friend is Hard to Find*, 8.

68. Corey, "The 'First' Cambodian Contemporary Artist," 64–65. Ingrid Muan, "Musings on Museums from Phnom Penh," in *Museum Frictions: Public Cultures/Global Transformations*, ed. Ivan Karp et al (Duke University Press, 2006), 257–85; Ashley Thompson, "Forgetting to Remember, Again: On Curatorial Practice and 'Cambodian Art' in the Wake of Genocide," *diacritics* 41, no. 2 (2013): 83–88.

69. The two most substantial exhibition histories dealing with Southeast Asia are both unpublished doctoral dissertations. Seng Yu Jin, "A History of Art Exhibitions: The Emergence of Critical Exhibitions in Southeast Asia, 1970s–1990s," unpub. PhD diss., University of Melbourne, 2019; Kathleen Ditzig (Ditzig Kathleen Elizabeth Li-Ying), "Exhibiting Southeast Asia in the Cultural Cold War: Geopolitics of Regional Art Exhibitions (1940s–1980s)," unpub. PhD diss., Nanyang Technological University, Singapore, 2023.

70. "A Good Friend is Hard to Find," *Reyum Institute of Arts and Culture*, January 29, 2006, accessed September 2024, http://reyum.org/exhibitions/exhibit20/exhibit_photo_gallery.html#A.

71. Erik W. Davis, *Deathpower: Buddhism's Ritual Imagination in Cambodia* (Columbia University Press, 2016), 77–78.

72. "A Good Friend" website.

73. Kong, "Translator's Note," 417. Emphasis in original.

74. Phatarawadee Phataranawik, "The Artist as Writer," *The Nation* (January 12, 2018), accessed September 2024, https://www.nationthailand.com/life/30336117.

75. Peter Schwenger, *Asemic: The Art of Writing* (University of Minnesota Press, 2019), 7.

76. David Teh, *Thai Art: Currencies of the Contemporary* (MIT Press, 2017), 156.

77. Phatarawadee, "The Artist as Writer," emphasis added.

78. David Joselit, "The Readymade Metabolized: Fluxus in Life," *RES: Anthropology and Aesthetics*, no. 63/64 (Spring/Autumn 2013): 190–200.

79. Joselit, "The Readymade Metabolized," 197.

80. Araya Rasdjarmrearnsook, solo exhibition catalogue, 1994, translated from Thai to English by Clare Veal, and quoted in Clare Veal, "Can the Girl be a Thai Woman? Reading the Works of Araya Rasdjarmrearnsook from Feminist Perspectives," in John Clark, Clare Veal and Judha Su, *Araya Rasdjarmrearnsook: Storytellers of the Town*, (4A Centre for Contemporary Asian Art, 2014), 63–4.

81. Araya Rasdjarmrearnsook, quoted in Apinan Poshyananda, "Roaring Tigers, Desperate Dragons in Transition," in *Contemporary Art in Asia: Traditions, Tensions*, ed. Apinan Poshyananda (Asia Society Galleries, 1996), 43.

82. T. K. Sabapathy, "Exhibitions of Southeast Asian Modern/Contemporary Art. Recollections, and Thoughts on Some Matters," unpub. paper presented at the Second Board Retreat of the Singapore Art Museum, September 13, 2017, 4. I thank Sabapathy for kindly sharing this paper with me.

83. One scholar has proposed that visual arts have developed more quickly than literary forms in Singapore, "if for no other reason than just the simple fact that the

physical infrastructure for their display is more spectacular." C. J. W. -L. Wee, "The Singapore Contemporary and Contemporary Art in Singapore," in *Charting Thoughts: Essays on Art in Southeast Asia*, ed. Low Sze Wee and Patrick D. Flores (National Gallery Singapore, 2017), 250, n. 16.

84. Unnamed Thai critic, quoted in Fuhrmann, *Ghostly Desires*, 164.

EPILOGUE

1. Quotes are from the 2024 version of *Reincarnations of Shadows* (2023–ongoing).

2. Paul O'Neill and Mick Wilson, "Introduction," in *Curating and the Educational Turn*, ed. Paul O'Neill and Mick Wilson (Open Editions and de Appel Arts Centre, 2010), 15–16.

3. Kunci Study Forum & Collective, "The School of Improper Education," *Critical Times* 3, no. 3 (December 2020): 566.

4. Kunci Study Forum & Collective, *Letters: The Classroom is Burning, Let's Dream about a School of Improper Education* (Ugly Duckling Presse, 2020), 1, 20.

5. Vuth Lyno, "Knowledge Sharing and Learning Together: Alternative Art Engagement from Stiev Selapak and Sa Sa Art Projects," *Udaya Journal of Khmer Studies* 12 (2014): 253–301.

6. According to one scholar, artists have been "reviving the *sanggar* tradition" since at least the mid-1970s. Elly Kent, *Artists and the People: Ideologies of Art in Indonesia* (NUS Press, 2022), 122.

7. Simon Soon, "Images Without Bodies: Chiang Mai Social Installation and the Art History of Cooperative Suffering," *Afterall* 42, September 20, 2016, accessed September 2024, https://www.afterall.org/articles/images-without-bodies-chiang-mai-social-installation-and-the-art-history-of-cooperative-suffering/.

8. Ho Tzu Nyen, quoted in Wong Binghao, "Ho Tzu Nyen on Time and the Tiger," *Ocula*, January 17, 2024.

9. Edwin Jurriëns, "'TV or Not TV': Spelling the Indonesian Media with Veven Sp. Wardhana," *Bijdragen tot de Taal-, land-en Volkenkunde/Journal of the Humanities and Social Sciences of Southeast Asia* 172, no. 1 (2016): 34.

10. Nissim Otmazgin and Eyal Ben-Ari, "Cultural Industries and the State in East and Southeast Asia," in *Popular Culture and the State in East and Southeast Asia*, ed. Nissim Otmazgin and Eyal Ben-Ari (Routledge, 2012), 7.

11. Several parts of episode 1, on Cheong Soo Pieng, are drawn from Kevin Chua, "Painting the Nanyang's 'Public': Notes towards a Reassessment," in *Eye of the Beholder: Reception, Audience, and Practice of Modern Asian Art*, ed. John Clark, Maurizio Peleggi, and T. K. Sabapathy (Wild Peony, 2006), 72–93.

12. Ho Tzu Nyen, "Afterimages: Strands of Modern Art in Singapore," unpub. Master's (Southeast Asia Studies) diss., National University of Singapore, 2008.

13. Russell Storer, "Ho Tzu Nyen: 4×4," *Broadsheet* (2006): 43.

14. T. K. Sabapathy, *Road to Nowhere: The Quick Rise and Long Fall of Art History in Singapore* (The Art Gallery at the National Institute of Education, 2010), 35.

15. Michael M. J. Fischer, *Probing Arts and Emergent Forms of Life* (Duke University Press, 2023), 2.

16. Joanne Leow, "Circumventing the Archive: *The Art of Charlie Chan Hock Chye* and *To Singapore, with Love*," *Verge: Studies in Global Asias* 6, no. 1 (Spring 2020): 58–67.

17. S. Gopinathan, "Globalisation, the Singapore Developmental State and Education Policy: A Thesis Revisited," *Globalisation, Societies and Education* 5, no. 1 (2007): 62.

18. Can-Seng Ooi, "Education and Becoming an Artist: Experiences from Singapore," in *Careers in Creative Industries*, ed. Chris Mathieu (Routledge, 2012), 258.

19. He Zhiyuan and Ho Tzu Nyen, "Stage Fright and Various Failures: A Conversation with Ho Tzu Nyen," *Performance Paradigm: A Journal of Performance and Contemporary Culture* 8 (2012): 6.

20. Ho Tzu Nyen, quoted in John Low and Ho Tzu Nyen, "A Conversation about 4×4 – Episodes of Singapore Art," in Jiazi Chen et al, *Singapore Art Show 2005* (National Arts Council, 2005), 126.

21. Lee Weng Choy, "On Wanting & Letting Go: Ho Tzu Nyen, the Screen, the Frame and the Edges of Narrative," in *The Cloud of Unknowing – Biennale Arte 2011, Singapore Pavilion*, ed. June Yap and Ho Tzu Nyen (Ho Tzu Nyen, 2011), 25. Storer, "Ho Tzu Nyen: 4×4," 42.

22. Ho, quoted in Low and Ho, "A Conversation about 4x4," 126.

23. Chanon Kenji Praepipatmongkol and Roger Nelson, "Araya Rasdjarmrearnsook: Between and Beyond (He and She)," in Araya Rasdjarmrearnsook, *I Am An Artist (He Said)*, trans. Kong Rithdee (National Gallery Singapore, 2022), 448.

24. Araya Rasdjarmrearnsook, *I Am An Artist (He Said)*, trans. Kong Rithdee (National Gallery Singapore, 2022), 99.

25. T. K. Sabapathy, "Premises for Critical Studies of Modern Art in Southeast Asia" (1982), in *The Modern in Southeast Asian Art: A Reader*, vol. 1., ed. T. K. Sabapathy and Patrick D. Flores (National Gallery Singapore and NTU Centre for Contemporary Art Singapore, 2023), 73–78.

26. "Ho Tzu Nyen 4×4 Project Forum and Exhibition," Juliana Yasin, Asia Art Archive, 2005, accessed September 2024, https://aaa.org.hk/en/collections/search/library/ho-tzu-nyen-4x4-project-forum-and-exhibition#.

27. Storer, "Ho Tzu Nyen: 4×4," 43.

28. Jacqueline Millner and Catriona Moore, *Contemporary Art and Feminism* (Routledge, 2022), 105.

29. Chanon and Nelson, "Araya Rasdjarmrearnsook: Between and Beyond (He and She)," 428.

30. Araya Rasdjarmrearnsook quoted in "Araya Rasdjarmrearnsook: A Woman Who Has Her Affection for Death. (The Female Artist Who Loves to Satirise and Irritate)," trans. Judha Su, ed. John Clark, in John Clark, Clare Veal and Judha Su, *Araya Rasdjarmrearnsook: Storytellers of the Town* (4A Centre for Contemporary Asian Art, 2014), 114.

31. Jordi Serrano-Muñoz, "Decolonial Theory in East Asia? Outlining a Shared Paradigm of Epistemologies of the South," *Revista Crítica de Ciências Sociais* 124 (2021): 15.

32. These quotes are attributed to Boaventura de Sousa Santos, *The End of the Cognitive Empire: The Coming of Age of Epistemologies of the South* (Duke University Press, 2018), 107. It is likely, however, that this work is not his alone, or perhaps not his at all. Allegations by several women, including Carla Paiva, Eva García Chueca, Gabriela Rocha, Aline Mendonça, Mariana Cabello, Élida Lauris, and Sara Araújo, claim that de Sousa Santos used their work without proper acknowledgement. They also allege sexual harassment and other abuses. At the time of writing, to my knowledge, investigations are ongoing. OpenDemocracy, "New reports of harassment emerge against sociologist Boaventura de Sousa Santos," *OpenDemocracy*, June 12, 2024, accessed June 2025, https://www.opendemocracy.net/en/5050/boaventura-de-sousa-santos-allegations-sexual-harassment-abuse-women-university-coimbra-wisconsin-madison/.

33. Santos, *The End of the Cognitive Empire*, 137. The authorship of this text is disputed, as noted by OpenDemocracy (see note 32).

34. Lorraine Code, *What Can She Know? Feminist Theory and the Construction of Knowledge* (Cornell University Press, 1991), 169.

35. Donna Haraway, "Situated Knowledges: The Science Question in Feminism and the Privilege of Partial Perspective," *Feminist Studies* 14, no. 3 (Autumn 1988): 575–99.

36. Code, *What Can She Know?*, 28.

37. Santos, *The End of the Cognitive Empire*, 6. The authorship of this text is disputed, as noted by OpenDemocracy, (see note 32).

38. Serrano-Muñoz, "Decolonial Theory in East Asia?," 20.

39. May Adadol Ingawanij, "Making Line and Medium," *Southeast of Now: Directions in Contemporary and Modern Art in Asia* 3, no. 1 (March 2019): 14.

40. Nguyễn Quân, "After Ten Years (1975–1985): Some Issues in Vietnamese Plastic Arts Today" (1986), trans. Dương Mạnh Hùng, in *The Modern in Southeast Asian Art: A Reader*, vol. 2, ed. T. K. Sabapathy and Patrick D. Flores (National Gallery Singapore and NTU Centre for Contemporary Art Singapore, 2023), 1174. Dương Mạnh Hùng (in an email to the author, August 2024) explains that the compound *lý luận-phê bình* combines *lý luận* (to interpret or theorize, to create sense or order) and *phê bình* (criticism).

41. Nguyễn Quân, "After Ten Years," 1175.

42. Miranda Fricker, *Epistemic Injustice: Power and the Ethics of Knowing* (Oxford University Press, 2007), 1. My interest in the concept of epistemic injustice builds on art-historical scholarship that mobilizes Walter Mignolo's concept of epistemic disobedience and Gayatri Chakravorty Spivak's concept of epistemic violence.

43. Theara Thun, *Epistemology of the Past: Texts, History, and Intellectuals of Cambodia, 1850–1970* (University of Hawai'i Press, 2024), 11.

44. Fricker, *Epistemic Injustice*, vii. See also Ian James Kidd, José Medina, and Gaile Pohlhaus, Jr., "Introduction," in *The Routledge Handbook of Epistemic Injustice*, ed. Ian James Kidd, José Medina, and Gaile Pohlhaus, Jr. (Routledge, 2017), 1–9.

45. Kimberlé Williams Crenshaw, "Mapping the Margins: Intersectionality, Identity Politics, and Violence Against Women of Color," *Stanford Law Review* 43, no. 6 (July 1991): 1241–1299.

46. Patricia Hill Collins, "Intersectionality and Epistemic Justice," in *The Routledge Handbook of Epistemic Injustice*, ed. Ian James Kidd, José Medina, and Gaile Pohlhaus, Jr. (Routledge, 2017), 116. Emphasis added.

47. Collins, "Intersectionality and Epistemic Justice," 122–3.

48. Santos, *The End of the Cognitive Empire*, 6. The authorship of this text is disputed, as noted by OpenDemocracy (see note 32).

49. Vann Molyvann, quoted in Helen Grant Ross and Darryl Leon Collins, *Building Cambodia: 'New Khmer Architecture' 1953–1970* (Key Publisher, 2006), 205. Emphasis added.

50. Vann Molyvann, "New Life Infused into the Arts in Cambodia" (1965), in *The Modern in Southeast Asian Art: A Reader*, vol. 1, ed. T. K. Sabapathy and Patrick D. Flores (National Gallery Singapore and NTU Centre for Contemporary Art Singapore, 2023), 704–5.

51. Sara Ahmed, *Living a Feminist Life* (Duke University Press, 2017), 10. Emphasis added.

52. Ahmed, *Living a Feminist Life*, 275, n.1.

Bibliography

Ahmad Mashadi. "Moments of Regionality: Negotiating Southeast Asia." In Patrick D. Flores and Singapore Art Museum, *Crossings: Philippine Works from the Singapore Art Museum*, 25–37. Singapore: National Heritage Board, Singapore and Ayala Foundation, 2004.

Ahmad Mashadi. "Regionalist Perspectives on Southeast Asian Art: Editorial Overview." In T. K. Sabapathy, *Writing the Modern: Selected Texts on Art & Art History in Singapore, Malaysia & Southeast Asia, 1973–2015*. Edited by Ahmad Mashadi, Susie Lingham, Peter Schoppert, and Joyce Toh, 332–339. Singapore: Singapore Art Museum, 2018.

Ahmed, Sara. *Living a Feminist Life*. Durham: Duke University Press, 2017.

Alfian Sa'at, Faris Joraimi, and Sai Siew Min, eds. *Raffles Renounced: Towards a Merdeka History*. Singapore: Ethos Books, 2021.

Aminudin T. H. Siregar. "He Who Comes as an Invalid and Wounded." In *Semsar Siahaan: Art, Liberation*. Edited by T. K. Sabapathy, 18–39. Singapore: Gajah Gallery, 2017.

Anadolu Agency. "British Museum to Display Ottoman Master's $7.4M 'Young Woman Reading' Painting in London." *Daily Sabah*, October 4, 2019. Accessed September 2024. https://www.dailysabah.com/arts-culture/2019/10/04/british-museum-to-display-ottoman-masters-74m-young-woman-reading-painting-in-london.

Anthology Film Archives. "Davy Chou – Interview (for *Golden Slumbers* 2011)." Accessed September 2024. http://anthologyfilmarchives.org/uploads/press_pdf/GoldenSlumbersDP-7.pdf.

Antoinette, Michelle. *Reworlding Art History: Encounters with Contemporary Southeast Asian Art after 1990*. Amsterdam: Rodopi, 2014.

Apinan Poshyananda. *Modern Art in Thailand: Nineteenth and Twentieth Centuries*. Singapore: Oxford University Press, 1992.

Apinan Poshyananda. "Roaring Tigers, Desperate Dragons in Transition." In *Contemporary Art in Asia: Traditions, Tensions*. Edited by Apinan Poshyananda, 23–53. New York: Asia Society Galleries, 1996.

Araya Rasdjarmrearnsook. *I Am An Artist (He Said)*. Translated by Rithdee Kong. Edited by Roger Nelson and Chanon Kenji Praepipatmongkol. Singapore: National Gallery Singapore, 2022.

Arbuckle, Heidi. "Performing Emiria Sunassa: Reframing the Female Subject in Post/colonial Indonesia," PhD diss., University of Melbourne, 2011.

Arch+ 243. "Contested Modernities – Postkoloniale Architektur und Identitätskonstruktion in Südostasien." April 2021. Accessed September 2024. https://archplus.net/de/archiv/ausgabe/243/.

Artling Team, The. "Interview with Hilmi Johandi." June 18, 2014. Accessed September 2024. https://theartling.com/en/artzine/interview-helm-johandi/.

Asia-Europe Foundation, Culture 360. "Digital Archive of Indonesian Visual Art." September 6, 2010. Accessed September 2024. https://culture360.asef.org/resources/indonesian-visual-art-archive-ivaa/.

Aton, Francesca. "LaToya Ruby Frazier Wins 2022 Carnegie International's Top Prize." *ARTnews*, September 26, 2022. Accessed September 2024. https://www.artnews.com/art-news/news/latoya-ruby-frazier-malcolm-peacock-hyphen-collective-win-58th-carnegie-international-prizes-1234640515.

Austin, Jessica. "Gender and the Nation in Popular Cambodian Heritage Cinema." Master's diss., University of Hawai'i, 2014.

Azzawi, Dia al-, Ismail Fattah, Saleh al-Jumaie, Muhammad Muhraddin, Rafa al-Nasiri, Hashem Samarji. "Accounting for the June 1967 War – Manifesto: Towards a New Vision (1969)" In *Modern Art in the Arab World: Primary Documents*, edited by Anneke Lenssen, Sarah Rogers, and Nada Shabout, 306–309. New York: Museum of Modern Art, 2018.

Bal, Mieke. "Citational Aesthetics: For Intermediality as Interrelation." In *The Palgrave Handbook of Intermediality*, edited by Jørgen Bruhn, Asun López-Varela Azcárate, and Miriam de Paiva Vieira, 461–492. Cham: Palgrave Macmillan, 2024.

Bal, Mieke. *Image-Thinking: Artmaking as Cultural Analysis*. Edinburgh: Edinburgh University Press, 2022.

Bal, Mieke. *Quoting Caravaggio: Contemporary Art, Preposterous History*. Chicago: University of Chicago Press, 1999.

Barnard, Timothy P. "Fauna in a Colonial Landscape." In *Imperial Creatures: Humans and Other Animals in Colonial Singapore, 1819–1942*, 52–102. Singapore: NUS Press, 2019.

Barnes, Leslie. "*Un cinéma sans image*: Palimpsestic Memory and the Lost History of Cambodian Film." In *Post-Migratory Cultures in Postcolonial France*, edited by Kathryn Kleppinger and Laura Reeck, 79–95. Liverpool: Liverpool University Press, 2018.

Barthe, Christine, ed. *Photographs 1842–1896: An Early Album of the World*. Beirut: Kaph Books, 2019.

Bartholomew, Richard. *Richard Bartholomew, the Art Critic*. Edited by Pablo Bartholomew, Rati Bartholomew, and Carmen Kagal. Noida: BART, 2012.

Basuki Resobowo and Oesman Effendi. "The Development of New Indonesian Painting: A Correspondence between Two Painters." In *The Modern in Southeast Asian Art: A Reader*, volume 1. Edited by T. K. Sabapathy and Patrick D. Flores, 381–393. Singapore: National Gallery Singapore and NTU Centre for Contemporary Art Singapore, 2023.

Bate, David. *Photography: The Key Concepts*. Oxford: Berg, 2009.

Becker, A. L. "Language and Languaging." *Language & Communication* 11, no. 1/2 (1991): 33–35.

Bennett, Lucinda. "Secret Languages, Stranger's Houses, Snakes: On Sriwhana Spong." *The Pantograph Punch* (June 2018): unpaginated.

Berman, Marshall. *All That is Solid Melts into Air: The Experience of Modernity*. Revised Edition. London: Penguin, 1988.

Bhargava, Aaina. "Vietnamese artist Thao Nguyen Phan is reviving the legacies of forgotten female artists and exploring her homeland's heritage." *Tatler Asia*, January 1, 2024. Accessed September 2024. https://www.tatlerasia.com/lifestyle/arts/thao-nguyen-phan-interview.

Bianpoen, Carla, Farah Wardani, and Wulan Dirgantoro. *Indonesian Women Artists: The Curtain Opens*. Jakarta: Indonesian Arts Foundation, 2007.

Bishop, Claire. "Information Overload: Claire Bishop on the Superabundance of Research-based Art." *Artforum* 61, no. 8, April 2023. Accessed September 2024. https://www.artforum.com/features/claire-bishop-on-the-superabundance-of-research-based-art-252571/.

Blake, Tara, and Janet Harbord. "Typewriters, Cameras and Love Affairs: The Fateful Haunting of Margaret Mead." *Journal of Media Practice* 9, no. 3 (2008): 215–227.

Blocker, Jane. *Becoming Past: History in Contemporary Art*. Minneapolis: University of Minnesota Press, 2016.

Bois, Yve-Alain, Denis Hollier, Rosalind Krauss, and Hubert Damisch. "A Conversation with Hubert Damisch." *October* 85 (Summer 1998): 3–17.

Bophana Center. "About Bophana Center." Accessed September 2024. https://bophana.org/about/.

Bourriaud, Nicolas. "Coactivity: Between the Human and Nonhuman." *Flash Art* 326, June-August 2019. Accessed September 2024. https://flash—art.com/article/coactivity-between-the-human-and-nonhuman/.

Bradway, Teagan, and Elizabeth Freeman, eds. "Introduction: Kincoherence/Kinaesthetics/Kinematics." In *Queer Kinship: Race, Sex, Belonging, Form*, 1–24. Durham: Duke University Press, 2022.

Breitz, Candice. "The First Johannesburg Biennale: Work in Progress." *Third Text* 9, no. 31 (1995): 89–94.

Brostoff, Alex, and Lauren Fournier. "Introduction: Autotheory ASAP! Academia, Decoloniality, and 'I.'" *ASAP/Journal* 6, no. 3 (September 2021): 489–502.

Buchanan, Sherry. *Tran Trung Tin: Paintings and Poems from Vietnam*. London: Asia Ink, 2002.

Burton, Deena. *Sitting at the Feet of Gurus: The Life and Dance Ethnography of Claire Holt*. Philadelphia: Xlibris US, 2009.

Butt, Danny. "The Promise of Artistic Research in the Asia Pacific." *Manusya: Journal of the Humanities* 23 (2020): 328–334.

Butterfield-Rosen, Emmelyn. *Modern Art and the Remaking of Human Disposition*. Chicago: University of Chicago Press, 2021.

Cao, Maggie M. *The End of Landscape in Nineteenth-century America*. Oakland: University of California Press, 2018.

Chairat Polmuk. "Affect: Notes from Southeast Asian Visual Culture." In *Routledge Handbook of Contemporary Buddhism*. Edited by Stephen C. Berkwitz and Ashley Thompson, 327–342. London: Routledge, 2022.

Chakrabarty, Dipesh. *Provincializing Europe: Postcolonial Thought and Historical Difference* (New Edition). Princeton: Princeton University Press, 2000.

Chandler, David. *A History of Cambodia*. Fourth Edition. Boulder, Colorado: Westview Press, 2008.

Chandler, David P. *The Tragedy of Cambodian History: Politics, War, and Revolution Since 1945*. New Haven: Yale University Press, 1991.

Chang, Jiat-Hwee. *A Genealogy of Tropical Architecture: Colonial Networks, Nature and Technoscience*. London: Routledge, 2016.

Chang, Jiat-Hwee, Justin Zhuang, and Darren Soh. *Everyday Modernism: Architecture & Society in Singapore*. Singapore: Ridge Books and NUS Press, 2023.

Chee, Kenny. "Robot Dog Spot Finds New Work: Scanning Worksites, Sending Results Over 5G." *The Straits Times*, October 19, 2021. Accessed September 2024. https://www.straitstimes.com/tech/tech-news/robot-dog-spot-finds-new-work-scanning-worksites-sending-results-over-5g.

Chen, Kuan-Hsing. *Asia as Method: Toward Deimperialization*. Durham: Duke University Press, 2010.

Chin, Lawrence. "The Value of Almost: Some Thoughts on Paintings by Hilmi Johandi." In *Stagecraft: Landscapes and Paradise*, unpaginated. Singapore: Ota Fine Arts, 2019.

Chotpradit, Thanavi, J. Pilapil Jacobo, Eileen Legaspi-Ramirez, Roger Nelson, Nguyen Nhu Huy, Chairat Polmuk, San Lin Tun, Phoebe Scott, Simon Soon, and Jim

Supangkat. "Terminologies of 'Modern' and 'Contemporary' 'Art' in Southeast Asia's Vernacular Languages: Indonesian, Javanese, Khmer, Lao, Malay, Myanmar/Burmese, Tagalog/Filipino, Thai and Vietnamese." *Southeast of Now: Directions in Contemporary and Modern Art in Asia* 2, no. 2 (October 2018): 65–195.

Chou, Davy, and Arts Network Asia. "ANA Grants 2010 Full Proposal: Documentary Film "Golden Slumbers" by Davy Chou." Accessed September 2024. http://artsnetworkasia.org/content/proposals/ChouDavy.html.

Chua Beng Huat. "Inter-Referencing Southeast Asia: Absence, Resonance and Provocation." In *Methodology and Research Practice in Southeast Asian Studies*. Edited by Mikko Huotari, Jürgen Rüland, and Judith Schlehe, 273–288. London: Palgrave Macmillan.

Chua, Kevin. "Exhibiting Modern Asian Art in Southeast Asia." *Yishu: Journal of Contemporary Chinese Art* 13, no. 2 (March/April 2014): 105–116.

Chua, Kevin. "Painting the Nanyang's 'Public': Notes towards a Reassessment." In *Eye of the Beholder: Reception, Audience, and Practice of Modern Asian Art*. Edited by John Clark, Maurizio Peleggi, and T. K. Sabapathy, 72–93. Sydney: Wild Peony, 2006.

Chua, Lawrence. *Bangkok Utopia: Modern Architecture and Buddhist Felicities, 1910–1973*. Honolulu: University of Hawai'i Press, 2021.

Clark, John. *Modern Asian Art*. Honolulu: University of Hawai'i Press and Craftsman House, 1998.

Clark, John, Clare Veal, and Judha Su. "Araya Rasdjarmrearnsook: A Woman Who Has Her Affection for Death. (The Female Artist Who Loves to Satirise and Irritate)." In *Araya Rasdjarmrearnsook: Storytellers of the Town*. Edited by John Clark. Translated by Judha Su, 110–121. Sydney: 4A Centre for Contemporary Asian Art, 2014.

Code, Lorraine. *What Can She Know? Feminist Theory and the Construction of Knowledge*. Ithaca: Cornell University Press, 1991.

Collins, Patricia Hill. "Intersectionality and Epistemic Justice." In *The Routledge Handbook of Epistemic Injustice*. Edited by Ian James Kidd, José Medina, and Gaile Pohlhaus, Jr., 115–124. London: Routledge, 2017.

Copeland, Huey, Leah Dickerman, and Pamela M. Lee. "Between Visual Scenes and Beautiful Lives: A Conversation with Saidiya Hartman." *October* 180 (Spring 2022): 81–104.

Corey, Pamela N. "The 'First' Cambodian Contemporary Artist." *Udaya: Journal of Khmer Studies* 12 (2014): 61–94.

Crenshaw, Kimberlé Williams. "Mapping the Margins: Intersectionality, Identity Politics, and Violence Against Women of Color." *Stanford Law Review* 43, no. 6 (July 1991): 1241–1299.

Cruse, Andrew. "Tropical Comforts in Vietnam." *ABE Journal: Architecture Beyond Europe* 19 (2021), online. Accessed June 2025. https://doi.org/10.4000/abe.12515.

Cumings, Bruce. "Biting the Hand That Feeds You: Why the 'Intelligence Function' of American Foundation Support for Area Studies Remains Hidden in Plain Sight." *Global Society* 28, no. 1 (2014): 70–89.

Dadi, Iftikhar. *Modernism and the Art of Muslim South Asia*. Chapel Hill: University of North Carolina Press, 2010.

Dan Soewarjono. "Dikitar Pelukis Dan Pengartja Wanita" [Around women painters and sculptors]. *Budaya Jaya* (January 1957): 26–54.

Darma Putra, I Nyoman. "From Balinese to Indonesian; Poetry from the Colonial and National Revolution Periods." In *A Literary Mirror: Balinese Reflections on Modernity and Identity in the Twentieth Century*, 67–110. Leiden: KITLV Press, 2011.

Davis, Erik W. *Deathpower: Buddhism's Ritual Imagination in Cambodia*. New York: Columbia University Press, 2016.

De Koninck, Rodolphe. "Wessex Estate: Recollections of British Military and Imperial History in the Heart of Singapore." *Asian Journal of Social Science* 31, no. 3 (2003): 435–451.

Dirgantoro, Wulan. *Feminisms and Contemporary Art in Indonesia: Defining Experiences*. Amsterdam: Amsterdam University Press, 2017.

Ditzig, Kathleen Elizabeth Li-Ying. "Exhibiting Southeast Asia in the Cultural Cold War: Geopolitics of Regional Art Exhibitions (1940s–1980s)," PhD diss., Nanyang Technological University, 2023.

Duro, Paul. "Why Imitation, and Why Global?" In *Theorizing Imitation in the Visual Arts: Global Contexts*. Edited by Paul Duro, 8–29. Malden: Wiley Blackwell, 2015.

Edwards, Peter, Global Cement Magazine. "Cement in Vietnam." April 19, 2012. Accessed September 2024. https://www.globalcement.com/magazine/articles/687-cement-in-vietnam.

Elkins, James. *The End of Diversity in Art Historical Writing: North Atlantic Art History and Its Alternatives*. Berlin: De Gruyter, 2021.

Emiria Sunassa. Letter from Emiria Sunassa to Professor Dr. G. F. Pijper, May 6, 1954, translated by Zena Vollenberg-Jenkins. In the Guilaume Frédéric Pijper archive and collection, Leiden University Libraries.

Emiria Sunassa. Letter from Emiria Sunassa to Professor Dr. G. F. Pijper, November 7, 1947, translated by Zena Vollenberg-Jenkins. In the Guilaume Frédéric Pijper archive and collection, Leiden University Libraries.

"Emiria Sunassa: How She Came To Be a Painter." *Indonesian Affairs* (April-May 1952): 54–56.

Everyday Museum, The, Singapore Art Museum. "Singapore Deviation: Wander with Art through the Rail Corridor." 2023. Accessed September 2024. https://www.theeverydaymuseum.sg/project/singapore-deviation/.

Farrar, Sarah. "Costume for a Mourner." *Museum of New Zealand Te Papa Tongarewa*, undated [circa 2017–2018]. Accessed September 2024. https://collections.tepapa.govt.nz/object/1045146.

Fischer, Michael M. J. *Probing Arts and Emergent Forms of Life*. Durham: Duke University Press, 2023.

Flores, Patrick D. "Address of Art: Vicinity of Region, Horizon of History." In *Charting Thoughts: Essays on Art in Southeast Asia*. Edited by Low Sze Wee and Patrick D. Flores, 12–21. Singapore: National Gallery Singapore, 2017.

Flores, Patrick D. "A Possible Coordinate." In *South by Southeast*. Edited by Patrick D. Flores and Anca Verona Mihuleţ, 6–15. Hong Kong: Osage Art Foundation, 2016.

Flores, Patrick D. "Art-Historical Alterity in the Post-Colony." In *Art History and Emergency: Crises in the Visual Arts and Humanities*. Edited by David Breslin and Darby English, 85–104. Williamstown: Sterling and Francine Clark Institute and Yale University Press, 2016.

Flores, Patrick D. "First Person Plural: Manifestos of the 1970s in Southeast Asia." In *Global Studies: Mapping Contemporary Art and Culture*. Edited by Hans Belting, Jacob Birken, Andrea Buddensieg, and Peter Weibel, 224–271. Ostfildern: Hatje Cantz Verlag, 2011.

Flores, Patrick D. "Moments of the Modern in Southeast Asia: Art, Region, Art History." In *Shaping the History of Art in Southeast Asia*. Edited by Patrick D. Flores and Kenji Kajiya, 5–8. Tokyo: Japan Foundation Art Center, 2017.

Flores, Patrick D. *Painting History: Revisions in Philippine Colonial Art*. Quezon City: Office of Research Coordination, University of the Philippines and National Commission for Culture and the Arts, 1998.

Flores, Patrick D. *Past Peripheral: Curation in Southeast Asia*. Singapore: NUS Museum, 2008.

Flores, Patrick D. "'There, Hapless State . . .': The Geopoetic of Co-Suffering." In *Interlaced Journeys: Diaspora and the Contemporary in Southeast Asian Art*. Edited by Patrick D. Flores and Loredana Pazzini-Paracciani, 7–15. Hong Kong: Osage Publications, 2020.

Flores, Patrick D. "Towards a Lexicon of Inclinations: Words Forming Worlds in Southeast Asia." *Asian Diasporic Visual Cultures and the Americas* 3 (2017): 35–53.

Ford, Thomas H. *How to Read a Poem: Seven Steps*. London: Routledge, 2021.

Fournier, Lauren. *Autotheory as Feminist Practice in Art, Writing and Criticism*. Cambridge, Massachusetts: MIT Press, 2021.

Fricker, Miranda. *Epistemic Injustice: Power and the Ethics of Knowing*. Oxford: Oxford University Press, 2007.

Fuhrmann, Arnika. *Ghostly Desires: Queer Sexuality and Vernacular Buddhism in Contemporary Thai Cinema*. Durham: Duke University Press, 2016.

Fyerool Darma. "Polymerized Heritage." *Future Anterior* 19, no. 1 (Summer 2022): 100–107.

Gawthorpe, Andrew J. *To Build As Well as Destroy: American Nation Building in South Vietnam*. Ithaca: Cornell University Press, 2018.

Geertz, Hildred. *Images of Power: Balinese Paintings Made for Gregory Bateson and Margaret Mead*. Honolulu: University of Hawai'i Press, 1994.

George, Kenneth M. *Picturing Islam: Art and Ethics in a Muslim Lifeworld*. Chichester, West Sussex: Wiley-Blackwell, 2010.

Gilroy, Paul. "Transcript: In Conversation with Achille Mbembe." Sarah Parker Remond Centre, University College London, June 17, 2020. Accessed September 2024. https://www.ucl.ac.uk/racism-racialisation/transcript-conversation-achille-mbembe.

Godfrey, Mark. "The Artist as Historian." *October* 120 (Spring 2007): 140–172.

Gonzaga, Elmo. "Regionalism as Anti-colonialism: Imaginaries of Area in South East Asian Omnibus Film and Database Art." *South East Asia Research* 32, no. 2 (2024): 125–141.

Gopinathan, S. "Globalisation, the Singapore Developmental State and Education Policy: A Thesis Revisited." *Globalisation, Societies and Education* 5, no. 1 (2007): 53–70.

Goris, Roelof. *Bali: Godsdienst en Ceremoniën* (Bali: Religion and Ceremonies). Batavia: Druk G. Kolff & Co., 1930.

Gosseye, Janina, Naomi Stead, and Deborah van der Plaat, eds. *Speaking of Buildings: Oral History in Architectural Research*. New York: Princeton Architectural Press, 2019.

Grant, Catherine. *A Time of One's Own: Histories of Feminism in Contemporary Art*. Durham: Duke University Press.

Green, Geffrey Corbett. "Walter Spies, Tourist Art and Balinese Art in Inter-war Colonial Bali." PhD diss., Sheffield Hallam University, 2002.

Guillermo, Alice G. "The Institutions of the Modern Art World in the Philippines." In *Modernity in Asian Art*. Edited by John Clark, 116–127. Sydney: Wild Peony, 1993.

Ha Thuc, Caroline. *Research-Based Art Practices in Southeast Asia: The Artist as Producer of Knowledge*. Cham: Palgrave Macmillan, 2022.

Halberstam, Jack. *The Queer Art of Failure*. Durham: Duke University Press, 2011.

Hamill, Sarah, and Megan R. Luke, eds. *Photography and Sculpture: The Art Object in Reproduction*. Los Angeles: The Getty Research Institute, 2017.

Haraway, Donna. "Situated Knowledges: The Science Question in Feminism and the Privilege of Partial Perspective." *Feminist Studies* 14, no. 3 (Autumn 1988): 575–599.

Haraway, Donna. *When Species Meet*. Minneapolis: University of Minnesota Press, 2008.

Hartman, Saidiya. "Venus in Two Acts." *Small Axe* 26 (vol. 12, no. 2) (June 2008): 1–14.

He Zhiyuan and Ho Tzu Nyen. "Stage Fright and Various Failures: A Conversation with Ho Tzu Nyen." *Performance Paradigm: A Journal of Performance and Contemporary Culture* 8 (2012): 1–21.

Hellqvist, Björn. "Referencing in the Humanities and its Implications for Citation Analysis." *Journal of the American Society for Information Science and Technology* 61, no 2 (2010): 310–318.

High, Holly. "An Introduction to *Stone Masters*." In *Stone Masters: Power Encounters in Mainland Southeast Asia*, edited by Holly High, 3–31. Singapore: NUS Press, 2022.

Hilmi Johandi. "Staging Illusion: Seeing Void," Master's diss., Lasalle College of the Arts, Singapore, 2018.

Ho Tzu Nyen. "About – *The Critical Dictionary of Southeast Asia* (2012–ongoing)." Accessed September 2024. https://cdosea.org/#about/b.

Ho Tzu Nyen. "Afterimages: Strands of Modern Art in Singapore," Master's diss., National University of Singapore, 2008.

Holert, Tom. *Knowledge Beside Itself: Contemporary Art's Epistemic Politics*. Berlin: Sternberg Press, 2020.

Holt, Claire. *Art in Indonesia: Continuities and Change*. Ithaca: Cornell University Press, 1967.

Holt, Claire, unpublished field note headed "Emiria to HBS," dated February 23, 1956. Claire Holt papers, 1927–1970. Collection Number: 14-27-2648. Cornell University Library.

Hsü, Marco C. F. *A Brief History of Malayan Art*. Translated by Lai Chee Kien. Singapore: Millennium Books, 1999.

Hutcheon, Linda. *A Theory of Parody: The Teachings of Twentieth-Century Art Forms*. Urbana: University of Illinois Press, 2000.

Huyssen, Andreas. *Memory Art in the Contemporary World: Confronting Violence in the Global South*. London: Lund Humphries, 2022.

Hyphen –. "About Us." Accessed September 2024. https://hyphen.web.id/about-us/.

Ingawanij, May Adadol. "Making Line and Medium." *Southeast of Now: Directions in Contemporary and Modern Art in Asia* 3, no. 1 (March 2019): 13–21.

Isaacs, Raymond. "The Urban Picturesque: An Aesthetic Experience of Urban Pedestrian Places." *Journal of Urban Design* 5, no. 2 (2000): 145–180.

Jack, Margaret. *Media Ruins: Cambodian Postwar Media Reconstruction and the Geopolitics of Technology*. Cambridge, Massachusetts: MIT Press, 2023.

Jacknis, Ira. "Margaret Mead and Gregory Bateson in Bali: Their Use of Photography and Film." *Cultural Anthropology* 3, no. 2 (May 1988): 160–177.

Jacobs, Julia, and Tom Mashberg. "U.S. Returns 30 Looted Antiquities to Cambodia." *The New York Times*, August 8, 2022. Accessed September 2024. https://www.nytimes.com/2022/08/08/arts/us-cambodia-looted-antiquities.html.

Java Creative Café. "Svay Ken and Chath Piersath: Outsider Art." April 25–May 25, 2003. Accessed September 2024. https://javacreativecafe.com/gallery/outsider-art-2003/.

Jerome Robbins Dance Division, The New York Public Library. "Gusti Rundu and son Sanuan, 25 November, 1956; Arie Smit and members of Gusti Rundu family." *The New York Public Library Digital Collections*. Accessed September 2024. https://digitalcollections.nypl.org/items/510d47dc-4a72-a3d9-e040-e00a18064a99.

Joselit, David. "The Readymade Metabolized: Fluxus in Life." *RES: Anthropology and Aesthetics*, no. 63/64, Wet/Dry (Spring/Autumn 2013): 190–200.

Juliana Yasin and Asia Art Archive. "Ho Tzu Nyen 4x4 Project Forum and Exhibition." 2005. Accessed September 2024. https://aaa.org.hk/en/collections/search/library/ho-tzu-nyen-4x4-project-forum-and-exhibition#.

Jurriëns, Edwin. "'TV or Not TV': Spelling the Indonesian Media with Veven Sp. Wardhana." *Bijdragen tot de Taal-, land-en Volkenkunde/Journal of the Humanities and Social Sciences of Southeast Asia* 172, no. 1 (2016): 33–65.

Karl, Rebecca E. *Staging the World: Chinese Nationalism at the Turn of the Twentieth Century.* Durham: Duke University Press, 2002.

Kee, Joan. *The Geometries of Afro Asia: Art Beyond Solidarity.* Oakland: University of California Press, 2023.

Kent, Elly. *Artists and the People: Ideologies of Art in Indonesia.* Singapore: NUS Press, 2022.

Ker, Yin. "Śāntiniketan and Modern Southeast Asian Art: From Rabindranath Tagore to Bagyi Aung Soe and Beyond." *Artl@s Bulletin* 5, no. 2 (2016): 8–20.

Kernbauer, Eva. *Art, History, and Anachronic Interventions Since 1990.* New York: Routledge, 2022.

Kidd, Ian James, José Medina, and Gaile Pohlhaus, Jr. "Introduction." In *The Routledge Handbook of Epistemic Injustice.* Edited by Ian James Kidd, José Medina, and Gaile Pohlhaus, Jr., 1–9. London: Routledge, 2017.

Klinke, Harald, ed. *Art Theory as Visual Epistemology.* Newcastle upon Tyne: Cambridge Scholars Publishing, 2014.

KonKhmerKounKhmer. "About Us." Accessed September 2024. https://konkhmerkounkhmer.wordpress.com/about/.

Krämer, Marie. "In Search of a Lost Cinema: Cinephilia and Multidirectional Moving Image Memory in *Golden Slumbers* (Davy Chou, 2012)." *Alphaville: Journal of Film and Screen Media* 21 (2021): 72–88.

Kunci Study Forum & Collective. *Letters: The Classroom is Burning, Let's Dream about a School of Improper Education.* New York: Ugly Duckling Presse, 2020.

Kunci Study Forum & Collective. "The School of Improper Education." *Critical Times* 3, no. 3 (December 2020): 566–578.

Kwon, Miwon. "Promiscuity of Space: Some Thoughts on Jessica Stockholder's Scenographic Compositions." *Grey Room* 18 (Winter 2005): 52–63.

La Biennale di Venezia. "Cinema: Bodeng Sar (White Building), Orizzonti." Accessed September 2024. https://www.labiennale.org/en/cinema/2021/lineup/orizzonti/bodeng-sar-white-building.

Lai Chee Kien. "The Enigma of Departure: Remembering Singapore's Railway Lines and Stations." *BiblioAsia* (October–December 2011): unpaginated. Accessed September 2024. https://biblioasia.nlb.gov.sg/vol-7/issue-3/oct-dec-2011/singapore-railway-lines/.

Lai Chee Kien. "Translator's Notes." In Marco C. F. Hsü, *A Brief History of Malayan Art*, translated by Lai Chee Kien, viii–xv. Singapore: Millennium Books, 1999.

Lambert-Beatty, Carrie. "Make-Believe: Parafiction and Plausibility." *October* 129 (Summer 2009): 51–84.

Larsen, Stanley Robert and James Lawton Collins, Jr. *Vietnam Studies: Allied Participation in Vietnam.* Washington, DC: Department of the Army, 1975.

Le Fleming, Rosalind. Rosalind Le Fleming to Florence Le Fleming, March 11, 1930, typed by Steven Fleming. In "Transcript of Le Fleming's Letters to Florence Le Fleming." Hugh Le Fleming Collection, Cambridge University Library.

Lee, Peter, ed. *Amek Gambar – Taking Pictures: Peranakans and Photography.* Singapore: Asian Civilisations Museum, 2020.

Lee Weng Choy. "On Wanting & Letting Go: Ho Tzu Nyen, the Screen, the Frame and the Edges of Narrative." In *The Cloud of Unknowing - Biennale Arte 2011,*

Singapore Pavilion. Edited by June Yap and Ho Tzu Nyen, 18–28. Singapore: Ho Tzu Nyen, 2011.

Lee, Sarah, and Sara Siew, eds. *Reframing Modernism: Painting from Southeast Asia, Europe and Beyond*. Singapore: National Gallery Singapore, 2016.

Leow, Joanne. “Circumventing the Archive: *The Art of Charlie Chan Hock Chye* and *To Singapore, with Love*.” *Verge: Studies in Global Asias* 6, no. 1 (Spring 2020): 58–67.

Leow, Joanne. “Confabulation as Decolonial Pedagogy in Singapore Literature.” In *Decolonizing the English Literary Curriculum*. Edited by Ato Quayson and Ankhi Mukherjee, 167–184. Cambridge: Cambridge University Press, 2024.

Lett, Michael. “Sriwhana Spong.” Accessed September 2024. https://michaellett.com/artist/sriwhana-spong/.

Lê, Việt. *Return Engagements: Contemporary Art's Traumas of Modernity and History in Sài Gòn and Phnom Penh*. Durham: Duke University Press, 2021.

Lewis, Cara L. *Dynamic Form: How Intermediality Made Modernism*. Ithaca: Cornell University Press, 2020.

Lewis, Su Lin. *Cities in Motion: Urban Life and Cosmopolitanism in Southeast Asia, 1920–1940*. Cambridge: Cambridge University Press, 2016.

Leydesdorff, Loet. “Theories of Citation?” *Scientometrics* 43, no. 1 (1998): 5–25.

Lim, Eng-Beng. *Brown Boys and Rice Queens: Spellbinding Performances in the Asias*. New York: New York University Press, 2013.

Loh, Joleen. “Relocating Kim Lim: A Cosmopolitan Perspective.” *Southeast of Now: Directions in Contemporary and Modern Art in Asia* 2, no. 2 (October 2018): 33–62.

Loh, Joleen. “The Photographs of Kim Lim: A Visual Essay.” *Art History* 44, no. 3 (June 2021): 532–552.

Loos, Tamara. “Reading *Gender Trouble* in Southeast Asia.” *The Journal of Asian Studies* 79, no. 4 (November 2020): 927–946.

Low, John, and Ho Tzu Nyen. “A Conversation about 4×4 – Episodes of Singapore Art.” In *Singapore Art Show 2005*. Edited by Jiazi Chen, Wengchoy Lee, Lindy Poh, Venka Purushothaman, Tony See and Constance Sheares, 118–145. Singapore: National Arts Council, 2005.

Low, Yvonne. “A ‘Forgotten’ Art World: The Singapore Art Club and its Colonial Women Artists.” In *Charting Thoughts: Essays on Art in Southeast Asia*. Edited by Low Sze Wee and Patrick D. Flores, 104–119. Singapore: National Gallery Singapore, 2017.

Low, Yvonne. “Women Artists: Becoming Professional in Singapore, Malaya and Indonesia.” PhD diss., University of Sydney, 2014.

Ly, Boreth. “Screening the Crisis of Monetary Masculinity in Rithy Panh's *One Night After the War* and *Burnt Theatre*.” In *Film in Contemporary Southeast Asia: Cultural Interpretation and Social Intervention*. Edited by David C. L. Lim and Hiroyuki Yamamoto, 53–72. London: Routledge, 2012.

Malaysia Design Archive. “About Us.” Accessed September 2024. https://www.malaysiadesignarchive.org/aboutus/.

Masahiro, Ushiroshoji. “The Birth of ‘Fine Art’ in Southeast Asia, 1900–1945.” In *Charting Thoughts: Essays on Art in Southeast Asia*. Edited by Low Sze Wee and Patrick D. Flores, 130–139. Singapore: National Gallery Singapore, 2017.

Mathur, Saloni. *A Fragile Inheritance: Radical Stakes in Contemporary Indian Art*. Durham: Duke University Press, 2019.

Mathur, Saloni. “A Retake of Sher-Gil's *Self-Portrait as Tahitian*.” *Critical Inquiry* 37, no. 3 (Spring 2011): 515–544.

Mattos, Claudia. “Whither Art History?: Geography, Art Theory, and New Perspectives for an Inclusive Art History.” *The Art Bulletin* 96, no. 3 (September 2014): 259–264.

Maza, Cristina. "All-male, All-gay Dance Troupe Stages its Cambodian Debut." *The Phnom Penh Post*, August 12, 2016. Accessed September 2024. https://www.phnompenhpost.com/post-weekend/all-male-all-gay-dance-troupe-stages-its-cambodian-debut.

Mesterharm, Nico (director), Lach Chantha and Meta House. "Svay Ken Talks (2008)." Uploaded May 9, 2023. YouTube video, 41:09. Accessed September 2024. https://www.youtube.com/watch?v=Wo87N13d_WU.

Mignolo, Walter D. "Decoloniality is an Option, Not a Mission." In Walter D. Mignolo and Catherine E. Walsh, *On Decoloniality: Concepts, Analytics, Praxis*, 211–226. Durham: Duke University Press, 2018.

Millner, Jacqueline, and Catriona Moore. *Contemporary Art and Feminism*. London: Routledge, 2022.

Mitter, Partha. "Decentering Modernism: Art History and Avant-Garde from the Periphery." *The Art Bulletin* 90, no. 4 (December 2008): 531–548.

Moxey, Keith. "Is Modernity Multiple?" In *Visual Time: The Image in History*, 11–22. Durham: Duke University Press, 2013.

Mrázek, Jan. "Ways of Experiencing Art: Art History, Television, and Javanese Wayang." In *What's the Use of Art? Asian Visual and Material Culture in Context*. Edited by Jan Mrázek and Morgan Pitelka, 272–304. Honolulu: University of Hawai'i Press, 2008.

Muan, Ingrid. "Citing Angkor: The 'Cambodian Arts' in the Age of Restoration 1918–2000." PhD diss., Columbia University, 2001.

Muan, Ingrid. "Musings on Museums from Phnom Penh." In *Museum Frictions: Public Cultures/Global Transformations*. Edited by Ivan Karp, Corinne A. Kratz, Lynn Szwaja, Tomas Ybarra-Frausto, Gustavo Butinx, Barbara Kirshenblatt-Gimblett, and Ciraj Rassool, 257–285. Durham: Duke University Press, 2006.

Muhammad Hafiz. "Fyerool Darma: Resurrecting the Archipelago – In Partnership with Gilman Barracks." *Ocula*, September 22, 2017. Accessed September 2024. https://ocula.com/magazine/insights/fyerool-darma-resurrecting-the-archipelago/.

Mutumbu, Tendai John. "Sriwhana Spong." *Ocula*, July 6, 2018. Accessed September 2024. https://ocula.com/magazine/conversations/sriwhana-spong/.

Nakayasu, Sawako. *Say Translation Is Art*. Brooklyn: Ugly Duckling Presse, 2020.

Nasar, Hammad. "Notes from the Field: Navigating the Afterlife of 'The Other Story'." In *Field Notes 4*. Edited by Lucia Kim, Hammad Nasar, and Chantal Wong, 50–63. Hong Kong: Asia Art Archive, 2015.

Nash, Jennifer C. *How We Write Now: Living with Black Feminist Theory*. Durham: Duke University Press, 2024.

National Gallery Singapore. *Annual Reports (of National Gallery Singapore)*. Accessed September 2024. https://www.nationalgallery.sg/about/about-the-gallery/annual-reports.

Ndlovu-Gatsheni, Sabelo J. "Provincializing Europe and Deprovincialising Africa: Prospects for Decolonizing the Humanities." *Présence Africaine* 197 (2018): 337–362.

Nelson, Roger. "Behind the Painting, A Pantoum: Literature and Art and Southeast Asia." In *The Routledge Companion to Art and Literature*. Edited by Neil Murphy, W. Michelle Wang, and Cheryl Julia Lee, 452–466. Abingdon: Routledge, 2024.

Nelson, Roger. "Curating as (Expanded) Art History in Southeast Asia: Recent Independent Projects in Ho Chi Minh City, Luang Prabang and Phnom Penh." *ARTMargins* 9, no. 2 (2020): 33–60.

Nelson, Roger. "Emiria Sunassa's Citational Paintings: 'Like a Boil on a Virgin's Lips.'" *Oxford Art Journal* 46, no. 3 (2023): 407–426.

Nelson, Roger. "Immersion, Fragmentation, and the Insidious Spectacle: Interview with Hilmi Johandi." In *President's Young Talents 2018*. Edited by Joyce Toh, 101–109. Singapore: Singapore Art Museum, 2018.

Nelson, Roger. "Locating the Domestic in Vann Molyvann's National Sports Complex." *ABE Journal: Architecture Beyond Europe* 11, special issue "Paradoxical Southeast Asia," (2017): 1–25.

Nelson, Roger. "'My World is Modern': Deprovincialising Chen Cheng Mei and You Khin, Artists from Southeast Asia Who Traversed the Global South." *Southeast of Now: Directions in Contemporary and Modern Art in Asia* 5, no. 1 & 2 (October 2021): 205–249.

Nelson, Roger. "Staging: Notes on Hotels and Hospitality in the Work of Svay Ken and Hilmi Johandi." Forthcoming publication in conjunction with the exhibition "*Guest Relations*" shown at the Jameel Arts Centre in Dubai, November 4, 2023 to April 28, 2024.

Nelson, Roger. "Thao Nguyen Phan's Parafabulations: Thinking Alongside *First Rain, Brise-Soleil*." In *Thao Nguyen Phan: Reincarnations of Shadows*. Edited by Lucia Aspesi and Fiammetta Griccioli, 125–142. Milan: Pirelli HangarBicocca and Marsilio Editori, 2023.

Nelson, Roger. "The Gap Which Separates: Simultaneity, Disparity, and Audiovisual Linking Technologies in 'Southeast Asian Contemporary Art.'" *positions: asia critique* 33, no. 1 (2025): 161–191.

Nelson, Roger. "'The Work the Nation Depends On': Landscapes and Women in the Paintings of Nhek Dim." In *Ambitious Alignments: New Histories of Southeast Asian Art, 1945–1990*. Edited by Stephen H. Whiteman, Sarena Abdullah, Yvonne Low, and Phoebe Scott, 19–48. Sydney: Power Publications and National Gallery Singapore, 2018.

Nelson, Roger. "Two Tales of Two Cities: Contemporary Art, Southeast Asia, Divergent Approaches." *Art Journal* 81, no. 4 (2022): 146–149.

Ng Yi-Sheng. "A Gate of Dragon's Teeth: A Decolonial Approach to Writing Precolonial Historical Fiction in Singapore," PhD diss., Nanyang Technological University, 2021.

Nguyễn Quân. "After Ten Years (1975–1985): Some Issues in Vietnamese Plastic Arts Today" (1986). In *The Modern in Southeast Asian Art: A Reader*, volume 2. Translated by Dương Mạnh Hùng. Edited by T. K. Sabapathy and Patrick D. Flores, 1171–1177. Singapore: National Gallery Singapore and NTU Centre for Contemporary Art Singapore, 2023.

Nordholt, Henk Schulte. "Localizing Modernity in Colonial Bali during the 1930s." *Journal of Southeast Asian Studies* 31, no. 1 (March 2000): 101–114.

Ok, Prumsodun. "Prumsodun Ok & NATYARASA." Accessed September 2024. https://www.prumsodun.com/natyarasa.

Ok, Prumsodun. *The Serpent's Tail: A Brief History of Khmer Classical Dance*. Self-published, 2018. Accessed September 2024. https://www.academia.edu/36957739/THE_SERPENTS_TAIL_A_BRIEF_HISTORY_OF_KHMER_CLASSICAL_DANCE.

Okeke-Agulu, Chika. *Postcolonial Modernism: Art and Decolonization in Twentieth-Century Nigeria*. Durham: Duke University Press, 2015.

O'Neill, Paul, and Mick Wilson. "Introduction." In *Curating and the Educational Turn*. Edited by Paul O'Neill and Mick Wilson, 11–22. London: Open Editions and de Appel Arts Centre, 2010.

Ooi, Can-Seng. "Education and Becoming an Artist: Experiences from Singapore." In *Careers in Creative Industries*. Edited by Chris Mathieu, 254–269. New York: Routledge, 2012. 258.

OpenDemocracy. "New reports of harassment emerge against sociologist Boaventura de Sousa Santos." *OpenDemocracy*, June 12, 2024. Accessed June 2025. https://www.opendemocracy.net/en/5050/boaventura-de-sousa-santos-allegations-sexual-harassment-abuse-women-university-coimbra-wisconsin-madison/.

OpenDevelopment Vietnam. "Agriculture and Fishing." May 14, 2020. Accessed September 2024. https://vietnam.opendevelopmentmekong.net/topics/agriculture-and-fishing/#ref-3846269-16.

Osborne, Milton. "The Passions of a Prince." In *Before Kampuchea: Preludes to a Tragedy*, 44–58. Sydney: Allen & Unwin, 1979.

Ota Fine Arts. "Hilmi Johandi | Stagecraft: Landscapes and Paradise." 2019. Accessed September 2024. https://www.otafinearts.com/exhibitions/67-hilmi-johandi-stagecraft-landscapes-and-paradise-hilmi-johandi/.

Otmazgin, Nissim, and Eyal Ben-Ari. "Cultural Industries and the State in East and Southeast Asia." In *Popular Culture and the State in East and Southeast Asia*. Edited by Nissim Otmazgin and Eyal Ben-Ari, 3–26. London: Routledge, 2012.

Palladini, Giulia, and Marco Pustianaz. *Lexicon for an Affective Archive*. Bristol: Live Art Development Agency and Intellect, 2018.

Park, J.P. "Art-Historical Fiction or Fictional Art History?: Zhang Taijie, Dong Qichang, and the Literary Making of the Past in Early Modern China." *Archives of Asian Art* 72, no. 2 (October 2022): 181–219.

Partington, Matthew, and Linda Sandino, eds. *Oral History in the Visual Arts*. London: Bloomsbury, 2013.

Pen Sereypagna and Thao Nguyen Phan. "Architecture is the Painting of Making Space: Pen Sereypagna in conversation with Thao Nguyen Phan." In *Thao Nguyen Phan*. Edited by Anne Barlow and Giles Jackson, 47–55. London: Tate, 2022.

Phan, Thao Nguyen. "Artist Statement." In *Poetic Amnesia*. Edited by Zoe Butt, 12–15. Ho Chi Minh City: The Factory Contemporary Art Centre, 2017.

Phan, Thao Nguyen. "Thao Nguyen Phan on Diem Phung Thi: The Metamorphosis of Signs." Artists on Artists et al. vol 2, *Cobo Social*. January 18, 2021. Accessed September 2024. https://issuu.com/denisetsui3/docs/cobo2021_artwork_preview_spread.

Phan, Thao Nguyen, and Zoe Butt. "Imprinting Parallel Histories: Thao Nguyen Phan in conversation with Zoe Butt." *Fondazione In Between Art Film*. 2021. Accessed September 2024. https://still.inbetweenartfilm.com/en/imprinting-parallel-histories/.

Phataranawik, Phatarawadee. "The Artist as Writer." *The Nation*. January 12, 2018. Accessed September 2024. https://www.nationthailand.com/life/30336117.

Powers, Martin. "The Art-Historical Art of Song China: Citation and Historicism in *Tao Yuanming Returning to Seclusion*." *Ars Orientalis* 49 (2019): 22–41.

Pramoedya Ananda Toer. *This Earth of Mankind*, part 1 of *The Buru Quartet*. Translated by Max Lane. New York: Penguin, 1996 [1981].

Protschky, Susie. *Photographic Subjects: Monarchy, Photography and the Making of Colonial Citizens*. Manchester: Manchester University Press, 2019.

Ranard, Andrew. *Burmese Painting: A Linear and Lateral History*. Chiang Mai: Silkworm Books, 2009.

Reyum Institute of Arts and Culture. "A Good Friend is Hard to Find." January 29, 2006. Accessed September 2024. http://reyum.org/exhibitions/exhibit20/exhibit_photo_gallery.html#A.

Riksa Afiaty and Charles Esche, eds. *Power & Other Things: Indonesia & Art, 1835–Now*. Ghent: Snoeck, 2017.

Robertson, Jean, Deborah Hutton, Cynthia Colburn, Ömür Harmansah, Eric Kjellgren, Rex Koontz, De-nin Lee, Henry Luttikhuizen, Allison Lee Palmer, Stacey Sloboda, and Monica Blackmun Visonà. "Preface." In *The History of Art: A Global View*, 12–13. London: Thames and Hudson, 2021.

Romey, Eliza. "King, Politician, Artist: The Films of Norodom Sihanouk," Master's diss., La Trobe University, 1998.

Roots, National Heritage Board. "Malaysian Golden Chersonese Malay States Railway Travel Poster." *Collection of National Museum of Singapore*. Accessed September 2024. https://www.roots.gov.sg/Collection-Landing/listing/.

Roots, National Heritage Board. "'Travel Through Malaya by FMS Railways' poster (Mount Ophir, Johor)." *Collection of National Museum of Singapore*. Accessed September 2024. https://www.roots.gov.sg/Collection-Landing/listing/1132482.

Rosenfeld, Gavriel. "Why Do We Ask 'What If?' Reflections on the Function of Alternate History." *History and Theory* 41, no. 4 (December 2002): 90–103.

Rosner, Daniela K. *Critical Fabulations: Reworking the Methods and Margins of Design*. Cambridge, Massachusetts: MIT Press, 2018.

Ross, Helen Grant and Darryl Leon Collins. *Building Cambodia: 'New Khmer Architecture' 1953–1970*. Bangkok: Key Publisher, 2006.

Roung Kon Project. "Lux Cinema." Undated (circa 2020). Accessed September 2024. https://www.roungkonproject.com/architectural-drawings.

Roung Kon Project. "Roung Kon Project, A Brief Introduction of Cambodian Cinema." Undated (circa 2020). Accessed September 2024. https://www.roungkonproject.com/about.

Sabapathy, T. K. "Developing Regionalist Perspectives in Southeast Asian Art Historiography" (1996). In *Contemporary Art in Asia: A Critical Reader*. Edited by Benjamin Genocchio and Melissa Chiu, 47–61. Cambridge, Massachusetts: MIT Press, 2011.

Sabapathy, T. K. "Intersecting Histories: Thoughts on the Contemporary and History in Southeast Asian Art." In *Intersecting Histories: Contemporary Turns in Southeast Asian Art*, 36–83. Singapore: School of Art, Design and Media, Nanyang Technological University, 2012.

Sabapathy, T. K. "Exhibitions of Southeast Asian Modern/Contemporary Art. Recollections, and Thoughts on Some Matters." Unpublished paper presented at the *Second Board Retreat of the Singapore Art Museum*, Singapore, September 13, 2017. T. K. Sabapathy Archives, NUS Museum, National University of Singapore.

Sabapathy, T. K. "Introduction *to Intersecting Histories: Contemporary Turns in Southeast Asian Art*" (2012). In *Writing the Modern: Selected Texts on Art and Art History in Singapore, Malaysia and Southeast Asia*. Edited by Ahmad Mashadi, Susie Lingham, Peter Schoppert, and Joyce Toh, 316–320. Singapore: Singapore Art Museum, 2018.

Sabapathy, T. K. "Premises for Critical Studies of Modern Art in Southeast Asia" (1982). In *The Modern in Southeast Asian Art: A Reader*, vol. 1. Edited T. K. Sabapathy and Patrick D. Flores, 73–78. Singapore: National Gallery Singapore and NTU Centre for Contemporary Art Singapore, 2023.

Sabapathy, T. K. *Road to Nowhere: The Quick Rise and Long Fall of Art History in Singapore*. Singapore: The Art Gallery at the National Institute of Education, 2010.

Sabapathy, T. K. "The Nanyang Artists: Some General Remarks" (1979). In *Writing the Modern: Selected Texts on Art & Art History in Singapore, Malaysia & Southeast Asia, 1973–2015*. Edited by Ahmad Mashadi, Susie Lingham, Peter Schoppert, and Joyce Toh, 340–345. Singapore: Singapore Art Museum, 2018.

Sabapathy, T. K. and Patrick D. Flores, eds. *The Modern in Southeast Asian Art: A Reader*. Singapore: National Gallery Singapore and NTU Centre for Contemporary Art Singapore, 2023.

Saelemakers, Samuel. "Foreword." In *Speculative Art Histories: Analysis at the Limits.* Edited by Sjoerd van Tuinen, viii–ix. Edinburgh: Edinburgh University Press, 2017.
Salguero, C. Pierce. "Honoring the Teachers, Constructing the Lineage: A *Wai Khru* Ritual among Healers in Chiang Mai, Thailand." In *Translating the Body: Medical Education in Southeast Asia.* Edited by Hans Pols, C. Michele Thompson, and John Harley Warner, 295–318. Singapore: NUS Press, 2017.
Santos, Boaventura de Sousa. *The End of the Cognitive Empire: The Coming of Age of Epistemologies of the South.* Durham: Duke University Press, 2018. [Note: the authorship of this work is challenged. See the report by OpenDemocracy, cited previously.]
Save Myanmar Film. "Preserving Local Culture Through Films." Accessed September 2024. https://www.savemyanmarfilm.org/.
Scharf, Aaron. *Art and Photography.* Revised edition. Harmondsworth: Penguin, 1974.
Schenck, Mel. *Southern Vietnamese Modernist Architecture: Mid-Century Vernacular Modernism.* Helena, Montana: Architecture Vietnam Books, 2020.
Schwenger, Peter. *Asemic: The Art of Writing.* Minneapolis: University of Minnesota Press, 2019.
Scott, Phoebe. *Familiar Others: Emiria Sunassa, Eduardo Masferré and Yeh Chi Wei, 1940s–1970s.* Singapore: National Gallery Singapore, 2022.
Seebass, Tilman. "Change in Balinese Musical Life: 'Kebiar' in the 1920s and 1930s." In *Being Modern in Bali: Image and Change.* Edited by Adrian Vickers, 71–91. New Haven: Yale University Southeast Asia Studies, 1996.
Seng, Savunthara, Alyssandra Maxine, and Duong Manh Hung. "Welcome to Issue 2 of MargIn Magazine: Traces." *MargIn* 2 (2025): 4–5.
Seng Yu Jin. "A History of Art Exhibitions: The Emergence of Critical Exhibitions in Southeast Asia, 1970s–1990s," PhD diss., University of Melbourne, 2019.
Serrano-Muñoz, Jordi. "Decolonial Theory in East Asia? Outlining a Shared Paradigm of Epistemologies of the South." *Revista Crítica de Ciências Sociais* 124 (2021): 5–26.
Shabbir Hussain Mustafa, ed. *Tropical: Stories from Southeast Asia and Latin America.* Singapore: National Gallery Singapore, 2023.
Shapiro-Phim, Toni. "Cambodia's *Seasons of Migration.*" *Dance Research Journal* 40, no. 2 (Winter 2008): 56–73.
Shapiro-Phim, Toni. "Mediating Cambodian History, the Sacred, and the Earth." In *The Routledge Dance Studies Reader.* Third Edition. Edited by Jens Richard Giersdorf and Yutian Wong, 262–273. London: Routledge, 2019.
Shapiro, Toni. "Dance and the Spirit of Cambodia." PhD diss., Cornell University, 1994.
Sini, Raffaella. *Singapore's Park System Master Planning: A Nation Building Tool to Construct Narratives in Post-Colonial Countries.* Singapore: Springer, 2020.
Siti Nuraishah Ahmad. "Malaysia as the Archetypal Garden in the British Creative Imagination." *Southeast Asian Studies* 3, no. 1 (April 2014): 49–84.
Smith, Linda Tuhiwai. *Decolonizing Methodologies: Research and Indigenous Peoples.* Third Edition. London: Zed Books and Bloomsbury Publishing, 2021.
Spirit of Friendship. "About." December 2018 version. Accessed September 2024. https://web.archive.org/web/20181225123916/http://spiritoffriendship.org.
Spong, Sriwhana. "*Scirinz* (A Running Sore): Particular and Ecstatic Scripts of the Body by Mystic Women in the Middle Ages and Early Modern Europe." PhD diss., University of Auckland, 2021.
Somerville, Alice Te Punga. "relative." In *Always Italicise: How to Write While Colonised,* 30–31. Auckland: Auckland University Press, 2022.
Soon, Simon. "Images Without Bodies: Chiang Mai Social Installation and the Art History of Cooperative Suffering." *Afterall Journal* 42, September 20, 2016. Accessed

September 2024. https://www.afterall.org/articles/images-without-bodies-chiang-mai-social-installation-and-the-art-history-of-cooperative-suffering/.

Soon, Simon. "What is Left of Art? The Spatio-Visual Practice of Political Art in Indonesia, Singapore, Thailand, and the Philippines, 1950s–1970s." PhD diss., University of Sydney, 2015.

Steinberg, Leo. "Introduction: The Glorious Company." In Jean Lipman and Richard Marshall, *Art About Art*, 8–31. New York: E.P. Dutton and Whitney Museum of American Art, 1978.

Storer, Russell. "Ho Tzu Nyen: 4x4." *Broadsheet* (2006): 42–43.

Stur, Heather Marie. *Saigon at War: South Vietnam and the Global Sixties*. Cambridge: Cambridge University Press, 2020.

Supartono, Alexander and Alexandra Moschovi. "Contesting Colonial (Hi)stories: (Post)colonial Imaginings of Southeast Asia." *Journal of Southeast Asian Studies* 51, no. 3 (September 2020): 343–371.

Svay Ken. *A Good Friend is Hard to Find: An Homage to Ingrid by Painter Svay Ken*. Translated by Helen Jarvis. Phnom Penh: Reyum Publishing, 2006.

Svay Ken. *Painted Stories: The Life of a Cambodian Family from 1941 to the Present*. Edited by Ly Daravuth and Ingrid Muan. Phnom Penh: Reyum Institute of Art and Culture, 2001.

Tate Etc. "Empathy not Erasure." *Tate Etc* 54 (Spring 2022), April 26, 2022. Accessed September 2024. https://www.tate.org.uk/tate-etc/issue-54-spring-2022/empathy-not-erasure.

Taylor, Nora A. "Introduction: Who Speaks for Southeast Asian Art?" In *Modern and Contemporary Southeast Asian Art: An Anthology*. Edited by Nora A. Taylor and Boreth Ly, 1–14. Ithaca: Cornell Southeast Asia Program Publications, 2012.

Taylor, Nora A. *Painters in Hanoi: An Ethnography of Vietnamese Art*. Second Edition. Singapore: NUS Press, 2009.

Taylor, Nora A. "Art without History? Southeast Asian Artists and Their Communities in the Face of Geography," *Art Journal* 70, no. 2 (Summer 2011): 6–23.

Taylor, Nora A. "The Southeast Asian Art Historian as Ethnographer?" *Third Text* 25, no. 4 (2011): 475–488.

Taylor, Nora A. "(Tran)scribed History: Thảo Nguyên Phan's Palimpsest Visions of Colonialism and Conversion." *Afterall* 47 (Spring/Summer 2019), 2019. Accessed September 2024. https://www.afterall.org/articles/transcribed-history-thao-nguyen-phans-palimpsest-visions-of-colonialism-and-conversion/.

Taylor, Nora A. and Karin Zitzewitz. "History as Figure of Thought in Contemporary Art in South and Southeast Asia." *Art Journal* 77, no. 4 (Winter 2018): 46–48.

Teh, David. *Thai Art: Currencies of the Contemporary*. Cambridge, Massachusetts: MIT Press, 2017.

Teh, David. "*The City in Time: Contemporary Art and Urban Form in Vietnam and Cambodia*. By Pamela N. Corey. Seattle: University of Washington Press, 2021. xi, 228. ISBN: 9780295749235." [book review]. *Journal of Asian Studies* 83, no. 2 (2024): 495–497.

Thompson, Ashley. "Forgetting to Remember, Again: On Curatorial Practice and "Cambodian Art" in the Wake of Genocide." *diacritics* 41, no. 2 (2013): 82–109.

Thompson, Ashley. *Engendering the Buddhist State: Territory, Sovereignty and Sexual Difference in the Inventions of Angkor*. London: Routledge, 2016.

Thun, Theara. *Epistemology of the Past: Texts, History, and Intellectuals of Cambodia, 1850–1970*. Honolulu: University of Hawai'i Press, 2024.

Tith, Kanitha, Casco Art Institute: Working for the Commons. "Kanitha Tith – How Heavy is Time? (2020)." Filmed June 16, 2020. YouTube video, 37:31. Accessed September 2024. https://www.youtube.com/watch?v=vs0e05Bc_Tc.

Townsend, Dabney. "The Picturesque." *The Journal of Aesthetics and Art Criticism* 55, no. 4 (Autumn 1997): 365–376.

Turnbull, Robert. "A Burned-out Theater: The State of Cambodia's Performing Arts." In *Expressions of Cambodia: The Politics of Tradition, Identity, and Change*. Edited by Leakthina Chau-Pech Ollier and Tim Winter, 133–149. London: Routledge, 2006.

Tythacott, Louise and Panggah Ardiyansyah, eds. *Returning Southeast Asia's Past: Objects, Museums, and Restitution*. Singapore: NUS Press, 2021.

van Tuinen, Sjoerd. "Introduction." In *Speculative Art Histories: Analysis at the Limits*. 1–11. Edinburgh: Edinburgh University Press, 2017.

Vann Molyvann. "New Life Infused into the Arts in Cambodia" (1965). In *The Modern in Southeast Asian Art: A Reader*, volume 1. Edited by T. K. Sabapathy and Patrick D. Flores, 701–705. Singapore: National Gallery Singapore and NTU Centre for Contemporary Art Singapore, 2023.

Vasko, Lydia. "Going for Gold: National Gallery Singapore Approaches Final Stages of Construction." *The Straits Times*, August 9, 2014. Accessed September 2024. https://www.straitstimes.com/singapore/going-for-gold-national-gallery-singapore-approaches-final-stages-of-construction.

Veal, Clare. "Can the Girl be a Thai Woman? Reading the Works of Araya Rasdjarmrearnsook from Feminist Perspectives." In John Clark, Clare Veal, and Judha Su, *Araya Rasdjarmrearnsook: Storytellers of the Town*, 56–77. Sydney: 4A Centre for Contemporary Asian Art, 2014.

Veal, Clare. "Nostalgia and Nationalism: Facebook 'Archives' and the Constitution of Thai Photographic Histories." *Journal of Southeast Asian Studies* 51, no. 3 (September 2020): 372–396.

Veal, Clare. "Water is Never Still: Araya Rasdjarmrearnsook's Sculptural and Installation Practice." *Afterall* 47, no. 1 (Spring/Summer 2019): 88–103.

Vellodi, Kamini. "Thought Beyond Research: A Deleuzian Critique of Artistic Research." In *Aberrant Nuptials: Deleuze and Artistic Research 2*. Edited by Paulo de Assis and Paolo Giudici, 215–232. Leuven: Leuven University Press, 2019.

Vickers, Adrian. *Bali: A Paradise Created*. Berkeley: Periplus Editions, 1989.

Vickers, Adrian. *Balinese Art: Paintings and Drawings of Bali 1800–2010*. Singapore: Tuttle Publishing, 2012.

Virtual Museum of Balinese Painting, The. "I Gusti Made Rundu, born 1918, died 1993, 56 works." Accessed September 2024. https://bit.ly/3NnLBLP.

Virtual Museum of Balinese Painting, The. "Welcome to the Virtual Museum of Balinese Painting." Accessed September 2024. https://heurist.sydney.edu.au/heurist/?db=balipaintings&website&id=40124#.

Vuth Lyno. "Knowledge Sharing and Learning Together: Alternative Art Engagement from Stiev Selapak and Sa Sa Art Projects." *Udaya Journal of Khmer Studies* 12 (2014): 253–301.

Wagner, Anne Middleton. *Three Artists (Three Women): Modernism and the Art of Hesse, Krasner and O'Keeffe*. Berkeley: University of California Press, 1996.

Wee, C. J. W. -L. "The Singapore Contemporary and Contemporary Art in Singapore." In *Charting Thoughts: Essays on Art in Southeast Asia*. Edited by Low Sze Wee and Patrick D. Flores, 246–266. Singapore: National Gallery Singapore, 2017.

Werron, Tobias, Jelena Brankovic, and Leopold Ringel. "Theorizing Together." *Distinktion: Journal of Social Theory* 25, no. 2 (2024): 228–249.

Wright, Astri. "Self-Taught All the Way: Three Contemporary Women Artists in Indonesia." In *Women Imaging Women: Home, Body, Memory: Papers from the Conference on Artists from Indonesia, Philippines, Thailand and Vietnam*. Edited by

Flaudette May V. Datuin and Patrick D. Flores, 118–154. Manila: Ford Foundation, Art Studies Foundation, Cultural Center of the Philippines, 1999.

Wright, Astri. "The Arc of My Field is a Rainbow with an Expanding Twist and All Kinds of Creatures Dancing: The Growing Inclusivity of Indonesian Art History." In *Producing Indonesia: The State of the Field of Indonesian Studies.* Edited by Eric Tagliacozzo, 105–132. Ithaca: Cornell Southeast Asia Program Publications, 2014.

Wong Binghao. "No Models: Sriwhana Spong's *Instruments.*" *Southeast of Now: Directions in Contemporary and Modern Art in Asia* 6, no. 1 (March 2022): 95–121.

Wong Binghao. "Ho Tzu Nyen on Time and the Tiger." *Ocula.* January 17, 2024. Accessed September 2024. https://ocula.com/magazine/conversations/ho-tzu-nyen-time-and-the-tiger/.

Wong, Susie. "Araya Rasdjarmrearnsook." In *Southeast Asian Art Today.* Edited by Joyce van Fenema, 234–238. Singapore: Roeder Publications, 1996.

Wood, Christopher S. *A History of Art History.* Princeton: Princeton University Press, 2019.

yamomo, meLê. "Acoustic Epistemologies and Early Sound Recordings in the Nusantara Region: Phonography, Archive, and the Birth of Ethnomusicology." In *Made in Nusantara: Studies in Popular Music.* Edited by Adil Johan, and Mayco A. Santaella, 75–82. London: Routledge, 2021.

yamomo, meLê. *Theatre and Music in Manila and the Asia Pacific, 1869–1946: Sounding Modernities.* Cham, Switzerland: Palgrave Macmillan, 2018.

Yap, June. *Retrospective: A Historiographical Aesthetic in Contemporary Singapore and Malaysia.* Petaling Jaya: Strategic Information and Research Development Centre, 2016.

Zoete, Beryl de, and Walter Spies. *Dance and Drama in Bali.* New York: Harper and Brothers Publishers, 1938.

Index

www.ingramcontent.com/pod-product-compliance
Lightning Source LLC
Chambersburg PA
CBHW070439080926
51106CB00029B/1164